THE

BRITISH ARMY IN INDIA:

ITS PRESERVATION

THE

BRITISH ARMY IN INDIA:

ITS PRESERVATION

BY AN APPROPRIATE

CLOTHING, HOUSING, LOCATING, RECREATIVE EMPLOYMENT,

AND HOPEFUL ENCOURAGEMENT OF THE TROOPS

WITH

AN APPENDIX ON INDIA

JULIUS JEFFREYS, F.R.S.

GYAN

Published by

Gyan Publishing House
5, Ansari Road
Daryaganj, New Delhi-110002
Phone: 011-47034999, 9811692060
E-mail: books@gyanbooks.com

Distribution Network
gyanbooks.com
India, USA, Canada, UK, Australia, France

ISBN : 978-81-212-9242-9 (PB)
First Published, 1858

2nd Impression 2023

Printed at: Gyan Press, Delhi.

THE BRITISH ARMY IN INDIA ITS PRESERVATION
Author: JULIUS JEFFREYS

THE
BRITISH ARMY IN INDIA:
ITS PRESERVATION

BY AN APPROPRIATE

CLOTHING, HOUSING, LOCATING, RECREATIVE EMPLOYMENT, AND HOPEFUL ENCOURAGEMENT OF THE TROOPS.

WITH

AN APPENDIX ON INDIA:

THE CLIMATE OF ITS HILLS; THE DEVELOPMENT OF ITS RESOURCES, INDUSTRY, AND ARTS; THE ADMINISTRATION OF JUSTICE; THE BLACK ACT; THE PROGRESS OF CHRISTIANITY; THE TRAFFIC IN OPIUM; THE VALUE OF INDIA; PERMANENT CAUSES OF DISAFFECTION, AND OF THE RECENT REBELLION; THE TRADITIONARY POLICY; MISGOVERNMENT BY NATIVE RULERS; ANNEXATIONS OF THEIR TERRITORY, ETC.

BY JULIUS JEFFREYS, F.R.S.,

FORMERLY STAFF-SURGEON OF CAWNPORE, AND CIVIL SURGEON OF FUTTEHGURH.

LONDON:

LONGMAN, BROWN, GREEN, LONGMANS, & ROBERTS.

1858.

TO

JAMES RANALD MARTIN, Esq., F.R.S.

Kingston, Surrey,
May 20th, 1858.

MY DEAR MARTIN,

It is not a friendly acquaintance of many years only which prompts my desire to address these pages to you.

I would fain by these lines connect a work on Tropical Prophylactics with your valuable writings on Tropical Pathology and Therapeutics.

It is doubtless well said that prevention is better than cure; and to the former you have, throughout your career abroad and at home, devoted your best energies, while, in bounden duty, as an army surgeon, you have likewise pursued, and with an equal success, the science and practice of curing disease.

Having propounded more *advanced* views on Tropical Pathology, you have established them by the surest means—an extensively successful practice; and you have shown, during the many years since your return to Europe, that professional talent and benevolence are not limited in their sphere to one clime alone, but are general in their efficiency and action.

For myself, accident, not choice, having found me a student of medicine, while it was impossible not to pursue with pleasure medical philosophy, as such, and as the foremost in secular knowledge, a natural temperament has ever caused me to seek release from the practice of an uncertain science, the subject of which was *the living man;* and to prefer operating upon inanimate matter (I cared not in how large or small proportions) through the agency, too, of more certain knowledge. I have been ready to pay the penalty, and it is not a small one, of being a member of one profession, but an amateur of others. To this cause is due the present, and former, efforts to avoid a sense of professional barrenness by performing a medical part through the agency of physical and mechanical science.

A member of the Health of Towns' Commission, and of the recent Army Sanitary Commission, you may view, with more than a friendly interest, the effort of a not unfamiliar pen to contribute something towards the preservation of the soldiers' health in the Tropics, which forms the prominent portion of this volume; and of which a part was in the press when the Report of your Commission was published. That Report, it would appear, for I have not seen it, is such, in ability and meetness of official style, as the names on the Commission would guarantee. In the following composition you will observe a contrast, and in the Introduction its apology.

I remain,

My dear Martin,

Very sincerely yours,

JULIUS JEFFREYS.

INTRODUCTION.

In placing before the public a work touching upon various questions of importance relating to India, the Author feels sensible that the many years which have elapsed since he left that country, and the many months since the first portion of this volume was sent to press, demand some explanation in justification of the publication.

Without venturing, with the great historian of India, to claim as an advantage for the task, the study of his subject in England removed from all such prejudice as may arise from a personal observation of the country, he may safely presume that a residence of many years in India of such *intensity* as his own, followed since his return by an attentive observation of the progress of events, will be considered as affording ample opportunities to any mind seriously devoted to the inquiry.

For arriving at information connected with India, of the nature briefly imparted in the following pages, a residence in the country of some years' duration was, he thinks, indispensable; but had its duration been doubled it could have resulted in little more than a repetition of the same observations and experience.

Such has been the rapidity of events during the time that this Work has been in the press, that they have already realized to a distressing extent anticipations in its pages, indited as a warning protest against the encouragements to brave the tropical sun published at the time on all sides, even in India, and not unreasonably copied from such local authority by the press in England. The delay in the publication of the work has been caused by the same hesitation to break a purposed silence upon Indian questions, which has been maintained since the first year of the Author's return, with one exception of an anonymous pamphlet. The present volume was commenced as a pamphlet, to be rigidly confined to one subject—*the Dress of British Troops in India.* On opening for the purpose his somewhat voluminous notes on India, matter which had been gradually accumulated upon a variety of subjects presented itself, and appeared to possess at least equal importance with that which was to have formed a monograph of small bulk; while it related to questions of much interest at the present moment—of more interest to many minds than the clothing of troops. Hence the body of the Work: retaining its military character, has expanded from one to five heads; while a quantity of matter, most of it upon wider and still more important questions, has found its way into the Appendix, and doubled the contents of the volume. To some of this matter, more especially to that relating to *the opium question,** and *to the development of the resources and industry of India, and the state of the useful arts there,*† the reader's attention is invited with an anxiety second only to that for the preservation and happiness, and hopes for time and eternity, of the British soldiery and their families in India.

Without the power to express himself upon serious questions in any other terms than such as are commensurate with their gravity, the Author must be prepared to find exception taken to the strength of

* Appendix I, page 323. † Appendix F, page 255.

some of his expressions. It is, however, to errors not persons they apply ; and he is but too conscious of his own supineness in failing to impart to others information long accumulated and convictions deeply felt upon the various questions contained in this volume, not to apply to himself a due share of the inferences deducible from the earnest deprecation of neglect which he has been constrained to make.

In 1824, the Author visited the Himalayas, at the age of twenty-three, for the purpose of studying their climate and its sanitary properties, and published the result of his observations in an essay,* in which the formation of stations at suitable elevations was recommended. The subject attracted the attention of the Government of Bengal, and the medical authorities, with whom he had correspondence† on the establishment of the military sanitary stations which were shortly afterwards fixed at Simla, Missouri, and Landour.

Ten years afterwards, in 1834, he laid before Lord William Bentinck, then Governor-General of India, certain views having reference to the mental and sanitary condition of British troops in that country, with a proposal based on them for offering the soldiery a certain employment, which would prove to them a cheering and remunerative occupation, keeping them from *ennui* and dissipation, and tending to promote their happiness, contentment, and health ; and which

* Appendix E, page 242.

† The late Dr. Burke, H.M. Inspector-General of Hospitals in India, and Mr. MacDowell, Superintending Surgeon of the Kurnaul Division (which included the Hill country), informed the Author that the perusal of that essay had led them to address: the one the Government, the other the Medical Board, inviting their attention to the formation of Military Sanitary Stations at the elevations recommended.

would at the same time be instrumental towards improving many of the useful arts in India, at present too rudely conducted to be a source of national wealth or of social advancement.

He has to acknowledge with grateful recollections the very encouraging reception his Lordship afforded to this and other proposals for developing the resources of the country, and advancing the condition of the natives. He did him the honour, more than once, of expressing a wish that his health might permit him to remain in India, with a view to giving effect to some of these plans. But multifarious exertions of mind and body had proved exhausting, and compelled him to leave. Nevertheless, he had endured for many years an amount of exposure to the sun and weather which would have proved fatal to a much stronger person clad in an ordinary manner. The exemption from serious illness, which was secured by simply clothing himself in a respectful obedience to natural laws, on the one hand, and the deplorable effects in others which he has, times without number, witnessed from long-continued exposure with defective clothing, on the other hand, have from an early period impressed him with the conviction that much more might be done to protect British troops exposed on duty in the Tropics. It was his desire, many years ago, to have attracted the attention of the home authorities to the question; but after some observation he could not flatter himself that he would succeed in impressing upon the minds of persons then in power convictions as deep as his own, as to the greater extent to which the health and lives of British soldiers in India might be preserved; the prevailing opinion appearing to be that whatever was practicable had been already done.

Upon the news of the mutiny reaching England, the extensive exposure of our troops which it would necessarily involve renewed the impressions of thirty years. Accordingly, he endeavoured to invite attention to the subject then. More recently he has found the Chairman and Deputy-Chairman of the East India Direction ready to afford every attention to the question, and fully alive to its importance.

For more general information of a sanitary character relating to the army, the reader is referred to the labours of the various military medical officers who have written on the subject; more especially to those of Mr. Martin, connected with India, in which it is difficult whether to admire most the judgment or the energy displayed. Such, likewise, would appear to be the character of the Report of the Army Sanitary Commission, of which he, with others of distinguished ability, is a member.

The author would regret not having had the opportunity of availing himself of that Report, published when these pages were in the press, had the object of his undertaking embraced anything like a treatise on the whole sanitary question. For the views and matter contained in the following pages he is solely responsible, as the result of his own observations.

To the ability and meetness of style of the Sanitary Report (which he has not himself seen) the public press has borne testimony as being such as the constitution of the Commission could not fail to ensure. A Royal Commission maintains a proper dignity by presuming that its authority alone: will command for the facts it reports, either the attention of the executive, or an appeal to public feeling through the eloquence of the politician. But for a private writer to imitate the impassive style of a Royal Report is a pedantry of the day which too often fails of its object. If a bare announcement of facts would avail anything, the evils which prevail on all hands, would have been long since remedied. The mind, in busy English life, cannot, or will not, take the trouble to nurse a bare and unsightly fact, and much less a progeny of them, until it has grown to such proportions as to hold possession of the feelings and impel them to action. A fact, unsupported by influential authority, before it can be *felt*, as well as known, by a reader or hearer, must be, as it were, weighed in his presence, and have its various aspects, hues, tendencies, and claims set fully and forcibly before him; or in general it had better not be stated at all; for the condition of all others most hopeless of good is a familiarity of the ear with grave facts unaccompanied by any influence of them on the heart.

It is under these convictions the Author writes; but, though he has not allowed any consideration how far his remarks may be acceptable or otherwise to some of his readers to cramp his expressions, he has to regret his inability to do more justice to the claims he advocates; and that, owing to various interruptions, this work, which has been a long time in the press, should not have been published last year.

CONTENTS.

APPENDIX.

ERRATA.

Page 254, line 12, *omit* "as."
„ 332, „ 5, *for* "exhudation" *read* "exudation."
„ 345, „ 15, *for* "though" *read* "through."

DIRECTIONS TO THE BINDER.

Figs. 2 and 3 .. .. *to face page* 59
„ 5 and 6 .. .. „ 78
„ 9 and 10 .. .. „ 92

THE BRITISH ARMY IN INDIA,

&c. &c.

GENERAL VIEW OF THE SUBJECT.

THERE are few questions which at the present moment have a greater claim upon the attention of the public, and especially of statesmen, than that of affording British Troops in India all possible protection from that hostile climate.

The subject treated under five heads.

The subject will be treated, in the following pages, under five general heads:—THE CLOTHING, HOUSING, LOCATING, RECREATIVE EMPLOYMENT, and HOPEFUL ENCOURAGEMENT of the Soldiery; and the amount of matter presented before the reader will be only such as shall suffice for inviting him to join in certain views upon the chief points of this wide question, which it is hoped will prove of sufficient importance and interest to repay his attention.

Since the exposure of British Troops to the weather will be much greater than hitherto, when nearly all military duty was in peace performed by a native army, and especially greater during the next two years, during which they may be frequently in the field, it is the dress of the soldier which claims primary attention. This subject, therefore, will be treated foremost in the following pages.

Before entering upon our subject, it is necessary *in limine* to protest against and refute an opinion at present too prevalent in India as well as in England, that, after all, exposure to the sun in India is not so injurious as has been hitherto believed. The apparent exemption from injury of the troops before Delhi, nay, the improved appearance of some, has been cited in both countries as evidence of the fact that, without any greater protection than they had, British soldiers may be employed in the field throughout the year with no great injury.

Recent opinions encouraging exposure to a tropical sun.

Their danger.

It is impossible to exaggerate the danger of such an opinion. If acted upon, it would before long issue in the destruction of the most vigorous army, had it to keep the field. The casualties from broken constitutions and death would be such as, in these days of prompt information, would very soon chill the military zeal of the youth of Britain.

If the question were not that of a commander watching over his army, but of an entomologist over the *cicadæ* in his garden, he might speak exultingly of their state, if most of them were found pretty vigorous after fluttering in the sun throughout one whole summer; but human health, even in India, is to be estimated at more than one season's duration. The *vis vitæ* is not so wholly without power against climatic influence, especially in the prime of life, but that some time will in general be occupied in forcing it to yield, even where *mental emotions do not come in to its aid*. As will be seen in the sequel, a stroke of the sun is but a casual effect of its rays. By far the more extensive and certain are those more gradual effects which, according to a man's constitution and *the state of his mind*, will occupy one, two, or three years in becoming established, excepting in certain abnormal cases where men possess not perhaps a more really vigorous, but what may be termed a semi-tropical constitution.

The immunity of some from a semi-tropical constitution.

It is unfortunate for others when a man of influence possesses the immunity it confers, unless he should happen to be a sound pathologist. Where this is not the case, however great his ability in other respects, he is too likely to measure the constitutions of others by his own, and to imagine that an acclimation which was almost spontaneous in his case, requires for its establishment in others only a like perseverance in braving the sun.

Mental excitement postpones the effects of exposure in most men.

It is the aid which mental emotions bring to the *vis vitæ*, especially hopeful excitement, that will enable most men to bear with apparent impunity for a time, adverse climatic influences even doubly severer than those which were gradually undermining their constitutions during the monotonous routine of barrack life. The extra heat and excessive bodily exertion also operate as an increased stimulus, forcing the secreting organs for a time into brisker action, and producing, with the aid of elevated spirits, even an improvement in the digestion, and a temporary relief of any congested organs. But a return to spirit-drinking will, not unfrequently, do much the same, in cases where its injurious effects had brought incurable disease upon the very organs now temporarily relieved, and apparently benefited, but in reality ruined by its resumption. We have it on the authority of Baron Munchausen, that on a return to a warm climate a bugle gave forth spontaneously tunes inaudible before, having been frozen into it by excessive cold. The fiction may offer to the unpathological some illustration of the effect of mental and other exciting causes in veiling, for a time, climatic effects which are, alas! too truly, accumulating in the system, to burst forth when those arresting causes are removed. Evidence of this will be adduced hereafter.

Casualty amongst troops exposed to the climate in India.

It is not too much to affirm that, if the British forces in India, caparisoned as they are, should have *to keep the field continuously* and with little support from native troops, the casualties from climate alone, after the first year, might be estimated at 50 per cent. per annum at the least,* and that of these a large proportion would be traceable to nearly avoidable causes.

To do all that is possible for preserving the lives of our fellow-countrymen after inducing them to enlist, and upon whose loyalty have to be made the largest demands, is an obligation of so solemn a character that men in power are not to be envied the responsibility it lays upon their consciences. It involves also the difference between an efficient and a perishing army.

Efficiency irrespective of appearance,

Surely then, compared with this important question, any notions of fashion or ideal proprieties of

* How far within the truth is this estimate, written some months ago, and then considered exorbitant by some, we have now a melancholy proof in the thinning of our ranks. One corps alone, and that presumed most acclimated, the Madras Fusileers, are stated to have been reduced, chiefly by disease, in six months from 850 strong to 190 fit for duty! Doubtless the rest of the gallant force under the late Sir Henry Havelock have suffered in much the same proportion.

form in dress ought not to be allowed one moment's consideration! In military matters, at least, the manly rule of Aristotle ought surely to be the only guide—namely, that those forms of things should ever be most esteemed which are best suited to their uses. Of how many a fine enduring soldier in the Tropics have not a defective head and body dress caused the death! **the true criterion of taste in dress.**

A despot in the East of Europe, setting no great value on human life, and having an unlimited command over his subjects by conscription, may, with the vanity of a woman at her toilet, be ever dressing his army, as he thinks, smart; but he cannot arrest the hand of Nature when she causes that army as a consequence to melt away before his eyes!

If the dress of the British army is ill-suited for the Tropics, its prospect is very different.

The exalted personage who is understood to be much interested in the question possesses not only moral feelings as elevated as is his position, and a mind highly cultivated, but is himself the especial patron of practical science. A like confidence, according to all reports, is due to the supreme official authority of the army. It is, then, not to be doubted, now that so considerable a portion of Her Majesty's forces will henceforth be stationed in India, and be much less relieved from exposure by the aid of native troops than hitherto, that the importance of a sound practical application of the laws of science to a protective clothing of the army in India will be fully recognised.

Others as well as myself have seen our fellow-countrymen (with whom, however humble their estate, we must desire to feel ourselves as of one national family) in the vigour of life *struck dead* or *rapidly destroyed* by causes for which those in command of them were in no wise to blame, having doubtless considered them inevitable; but most of which physics, pathology, and experience have taught me to believe nearly preventible. If the feelings natural to such a recollection and such a belief should betray themselves in any fervent expressions to which the reader might be disposed to take exception,* I can only make my appeal from his sensitiveness to his generosity, patriotism, and humanity, and, relying upon these, earnestly hope that the soldiers, of all ranks, who are winning back our Empire under the northern Tropic, may have the benefit of any truths these pages may contain.

Appeal to the benevolence of the reader.

With respect to most of the points discussed in the following pages, I do not know what improvements may have been proposed to the governing authorities by others. I know what has yet been done. In proportion as any reader can show that the measures advocated here are approached or anticipated by the suggestions of others, he will be welcomed as bringing other authority in support of them; and he will be more welcomed if he can supersede them by any suggestions of his own, the superiority of which he is prepared to establish incontestably. If there is a shade of difference in the merits of any plans, let the soldier have the benefit of it.

His efforts invited.

* A dry statement of facts, suitable from official pens, savours of indifference from a private one. Vide Introduction.

Knowing that an insight into the physics and pathology of the question is indispensable for anything like a clear view of it, or anything better in practice than mere empiricism, I feel the necessity of inviting the reader to a brief review and arrangement of the principles in science concerned, before inviting him to join in the search for means by which to concentrate those principles in such practical forms as shall prove both efficient and convenient. At the same time, bearing in mind that, of those who may favour these pages with a perusal, the most responsible may not be pathologists, I shall endeavour to be as brief as is compatible with clearness, and to avoid obscure details and unfamiliar terms.

It is indeed surprising to witness the courage with which some will dash into the thick of complicated questions with minds unarmed for the purpose, and will, upon the ground of personal experience alone, or with no experience, pronounce decisions which would imperil the lives of their fellow men, and the efficiency of armies! A mere casual acquaintance with certain uses of matter, and local practices, which produce some approximation towards the desired result, may lead us but a small way, nay, will often mislead us, as long as we are contented to let our minds float vaguely over the surface of the question. The case is urgent: men are dying, and will die in increasing numbers if we do not enlist for their protection all those principles in science, and properties of matter, which are ready, if but called upon, to flock to the rescue!

The aid of science indispensable.

We *must* make solar radiation and the laws of heat

our study, and also the properties in relation to heat of terrestrial matter in its various forms, especially of that most wondrous form of matter, which, tabernacling a spirit, lives, breathes, and thinks—a prey to outward influences and inward commotion! *

Objections to theory prevalent but crude.

Much indeed is said on this, as on all other questions, of the prudence of avoiding all "*theory*," and relying solely upon "*practical experience*." The writer of these lines cannot be accused of contemning "practice." Few have been urged by a "practical" turn to originate a greater variety of practical appliances. If in *practical* effect they have

* While these pages were in the press, their publication has been interrupted, amongst other causes, by the task, to which I have been happy to give the time, of superintending the constructing of pattern helmets of different kinds, at the request of the Chairman and Deputy-Chairman of the Court of Directors of the East India Company, whose attention had been invited to the subject. Though far from being *working patterns*, they are, considering the difficulty attending all first productions, a satisfactory exhibition of their principles, and such as would amply suffice to place at once before the view of a committee in which the different branches of science concerned were as duly represented as the military, the various important objects sought, and the design of each of the several parts, and of their respective proportions. It was my endeavour to put before the Military Committee at the India House such a view of the prophylactic requirements and details of the case as could be embraced in the limited period of a single interview, and I have to acknowledge the polite attention afforded me by the members generally. But the subject is one demanding repeated scientific discussion, and that close examination into all requirements, with *that apportioning to each its due relative weight*, which it would be unreasonable to expect from the members of a single profession.

These helmets have been lying some time at the India House, and may have been seen by army accoutrement makers, disposed to exhibit constructions of their own to the military authorities. Any such, who may be desirous of producing specimens of protective helmets, are welcome to adopt the suggestions offered by those patterns; but they are earnestly cautioned not to carry too far, with the view of rendering their constructions inviting, a reduction in the size, nor to think that havoc can be made of the embodied principles without a proportional injury to the result.

not proved unsuccessful, it has been because they have never been attempted but upon "theory" based on scientific truths accumulated by others, and whenever it was possible confirmed by experiments of his own. Thus on this very question of Tropical dress, it was because he was no less attached to *theory* than to *practice*, to science than to art, that, with a constitution more than usually disqualified to endure a tropical sun and a raging hot wind, he was enabled to insulate himself under the rays of the former, and the exsiccating action of the latter, and as a consequence to persevere for many years in occupations demanding exposure of the most trying kind; and though ultimately exhausted, to escape acute attacks and prevailing epidemics of every sort.

The author protected by theoretically constructed dress.

Upon this experience, and upon too much of a converse nature in the case of men of much greater vigour, and less tendency to suffer in the head from the sun, but not thus protected, these two axioms have been founded. 1st. That when a man is struck by the sun, there is in general no better reason for it than for another's being drowned through shipment in a leaky vessel. 2nd. That very few natives of Britain can long endure exposure to the sun on a Tropical continent without serious damage to the constitution, unless thoroughly, or, in other words, scientifically protected.

Axioms relating to protective dress.

It must, on reflection, be manifest to every one, that since an acquaintance with the properties of matter is essential to theory in Natural Science, as the very basis of the reasoning on which it is built, to speak of theory and practice as not agreeing together involves a contradiction. If there is a disagreement apparent in any case, one or other, or both, of what we term "theory" and "practice" must be unsound.

That the knowledge possessed by the ablest minds is but imperfect, and unable to protect them at all times from error, is too true; but if on that account we contemn that knowledge in our own practice, we must either be content, as so many are, to remain without progress, persevering in a defective course of action, so long as it does not bring us to dead a lock, or we must go stumbling forwards in the dark, since we refuse to be guided by the only and proper light to practice—*Theory.*

Right practice inseparable from theory.

It is a truth worthy of note that the more the mind shrinks from "theory" (the comprehension of causes and consequences), and is set upon being "thoroughly practical," the more barren in resources and instruments does it become—the more wanting in practical means—the more *unpractical*, until to be "thoroughly practical" comes to mean little more than to close the understanding and feelings —the eyes, ears, and heart—to the consequences, often deplorable, of blundering on from generation to generation with meagre and defective appliances.

Practical experience. Its true character.

"Practical Experience" cannot be too highly estimated in all mundane undertakings; but how commonly is the term misapplied, or its comprehensiveness not discerned! As practice without theory is mere stagnant empiricism, so a boasted "practical experience," without *experiment*, is merely a constant reiteration of the same course of action, which may be faulty, and is sure to be incomplete; in which case the less of such experience a person has the better; and, at best, it can afford no information beyond its own narrow bounds. Hence the value of men's experience is often in an inverse proportion to its duration, which only serves to rivet imperfection, if not error also, more firmly on the mind.

Can any man of judgment and feeling who may, by the perusal of these pages, have his attention drawn to such considerations, fail to have the following questions forcibly intruded on his thoughts: "Whence is it that a thoroughly philosophical and practical inquiry, with all the resources of the State, has not long since been instituted upon a subject of so great importance as the preservation * of British soldiers in the Tropics?" "Whence is it that there should still prevail all that discordance of opinion upon it which results from, and proves, the absence of an authoritative decision of the question meriting that general respect which would be commanded by a persevering investigation of it by qualified minds?" Is it possible that a conclave of military officers alone, whatever may be their rank and experience, should command that confidence by merely calling in, when they may judge it necessary, the passing opinions of men of science? Of the two, it would be better for the result that the latter should form the standing committee, and the former be consulted upon exclusively military points. Yet the defects of such a proposal would be at once glaringly manifest

The prevalence of discordant opinions on sanitary questions, and their cause.

* By the choicest system of Clothing, Housing, Locating, Dieting, Recreative Employment, aud Hopeful Encouragement.

from its not having the sanction of custom, while the greater defects of the existing system are little considered, though they inevitably deprive it of respect, and, what is worse, cause it to remain so barren of useful results. But is it well that men, dignified and able in their own profession, should be placed in so false a position? Is it fair that omniscience should be expected of military men; that all science, and all art, should be supposed to lie open before them?

Other branches of science besides military indispensable.

The question of combining, in the highest degree, the sanitary protection of the soldier with his military efficiency, is one into which physiology, pathology, natural philosophy, with a knowledge of the properties of matter, and a skill in employing them, enter quite as much* as does military science. Any conclave in which they are not fully represented cannot merit respect, nor master the subject.

It is grievous to think, that while every village in the land is being searched for recruits even of the average stature of women, every department of science and of art should not long since have been ransacked, and all their available resources enlisted, for the preservation of the soldier when he is obtained!

Is it, or not, under the authority of the government itself that our uninformed fellow countrymen are invited to throw themselves confidingly upon the honour and affection of their country to protect them, while risking their lives in its battles, from all such suffering as is avoidable and unavailing to the

* This truth is abundantly evinced in the evidence given before various parliamentary committees; especially in the very important evidence of Mr. Martin before the Committee of the House of Commons on Indian Territories in 1853.

The duty of the soldier and his employers reciprocal.

objects of their prowess? When the soldier is not permitted to choose his own equipment, as of old, and would only err if he did, when discipline of necessity demands of him in all things a confiding trust in his superiors as heroic in the Camp as in the Field, is the reciprocal duty on their part a whit less morally imperative? Upon what is he asked to base the patriotic love which is to fire his breast, and carry him, as it does, through the serried ranks of any foe that may be opposed to him from the pole to the equator? Is there amongst the unenviable responsibilities of government a more solemn obligation than that the very best measures which science can dictate, and art can realize, should be preconcerted and provided for his protection before he is invited to step in a moment from the fields of freedom across the Rubicon into the dominion of absolute command?

It is indeed painful to observe how many persons, while exulting in the successful devotion of our soldiers, are so much engrossed by political considerations as to be sadly oblivious of the debt of gratitude and humanity which they themselves individually, and the whole nation, are thereby incurring; how many appear to be more concerned with the question whether reinforcements will abound, than with the *suffering* and DEATH which create the demand for them! While it is frankly admitted that a concern for the preservation of British life imperilled in India, much more than of India itself as a possession, has prompted this publication, the objects of those with whom the latter is the prior consideration will also be most effectually promoted by the means which it advocates; by devoting as strenuous efforts to the preservation of lives *there* as to the replacing of them from *hence*.

Sickness of Europeans; its effect on the native mind.

Not only would a great mortality in the army check* the ardour of recruits, but its effect upon the natives would be more serious still. I had frequent opportunities of noting the impression produced on their minds by the sickliness of Europeans in India, and have at times elicited their opinions upon it. They differ nothing from mankind in general in being universally disposed to plume themselves upon any advantages they possess over others, and especially upon the solitary advantage over us in possessing tropical constitutions. Man, everywhere, is likewise disposed to look upon that climate which suits him best, as the proper one, and upon the native of a different clime, who sickens and declines in the former, as a "poor creature" of a feeble constitution. The natives of India look upon us as white bears from the cold unhealthy North, ferociously brave, but of sickly constitutions, disabling us from occupying their country without their aid. That the rebellion was long meditated,† and purposely timed to commence in the hottest season, I cannot entertain a doubt. The rebels were not wrong in their estimate of the power of their sun; but they miscalculated the time it would require for doing their work. It

* Does not common humanity prompt the desire that it should, and thus ensure a change of system?

† Certain inquiries led me to entertain, and to express in print, twenty-five years ago, the apprehension of a wide-spread disaffection in the families from which the sepoys are drawn, especially in Bundelkund. These causes have been frequently referred to in the letters from politicians in India recently published, as now manifesting themselves.

was true that it could destroy a whole army of British soldiers, but too gradually for their purpose. Aided by elating excitement, the former are enabled to last through one, two, or three seasons, according to their power of endurance severally, and to strike down rebellion before they are themselves struck down by the climate. But we may rest assured that the hopes of the disaffected are watchfully directed to the thinning of our ranks by each year of exposure; and that they rightly draw more encouragement from this, than from the prospect of meeting our forces with success in the field. Extensive casualties amongst the soldiery from disease would too probably keep alive the embers of insurrection, which again would prolong the necessity for the exposure which, equipped as the troops are, would prove a cause of sickness constantly increasing in its effects. Should this vicious circle ever become fully established through equal perseverance on both sides, there can be little doubt in what it must eventuate. If our soldiers, therefore, can be indued with more lasting persistence under exposure in the field, a moral effect of great influence will, I am persuaded, be produced.

Dress prior in order, if not in importance.

The subject, DRESS, has been given a primary position, not from its possessing a superior importance to the HOUSING and OCCUPATION of the soldier, for, on the return of tranquillity, these will assume greater dimensions, but because he is now in the field, and in danger of dying there before the question of rightly housing and employing him can have a practical solution.

Caution against a prejudgment of the dress proposed,

To guard against any prejudgment of the dress proposed, it may be well, without anticipating the subject, to invite the reader's attention to a few points here. In the first place, in the dimensions adopted in the several forms of helmets, it was felt to be necessary that some standard should be selected. It might be a maximum, a medium, or a minimum. Upon consideration, the first has been chosen, the primary point being adequate protection. The several parts, divisions, and materials, and their respective *proportions* having been decided, as nearly as was possible beforehand, the dimensions may be reduced to such an extent as may be deemed necessary for the efficiency of the soldier. In the case of cavalry, with their quick movements through the air, and against wind, it may be requisite to squeeze down the dimensions of the head-dress more than were to be desired for security; but it would be indeed a folly to let the mind be so carried away by partial and commonplace views as to rush into the extreme of scantiness, and to ruin the constitutionsof a whole corps in a season or two, from an overstrained desire not to encumber them.

and objections anticipated.

The effect of size in the head-dress,

It should be kept well in view, that in the question of *size*, so far as encumbrance is concerned, we have only to consider the *resistance of the air*. The helmet must not be so large that in riding against a wind a man will experience more inconvenience than is repaid to him by the increased protection those dimensions afford. But we must not look to the inconvenience of resistance alone. If men, being only somewhat inconvenienced by the size of their helmets, should have them exchanged for others so much reduced that they began again to suffer seriously from solar effects from which their larger helmets had protected them, it is manifest that the reduction in size would have been carried too far.

Again, as is explained in the sequel, if the weight be rested on the top of the head, and not supported by the tension round the brows and sides, and if the hat be low in proportion to its breadth, and its centre of gravity be kept below its centre of support, it might have double the weight of many helmets (not that this is necessary) without being felt as heavy or encumbering. and of weight.

Furthermore, there is an express provision enabling the soldier to vary the dimensions of the hat round his head, that he may not have to endure as tight pressure around it as when the weight is mainly *supported* by such pressure. But though the soldier is thus enabled to relieve his head of much constriction, and to wear his helmet as easy around his brows as circumstances may permit, it is not of course intended, nor is there any necessity from this provision, that it should be worn insecurely loose. The tension requisite for security may be regulated to any desired extent, without interfering with the support of the weight on the top of the head by means of the draw-cap. Variability in the dimensions of a hat desirable.

It would be found, indeed, in practice, that if the weight be thus supported, and its centre of gravity placed as low as possible, much less tension round the brows would be necessary to prevent the helmet from being shaken off in the prancing of a horse than might be supposed; but the very provision secures to the trooper the option of increasing that tension to any extent, and at any moment he pleases. So far is it from involving, as has been imagined, an insecure looseness of his helmet, that when he comes out of hospital convalescent, with his head emaciated after having been shaved and blistered, as is the fate of many, it would provide for the contraction of his helmet to the reduced dimension of his head, whereas an ordinary irreducible helmet would have to be stuffed perhaps with hard leather to be made to fit him.

Bright exterior in helmets.

Again, the protective power of a bright metallic exterior is fully noted, and applied in most of the constructions proposed; but, as will be seen, the inconvenience to foot soldiers of a reflection of the sun's rays from each other's hats has been by no means overlooked, neither has the philosophical provision against it, of avoiding all spheroidal forms in *their* helmets, and giving them only *vertical* and *horizontal* faces. An ordinary fashionable hat, a shako with upright sides, or an inverted saucepan, offer forms for metal surfaces secure against that defect, however bright they may be; nay, in proportion to their brilliancy.

When, therefore, it is objected that bright helmets are inadmissible also for cavalry, upon the ground that they render them more visible to an enemy, we may simply propose that their helmets for the Tropics should likewise be given the above homely form, instead of a more elegant spheroidal, without asking the question, "Why then have so many regiments splendid helmets if they are useless in the field until covered, and how much does it avail to cover them if the broad scabbards, trappings, and mountings remain bright, which, tilting their *planes of reflection* in all manners of directions, would, one would imagine, be sure to catch the sight, and exhibit the trooper?"

Under the heads, THE HOUSING, LOCATING, ENCOURAGEMENT, and EMPLOYMENT of soldiers in India, will be found matter inviting contemplation and inquiry. Before the hope can be with reason entertained of repressing the intemperance of the soldiers, which in India appears to be bounded only with the opportunities they can command, and which is so destructive to them, and so disgracing* to their Christianity, the causes of it must be sought out, and as far as is possible removed. We shall find that in addition to the hereditary, pernicious views, and habits, which they bring with them from England, an uneasiness of body and mind, occasioned by a climate which keeps them gloomily within doors, and worries them

Causes of intemperence amongst soldiers in India.

* Intemperance and Christianity are to a lamentable extent associated together in the minds of the natives, both Hindus and Mahomedans, as every missionary knows too well, from the obstacle it offers to his labours. The following is a remarkable instance. On my making inquiries into the creeds of certain black descendants of Europeans scattered about the upper provinces (not the "Eurasians"), a well-informed Mussulman stated that they were Christians. Upon my asking how he came to know it, as they had no places of worship to frequent, he said, not disrespectfully, but in all simplicity, that he knew it from their being nearly all of them drunkards. It is a grievous fact that the example of "Christians," and the efforts of the government to multiply spirit-shops for the sake of revenue, are changing the habits of the natives. Drunkenness is becoming gradually prevalent, whereas formerly there were few who touched alcohol in any form.

there, and by other grave causes, is their especial incentive to intemperance in India.

An anxiety for them, and for their example, combined with a desire that a British spirit of progress (not the mere rhetorical aspirations of politicians, the easy curricles to reputation endlessly employed, but) a thoroughly practical effort, through the aid of the soldiery, should be applied to the improvement of the arts and development of the resources of India, led me to devise* (most of them many years ago) various amusing employments for their minds, and measures for rendering their barracks more healthy and enjoyable. To this subject the attention of the reader will be earnestly requested in the sequel.

* Vide Introduction.

ON THE SPECIFIC PROPERTIES OF MATTER THROUGH WHICH HEAT OPERATES AND IS TO BE RESISTED.

We cannot move a step towards obtaining a clear view of the agencies by which a climate operates injuriously, so far as heat is concerned, or of those at our command for resisting it, until we have so well arranged before our minds the following six properties of matter in relation to heat that we can at once discern when any of them are acting against us, and how to win them over to our aid, either for separate or combined operation.

These properties are, Conduction, Absorption of Heat by Evaporation, Reflection, Radiation, Convection, and Subterranean Absorption of Heat. The properties of matter through which heat operates.

Conduction.—*Quick* conduction of heat operates far more often unfavourably by letting in outer heat, as in the case of imperfect roofing and walls of a house, or of defective head-dress and clothing of the body, than favourably by carrying off internal heat; though its value through the agency of light clothing, under certain conditions, is doubtless great. Slow-conduction (commonly but incorrectly termed *non*-conduction) is the operative principle in the various familiar means for warding off heat, which have forced themselves upon the attention of the natives of the Tropics, who were ignorant of Conduction.

causes. The shelter of shade would suggest their calico as a general covering, which experience would reduplicate into a turban for the more sensitive head; and stiffer materials would be substituted, when stiffness was wanted for a raised crown and sides, to relieve the head from oppression by giving space over it, as in the hats of all countries; and in India the pith "*Sola*" offered the same effect in a high degree, by combining the extreme of slow-conduction with that of lightness; but with too fragile a texture for any but gentle usage; moreover, as we shall see, its slow-conduction will not alone suffice.

Slow-conduction the agent chiefly relied on by the natives for resisting heat.

When therefore it is affirmed that we cannot do better than copy the example of the natives of hot climates, a double oversight is committed. In the first place, their sensibility to climatic influences is altogether different from ours, so that what suffices for them may not by any means for us, of which there is evidence at every turn in India; and in the next, since they have no light from science to open to their view any resources beyond those stumbled over in the obscure path of experience along which they grope, it is highly improbable that they should have fallen upon the best means of effecting their ends. No small part of my time in India was devoted to examining their agricultural and manufacturing mechanics, as well as several of their chemical arts, and in an endeavour to improve some of them. With few exceptions I found the result no other than was to have been expected in a country where science had no existence, where material property, until our rule, had had little

Their example an imperfect guide.

protection, and where *mental property* was still without any protection whatever, and that amongst a people singularly wanting in enterprise. These remarks are necessary to clear the ground from the constant appeal made to native usage. If it offer the best example it will bear the test of theory and of trial; now, as will be seen, it is not theoretically perfect; and as for trial, taking the instance of the turban, so often referred to as a perfect head-dress, though it is doubtless much better than a British head-dress, it has repeatedly failed to give that immunity to necessary exposure which we have a right to hope for from modern resources, and are bound to seek for our gallant countrymen. Men are still not unfrequently struck by the sun, and many more graduate under it for inflammation of the liver, cholera, and fever, though it may take one or even two years of exposure to qualify them for candidature.

Turbans imperfect in action.

Nor will any single layer, or even two, of the pith of "sola," though pre-eminent amongst slow-conductors, exclude the sun's heat sufficiently to guard all persons, even against sun-stroke, which is an effect proving a *large penetration of heat* to have taken place. At the storming of Rangoon, in the late Burmese war, officers wearing sola hats were struck by the sun. How many more, then, must have been receiving its more gradual, but in the end scarcely less deleterious impressions!

Also "sola" hats.

That the principle of slow-conduction operating in the turban and the sola hat, should, *when employed alone*, fall short in resisting power, will surprise no one who bears in mind that a masonry roof of 1½ or even 2 feet in thickness fails to keep the upper rooms of houses in India from being perceptibly affected by the sun's rays; and that much heat penetrates even through the thatch of a bungalow when a foot or more in thickness; the air near its under surface being much heated. The eight layers of thick cotton cloth in the two *flies* (roofs) of an officer's tent in India, even though much aided by the convection of heat from them (a large body of air circulating between them), fail to prevent the solar heat from penetrating. With such power is it projected down by the radiant cloth that it will often drive the inmate under the table for further shelter, unless he protect himself by a wetted cloth on the head.

Solar heat penetrates even thick roofs.

The reason of this becomes obvious when we reflect upon the nature of *slow*-conduction. Its very name (there being no such thing as NON-conduction) shows that after all it does but operate against time, which will beat it at last. The property of slow-conduction possessed by any matter promises nothing to it against the entrance of heat radiated upon its surface. On the contrary, nearly in proportion as bodies are the slowest conductors of heat, are they the readiest admitters of radiant heat falling on their surface. Hence clothing which is simply slow-conducting, though it may so retard the progress of the fiercest rays, as for a time to afford complete protection, must, since it passively receives nearly all the rays that fall upon it, by degrees convey a large part of them inwards to the body it covers. The

Slow-conductors only temporary in action, and receive heat readily at their surface.

slowest conductor would transport heat much more rapidly than it does, did it not get rid of a portion, immediately on its entrance, by imparting some of it by conduction to the air, and by re-radiating some; but these are feeble aids when the air is very hot, and other solid bodies near are as hot as the radiating surface.

Yet the principle is of value.

Nevertheless, slow-conduction is a principle of high value in aid of our object when it is employed in conjunction with others.

Evaporation. Its cooling power in India in "tattees."

EVAPORATION.—The absorption of heat in the evaporation of water is the next property which has been fortuitously employed, not only for mitigating atmospheric heat, but also for absorbing the solar rays. With the use of the "*tattee*" or bamboo frame covered with the fragrant "*khus-khus*" root, or with the "*jewassee*" grass, and kept drenched with water, every one is familiar; but perhaps few have taken note of the prodigious quantity of water which is required to supply the evaporation from each single tattee of the size of a doorway. I made some experiments for successive days in a hot season of average temperature; the mid-day heat ranging from 110° to 115°. I regret that I have not at hand a memorandum of the results to refer to, but I believe the evaporation amounted to several hundred pounds when the wind blew briskly through the "tattee." The air would thus fall readily 30 degrees and sometimes nearer 40 degrees in its momentary passage through it.

There is then in evaporation an agent of abundant

power, where plenty of water and a current of air to maintain its evaporation can be commanded. Even when a person is sitting still in a tent a wetted cloth or turban on the head will, as already remarked, mitigate the heat penetrating through the tent in no small degree. In the outer air also the cooling power of evaporation can master the heat of both the sun and the atmosphere if there be wind to excite it. Every resident in the western provinces of India is aware how soon a piano will be warped out of shape and value in a house which is not artificially cooled, and how soon it loses its tune even in a cooled one. In the height of the hot winds I sent a piano in full tune from Cawnpore to friends at Meerut, a distance of near 300 miles, who, as it was brought in through a fierce hot wind, expected to find it destroyed, and at a baking heat. They informed me that, when they opened it, it actually cooled the air of the room near it, and was still in tune; and in fact had suffered nothing. Relying on the power of evaporation, I had it wrapped in cerecloth well *payed* with melted wax to secure it from the wet, and then enveloped in several layers of an open-wove cloth,* the warp of which was thick cotton wick, made for the "Refrigerator," the machine for cooling houses, described under a future head. A slight awning of "sirkee" (a fine reed) was suspended above it. It was carried, like a palanquin, by bearers, and was accompanied by two or three "bheestees" (water-bearers) whose duty it was to keep it drenched with water day and night, and whose reward double pay

A piano protected through great heat by evaporation.

* Any equally retentive substance would answer.

if it arrived in tune. I mention this incident not only as strongly illustrative of the power of evaporation to combat heat both of sun and wind, but as an allowable digression, since it may afford information useful to some of our fair countrywomen yet surviving the horrors of the time, whom conjugal duty may keep in or call back to India, and whose renewed homes may well need the solace of music. They will find the above, if rightly managed, the safest and quickest way of conveying their instruments by land, and not very expensive.

If any reader should think this episode to oppose the future statement that the evaporation of cutaneous perspiration cannot protect the brain and body from the solar rays, I would remind him that not only is the quantity of evaporable perspiration insufficient, but that the brain and other organs when they suffer are no more heated *directly* by the sun than was the inner organism of the piano. Had the piano had life, and had a delicate nervous tissue irritable by heat pervaded the evaporating surface around it with which its organism within was in close sympathy, it also would have lost its tune, and been destroyed, though the heat could not reach its interior.

Solar action on the skin different.

Though the skin, owing to its sensibility, cannot by evaporation from its own surface ward off all the effects of radiant heat, copious evaporation from an *inanimate* surface, like clothes thoroughly wetted, and in a current of wind, possesses abundant power to do so; but unfortunately it is a power which cannot be placed under safe control, nor be always at command when most needed. Varying with every current of

Evaporation a powerful but critical agent;

wind, it may at one moment just suffice to keep down heat so far as to produce the impression of a tepid bath, soothing and relaxing the skin; and at another, suddenly and severely chill the skin it had just relaxed—an effect which must not be mistaken for, as being very different from, the Russian *douche* succeeding the steam bath. It is therefore an agent which, even for the head, has to be employed with caution out of doors, though in the steadier atmosphere of a tent or house it may by most persons be safely employed. But it is liable also to be not at command when most needed, as on a line of march. Few persons have perhaps considered how much water, if evaporation alone were relied on, would have to be supplied to each man even to keep the head alone cool. As to the trunk and limbs, though soldiers are often compelled by duty to wade through rivers, and occasionally up to their very shoulders, and may under excitement bear the subsequent evaporation with apparent impunity, it is a cooling process the pathologist would be sorry to recommend as a rule. The occasional chills of their own perspiration are in the Tropics quite trying enough for them to endure.

yet valuable at times.

Nevertheless, as a subordinate auxiliary means for protecting the head when the atmospheric heat rises above 100° (Fahr.), evaporation may with due provisions be employed with much advantage.

Reflection a highly protective power.

THE REFLECTION OF HEAT.—The great protective power of this principle has not, so far as I am aware, been employed by the natives of the Tropics; the gilding of their chattas of state (large parasols), in accordance with their other gorgeous paraphernalia, being apparently used solely with a view to pomp.

Familiar as the natural philosopher is with the properties of heat, so far as they are known, and of matter in relation to this wonderful agent, the useful application of these properties has not in every direction kept pace with this knowledge. We are familiar with the use of reflectors for the purpose of *utilizing* the heat reflected, as in the case of reflecting sides to a fire-grate, but reflection has not been as freely employed as it might for *warding off* heat. A striking illustration of this power happened to be afforded by a construction I contrived some years ago for burning coke and anthracite brilliantly in an open fire-grate, and for carrying off the products of the combustion effectively. This was attained by simply placing a plate of metal, *d*R, Figs. 1 and 1*a*, immediately over the

A striking illustration of this power.

Fig. 1.

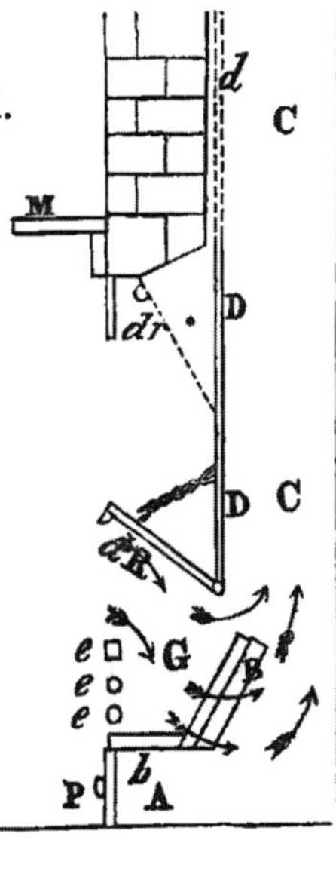

Fig. 1*a*.

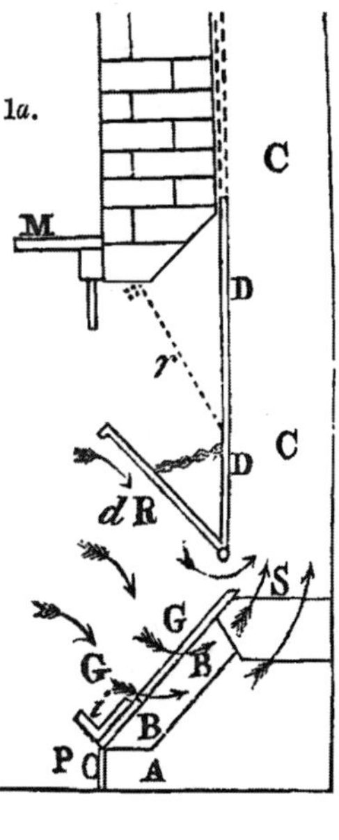

fire, inclined at a certain angle, and suspended to a shifting plate D D, which nearly closed the chimney-way. If the grate be otherwise rightly formed, and the current at bottom be duly checked, the air is *deflected* by the inclined plate down upon the fuel, and keeps the front and top of it in a high state of brilliancy. It then occurred to me, that by facing this plate with one of burnished steel I might *reflect* into the room the heat from the whole top of the fire which usually shines to waste up a chimney. The effect was to give a double image of the fire, and very nearly a double effect, and even more than double when the fire was low, and its upper surface larger than its front. The power of this reflector (R) is so great that it would roast a joint in front of it as readily as the fire itself, and it cannot be approached by the hand within two or three feet. Yet the hand can actually be kept pressed against the back of the inclined plate itself while a brilliant fire is within a few inches of it, and has been shining upon it the whole day. But had a facing of calico or leather been substituted for the steel mirror, not only would any such substance have been instantly scorched, but the skin of the hand pressed on the back of the plate would have been immediately destroyed.

The value of bright metallic surfaces for dress.

Now, since the relation of the solar rays to *metallic* surfaces is nearly the same as of rays from a fire, how powerful a resisting property have we, in bright metal, available for warding off the sun from the head and body of the soldier! Moreover, in the case of the head, a metallic covering possesses mechanical qualities of resistance and durability so well suited for a military head-dress, as, on account of these alone, to have been employed for helmets from the earliest days. In this instance, at least, we have that scowling phantom Custom, so troublesome and obstructive to improvement, for once on our side.* We cannot, indeed, command so dense and brilliant a reflecting surface as the polished steel mirror, which turns off nearly the whole heat, but a degree of smoothness which can be easily preserved will reject three-fourths of the heat which will enter cotton; and, as will be shown in the practical application of the principle, since the property of reflection rests in the surface alone and has nothing to do with the thickness, so thin metal may be employed that we may have a wide space within it, and a second face of metal to arrest such heat as shall have penetrated and been projected inwards from the first.

Slow radiation. Its value.

SLOW RADIATION.—This property is also very valuable for our purpose, though in a minor degree to the former. It is happily possessed by the very same matter which enjoys the property of high reflection, and is in fact its reciprocal property.

Since some portion of the sun's rays must be expected to enter the reflecting barrier even when it is bright, and a considerable portion if it is allowed to become tarnished; and since such rays will then be conducted through the substance of the metal to its inner surface, if we leave this unlined by

* The objection which may be raised to the employment of bright surfaces, that they would render their wearers too dazzling to comrades, and too visible by enemies, has been already touched upon, and will be found fully discussed and obviated in the sequel.

cloth or any fibrous substance, and simply tinned, it will radiate heat very slowly and feebly upon the head or other contents within it, compared with cotton cloth, felt, or leather; the radiating power of any of these substances being from six to eight times as great as of a bright tinned or brass surface, and four or five times that of a dull tinned one.

If, in our construction, we can employ this retarding property of slow radiation more than once between the sun and the surface to be protected, we shall materially improve our results.

Convection of heat. Its value.

THE CONVECTION OF HEAT.—This property of fluids may be also employed with much effect as an auxiliary against solar influence. Air, like water, receiving heat from any warmer surface, expands, rises, and is replaced by other air from below. If a free exit above be given to the rising air and free entrance below to the air replacing it, we may have such a current over the hot surface as shall sweep away a large part of the heat it has to give, provided the air be cooler than itself by some degrees. When the force of any wind is added to the current, the convection of heat is materially increased.

Of this principle of convection we must therefore be careful to avail ourselves in our undertaking. It is readily applicable both to the head and body dress; and also to buildings, especially to their roofs.

THE SUBTERRANEAN ABSORPTION OF HEAT is the last agency which it is necessary to include in our means. As it is applicable solely to the cooling of dwellings, and will be noticed under that head with certain practical suggestions, but a brief reference to it can be afforded here.

Although there is every reason for believing that a very high temperature prevails in the bowels of the earth, and at no greater depth than some miles from its surface, yet the diffusion of heat upwards is so gradual as not to affect appreciably the temperature of the soil within forty or fifty feet of the surface. To about that depth, though varying in different countries, it is well known that the temperature of the earth is entirely due to climatic causes, mainly to solar influence, and to the great power of throwing off heat by radiation possessed by the earth's surface. Earthy matter is so moderate a conductor of heat that at about that mean depth any heat of the hot months ceases to descend, being invited back to supply warmth to the surface when it is chilled in the cold months of the year. So that at a certain depth the temperature scarcely varies at all all the year round, and is very nearly the same as the mean temperature of the surface. It is plain then, that the whole body of this upper stratum of earth is, to that depth, cooler in the hot months than the air at the surface; the lowermost part of this stratum being in the hot winds in India as much as thirty or forty degrees cooler than the wind. Hence the walls and floor of the underground dwellings, called in India "*Thie Khanus*," cool their atmosphere in hot weather by many degrees; an effect increased materially when they exhale moisture which evaporates into the air. Some of the most effective of these *Thie Khanus* that I have noticed were at Delhi, and one in a garden

Coolness in summer of the stratum subjacent to the earth's surface.

Thie Khanus.

near Agra. I also made one myself, but it was only a single apartment for a study.

Such apartments are well enough for occupation by day when no unwholesome malaria enters them and when their cubic contents are large in comparison with the number of the occupants, but they are altogether unsuited for day barracks even, for which I have heard them more than once proposed. The ventilation necessary in a barrack for health would altogether overpower the cooling action of the comparatively limited surface of wall in the largest barrack, even if it were deep under ground. From the same cause a tunnel of considerable size and length, constructed at Cawnpore in 1824, for ventilating a large hospital with cool air, failed to have an adequate effect. Both its depth below ground and its cooling surface of earth were not sufficient; though it was otherwise ingeniously planned,* the air after passing through the tunnel being conveyed up into the hospital. At the same time my experiments lead me to believe that this agency of subterranean absorption of heat may be rendered available in a manner both remarkably economical and effective; since a cooling surface of great extent may be commanded, aided by a large evaporative surface. The details of this plan fall under another head—the housing of troops.

Their inadequate effect.

But the principle of subterranean absorption is a powerful resource.

* The plan was, I believe, adopted from a hospital in England.

GENERAL REMARKS ON TROPICAL VIRULENCE AND VITAL RESISTANCE.

In India the British soldier on duty, surrounded by *the atmosphere*, with *the sun* over his head, and *the ground* under his feet, presents to our view the unfortunate subject of three hostile agencies. It is the influence of these agents upon him, both in their distinct and in their combined operation, which must be studied before we can successfully avail ourselves of the best means which nature affords for insulating him so far as to enfeeble their power.

The functions of the skin of prominent importance.

It is manifest that his internal economy of vital organs cannot be reached or in any way acted upon by external agencies but through the medium of his outer or inner surfaces—his skin or the membrane lining his air passages.*

The functions of his skin then are of prominent account. It is active in throwing off the internal or animal heat by perspiring, and where it is uncovered by radiating off heat; and in this it is aided by the atmosphere, when colder than itself, carrying off heat by convection. But when the heat of the air is above that of the skin the convection is reversed, bringing heat to the skin and putting its active powers to the double trial of having to throw off, not

* The action of climatic, and especially of barometric, influences upon these surfaces was expatiated upon in an Essay by the author, on the climate of the Himalayas, published in 1824, and referred to under the head Locating of Troops.

only the animal heat, but invading atmospheric heat also. Nevertheless the skin, when aided by suitable clothing, possesses the power of warding off a large amount of heat when brought to it simply by the process of atmospheric convection.

The skin feeble in resisting radiant heat.

Against *radiant* heat, especially solar, the skin has much less power, being chiefly dependent upon the passive provision of that peculiar nervous impression —the sensation of heat—which serves as a warning that the sun's rays should be avoided, and those likewise projected, when the solar heat is intense, from the ground he stands on and from buildings upright before him.

Confined as he is to the ground, his pulmonary and outer skins become assaulted, and too often carried, by malaria in its nascent and direst form. But subtile and baneful as are all forms of malaria, they may to a considerable extent be neutralized by various means; especially by combating in the first instance their powerful coadjutor the sun's rays, and in the second their great opportunity, atony in the cutaneous defences, manifested by a suppressed perspiration.

Ordinary hats and helmets, boxes vapour-tight, or nearly so. Their injurious character.

With respect to the head, the exhalation from its surface ought to be especially encouraged, and in all cases we ought to be very jealous, not to shut the head up in a vapour-tight box, or one which is nearly so, with the feeble means of ventilation to be found in any hats or helmets in England. When exhalation is quite or nearly cut off, and the perspiration lies wet upon the surface, the skin of the head learns to throw out less of it than is natural and necessary.

There can be no doubt that to not a few persons in England, especially those advanced in life, the consequences of smothering, for many successive hours, the exhalation from the head, of all parts of the body, are not a little serious, though the effect may progress too insidiously to be observed. But as fashion is pleased to form our hats, supposing that most capricious and inexorable of despots, and most ignorant, could be induced to permit their walls to be encircled near the crown with a line of perforations, the free ventilation would in these climes chill the head in cold weather. Such insubordination to her is therefore not even attempted. But if our hats had a circle of such ventilating perforations, and below their level a flat inner crown of porous cloth similar to the concave moveable crown, BB, in all the following figures of helmets, the head would be kept from chills and even warmer in severely cold weather than at present; while it would be cooler in hot, and the exhalations might proceed to a natural and desirable extent.

Hats in England faulty, but easily improveable.

Even in the hottest weather, however, in England the smothering of the head by our defective hats is of small moment when compared with its effect in India, where the atmosphere is often at, and above, the blood heat, and the sun's rays so powerful. In such climatic conditions the only known process by which the head can relieve itself of accumulating animal heat (leaving out of account the large amount of intruding external heat) is by a free evaporation of moisture abundantly exhaled.

What then is to be said of coverings for the head

which not only let in solar heat to a large extent, but, as if they were intended as instruments of *capital* punishment, lock up the only door of escape by smothering the scalp altogether or tantalizing it with a few ventilating holes of the size of a pin, or at most of a pencil, and at the crown only! The marvel is, how any warm-blooded animal should, with the head in such a predicament, escape apoplectic destruction, even though it were of the coolest temperament, emasculated and bovine! But, that manly brains,—bulky and busy,—turgid with blood and with thoughts of blood!—with the spirits on fire and excited to the combat!—should endure for one hour the double culinary process of roasting from without and stewing within, is what no reflecting physiologist could have anticipated! The brain does, however, through the aid of the *vis vitæ*, make shift to endure it for the time; but, for the most part, by shifting the oppression from itself to some distant organ, and to the *whole skin* of the body. The man sooner or later *shudders* (a skin impression), vomits, and is in for cholera! or *shudders*, and starts at more than a bayonet in his liver, the commencement of acute inflammation in that organ! or he *shudders*, and dejects blood, while, if there be reality in feeling, his bowels are being twisted into viol strings! Acute dysentery with its long train of suffering is his lot!

Destructive character of military hats.

Especially the portion pressing against the head.

Again, with respect to that portion of a hat more especially which encircles and presses against the head, what are we to think of it? Of the mariner it is said he has but a plank between him and death; but in a good ship and true, that plank effectually keeps out the dangerous liquid. Of the white soldier on the plains of India it may with more force be said, he has but a film between him and death, of leather, pith, or fur, with perhaps a little calico to boot, through which the ethereal fluid leaks in to his destruction! It is positively frightful to contemplate the passive spectacle of the sun above in *Cancer*, British skulls below hard by that tropic, and between them scarce a quarter of an inch of matter, and that the most receptive of radiance, and at the crown only at any distance from the skull, but pressing close against its sides all round. It would be thought a reprehensible waste of property to subject to such solar influence empty caskets of ivory inlaid with goodly stones, seeing they would be warped and cracked to pieces very soon; but that more precious casket, the British skull, filled with a living brain and jewelled with eyes and other organs, has been thus exposed to ruin by thousands! Would that one had the command of rhetoric and of leisure adequately to depict the cerebral ruin and constitutional destruction pacing on in an army marching in such shakos and helmets, and throttled with neck stocks!

But if feeble in depicting the evil I would fain hope to succeed better in the more grateful and important task of attempting a remedy, and will have to beg the reader to contrast with such nominal protection any of the following constructions.

THE SUN.—The Sun then is the foe whose assaults we have first to ward off.

When a man falls, felled like a bullock, by a stroke of the sun, we have its power exhibiting one of Lord Bacon's "glaring instances" of a truth too literally. But so far is this from being its whole, or its chief, offence, that these cases of sun-stroke, while sad indeed for the sufferers, would have their account did they but impress the sight as forcibly as loud military bugles the ear, warning commanders in the Tropics to recognise a discipline more absolute than their own, and, with all despatch, to rid their men of their present shakos (cotton cloth covered though they may be), their bear caps, foraging caps, and throttling stocks, and otherwise to clothe them more in obedience to the laws of natural science.

Sun-stroke an important warning to commanders.

In all but delicate persons the skin may, by a little aid from right clothing, as has been already remarked, be enabled to guard itself against a large amount of atmospheric heat; but reflected and radiated heat, that of the sun especially, possesses a peculiar penetrating power, causing it, before it can be carried off by perspiration, to act upon the nervous expanse of the skin with various degrees of effect in different races: with little or none in many Indians, who can bask in the sun with pleasure; in a modified degree on some few Englishmen who, happening to possess a semi-tropical constitution, can acclimate themselves to it by dint of exposure; but in a very hostile degree on the great majority of them, who are much to be pitied when they fall under the command of one of the former, should he, as has more than once occurred, measure their constitutions by his own and

Action of the sun on the surface in Englishmen and other races.

think to inure them to the sun by forcing them to brave its assaults.

This difference in solar endurance is traceable to various causes. In the first place the scarf-skin of the native of the Tropics (and just in proportion as he has a hereditary habituation to the sun) has a thickness greatly surpassing that of the European, and especially of the enjoyers of our cloudy skies. Even amongst the natives themselves I had occasion to remark, when superintendent of vaccination at Futtehgurh, a surprising difference in the thickness of the skin in infants as well as in adults. *Coolies* and *Assamees*, whose naked bodies are exposed to the sun throughout the day, impart a hereditary thickness to the scarf-skin of their children. To penetrate the outer skin of such infants it was necessary to employ a lancet ground with a strong obtuse point. It was a horny hide when compared with that of the coarsest European adult, or even with that of well-clad and less exposed natives. The reader has doubtless felt, upon some accidental abrasion of the outer or scarf-skin of the finger, how acutely sensitive is the nervous surface of the true skin under it. Perceiving so thin a scarf to have been thus protective, he will the more readily appreciate the resisting power of the Indian's hide many times the thickness of his.

Remarkable thickness of the outer skin in some Indians.

Again, in the Indian the nervous expanse itself has, in the course of many generations, gradually lost much of its sensibility to heat; while the vitals within have also lost much of their irritability to it. Moreover his heat-generating system has long since acquired the habit of a temperate production, so as not to trouble him with such a surplus of animal heat as helps to destroy the European.

Error of attempting to acclimate an Englishman by exposure.

When therefore it is proposed that the Englishman shall inure himself to the climate of India by bravely exposing himself to it, the work of generations is attempted to be effected at once; a work which, by the time it was thoroughly complete in the constitutions of his few surviving descendants, would have simply *re-transformed* them into Asiatics, stewed and torrefied under the same skies which have gradually concocted the Indian. By that time they would probably have become in no way superior to him; since the haughty Englishman has now to acknowledge with him the same Iranian or *Indo*-atlantic stock.

The acclimating experiment has been often made. When aided by hopeful excitement it promises so well for a time, that the lessons of experience are being constantly forgotten. The following were pretty large experiments of the right kind for a prompt decision of the question; not being complicated by any circumstances of mental excitement or change of scene and air tending to modify or postpone the effects.

Instances of its injurious effects.

A finer body of men than Her Majesty's 44th regiment in 1823 could not be found now in the British army. I believe it was 900 strong. The commanding officer was said to have contemned confinement of the men during the day as effeminate, and especially to have continued drilling them in the forenoon after the hot season had begun. Before the error was discovered its dire effects had commenced. For some months not less than one third, and for some weeks one half of the men were in hospital at once; chiefly with fever, dysentery, and cholera. I remember to have seen for some time from five to ten bodies in the dead-room of a morning, many of them specimens of athletics. Again, during a tedious voyage up the Ganges, in medical charge of 800 recruits and drafts, with their families, for different branches of the service, in about 100 boats (there being no steamers on the river in those days), I found that the sickness fell almost entirely upon the men who exposed themselves to the sun by truanting on the shore, and very great and harassing it was. Again, when I was Staff Surgeon of Cawnpore, the field army was moved from their quarters, in the hot winds of 1825, towards Bhurtpore, but the troops were rightly recalled by the Governor-General till the cold season. During their exposure of two months, the usual effects of elating excitement were manifested; the men stood the march as well as the natives; but soon after their return to their barracks the previous exposure to the sun took effect upon them, and filled the hospitals with sick, many with a severe form of cholera, although in the station generally the disease was not at all prevalent at the time; marking the fact I have already emphatically noted, how trifling an amount of the mephisis of any epidemic will suffice to affect the system when the sensorium and the skin have been debilitated by solar action.

At the end of another generation we hear of

precisely similar effects. Hopeful excitement sustains our soldiery of the different forces a time; but sooner or later they begin to yield, and in a year or two long-continued exposure with no better protection than they have at present will, if it shall continue necessary, too certainly shatter the constitutions of nearly all.

Sun-stroke but a small part of the solar effects.

We have abundant evidence that a stroke of the sun is but a small part of the ill-doing in India of that powerful luminary; and it is its direct rays, much more than the high atmospheric temperature which it occasions, which do the mischief, of which notice will be taken under the head "*atmosphere.*"

Each portion of the nervous expanse pervading the skin possesses a close and peculiar sympathy with the vital organ subjacent to it, although it has no continuity of texture with it. This is especially the case with the brain and spine; and there is a peculiarity in the nature of this sympathy in their case, more particularly in that of the brain, which renders heat acting upon the skin of the head invariably trying to the organ within.

The action of the sun's rays in inducing disease,

Now, as has been already observed, reflected and radiant heat, more especially solar, is impinged with a force which eludes the perspiration-barrier of the skin, and excites its nervous expanse. When it is the skin over the head which receives the impulse, either directly or through an imperfect hat, the brain accepts the impression, and sometimes so acutely as to rule its own destruction by apoplectic congestion. The man falls struck by the sun. But much more frequently the brain, *the fountain of vital influence,* impresses its infirmity upon all the other organs, especially on the liver, intestines, and skin, which are already oppressed at such a season by accumulated animal heat, and, in the case of the two former, by sympathy also with the oppressed skin. The brain, instead of ulcerating itself, will often stamp an abscess in the liver, or an ulcer in the bowels, in the smallest number of hours in which the preliminary inflammation can be hurried on to its termination. More frequently still, the debility in the sensorial citadel is transmitted to every part of the outer wall. The whole skin is debilitated, or even paralysed, and *the skin's debility is malaria's opportunity.* The *Mephites* of Fever, Dysentery, and Cholera, stalking over the bodies of a sleeping army, which has been thus exposed to the sun by day, quickly scent out the enfeebled skins, and divide the prey! Thus it is that exposure to the sun renders men obnoxious to all manner of Tropical disease.

and in aggravating the effects of wounds.

To the soldier in action, moreover, the shafts from the solar adversary commingling with those of his human enemies seriously aggravate the effects of the latter. *Traumatic Tetanus*, lock-jaw from wounds, may be considered as more especially a *Tropical* affection. Wounds shattering the nerves to not one fourth the extent which in a temperate climate would be needed to produce this dreadful complication, will suffice to induce it when the *sensorium commune*, the brain and spinal cord, have been daily wrought up to a state of irritation which needs but a hint, as it were, from some distressed extremity, for them to lose all self-control and set the whole frame in convulsion. And in the case of a "*stump,*" is it possible that the exuding and organizing of nature's glue, under the guidance of a subdued and healthy inflammation, can proceed aright when the centre of all command, the brain, is thrown out of tone and tune? —that a brain, which was on the eve of giving itself, some organ, or the whole system, up as a prey to disease, can conduct the delicate and abnormal process of closing up a great wound to as healthy a termination as if that brain had been thoroughly guarded from all solar violence from the moment it received the order to take the field?

It would be painfully interesting to note the possible diminution of death and damage in field hospitals in the Tropics, after, if ever, a perfect system of clothing, housing, and mental recreation (with a consequent diminished intemperance) had been for a sufficient time established.

The spine also suffers from solar action.

The brain's auxiliary, the spinal marrow, is to a great, though minor, extent in the same sympathetic predicament with it. Next to the sun's action on the head, its action on the spine is the most trying, and most to be avoided. But the direct rays of a powerful sun upon the rest of the trunk are also sufficiently injurious to render a repulsion of them desirable.

Atmospheric heat, and the power of perspiration in absorbing it.

THE ATMOSPHERE next demands attention. The temperature of the blood in the Tropics being slightly above what it is in colder zones, or about 100°, and of the skin when not uneasy about 90°, when the atmosphere rises to 100° or more, it would impart heat rapidly to the body but for its being a gaseous fluid which both conducts heat very slowly, and at the same time admits the vapour of perspiration freely into its pores. This vapour absorbs all the heat the air is able to convey to the skin as fast as it is presented. The extent to which atmospheric heat thus assaulting the body may be absorbed, appears to be limited only by the power of the skin to supply moisture.

I have known instances of officers who never used tattees nor closed their glass doors against the hot wind which found its way freely through the venetian doors, and who enjoyed very fair health at the end of a long residence; but in all such cases the sun had been as much as possible avoided. In the few instances in which it had been long braved with apparent impunity there was invariably, as far as my own observation went, an amount of chronic disease, of long continuance, manifestly present, which would render the attainment of anything like longevity out of the question.

The importance of husbanding the tone of the skin.

It is not with any purpose of recommending a habitual exposure to hot wind, that this fact is mentioned; for I have had too much experience of its exhausting effects in my own case, and that of others; but to show that, if the soldier, whom duty compels to expose himself, can but be thoroughly protected from the sun, he will, if in ordinary Indian health, bear, with no great injury, the hot winds of any campaign; and he will bear them all the better if no attempt is made to accustom his skin to them, when he is in quarters, by letting them blow untempered by art through his barrack. The more the skin can be saved from repeated exhaustion, the better tone will it preserve for each necessary emergency. There is no such thing possible as to gain tone by endurance. It is a notable fact that the percentage of mortality does not decrease amongst troops by residence in the country, as it would at the prime of life if an advantageous acclimation were going on, but it steadily increases, showing that exhaustion and not acclimation is the general result.

The real cause of diminished illness in regiments after some residence in India.

We must not mistake the prevalent illness and mortality in a corps recently landed from Europe, and the decrease of illness subsequently, to a want of acclimation at first, and its establishment afterwards. The case is mainly this. In every large body of men, there are some whose constitutions, though perhaps vigorous in a temperate climate, are totally unfitted for a Tropical. These die off at once by acute disease. There are others, generally those who are somewhat feeble anywhere, who sicken early, and are frequently ailing; some of them dying soon, others becoming early invalided. There are also some men of all degrees of vigour so recklessly, sometimes wilfully, careless of themselves, or so dissatisfied with their lot, that they soon fall a prey to the climate, the effects of which they universally precipitate by intemperance and exposure. When all these are sifted out of a regiment, the sickness and mortality, as a matter of course, decrease greatly, but not because the survivors have become climate-proof.

It is not here meant to be affirmed that acclimation of no kind or degree takes place. There is some effect, but it simply amounts to this. To the impressions of malaria, *where they have not taken effect* upon a man, his cutaneous and pulmonary surfaces become in some degree blunted by habit; but *where they have produced disease*, so far is acclimation from following a recovery, that in nearly all cases the susceptibility greatly increases. A man who has had jungle or remittent fever will have relapses, and generally die, if he has not *change of climate*; and he is ever afterwards more susceptible than previously. This is also the case, though in a somewhat less degree, with cholera and dysentery. Again, the diminution in India in the quantity of the blood, and the impoverishment of its quality, which take place, especially in those who have been frequently ill, do certainly lessen the tendency to acute inflammation, and to acute affections of head; but this progress towards decay is a poor sort of acclimation. Lastly, the skin, *in general*, ceases, after a time, to drench itself so immoderately with sweat upon the least exertion, or in a hot atmosphere which is motionless, as at first, and is therefore less open to sudden impressions, especially to chills from a redundant evaporation. If there is any change meriting the name of acclimation it is this. But the main difference between a newly landed and a long resident corps is to be traced to the sifting out from it of the anti-tropical constitutions, the utterly reckless, and the desponding; and to some growth of prudence amongst the rest.

To return to our subject—the action of a tropical

The different phenomena of the conflict between atmospheric heat and cutaneous action.

atmosphere upon the skin and system. If a man sat naked in a perfectly still atmosphere, it would cause him little inconvenience though it were twenty or more degrees above the heat of his blood, were it not for the accumulation of his own animal heat. In such an atmosphere he would run down with perspiration, which would effectually prevent outer heat from being conducted inwards; but it would not at the same time carry off his own internal heat quickly enough to prevent his suffering, unless that air were put in motion. When in motion, however, the quickly renewed visits of dry air so accelerate the evaporation, that not only the atmospheric heat, but also that portion of animal heat which has to pass off by the skin, is absorbed by it. When the current of the hot air is regulated just to this point, either by letting it pass with moderate force through a house or by agitating it moderately by means of a punkah, we have this endurable condition of skin as to heat, and with no such excessive demands made upon it as to exhaust its powers *rapidly*. This is about the general state of the persons mentioned above who let the hot winds have more or less free access to their houses, throwing upon their own skins much rude evaporative duty which had better have been done for them by "*tattees*" *temperately* indulged in. Again, if the motion of the air amounts to a breeze, the absorption of the heat is so rapid that the skin falls much below the heat of the blood, causing the *hot* wind to feel *cold*. We have the curious and frequent, though commonly unobserved, phenomenon of the air without being at 110° or 120°, the blood within at 100°, and a film of moist skin between them at 80° or 90°. While this is going on, the man if hearty, will, for the time, feel refreshed, if delicate, chilly. But it will not last long. Such evaporation soon overtakes the power of supply of any skin, especially of the mummied skin of the old campaigner. The sensible perspiration dries up, and the insensible is not equal to the demand of the inner and outer heat. The skin becomes dry and hot; and its heat will rise in proportion to the insufficiency of the perspiration.

We have here then three unsafe conditions, when the skin is naked, or imperfectly covered, and the air very hot. At one moment, in air absolutely still, the internal heat accumulates; at another, in a breeze, there may be, and often is, such a chill as to cause suppressed perspiration; and, at another, there may be direct febrile irritation from the drying up of the skin and positive ingress of heat.* Again, in the rainy season, when the atmosphere is from 10° to 20° *below* the temperature of the blood, and between showers in a semi-humid state, its conductive power is so considerable that, aiding its remaining evaporative, it becomes especially chilling. Hence the rainy is the season of chills. It is the season also, as it advances, for malaria, of which its humidity appears the solvent and ready vehicle for its mephitic action on an enfeebled skin or pulmonary membrane. Cutaneous phenomena.

Now the skin will be subject to all these liabilities in proportion as the atmosphere *has unrestrained ac-*

* In a work on the statics of the chest and animal heat, published in 1843, and in previous writings, I have dwelt on these points more fully.

cess to it; but especially in proportion as the sun's rays have access to the head and spine, with all their evil effects already detailed.

A hot atmosphere fails to dissipate the sun's rays.

The indirect effect of a hot atmosphere in its neglecting to dissipate the rays of the sun is worthy of notice; since some persons, who have experienced little inconvenience from a tropical sun at sea or on mountains, are apt when suffering from exposure on continental plains to charge their distress to the atmospheric heat directly, more than to the sun, which used not to distress them under the former circumstances, though it was at an equal altitude.

I have heard this fact argued in favor of accustoming oneself to a tropical sun. It is true that the hot air is in one sense chargeable with the whole assaults of the continental heat, both its own heat and the sun's; but it is much in the same way as a sleeping guard is chargeable with the inroad of an enemy. A cool, and especially a cold atmosphere, is vigilant to carry off by convection very fierce solar heat, directly it is, by lighting upon the surface of any opaque matter, changed from a radiant to an operative state. Thus; although the highly transparent atmosphere, often obtaining on lofty mountain heights in the Tropics, transmits the sun's rays with unimpeded force, it is so cold that it catches them up, the instant they have alighted, wherever it can circulate with freedom over the impinged surface. That struggle for dominion between the empires of cold and heat—so majestically described by Milton—the summer traveller in Switzerland may see to some extent exemplified; but

Remarkable mountain phenomenon.

more forcibly he, who, toiling over the passes of the Himalayas, shall be careful to note how, of two contiguous spots, both of them beaten upon by a sun of high ascension, the one may be—not merely a surface of melting snow or *glacier*, but a region of *active frost*—the subject of a keen wind sweeping away from it all solar heat it had in mockery transmitted to it! while the other spot, sheltered from that wind by a rocky prominence, or a lofty cliff of ice itself, and replete with those calorific transmissions, may be luxuriant with vegetable and even with insect life!

In a cold mountain wind the ordinary head-dress of the soldier might suffice if it were more shading.

To descend to the plains. Could we bring down to blow over the soldier's head-dress that cold wind, even the little things he is now provided with, while acting as ray-traps to feed the keen air with heat, all of which it would lick up at their very surface, would suffice to protect the heads they covered, and would cease to present to the eye of science the pitiful and painful aspect they do. But, unfortunately, on the plain and solid surface of the earth, where the sun has great power, the air will be hot, and will then but feebly catch up from any surface its impinging rays.

THE GROUND.—Omitting as foreign to the present undertaking any inquiry into the action of the earth and its productions as the sources of malaria, we have to confine our view to the action of the ground in radiating and reflecting heat upon the body of the soldier. That this mundane heat proves a material aggravation of the direct action of the sun from above, every observant person in the Tropics must have perceived, when standing upon a glaring soil; especially if he contrasts its effects with that of a green sward, or an elevated position, as an upper balcony.

THE SOLDIER'S DRESS.

HAVING taken a glance at the mode of action of the SUN, the GROUND, and the ATMOSPHERE upon the skin, and through it upon the brain and the system in general, and having taken as full a view, as was compatible with brevity, of the various properties of matter in relation to heat, which are available for protecting the body from radiant and reflected heat, and, to a certain extent, from atmospheric, I purpose deferring a further consideration of the latter until the body dress is treated of, and now proceed at once to the point first in importance.

Character of an effective head-dress.

THE HEAD DRESS.—A head-dress to be effective should possess such resisting power as to ward off entirely the whole rays of the sun throughout an exposure to its action of any duration; and not only from the skull, but also from the sides of the head, face, and neck. It ought also to transmit so copious a ventilation over the head as to encourage the perspiration to evaporate freely from it; and yet with a provision by which in cold weather the circulation of the air could be, at once, reduced or cut off. At the same time, such a head-dress should be no more cumbrous than was necessary to fulfil all those conditions completely.

It is here proper to remark that while all unnecessary weight and bulk should, as a matter of course, be avoided, to object to that which was really necessary for his complete protection, would be not a whit more reasonable than to complain of the size and weight of the soldier's rifle and ammunition, and to substitute for them an air-gun and its pellets, which would better defend him against his human enemy than does his present head-dress against his solar. It may at once be affirmed with confidence that the soldier will be abundantly repaid the trouble of carrying every inch and ounce of helmet which is necessary for a total repulsion of the sun and prevention of its dire and complicated effects.* We may in England, in the effeminacy of luxurious life, foster sensitiveness to weight and consult levity in our hats until "the grasshopper will be a burden" should it settle upon them, but in the Tropics the *weight* of the sun's rays is such that even the effeminate would be thankful to bear any weight of defensive matter on their heads in lieu of that crushing sense of weight which knocks the strongest down at last. Well would it be worth while to reduce, if needful, his accoutrements by a pound or more, and add it if required to his head-dress. In fact, the head readily acquires the habit of carrying with ease ten or twenty times that necessary weight. Not to mention our maiden carriers at home of fruit and fish, and Welch butter-women balancing their firkin to market on

The question of weight and bulk considered.

The head well fitted for carrying weight.

* The subject is further considered in p. 95.

their heads, walking, knitting, and singing as they go, we find in India itself the head to be the chief seat of carriage ; *kuhars* (bearers) only employing the shoulders. The coolie trotting many miles with his five to eight stone of grain, the milk and well girls with their spherical foot or even eighteen inches of liquid, and women and children with their "*cowrie khapes*" of mud *running eight hours a day* and rearing the most formidable of fortresses, prove that by choice the head is selected for carrying loads, and for great distances rivals the back and shoulders. With these facts before our minds we must perceive how wanting in judgment it would be to object to any addition of weight *necessary* for an effective head-dress. Indeed that costly erection the bearskin hat, so formidable to nursery children but otherwise so useless, is even now, though much lightened, weightier than a thoroughly protective helmet or shako need be, and far more so from its being top-heavy. Owing to the large surface it presents to the wind it subjects the neck also to horizontal strains in all directions, which are beyond measure more trying than a steady vertical weight of much greater amount.

The bear-skin hat.

A variety of trials leads me to believe that a really sun-proof head-dress may be produced weighing about two pounds; but were the weight as much again, if properly poised, as explained hereafter, it would be of small moment in comparison with any short-coming in the protection.

Placing in order before our view the six available properties of matter concerned in the movements of heat, which we have already examined, we may endeavour to enlist on our side for our present purpose all but one of them—*the subterranean absorption of heat.*

While, on the one hand, we must on no account defraud our principles of one inch of space or one ounce of matter which is really necessary for their development—while we must, as we would acquit ourselves of a solemn responsibility, crucify fashion in a moment wherever we find it treacherously doing the work of our enemies in betraying our soldiers to the attacks of climate, it behoves us, on the other hand, to husband our means so well, as to avoid all redundance of bulk and weight, no fraction of space or particle of matter employed being superfluous or inoperative. We shall find it impossible to jump to our conclusion at once,—to arrive at so desirable a result by a single construction. Not only do bulk and weight, but durability, and facility of repair on the spot, enter as important elements into the question of practical utility.

A rejection of fashion and proper economy of space and weight.

Let it not be imagined any longer that this is the trifling question it has been supposed. We may no doubt command a comparatively considerable amount of protection by seizing upon some one form of matter having the familiar property of slow conduction, as cotton cloth, or "sola," and by a reduplication of it into a thick mass, as a turban or a hat of pith some inches thick. But such protection is temporary only; and unless we are careful to set that hat out at night under a clear sky, that it may radiate away a portion of the heat accumulated in its substance under the sun by day, it will begin to heat the head even as soon as it is put on; and at best

Protection of cotton cloth but temporary.

we cannot prevent substances, which are such ready receivers of radiant heat as these, from becoming gorged with it.

Slow-conducting impervious matter, next the head, injurious.

Moreover we must be careful how we place a mass of slow-conducting and impervious matter *next to the head* and pressing round its sides; thereby, not only shutting in perspiration, but also retarding the conduction of the animal heat outwards, as much as of the solar inwards. In all solar hats in use, and also in all ordinary military helmets, it is only when the atmosphere has risen to above 100° (a state rare except in Western India, and during the hot winds) that the detention of the animal heat of the head by such coverings ceases to be chargeable to their slow conducting nature.

As already remarked, no single principle or property of matter in relation to heat will alone give that complete protection which we are bound to strive after.

A thick roof even, is penetrated by the sun's rays.

Any one who would trifle with the difficulty ought, towards a hot weather afternoon in India, to be stationed on a ladder in a room having a masonry roof, of even a foot and a half in thickness, with his head not as near to it indeed as the soldier's to his helmet, but at some inches from it. He will very soon be thankful to descend from his elevation and escape a radiance of heat which neither the massive thickness nor the slow-conducting character of the materials of the roof has prevented from penetrating through it. The officer in a tent having double walls and flies, of many plies of cloth each, who is yet compelled to sit with a wetted turban on his

Fig. 2.

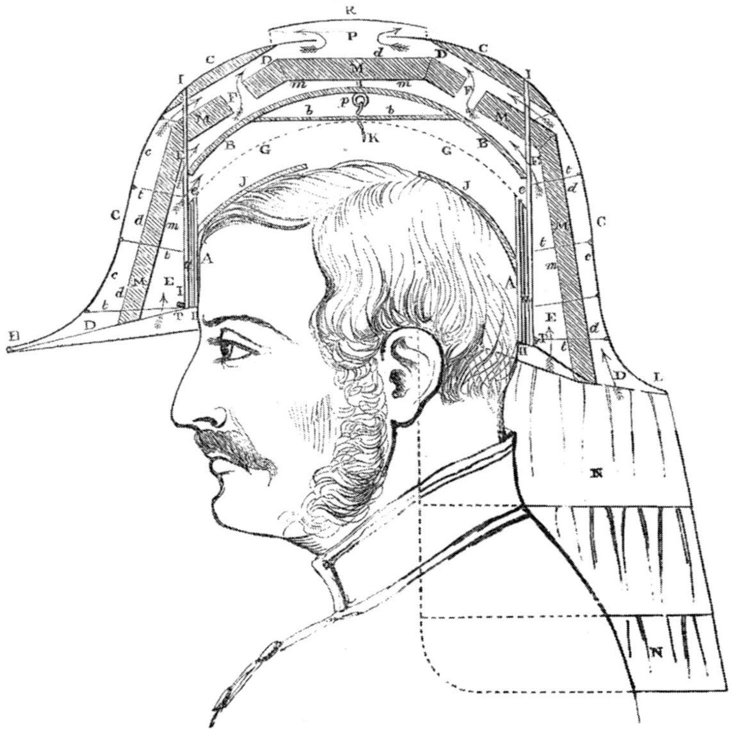

Fig. 3.

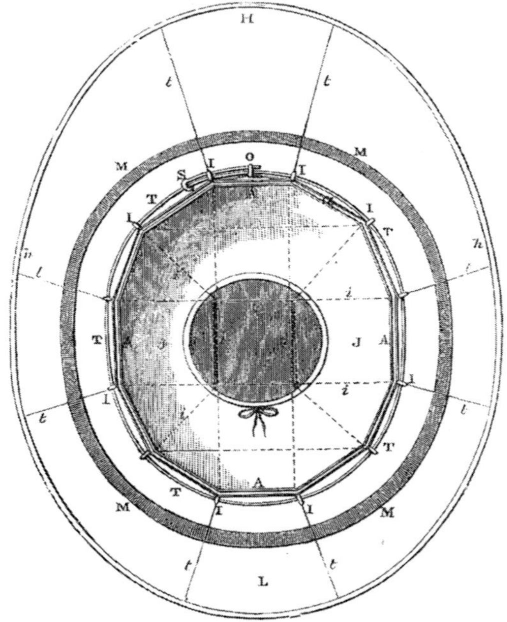

head, will assuredly not trifle with the difficulty of our undertaking. Neither will the experimental philosopher, who well knows that theory, indispensable as it is, can only guide us to general principles, and that his sciences have not, as yet, so far advanced, as to admit of that mathematical exactness which would enable us to decide *without experiment* in what relative proportion to employ our several principles, if indeed we should be able to select beforehand the best *order* for their successive operation.

HELMETS FOR MOUNTED TROOPS.

COMMENCING with one form of head-dress for mounted troops, and ranging our defensive principles in one of the different orders in which they may be more or less effectively employed, we may place *Reflection* in the van; next to it *Retarded Conduction;* then *Slow Radiation*, then *Convection*, then *Reflection* again; then *Slow Conduction*, then *Slow Radiation* again; then, to carry off the animal heat, &c., *Ventilation* and *Exhalation;* and lastly, and occasionally, artificial *Evaporation*.

The defensive principles available in the construction of head-dress,

Commencing with helmets of one type, Let Fig. 2 represent a vertical section from front to back of a soldier's head-dress. The cross section from ear to ear differs from the former only by the smaller cross diameter of the head, and by the absence of the front and back peak.

embodied in a helmet proposed.

Fig. 3 shows the plan or base of the hat as seen from below. The letters in both figures denote the same parts. Deferring all details of the construction;

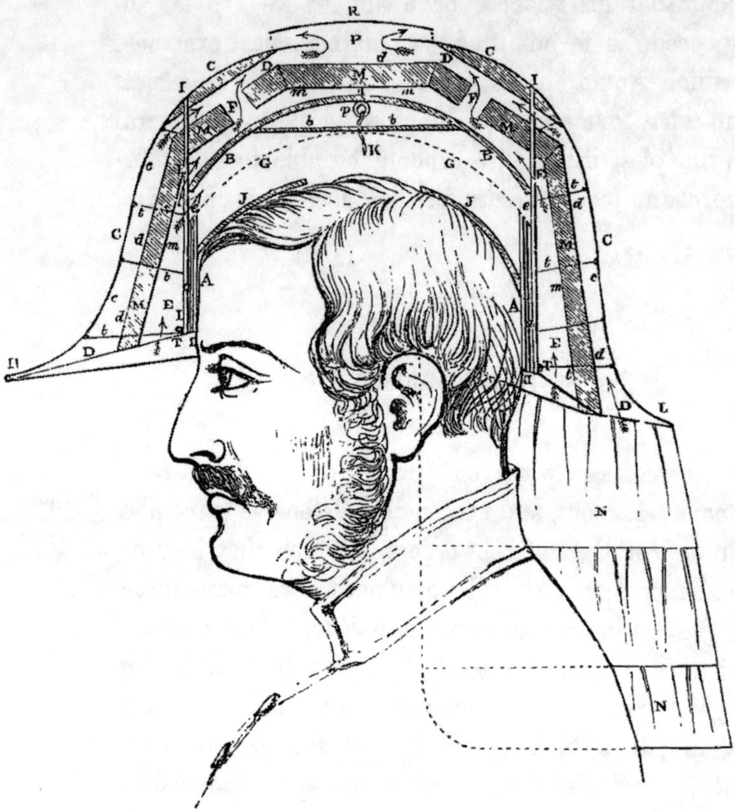

Fig. 2.

the walls of the hat round the head, from A to C, will be found an inch and a half thick, and to comprise the following matter, space, and virtue. The outside shell, C C, of this hat is either a bright metal shell of brass or German silver able to support itself, or a strong fine canvas coated on the outside and inside with bright tin; or lastly, should a reflecting exterior in a *spheroidal* helmet be considered, even for cavalry, so objectionable as to overrule the

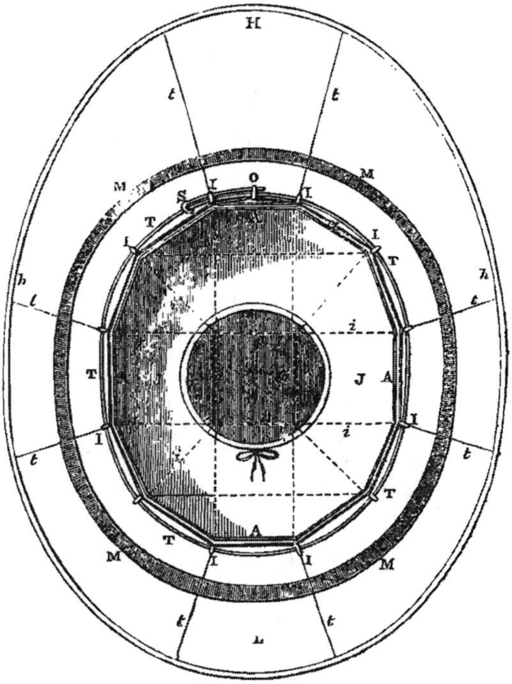

Fig. 3.

great advantages it offers to its wearer—whom its visibility in certain positions would not expose to one-tenth the danger from the missiles of his human enemies which its reflective power would avert from his solar—should it be demanded that in this type of helmets the surface shall not be reflective, we must sacrifice *the exterior* metal and leave the canvas bare, or coat it with a thin varnish of a slate colour. Clinging, however, to a metallic exterior until forced

The value of tin as an outer and inner surface.

to renounce it, a surface of tin claims our preference; inasmuch as, next to a gold surface, it is the least given to tarnish. It is so brilliant, that, could it retain its face, it alone would repel at once the larger part of the impinging rays; but though less affected chemically by atmospheric agents than silver, the surface of which falls so ready a prey to sulphur, both this agent in the atmosphere and the oxygen slightly damage its face; while its softness causes it to be so easily scratched that it soon loses its brilliancy. Nevertheless when tin, as an old tin teapot, has lost, in common with the aged housewife who may own it, the brilliant complexion of early freshness, and can with her claim homage only for thriftiness, it will be found to have still a surface very *slow to lose* and therefore *slow to receive* heat by radiation. It will economize her tea far better than if enclosed in a cotton or leather surface. And many a poor fellow's life would have been saved could he have inverted over his shako any clean tin pot, however old, but not blackened by smoke.

Outward reflection.

This tin surface C C then will be found, even when damaged, to throw off so large an amount of rays as to render it an agent well worthy of employment. It is fixed down upon the canvas casing by processes which promise with proper appliances to acquire much durability.

Retarded conduction inwards.

This canvas, while it carries the metallic surfaces and forms a strong casing for the hat, is equal to a layer of stout calico as a *retarding* conductor of the heat that has penetrated the outer surface, in its progress to the surface of tin-foil lining the inside of the canvas. This inner metallic face, c c, being protected from injury, will retain much of its brilliancy, and will prove, as when retaining the heat of a housewife's tea, an *unwilling radiator* of heat to the surface, *d d*, opposite to it; thus bringing into action the principle of *Slow Radiation.* Whatever objections may be entertained to exterior surface brilliancy, there can be none raised to our indulging ourselves, or rather the subjective brain within, to a repetition of it in the cavernous walls of the helmet wherever its virtues of prompt *reflection* and stint *radiation* can be brought to act with effect. Between the surfaces, *c c* and *d d*, is a space D D, &c., half an inch wide, all round the hat, open at bottom to the atmosphere, and having a free vent at top through the aperture P, and the openings around the ventilating cover R. This space then is devised both to give play to the virtue of the surfaces *c c c* and *d d d*, and as a free way for air which can rush up it without interruption, rising either by its buoyancy when heated, or by the pressure of the current caught by the curtain N of the hat, and turned upwards. To the air flowing up the space D D, the unwillingly radiating metallic surface, *c c*, imparts its heat readily by conduction, which the air carries away with it by *convection.* Which principle is here brought into action.

Slow-radiation.

Internal brightness free from every objection.

Inter-laminar convection.

But it would not do to suppose that no heat is radiated inwards from the tin lining of the canvas. To repel as much of such heat as possible we have a bright tin surface, *d d*, on the inner side of the air space D D. This surface brings the principle of *Re-*

Reflection repeated.

flection a second time into play, and with power, owing to the brightness of its protected surface. It is true that it operates so far disadvantageously compared with the outermost reflecting surface C C, that, whereas the latter gets rid altogether of whatever heat it has repelled by reflection, the heat being projected away into space or to distant objects, the inner reflecting surface *d d*, on the contrary, has opposed to it, at half an inch distance, a reflecting surface *c c*, as bright as itself, which beats the rays back again. While the rays are thus tossed forwards and backwards like shuttlecocks between battledores, they by degrees obtain some entrance into the metallic surfaces; but then, they become, as combined heat, readily imparted to the current of air ascending between the surfaces, which, as just explained, will take away much of them by *convection*.

Slow-conduction, medium for its action.

This third metallic surface, *d d*, overlies a body of soft wadding, M M, three-eighths of an inch thick, which receives from it and transmits tardily whatever heat has not been intercepted by the previous agencies; and thus brings into play in an efficient manner the principle of SLOW-*Conduction*. This principle is not placed in the van, but is introduced as a powerful reserve, to retard the progress of rays which have broken in through all the previous barriers, and are coming by dead pressure for conduction; against which such fibrous matter is effective, whereas it can offer but poor resistance to the solar rays if it is so placed as to receive the brunt of them direct, when they come vibrating down through space as projectiles. It is of importance that we should keep efore our view the fact already noted, that fibrous matters of all kinds, both vegetable and animal, are most ready recipients of *radiated* heat. Thus the leather of a shako and the cotton rag above it, when a cover is used, or the flimsy pith named "sola," take in the solar rays readily. The virtue of all these porous matters rests solely in their slow-conducting power; and so valuable is this property that where the exposure is of short duration, as for an hour or so, they will, if thick, answer that purpose. But since they absorb most of the rays of heat that fall upon them, they become in time gorged with heat, which their under surface then, not being metallic, radiates to surfaces near to them, as the head, with great facility. Hence fibrous matter, unless it be employed in two or more layers, far apart from each other, and each of them of such substance as to be thick, bulky, and cumbrous indeed, can never give anything like complete protection. While, if they touch the head, or there be not much ventilation going on, they detain animal heat as already explained.

Defect of cotton, leather, &c., as absorbing heat.

Having placed our slow-conducting medium M M, &c., in a favorable position, protected by successive metallic shelters from all direct rays, and saved also from much of their heat, which has penetrated, by the brisk convection of it going on up the channel D D, we shall yet do well to keep our view upon such heat as does still pervade this slow-conducting case M M, &c., after all our precautions. We shall do well to retard the propulsion of such heat from the otherwise freely radiant inner surface of our slow-conducting medium M M, by coating it also with tin-foil, and

The action of slow-radiation repeated.

thus again employing the principle of *Slow Radiation.* Of the small amount of heat this *metallic face* may receive, it will project no appreciable amount to the fabric A A, opposite to it, which is in contact with the wearer's head.

A second interior and ventilating channel.

Between the surface *m m*, and the woollen fabric A A, is a space E E, similar to the exterior space D D, in being open to the atmosphere below all round the bottom of the hat, and in having a free ventilation above; but the air rising in this space has no communication with the exterior and hotter current in D D, until it falls into it near its exit at top by passing out through four holes F F, in the slow-conducting case M M, which casing is made thicker at the crown where the sun's rays beat more severely than at the sides. The value of a slow-conducting medium M M, between the heated current rising in the channel D D, and the comparatively cool current ascending in E E, and ventilating the head, will now be apparent.

Fabric next the head. Its especial property.

It is to be noted that the fabric A A, which presses against the head, is not impervious to moisture like the substance composing all ordinary hats, shakos, or helmets, which consequently heat the forehead and detain the perspiration, but is of so porous a texture as to permit the perspiration to be exhaled freely through it into the fresh ascending current in E E. So likewise the top of the head is freely ventilated by the ascending current passing over it through the broad aperture *e e e*, all round between the sides A A, and the shifting crown B B. This ventilation permits the head to throw off perspiration copiously, while the wearer's hair, acting on the principle of the body dress described hereafter, detains the sensible perspiration sufficiently to prevent its being carried off too rapidly by a very dry air. Where a person is bald, the inner crown, B B, which is moveable, may be drawn down if the drying is too rapid. This crown being very porous will permit exhalations from the head to pass freely through it, and be carried off in the ventilating air, which can also permeate this crown sufficiently. This casing A A, and crown B B, while porous themselves and permitting a free exhalation, are sheltered by the inch and a half of gaseous and solid matter (just described) of different kinds and properties, and variously arranged; some for repelling and others for intercepting all intruding heat, even to tripping up such of its last straggling portions as reach and fall in the way of the inner ventilating current E E.

Inner crown shifting.

Furthermore, the case may arise in a very hot and arid atmosphere, when additional moisture would be desirable for tempering the heat by more evaporation than the head can supply. Such moisture can be readily introduced through a tube T, Fig. 8, fixed through the ventilating top R, and the casing M, and ordinarily closed by a cork, with or without a feather or other military ornament connected to it. Water-bearers, "*bheesties*," accompanying an army, might, as opportunities were offered, pour water into soldiers' hats through these tubes with their "*dolchees*," leathern mugs; the water would pass to the top of the inner crown B B, and soaking it would trickle down the porous side A A. While the hat itself ought to be proof against all *solar* heat, this additional evapora-

Supply of moisture for evaporation.

tion would be valuable in absorbing *atmospheric* heat when it was intense, so long as the supply of moisture lasted. If five or ten gallons per hour could be supplied for the purpose to every hundred men, it would be worth while to overlay these inner crown and walls with several folds of thick and porous cotton cloth, that they might hold as much as a pint at a time. The uncertainty of the supply and the inconvenience of the detention (though the watering might take place at each halt of the troops) offer some obstacle to this provision. Nevertheless, it is worthy of attention.

It is, however, only during about three months of the year, and in the more arid parts of India, that the temperature rises above blood heat. At other times, provided the sun's rays can be completely prevented from penetrating to the head, and there is a free flow of air over it, and over such a porous and evaporating fabric as surrounds the brows in this hat, the natural perspiration, husbanded in this fabric and in the hair of the head, would in general suffice to carry off the animal heat readily enough.

Shifting inner crown.

The inner crown B B is suspended by a cord K, with a sliding button P, by drawing which and pulling on the tape *b b*, the crown is brought down into the dotted position G G, or to any intermediate position. When this crown is raised, the air of ventilation flows both above and below it,—above, to carry off any heat that has stolen downwards through all the intercepting media exterior to it, and below it to ventilate the head.

When the crown B B is drawn down, it rests upon

the upper edge of the inner walls, or fabric A A. The *current* of air is then entirely cut off from the head of the wearer, and his helmet becomes as warm a cover in cold weather, as it is cool in hot. At the same time the head is by no means suffocated, even when the crown is quite down. The crown being itself composed of like porous fabric with the sides, A A, would permit an exhalation to take place through it, abundant for cold weather.

Such a provision of a shifting crown is important on more than one account. It appears to me desirable that the same helmet should be worn at all seasons, that the head may be habituated to one size and weight of helmet. Every change is irksome at first, and campaigning in hot weather is at best so trying, that every irksome change that can be avoided at that time should be. On the other hand, use is second nature. The mere habit of wearing any one form of head-dress constantly would render it, provided it did but fit the head well, more acceptable to the feelings than any other. Again, even in the cold weather in India, men, suffering from chronic disease of the liver, are frequently distressed and injured by the mid-day sun, and require more protection for the head than may appear necessary to the vigorous. In the valleys in the more hilly parts of India, as in Bundelkund, there is often in the colder months a difference of temperature of 40 degrees between sunrise and two o'clock in the same day, at which hour the sun by contrast is oppressive to most men as early in the year as February, and as late as November. With this helmet the soldier might com-

Its importance.

mence his march of a raw morning, with the crown drawn snugly down, and his head comfortably warm. But when the day grew oppressive, especially if he were preparing to engage in the heat of combat, he would find great relief from simply raising up the crown, more or less, to admit ventilation.

Description of the fabrication and materials of this helmet.

We have now to consider the materials and fabrication of this helmet.

In one form, the whole fabric is supported by a cage or frame, Fig. 4, of steel wire, consisting of six vertical arches, crossing over the summit at two centres *x x*, and forming twelve equidistant ribs *v v*, &c. all round. A spiral steel wire, winding round them to the top, forms with them an elastic cage of steel, which may be sword-proof, and at the same time light.

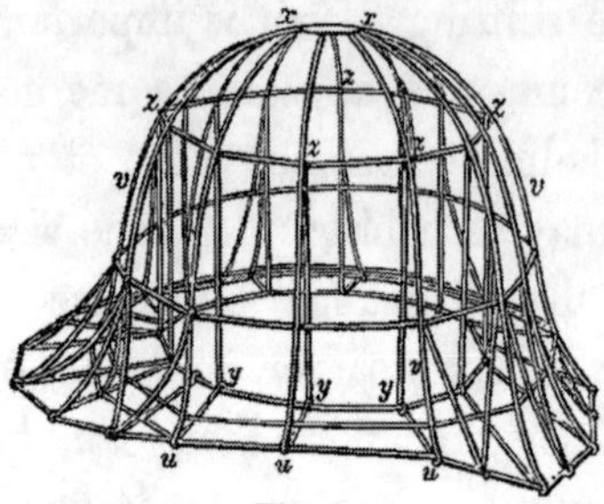

Fig. 4.

The lower ends of the ribs are bent at a right angle *u u*, converging towards the centre of the helmet, and at a distance of an inch and a half at another right angle *y y*, upwards; their extremities *z z* being firmly secured each to the rib of which it is a continuance. Thus are formed a number of brackets, *u y*, pointing inwards.

In this simple manner a strong framework is formed, over the exterior of which the strong canvas cover c c, Fig. 3, faced on one or both sides with tin-foil, is stretched. The pliancy of this cloth covering, and the elasticity of the steel frame carrying it, would render it proof against injury from ordinary accidents, as falls or pressure; while any abrasions of the surface by violence may be easily repaired by an instructed person.

The inner casing M M, Figs. 2 and 3, designed to act as a slow-conducting medium, is formed of compressed cotton wadding, or the pith "sola," lined on both sides with tin-foil, for the reasons already detailed.

Provision for varying the size of the helmet.

The casing or sides A A, Figs. 2, 3, and 8, next the head, is formed of fine thick flannel, or other porous woollen cloth, and is firmly attached to the twelve upright wires, *y z*, of the basket, Fig. 4, or in Figs. 2 and 3 to the twelve wires I I I, &c. A worsted band *a a*, about two inches wide, surrounds the fabric A A, between it and the wires I I I. This encircling band *a a* is grasped across its breadth, at O, Fig. 3, by a wire staple O, with an eye at top, by twisting which with the thumb and finger the band is wound upon it, and the sides A A are compressed from an oval to a polygonal form. By this arrangement the size of helmet round the head is variable instantaneously, and to a considerable extent. A wire pin S, sliding by eyes on the oval wire at the base of the frame I I I, &c., is passed into the eye of the pin, O, to keep it from untwisting.

The weight supported on the top of the head.

A fold of open canvas or fine net, J J, Figs. 2 and 3, is attached to the upper edge of the cloth A A all round, and to all the wires I I I, and its loose fold is drawn with a tape into a cap J J, resting on the head of the wearer. This causes the whole weight of the helmet to rest upon the head, instead of being in any degree supported, as in common hats, by tight lateral pressure against the sides of the head; than which nothing can be more disadvantageous. A weight which habit would render almost imperceptible, if it were distributed equally upon the head, becomes insupportable if it has to be suspended by tight pressure against the sides of the head.

Important uses of the provision for varying the size or tightness of the hat.

As already observed, the encircling wall or cloth A A, as seen in the base view Fig. 3, does not form an oval, but a polygon, stretched loosely from bracket to bracket, and brought into the angular form by tightening a band *a a*, surrounding the fabric. When the band is loosened, the cloth wall A A can be stretched into a more oval form, and its calibre much increased. By this provision, not only may the same size of helmet be made to fit a considerable range of heads; but to each man the fitting will be more comfortable than the ordinary hat of fixed dimensions. In the latter case a trifling difference of size makes all the difference between insecure looseness and painful tightness. Also one size of hat does not suit a man well at all times. A hat, as tight as can ordinarily be worn with comfort, feels insecure in a high wind, and has to be pushed farther down on the head; whereas a helmet in India ought not to be so shallowly worn as to admit of this. Moreover a hat pleasantly easy for ordinary weather, urges the wearer in a high wind to keep his *occipito-frontalis* and *temporal* muscles in a constant state of contraction, in order to swell out the integuments of the head against the hat and keep it from being blown out of position if he has a chin-strap, or off altogether if he has none. This continued contraction of the muscles of the head is one chief source of weariness in marching long in a high wind, and a cause often of head-ache. Whereas in this helmet the soldier can, without removing it even, tighten or loosen the enclosing band at pleasure, and thus make any difference he pleases in the degree of pressure round the head; tightening it in a strong wind or when he is preparing for combat. Again; the pressure against the head, being that of many flat facets instead of a rigid oval, will have a pleasant elasticity from the springiness of each face.

The front peak H is in this helmet, as shown in Fig. 3, as wide at its base *h h* as the whole diameter of the sides, and projects so well forwards that all the front and sides of the face will be guarded from the sun. The hinder peak L may descend as far down behind the neck as the motion of the head in looking upwards will permit; but for the protection of the neck, reliance must chiefly be placed in an effective back curtain N N.

Peculiar pliancy of the construction of Figs. 2 and 3 helmets.

The helmet, as shown in Figs. 2 and 3, is not constructed upon the wire basket, Fig. 4, but, with a view to lightness in the following manner. The lines *i i i i*, Fig. 3, show the crossings at top of a strong wire frame or basket, the sides of which are twelve upright wires I I, I I, Figs. 2 and 3, terminating below in eyes which a stout oval wire, T T, passes through, and is firmly secured to all round.

The outer casing C C, of canvas lined with tin, is

not rigidly fixed to this wire frame, but is simply stiffened out (as fashion distends female skirts, but with more of reason and stiffness) by spiral coils of fine steel wire crossing each other within it from top to bottom. This case C C, then, is simply placed over the stout wire frame I I, I I, after the inner casing M M has been built into it, and is firmly secured to the frame round the upper line I I, Fig. 2. It is then maintained concentric with the enclosed frame by means of stays of cord *t t t t*, stretching from it to the upright wires I I of the inner frame. These stays pass through the inner case M M at different levels all round, and are firmly secured to it in their passage, so as to keep it suspended in its midway position between the outer case C C and the frame I I.

By this construction, rigidity is only needed in the small inner frame or basket of wire I I I I, which forms the basis on which the whole rests. The casings C C and M M, while stiff enough to maintain their position and scarcely to vibrate perceptibly in a strong wind, are pliant and yielding to pressure or blows. To give a *rigid* support to so large a case as C C, requires an addition of more than half a pound of wire, and even then the durability would probably be less than in a construction elastic and yielding. At the same time such a helmet, while its main object is protection from the sun, would afford no small protection from sword-cuts. To cut through the crossings *i i i i*, Fig. 4, of stout steel wires at the crown, and then through the several media down to the head of the wearer, would require no ordinary stroke of the arm and temper in the blade. Of

Protection against sword cuts.

oblique cuts the force would probably be exhausted, on the tough yielding casings and the stout upright wires I I I I, within them, around the head, before the latter was seriously cut or contused. It has to be borne in mind that it is not the wound alone, but the concussion also which the brain receives from a blow coming with unbroken force, which renders cuts on the head so dangerous. No contemptible advantage of the size necessary for a perfect solar helmet would be its interposing matter like an advanced guard or a buffer, to receive the first shock of blows at some distance from the skull.

Cuts on the head. Their peculiarity.

The trial helmets which have been made of this and the next following kind have, in addition to the parts above described as essential to them, four ventilating ports, dotted outlines V V, Fig. 8, each screened with a projecting hood, which are the mouths of tubes fixed midway up the sides of the helmet, and crossing from the outer casing C C, into the chamber over the head, as at G G. These ports allow air to be blown through the helmet over the head, and materially increase the ventilation.

Lateral ventilators in some hats.

Metal Plate Helmets.

METAL PLATE HELMETS.—Holding still to the same general form and operative parts, trial helmets having a sheet-brass surface have been made in lieu of one of metal-faced cloth on a wire frame, as Figs. 2 and 4. The brass being bright on the outside, and tinned within, affords at once the two operative properties of reflection outwards and slow radiation inwards, and is itself a stiff case into which the softer inner casings, &c., can be conveniently fixed. The only objection to this construction has been the difficulty of combining together adequate size, rigidity, and lightness. Through the superior skill and appliances of a London House largely engaged in the brass manufactures, Messrs. Tylor and Sons, of Warwick Lane, these requirements have been realized to an extent which was not anticipated, and to the zealous interest they have taken in the matter we may be indebted for the utmost combination of lightness and strength in the outer shell for such helmets which hardened metal admits of. Trial will determine the comparative advantages of this metal plate, and the steel frame helmet covered with the metal-faced cloth, or with cloth lined within only with metal. By adding about three-quarters of a pound to the weight, the metal plate helmet can be given a rigidity proof against any but severe blows, and with the interior provisions quite proof against a sword-cut. Since the tendency of brass to become tarnished might involve more frequent cleaning than was convenient to a marching army, white metal may be substituted for it, which possesses even greater hardness and powers of resistance, and is much less affected by the atmosphere and other chemical agencies causing tarnish.

The brass shell made by Messrs. Tylor for a helmet of the patterns Figs. 2 and 3, has its interior construction somewhat varied from that in the figures. The intermediate casing M M, of slow-conducting matter, lies in contact with the outer brass shell as a lining to it. In this, the current of *convection* in the passage D D, and the inner *reflecting* surface *d d*, are omitted. Trial would determine with what loss of effect. Were the exterior surface not bright, such a sacrifice of principles within the walls would be indeed an error.

Double Shed Helmet.

THE DOUBLE SHED HELMET.—This helmet is also of metal plate, and acts upon the same general principles with the former, but has not quite so many protective provisions. Yet from the great freedom with which the air circulates amongst its parts, it may prove in no way inferior to the former kinds with concentric layers and ventilating currents. The objection taken to a bright metallic surface that it renders the wearer more visible to an enemy than any other has been already noticed in the commencement of the work. To what is stated there and in the sequel, it may be added, first, that, admitting the validity of the objection, it is a question whether a loss of life or of military results could arise from this cause, amounting to a tithe of the loss which might result from sacrificing so valuable a principle at the surface as *Reflection*; and secondly, that even if we retain the conoidal or spheroidal form we may, as will be more fully explained, convert this very property of reflection into a means of obscuration, rendering a helmet, in proportion as it is most bright, least visible. This may be effected by breaking up the curved surfaces into a multitude of steps, presenting only vertical and horizontal planes, which cannot but reflect all solar rays up to the heavens or downwards to the ground, excepting those at the moment of sunset, or sunrise.

A bright exterior vindicated.

Its visibility obviated.

Construction of the Double Shed Helmet.

Fig. 5 is a vertical section of this helmet from front to back.

Fig. 6 is a base view, or the aspect of the helmet when inverted. In both figures the letters correspond with the same parts.

This helmet consists essentially of the following members.

1st.—The upright sides A A, forming an upright oval, as in ordinary beaver hats.

2nd.—The inner shifting crown B B.

3rd.—The exterior crown or upper shed C C, united to the sides all round their summit at D D, and projecting as a shed E E, beyond them.

4th.—The Lower Shell or Shed F F, encircling the sides a little above their mid-way at G G, and sweeping down to form a shed exterior to them. In front this shed projects forwards to form a peak H, and behind downwards to form, with a curtain as in Fig. 3, a shield for the neck, L.

Its surface reflection and slow radiation inwards.

It will be seen at once that the roof C C, and the shed F F, are the parts which receive the brunt of the sun's rays. They are of sheet metal, more or less bright both on the outer and inner surfaces—on their outer to give action, as in the helmets just described, to the effective principle of *reflection*; and on their inner to bring into play *slow-radiation*.

Important provisions.

Commencing with the inner upright casing A A, D G, next the head; the lower portion of it is of soft porous cloth formed into a twelve-sided prism A A, Fig. 6, by attachment to the wire brackets I I I, &c., which support them. Enclosed by a worsted band, contractible by a draw tie, S, or still better,

FIG. 5.

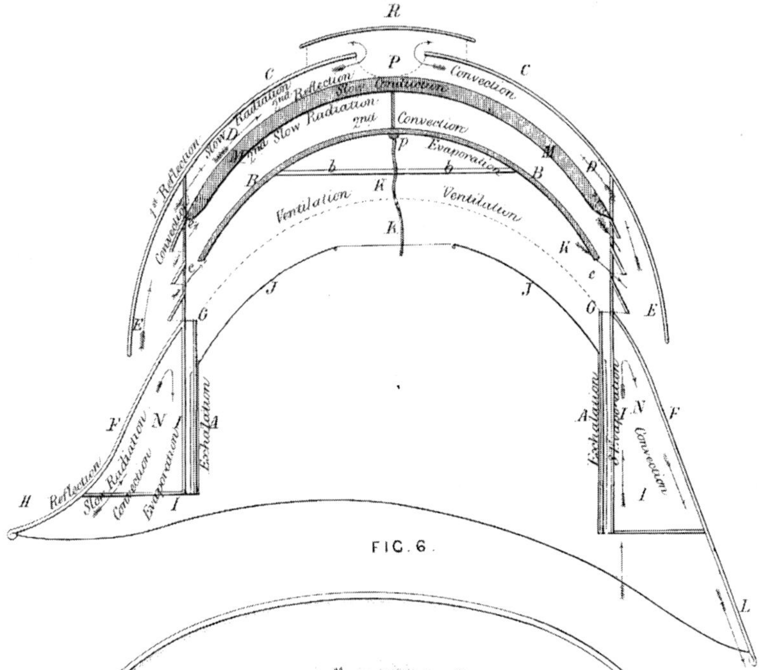

R
P
C
C
Convection
2nd Reflection
Slow Radiation
Slow Conduction
2nd Slow Radiation
2nd Convection
1st Reflection
Evaporation
Ventilation
Ventilation
Convection
Exhalation
Evaporation
Reflection
Slow Radiation
Convection
Evaporation
Exhalation

FIG. 6.

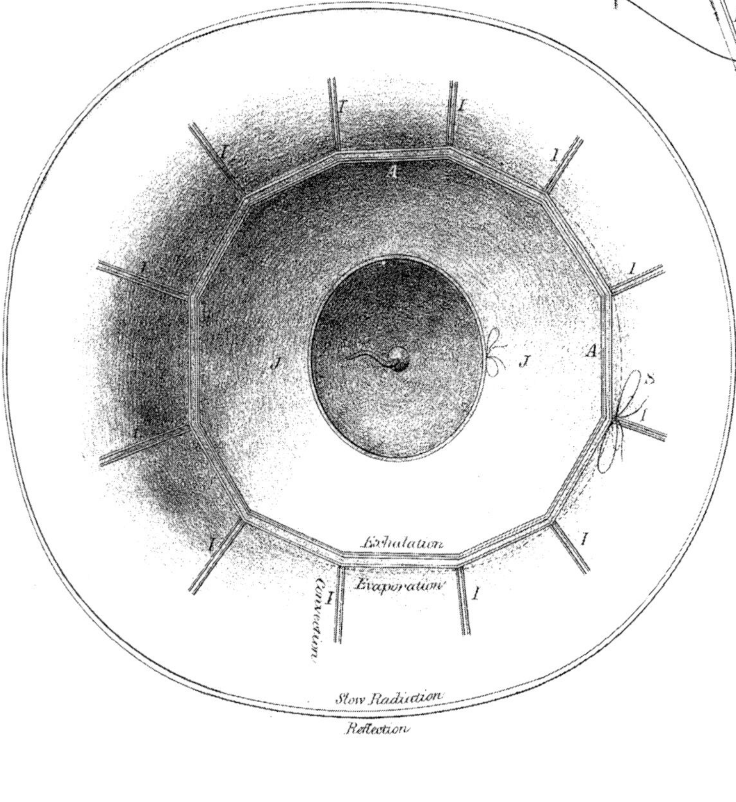

Exhalation
Evaporation
Convection
Slow Radiation
Reflection

as in Fig. 3, by a twisting pin O, the sides A A can be tightened round the head or loosened at will; the whole *weight* resting on the crown of the head by means of the drawn cap J J, of open canvas, while its centre of gravity being lower down takes off the sense of weight. The helmet may then be ordinarily worn quite loose. The portion of the sides or walls which surround the head, consisting of a porous absorbent fabric, permits a free exhalation of perspiration through it into the air circulating in the space N N, within the outer shed.

The upper half, D G, of this casing, is not made of cloth, but of thin sheet metal, shaped into a cylindrical oval, and abounding all round with free ventilating fissures *e e*, opening downwards, the metal above each fissure being stamped out into little sloping semicircular hoods, preventing any ingress of rays projected from the under surface of the outer shell downwards or sideways. Between the lower edge E E of the roof C C, and the upper edge of the shed F F, will be observed a wide opening all round leading to the numerous ventilators *e e e* in the casing D G, and giving an uninterrupted passage to every current of air.

Within the outer shell C C, and concentric to it, is a fixed crown M M, leaving between them a space, D D, of about half an inch, into which air enters through twelve holes all round, being the uppermost of the tiers of holes *e e*; such air constantly rising passes out above through the free ventilating opening P, under the top plate R.

This crown, M M, consists of a thick body of wad-

The fixed and moveable crowns.

ding, having both its convex and concave surfaces coated with the thinnest foil of tin. Concentric with this fixed crown M M, at a distance within it of half or three quarters of an inch, is a moveable crown B B, composed of one or two layers of thick flannel or other porous woollen cloth. It is suspended by a cord and sliding button P; by easing which, and pulling on the cross tapes *b b*, it may in a moment be drawn down near to, or into the position of, the dotted line G K G; so as to lessen or to cut off the copious "*ventilation*" (vide figure) which ordinarily flows across through the two lowermost tiers, *e e*, of twenty-four holes. The crown, when quite down, fits upon the walls A A, round their summit G G. At the same time the porosity of the crown and sides enclosing the head (while they keep the head snug in cold or damp weather) will permit a free exhalation of the perspiration to take place.

Provision for copious ventilation.

This crown, in hot weather, and in active exertion in cooler, should be suspended high, as in the figure, that copious ventilation may go on below it, through the two lowermost tiers of holes *e e*. The copious ventilation going on between this crown and the wearer's head will not only favor a free exhalation of perspiration from the head, but when the air is at all cooler than the head will conduct off animal heat from it. When the wearer is bald, and the wind very hot, either a flannel cap should be worn or the crown be drawn down, upon the principle set forth under the following subject of *Body Dress*. As has been fully set forth under the head of Ventilation, it is scarcely possible to exaggerate the importance of giving to the head the power to exhale perspiration freely, or the danger on the other hand of shutting the head up in an air-tight helmet under a powerful sun; and the ventilation must not be the sham ventilation of ventilating hats, so called, *but large and free.* The functions of all the surfaces, spaces, and variety of materials in this helmet are set forth in writing in the figures opposite to each part. We have at top, "*Reflection,*" first from the *convex* exterior of the shell C C, and secondly from that of the fixed crown M M. Again we have "*slow-Radiation*" from the *concave* interior faces, first of the shell, and secondly of the fixed crown. We have Convection, first between the outer shell and the fixed crown, and secondly between this and the moveable crown B B. In the region of E E, all round, where the shell C C shelters the hoods *o o o* of the ventilating holes *e e e*, &c., we have the *reflection* as before of the exterior of the shell, and again from the convex of each little hood *o*. Also the *slow-Radiation*, maintained by the inner face of the shell at E, is repeated at the inner concave of all the little hoods *o o o*. Proceeding lower, we have the shed F F *reflecting* heat *freely* from its exterior, and *radiating* it *tardily* inwards from its under surface; while we have in the large space N N, *Convection* freely maintained, not indeed by the continuous ascent of the heated current, but through its constant displacement by every movement of the wearer or of the atmosphere. This current might be allowed to pass out at the top of the gorge through numerous perforations, but then it would flow into the ventilating current *e e*, and might bring into it

This helmet possesses Reflection twice.

Slow-Radiation twice operating; also Convection.

heat swept from the interior of the shed. Moreover such a provision is quite unnecessary.

Slow-Conduction also operates in the crown.

Lastly, we have the principle of "*slow-Conduction*," introduced in the action of the body of wadding, or "sola," forming the substance of the fixed crown M M, where it will be of good service in retarding the progress of any heat coming down from above, which may have escaped all previous interception, and it cannot operate adversely by confining the animal heat. It might be of advantage to give the shed F F, to the extremity of its peaks H and L, a lining of such matter, which should be faced inwardly with tin-foil to perform the retarding duty of the present tinned under surface of the shed and peaks, which would be covered up by it.

This helmet, like the others, Fig. 2 and 8, is fitted with a back curtain to protect the neck, and in part the shoulders, from reflected rays. It is made in three rows of flounces, very full and connected to each other at points only, by which arrangement the air can flow freely through the curtain while rays are kept off. The metal double-shed helmet, which has now been fully described, would probably be found as efficient as any that could be proposed. One that has been finished weighs only 2 lbs. 4 oz. with all its fittings. The metal work by Messrs. Tylor and Sons, though it has a large extent of surface, weighs under 1¾ lb. Other specimens have been made of stouter brass and proportionably heavier, but yet of no really objectionable weight.

HELMETS FOR INFANTRY.

THE proximity of foot soldiers to each other presents a serious obstacle to the combination of a bright reflecting exterior with an elliptical or spheroidal form of helmet. Owing to the infinity of *tangent planes* presented by such curved surfaces, whatever may be the position of the sun, some rays of light falling upon them are sure to be reflected into the eyes of neighbouring soldiers. Into the same eye, as shown below, Fig. 7, rays will be projected from Spheroidal helmets dazzling, but cylindrical the contrary.

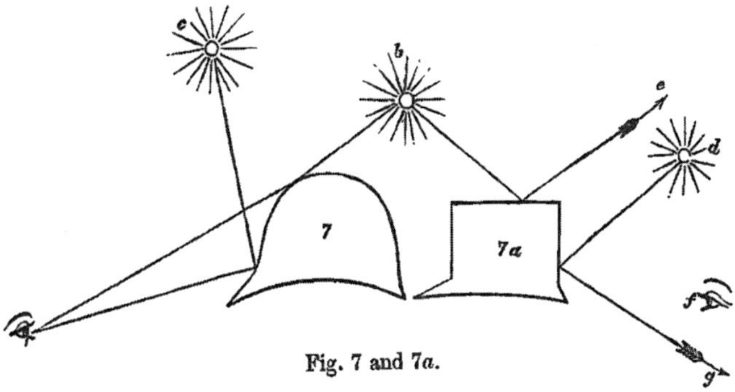

Fig. 7 and 7*a*.

the helmet, whether the sun is at *c*, or at *b*. Though each reflecting plane of such a surface is infinitely small—a mere point—and though, proceeding from a convex surface, the rays from expansion are much diluted, their brilliancy, even from somewhat dull metal, might be trying to the sight of a comrade close at hand. Whereas, let a bright helmet be given the simple form, Fig. 7 *a*, of an ordinary fashionable hat or inverted saucepan, and let the sun be at *b*, *d*, or anywhere, excepting near the horizon when shining feebly at the moment of its rising or setting. All rays from it falling upon the flat top of the helmet are sure to be reflected more or less skyward, as in the direction of the arrow *e*, while all rays falling upon the vertical sides are equally certain of being given a groundward direction, *g*, below the eye of a man even within two feet of the wearer, excepting when the latter happened to be much the taller of the two, and the sun getting low.

To provide then against the contingency of reflection dazzling to foot soldiers, we must in their helmets either sacrifice shape for the sake of surface-reflection, or surface-reflection for the sake of shape. Trial helmets of both kinds have been made.

Shako or saucepan-shaped hat: its virtues.

Fig. 8 exhibits an instance of the former. It is a vertical section of a saucepan-shaped helmet or shako, having no other pretension to beauty of form than what it can claim upon Aristotle's rule; but according to that standard its pretensions for admiration are high. The soldier owning it, while carrying off the field some poor comrade, snorting with apoplexy, his crown half covered with a foraging cap of a measure taken in some nursery, or closely fitted with a shako helped out with calico, would assuredly contemplate with admiration his own redoubtable protector, though homely in form. And where is the fastidious consultor of shapes who with such a sight before him would not do the same? As above shown in Fig. 7 *a*, all rays reflected from its horizontal top, even the most oblique, will be thrown far above the eyes of neighbours, while rays reflected from its vertical sides will be thrown altogether below them, excepting near sunset, when they are feeble. Such a helmet, so far from being glaring, would be least visible in proportion as it was most bright. The windows of a house, if there be no white blinds behind them, are in the day-time the darkest parts of its surface when viewed from without, owing to their being vertical; but at sunrise or sunset, to a person at a somewhat lower level, they appear on fire, so brilliantly does the glass reflect the nearly horizontal rays into the eyes of a person below the points of reflection. During the day, while the glass is to the sight darker than the neighbouring brick wall, it is reflecting rays downwards upon the ground so powerfully, that in the summer the grass of a plot near low windows or glass doors is often-times burnt up, while the rest of it may be verdant. Were bright metal substituted for the glass, this effect would be more remarkable, for in the case of glass the greater part of the rays penetrate it and enter the room.

Illustrated by reflection from windows.

This unpretending hat or shako, with its flat top and vertical walls, contains all the same operative parts with the metal helmet of the first construction, Figs. 2 and 3, viz.:—

Operative parts of this hat.

1st.—A metal-faced canvas or metallic shell C C, *reflecting* heat from its outer, and *unwillingly radiating it* from its inner surface *c c*.

2nd.—A free passage D D, all round, and at top, for the ascending current of *convection*.

3rd.—A metallic surface *d d*, coating the casing M M, round the sides and at the top, facing outwards to act as a *second reflector*.

4th.—A thick inner casing M M, of wadding or "sola," as a *slow conductor*.

5th.—A metallic surface *m m*, lining M M, facing inwards as a second *tardy radiator*.

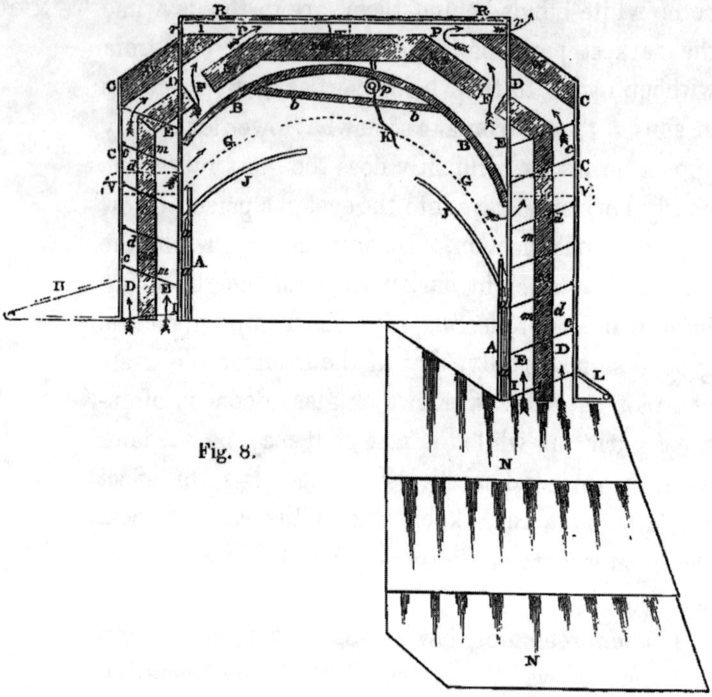

Fig. 8.

6th.—A free ventilating space all round, E E, communicating with the head under the crown B B, and with the space above it, and also with the four lateral ventilating ports *v v*, where these are introduced.

7th.—A porous casing of cloth A A, encircling the head and absorbing and exhaling the perspiration freely into the current of air ascending in the ventilating space E E.

8th.—A shifting crown B B, also of porous woollen cloth, which when raised permits a current of ventilation to pass under it as well as over it, and when drawn down in cold weather still transmits through its pores the exhalant perspiration.

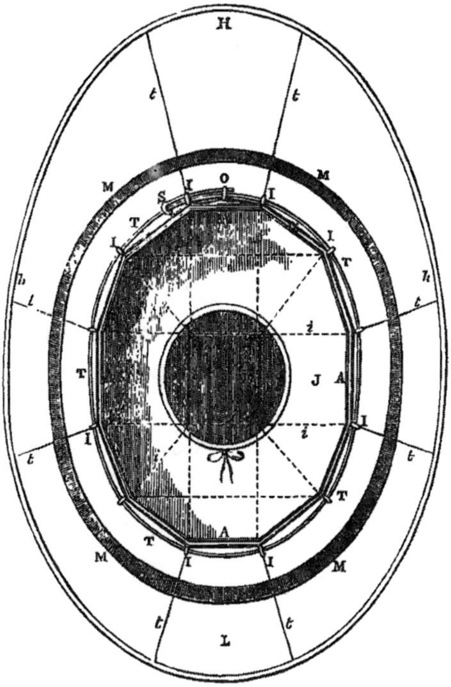

Fig. 3.

This helmet is so similar in its construction to the spheroidal one, Fig. 2, that the same base view, Fig. 3, will suffice for both of them. They are both built upon a wire frame, I I I I, *i i i i*, which in Fig. 8 only differs from the frame in Fig. 2 in being a flat-topped cylinder. Hence the top cover, R R, extends across it, and the ventilating currents make their exit at the fissure *r r r*, all round it. The outlet, P P, of the passage, D D, is also an annular opening, and not a central one as in Fig. 2.

The structure of the outer casing C C of this helmet is also peculiar. It consists of a strong open-wove canvas, such as forms the basis of worsted work, overlaid without with sheet tin. The sheet tin employed is that peculiar manufacture known by the name "*taggars;*" which though used for humble purposes is certainly a beautiful manufacture. Though the body of it is iron, with a rich coating of tin on both sides, it weighs only 2½ ounces per square foot, and may even be obtained thinner. When supported on the canvas it forms a pliant but very tough coat, abundantly reflective on its outer surface; while the open meshes of the canvas under it leaves its inner surface sufficiently denuded for it to operate as a *tardy radiator*. While the top and upright sides can reflect no solar rays in a troublesome direction, it may be necessary to paint the small inclined surface from *r* to *c* of some dark colour, as slate. For this reason, and to shelter the four holes F F, the inclined part is wadded within, at W W, which may compeusate for the loss of exterior reflection there.

Coated with the thinnest sheet-tin.

As in the spheroidal helmet, Fig. 2, the casings, C C and M M, are also kept in a distended state by spiral coils of fine steel wire within the canvas of C C, and they are kept concentric with the inner frame by similar cords *t t t t*.

The front peak H, and back L, are simply folds of

canvas lined with metal on their upper surface, and kept distended by an encircling steel wire, but pliant in all directions, yet always resilient into the right position.

Of the effectiveness of this hat or helmet there can be little doubt. Its shape, with none but horizontal and vertical planes which the sun could reach (for the hat would shade the peaks from the sun when in a troublesome direction), would command all the advantages of external reflection without any dazzling effect. At a little distance the helmet would be scarcely more visible than if covered with dark cloth. The very fact that rays from a bright metal surface are so trying when thrown on the face, proves the value of the principle of Reflection for repelling a large amount of heat; for, in the sunbeam, rays of heat accompany and are reflected with those of light, and observe the same laws so far as our present matters are concerned. If rays coming from one only out of ten thousand simultaneously reflecting points on the hemisphere of a helmet facing the sun, are so dazzling, what must be the amount of heat the head within that helmet is being protected from by this vigilant principle of Reflection? A grey cloth cap looks cool to a neighbour's eye, whose estimate is instinctively taken from his own convenience. It is *cool*, non-reflective, in the direction of his eye, and in ten thousand other directions, because it is passively admitting nearly all the rays, and conveying them sooner or later, according to the thickness of its texture, to the martyred head within. The *cylindrical* bright helmet

Effective properties of this hat.

would look cool, also, having a shady aspect from the rays not visiting the eyes. But it would not only look cool to the beholder, but be cool also to the wearer.

The troops in India already perishing from imperfect dress.

A fair estimate of the casualties in the gallant force with which Sir H. Havelock commenced his heroic campaign, which have taken place in excess of those which would have occurred had the sun been in the southern instead of the northern Tropic, of the men who suffered directly and indirectly from its rays aggravating the effects of *diseases* and of *wounds*, would show a proportion of the whole force to have suffered from solar action most distressing to contemplate;* and if to these were added the *constitutional shock* which the rest have sustained, and which will cause them to break down in another such season or two, the havoc exhibited in that little army alone would be such as would make the most pedantic stickler for appearance to throw elegance and fashion to the dogs! Would that the men of our hope and pride had had good saucepan or Tower of Babel shaped helmets as redoubtable as themselves—convulsive to the sons of polite art, the fastidious devotees of sweeping curves, but beautiful to the philosophic eye, as vigilantly parrying ten thousand solar darts, and at the same time sending them all flying off to the skies or down to the ground, so that not one chance ray can find its way to distress a neighbour's eye, or give him any but a shaded view of the bright and busy surface

* We now hear that of that force scarcely one fourth remained at the end of six months.

over which the defensive process of Reflection is going on!

With such a head-dress, and with their body guarded in a corresponding manner, what might not the state of that force have been, compared with what its remnant, lost amongst many reinforcements, has already become!

Helmet not reflecting at the surface.

But if virtue must needs be sacrificed to a more graceful shape, the endeavour must be made, in adopting some spheroidal form, to dispense with reflection at the surface, and to carry out the other provisions so fully as to compensate if possible for the loss of that valuable agency.

A trial helmet of this description has been made. It differs from the one just described only in its shape, which is ellipsoidal, and in having a cloth in place of a metal surface, the several concentric parts being carried by a frame of steel busks. That these helmets will greatly surpass any in ordinary use may be safely assumed; but whether surface-reflection can be dispensed with without a marked loss of effect is doubtful. It is not enough that the protection shall surpass any yet enjoyed by the soldier. It would be a blind, spiritless, and unworthy course to stop short of anything that science can dictate and art afford. We know too well what the climate of India can do while imperfectly opposed; we have yet to learn what may be the immunities conferred by the most perfect protection at our command!

Such helmets may be effective.

In committing so glaring a departure from principle as to countenance trial helmets having a cloth, or any but a metallic surface, I venture upon it only under the impression that they may possibly be constructed absolutely proof against a vertical sun, if a proportional jealousy be observed to maintain in the highest efficiency the several interior provisions which have been fully described. But perhaps we might, by the following conformation, compound the matter between homely virtue repelling the advances of Apollo, and comely frailty receiving them—between a bright inverted saucepan rejecting his rays, and a cloth ellipsoid admitting them. Thus a helmet may be constructed, elliptical in its general form, but with its metallic shell stamped or wrought up into a series of steps presenting none but horizontal and vertical faces. Such a helmet would reflect nearly as well as one with a plane surface, while, like the flat-topped cylinder, every little step up to the summit would throw rays off skyward and groundward. At the same time it would, I understand, be not difficult to construct, and would acquire much rigidity by having bands or wires soldered within the shell so as to form diagonals to the steps. The interior organism of this helmet would be similar to the others.

The double shell helmet, Figs. 5 and 6, might have its surface brought up in like manner into steps.

A helmet of another kind suggested as worth trying.

The lithographed Figs. 9 and 10 exhibit a helmet consisting solely of successive casings, the outer layer, of the very thin sheet tin already described, being laid on open canvas. Lines of perforations, *i i i i*, run round the sides of all of these casings from top to bottom. As the air could blow through this hat freely in all directions, and the principles of *Reflection*

FIG. 9.

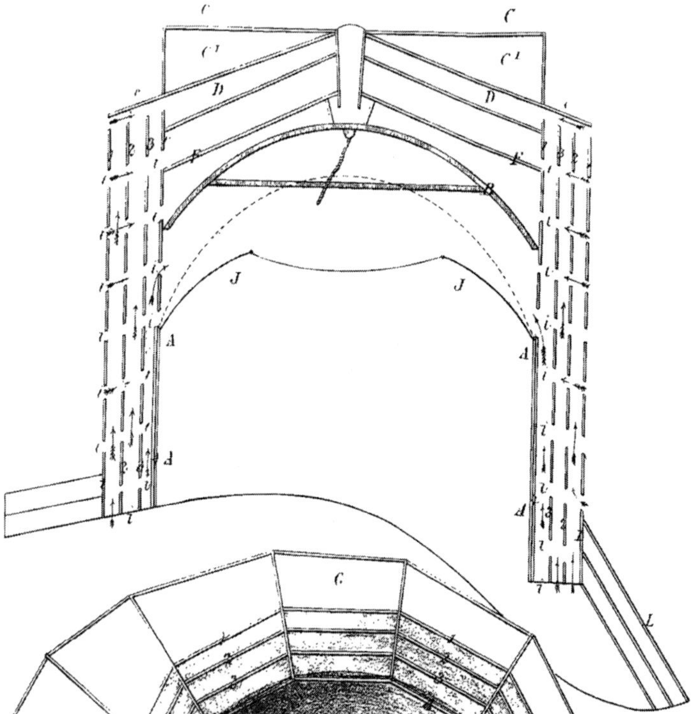

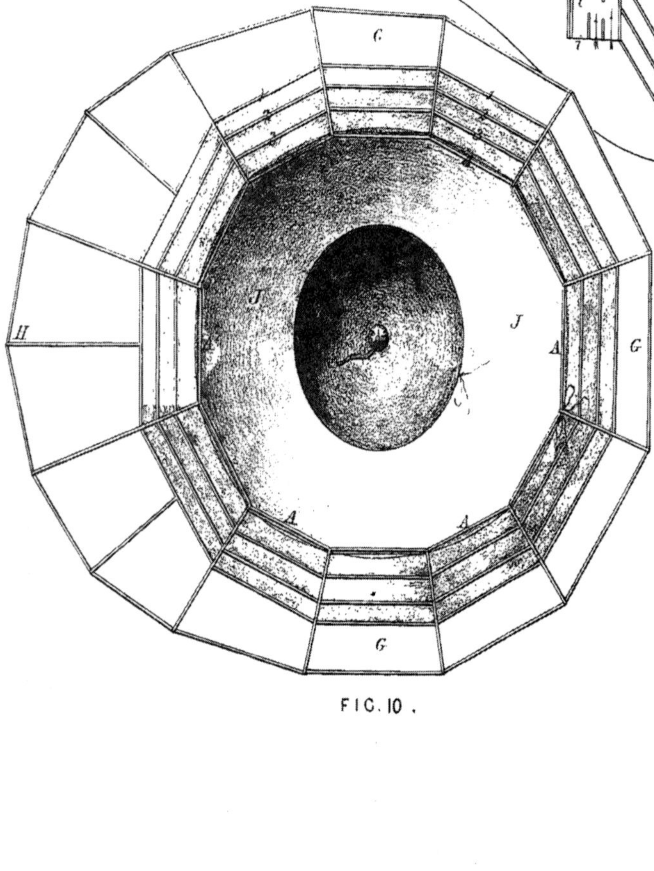

FIG. 10.

and *slow-Radiation* would be frequently repeated in it, it might prove a light, easily constructed, and effective helmet. Although the principle of *slow-conduction* is omitted in it, and the air after penetrating the heated exterior casings finds access to the head, the large quantity of air which would flow through such a structure might carry off heat as fast as it was deposited without becoming itself heated to an extent which would distress the head. This construction from its toughness and ready pliancy would not be wanting in durability, while its principle would be worth a trial. At the same time it cannot be viewed as having by any means equal certainty with the others. The ventilating air, when the current is not rapid, is likely to become heated to an extent which might prove oppressive.

CURTAIN FOR THE NECK.

HELMETS of sufficient variety for protecting the head having been described, the wants of the neck and side of the face must not be overlooked. The spinal marrow, its upper part especially, is highly sensitive; and shading though these helmets are, they cannot always protect the lower part of the neck from the sun, and the sides of the face from the fierce glare of the ground and walls. Figs. 2 and 8 show a helmet with a curtain such as it is proposed should be attached to all helmets. It consists of three flounces, the lower edge of each being fuller than the upper edge of the one next below it, and attached to it at certain points

Protection of the neck necessary.

only. In this way numerous ventilating loops are formed facing downwards, so that there can be no confinement of the air round the neck, and a wind from behind can find its way through to the neck and face. Moreover, the suspension of the curtain from the edge of the shed leaves a wide space between it and the neck for a free circulation of air. This curtain may be composed of two or three layers of jean or other closely wove cloth; but a single layer of a fabric having a metal face on both its surfaces would be more effective. Small squares of the sheet tin already described, about an inch or an inch and a half each way, sewn down to a piece of canvas net, or linked together, would afford a better protection than a considerable thickness of cloth, and would be lighter and less bulky; though the latter would not offer any encumbrance worthy of a thought compared with the ruinous effects to the constitution of spinal exposure.

Fashion conflicting with indispensable bulk.

In concluding the subject of Head-dress, while enough has been said respecting the question of form, it is well that we should be prepared for the first impressions which may be excited by the bulk requisite for commanding an absolute security. The times in which we live are no doubt unfortunate for this necessary increase of bulk. Fashion, the arbitress of taste, making the ceaseless round of her Zodiac in the "Limbo of Vanity," is now, in the matter of head-dress, moving slowly through the sign of Lilliput. She sends ladies for bonnets, and soldiers for foraging caps, and sometimes for shakos, to fit themselves in "baby warehouses." In this she may be borne with in our climate, where the sun's declination through three-fourths of the year is so considerable, and where at most times the welkin hangs thick over our heads, a gigantic helmet common to all.

The region of taste too much resembles Milton's bog for one who is simply depasturing in the fields of science to venture upon it. Fashion's horoscope, revealing mysteries too deep for human reason, has pronounced it to be good taste, *for the current hour*, that the cover for ladies and soldiers' heads should not be a cover at all, but one-half or one-third of a cover. If we must bow to this her inscrutable arbitrament, we may surely complain at her inconsistency in not extending the rule to our furniture where it would be comparatively harmless. Why may not the man who would dwell consistently, having feasted his eyes on the semi-bonneted head of his wife, cut away one half of the cover of his table, of his sofa, and of his chairs, and leave his furniture in strict accordance with her head, both as to elegance and protection?

Fashion fatal in military dress.

All this is comparatively * endurable, but when Fashion is playing into the hands of Death, and filling the grave with her victims, her despotism becomes insufferable. Losing sight of the foraging-cap for the time, and conceding to the ordinary dress-caps,† shakos, and helmets, a suitableness for our particular climate, we need not go further southward than the Mediterranean‡ stations for their defi-

* Comparatively only. How many a constitution has not the ladies' bonnet victimized, both in the cold of winter and sun of summer, in Europe?

† Saving that ingeniously faulty conceit the bear-skin cap.

‡ An officer some time ago remarked to me that it used to distress him

ciencies to tell upon the health of troops exposed to the sun. But when we approach the tropics, we have the atmosphere, for six months, ranging fifteen degrees on either side of blood heat. Being already surcharged with heat, it is little able to wash away by convection the sun's rays, as they fall upon any surface; the inadequate thickness of all ordinary head-dress, even of the best in use, would be glaringly manifest to any one who could have witnessed the preservative power of one of adequate dimensions. As it is, the sudden or gradual destruction of life or health is viewed as somehow inevitable, or referred to various auxiliary causes, not wanting, indeed, in number and power, arising out of the imprudence and irregular habits of soldiers.

Unsuitable forms contemptible however elegant.

A London wherry, or a cock-boat, might answer well for conveying soldiers over the gentle stream of the Thames, above-bridge, and many of these "funnies" are beautiful in their construction and form, when viewed in their proper place and element; but ship an army into wherries off Portsmouth, to cross the Atlantic, or even the Channel, and the scant size and flimsy structure which, on the gentle Thames, were pleasing to the view, would now appear contemptible and disgusting; and the man would be thought inhuman and insane, who should propose thus to harden men to the boisterous element. Yet to the man who dies apoplectic under the sun in India, but had been well enough within

at Gibraltar to see orderlies of a morning, with the sun, already high, shining upon the uncovered half of their heads, to which it would be informal for them to pull over from the other half the scanty foraging cap, a pitiful protection at the best!

doors, his dress has, in fact, proved just as fatally unequal to his protection as would the wherry, which would have swamped with him in a sea where he would have been safe enough in a ship.

Furthermore, to think to render a shako duly sun proof in the Tropics by slipping over it a calico cover,* though more reasonably hopeful than to think to render a wherry seaworthy by slipping over it a coracle, would be so by some degrees only.

In fine, when experience shall hereafter confirm what philosophy may safely now affirm, when by giving a suitable bulk and structure to the head-dress, and suitably modifying the body-dress, the soldier shall be enabled to march over the plains of India at all seasons, with a security approaching towards that with which he may go to sea at all seasons, in a ship of suitable dimensions and structure, there cannot be a question that habit, and the exhibition of such redoubtable properties, will give to the lateral increase of bulk requisite, not only a grateful effect, based on a sense of its adaptation to the highest purpose, but that commanding one also, which is at present sought in the case of the bear-skin cap of the Guards, by a vertical extension worse than useless.

Its redoubtable properties will give to lateral bulk in the head-dress a commanding effect.

It is vertical extension which renders top-heaviness, and especially the resistance of wind, so trying. Now, the sun-proof helmets require little, if any, increase of height above that of ordinary hats.

* Nevertheless it was doubtless the best means at hand for mitigating the defects of the shako, and was therefore with proper judgment adopted, though with what short-coming in protective effects the tragical result of almost annihilated regiments has already too plainly shown!

The weight of a well-poised hat little felt.

On the question of weight it has already been fully explained, that if the weight is, by means of a draw-cap, made to rest on the crown of the head, and not supported by lateral pressure round the brow and sides, and the centre of gravity is placed below that of support, a greater weight than that of any of the helmets proposed would, by a little habit, become unnoticed. Four times the weight that is distressing, when suspended by lateral pressure, will be carried easily if rested fairly upon the head.* *Easiness round the head* is so important for comfort, especially in hot weather, that, as already explained, the construction of the inner lining of the helmets has been adapted to this especial object. The soldier can wear such helmets, ordinarily, as easy as he pleases, secured from accidental displacement by the chin-strap; and when a strong wind or unusual exertion renders it necessary, he can, without uncovering his head, tighten the lining of cloth round his head to any extent in an instant, and loosen it again with equal facility.

The weight of the trial helmets.

With respect to the weight of the helmets, the majority of those which have been made range between two and two and three-quarter pounds. It appears very practicable to have steel wire basket helmets, which promise to be very effective, of from two, to two and a quarter pounds weight, and durable plate metal helmets, equally effective, half a pound heavier. Of one of the latter kind, which, complete, weighs only two pounds two ounces, the metal is rather too slight.

It is a common but not altogether fair remark,

* Appendix C.

The negligence of soldiers a futile objection.

that soldiers are indisposed to appreciate changes made for their benefit, or to trouble themselves to understand any novel construction, however simple. Were it so, the discipline they are under is abundantly absolute to ensure the result desired. We see the dullest men soon drilled into difficult and complicated movements and the management of fire-arms, all fifty-fold more intricate than simply to tighten a draw-cap or band round the head.

It is true with them, as with their betters, that dullness and prejudice are rather abundant; but having seen something both of soldiers and of workmen, I had rather undertake to introduce any new rule or use amongst the former, owing to their habit of prompt attention and their subordination, than amongst the latter; yet these have continually to adapt themselves to new appliances.

In introducing a new dress, a commanding officer could, on parade, address his men, informing them that it had, at great pains, been provided for their protection; that it would undoubtedly tend to preserve their health and lives; and that every part of it was of use, and necessary for that object; also that the serjeants would explain the use, and see that no wanton mischief was done to it by any man, whose punishment would be all the more severe, as marking his ingratitude for the anxiety shown for his benefit.

THE BODY-DRESS FOR BRITISH SOLDIERS IN INDIA.

Limits of the subject in hand.

To attempt any detailed examination of the several articles of dress with which it may be expedient to provide the soldier, would be foreign to the objects of this Essay, which are confined to his protection from the assaults of the climate, and especially of the sun. Their effects upon the spine, skin, and system generally have been sufficiently examined under former heads for guiding our attempts to make such modifications in, or additions to, the soldier's body dress as shall go far towards protecting him from the injurious action of the sun and atmosphere.

It has been shown* how the excessive heat in the atmosphere, combined with its evaporative power from dryness, in the hot season, or a relaxing heat alternating with conductive dampness in the rainy, produce, according as the air happens to be still or in motion around the body, various injurious transitions; as from a drenched state of the skin with an oppressive accumulation of animal heat, in a still atmosphere, to either a febrile dryness, or a sudden chill with suppressed perspiration, in one that is briskly in motion.

Circumstances in which the lightest dress is suitable.

In a still atmosphere within doors, in no extreme condition as to temperature, or to dryness or dampness, the majority of persons find the freest access of the air to their skin to be most suitable to them;

* Pages 50 and 51.

and hence the smallest amount of covering permissible by the proprieties of European life. As such a slight dress also appears to suffice out-of-doors so long as exposure to the sun is limited, and the exercise taken moderate, most persons have presumed that the lightest cotton dress, is the best under all circumstances during the warmer months. The press, both in India and England, has been furnished with complaints of the oppressive nature of the clothing of some regiments which had recently landed in that country from England, and such clothing has been contrasted with the supposed comfort of a light cotton dress. On the other hand, experience has led others to defend the regulation clothing as best suited for India.

A thin dress ill suited for much exposure to a hot atmosphere.

This is one of those questions in which "experience" will tell opposite ways, according to circumstances, and which can never be settled by looking to particular effects, but requires for its safe solution a careful investigation of causes. With this view, a brief examination has been already made of the physical and pathological action upon the naked skin of the body, of an atmosphere of high temperature, and in different degrees of dryness and of motion. It was shown how unfitted is the European skin, when uncovered, to cope with the exactions and caprice of such an atmosphere. Now, next to a state of absolute nudity, a flimsy dress of cotton gives far too rude an access to an out-door atmosphere, with its rough practice on the skin already described.

A barrier needed between the skin

What is required for the *campaigner's* skin in India, is a protective partition between it and the and the atmosphere. atmosphere, to act like a wicketed, or turnstiled barrier, preventing too rapid a passage of an impetuous crowd—a barrier against the atmosphere which shall prevent too hurried a passage both of heat and of gaseous particles either way—a *slow-conducting*, *porous*, and *spongy medium*, to husband the resources of the skin, and to ward off too rude and rapid an action of the air. It must be slow-conducting, to check as far as may be, at one time, the positive entrance of heat into the body from air hotter than the blood, and, at another, the opposite chilling action, of a rapid evaporation of the sweat, or of a damp air, somewhat cooler than the skin. It must be spongy to receive and husband all sensible perspiration. It must be porous to afford a sufficiently free, but controlled ingress, to the atmosphere, and egress again of its particles, moderately charged with perspiration. For such a medium, what so good a material as soft thick flannel, next to, and enclosing the whole skin? Men engaged in athletic exercises in England, as rowers and cricketers, find at once the advantage of such a flannel dress; but in the high temperature of India, the danger of a flimsy cotton dress is veiled by its being at times more comfortable, especially in the still atmosphere of a house. Whereas, the importance of flannel is greater there than in England, where there is no fear of febrile dryness from outer heat above the blood heat; and where the consequences of suppressed perspiration though dangerous, are not so deadly.

Its nature and properties.

The author's personal experience.

Having, during a period of eight years, to undergo exposure to the atmosphere, often throughout the whole day, at two of the hottest stations in India, Cawnpore and Futtehgurh (now of such fatal notoriety), the ruffianism of the atmosphere, against the assaults of which nature had given him but indifferent cutaneous powers, soon urged the author to trace out its various modes of action, and to clothe the whole body, and next the skin, from the neck to the ancles, with thick flannel. But at first the arms were not covered with it. The exterior clothing was the usual cotton dress of Europeans in India. When out in the hot winds, usually at a hundred and ten or a hundred and fifteen degrees, the temperature of the surface of the arms under the cotton covering only, was frequently above that of the blood, and the skin was dry and often febrile, while at other times, when loaded with perspiration, a current of wind would suddenly cool the arms with distressing chills. Whereas, everywhere else under the flannel, the skin was at all times moist and cool, never so drenched, and never dry and hot. The effect was so remarkable, that the flannel was very soon extended to the wrists, and thus he was enabled, during the long period named, to pursue a most trying course, suffering indeed from chronic disorder of the liver (which was, however, mitigated from the time the dress was adopted), but escaping, altogether, cholera, dysentery, and fever, excepting one slight attack of the latter, although they were often epidemic. With the head thoroughly protected from the sun by a hat of an effective construction, he has oftentimes, while at Futtehgurh, after remaining some time in the verandah of experimental furnaces, where the atmosphere was as high as a hundred and thirty degrees (Fahr.), come out into the sun to cool himself in a wind at above a hundred degrees. As this course was pursued many years by one to whom a tropical climate was more than usually hostile, it is one of the many instances confirmatory of the fact, that it is the solar ray and malaria, much more than simple atmospheric heat, which are destructive to nearly all European constitutions exposed to their influence. Undoubtedly, a high atmospheric temperature is eventually exhausting to all; and to not a few, to females especially, is often a cause of derangement of the health from the commencement of a residence in the country; but persons possessed of any vigour of constitution can stand a high atmospheric temperature for a long period, more particularly if it be not overcharged with moisture. But then the skin must not be exposed to the *direct* and *unrestrained* action of the hot air.

Flannel next the skin, but not thick clothing, desirable.

While advocating strongly the use of flannel over the whole body by British troops exposed in India, as less exhausting, after the skin is accustomed to it, than the unrestrained drought of the hot winds, and as a great protection against the alternations of heat and chill, especially in the rains, I would, on no account, be understood to defend the use, in hot weather, of a tight outer clothing of dense woollen cloth, which is a very different thing, and which is often, by its tightness and density, suffocative to the skin, and far too retentive of the animal heat. It is not unfrequently defended by persons who certainly do not enter deeply into principles, by the practice, supposed to be analogous, of wrapping up ice in blankets to preserve it from melting in hot weather. There might be some parallel in the two cases if a man had no internal heat to get rid of, which must, otherwise, prove destructive to him: if the skin also had no transpiring and exhaling duties to perform: and if, at the same time, his blood like the ice, were *at all times* many degrees cooler than the air against which it is blanketed. But, as matters are, there is in the imagined parallel, little that is similar, and much that is deceptive.

With respect to the cold season, there can be no question but that soldiers should be so clad as to be comfortably warm. To men who have been several years in the country the cold season, especially in the western provinces, is frequently that of most ailment. The skin having become exhausted and enfeebled by a long continued action of the climate is liable to be more chilled than braced at that season, and as a consequence the liver and other organs suffer from congestion and torpor. Warmth in the cold season needful.

It has to be borne in mind that the extent to which winter cold is trying, depends, not upon the actual degree of cold only, but also, and still more, upon the severity and duration of the previous heat.

Now in Western India the annual extremes of temperature even surpass those of England, a range of seventy and eighty degrees of Fahr. being common. At Kurnaul in 1824 I found the air some feet from the ground to sink as low as to the freezing point, more than once, in January; and in July, a friend Annual extremes of temperature great in India.

who noted the temperature while I was absent in the hills, found it to rise to a hundred and twenty-two degrees in a northern aspect and sheltered position.* Here was a difference of ninety-two degrees—an extreme instance, certainly, as far as my own observations went.

Many soldiers and officers likewise think that because they are in India they cannot suffer by any carelessness with respect to cold, and many, as a consequence, bring themselves upon the sick-list, and with ailments often of a tedious character.

A SUN-SCREEN TUNIC.

HAVING sufficiently considered the effects of atmospheric vicissitudes, and the body clothing suited to counteract them, we have still a serious and troublesome problem to deal with, namely, the protection of the spine and trunk of the body from the rays of the sun and from those reflected and radiated from a heated ground and from walls.

A sun-screen tunic for the back necessary.

Although the head is, undoubtedly, by far the most sensitive part of the body, a protection of it alone will by no means suffice. The spine is also highly sensitive. Radiant heat acting upon the back will, if powerful and long continued, put the strongest constitution to trial. Every one is familiar with the sickening effect of sitting for any time with the back towards even an ordinary house-fire of any

* This is the highest temperature in the shade I have known in India.

power. For the back of the marching soldier to be exposed for many successive hours to the fierce impulses of a tropical sun, with merely a few layers of clothing between them, and that of matters willingly receptive of radiance, and applied close to the body, so as to conduct the heat into the skin at once, is a condition of things too painful to contemplate with the mind impressed with the conviction that it is not unavoidable. It may be difficult to attain, at once, to the complete protection which a flexible metallic medium would afford, if so placed as to bring three of our principles,—Reflection, Slow-Radiation, and Convection—to bear with their utmost effect; but much may be effected by ordinary means.

If it should prove more difficult, than in the protection of the head, to bring into play the reflective and slowly-radiant properties of metallic surfaces, the principle of convection may be largely employed. To protect the back, we may suspend behind it, at a distance of some inches, an apron or curtain (Fig. 11) composed of two or more layers of closely wove linen or cotton cloth, to receive the sun's rays and to detain much of them until they are imparted to the air circulating between the curtain and the body, which will carry them off into the general atmosphere. If the curtain hangs free and at its full distance from the body at bottom, and is constructed like the neck-curtain, of a succession of flounces abounding with ventilating fissures facing downwards not to admit the sun's rays, the circulation of the air will be sufficiently quick for the process of convection to operate with much effect, especially when there is any wind or the body is in motion. We may certainly by this simple means reduce the solar influence by more than one-half. But there is no reason why we should rest satisfied with materials for our curtain so glaringly deficient in virtue—why

Fig. 11.

we should not determine to command the two bright metallic surfaces we need, in some form or other.

A flexible metal-faced cloth a desideratum.

Although it has been with me an interesting pursuit to acquire some knowledge of most processes employed in the arts both in England and India, the giving to textile fabrics metallic surfaces is one which had not attracted my attention. I applied to Messrs.

Bishop, of Godliman Street, Doctor's Commons, ornamental painters and banner-makers, as persons whose experience and skill might enable them to produce a fabric resplendent with metal, which might be placed between the poor soldier's body and the sun as a rampart, proof against its most penetrating projectiles. I could not learn from them or others that any cloth of such a nature available for the purpose has as yet been manufactured. Cloth covered with metal-leaf does not admit of being folded up closely. It cracks at the creases and angles, and soon gives way; the metal not only scaling off, but even the silk, which is the substance usually employed, soon becoming cut.

As it was plain that the extreme tenuity of the metal leaf itself would enable it to be bent at the sharpest angle, and would prevent it from having any cutting power, it appeared evident, upon a little reflection, that the defect was chiefly due to the brittle nature of the cement employed for fixing the leaf upon the cloth. It appears that a "size" composed of the more or less brittle "gums" of commerce is employed. It consequently occurred to me to suggest to Messrs. Bishop the trial of a "size" made of India-rubber; and that, perhaps, the article known as India-rubber cement would answer the purpose.

They politely adopted the suggestion, and have produced a specimen of a few square feet, which possesses all the flexibility to be desired, and which, as a first trial, is a creditable and promising production. The metallic surface completely shields the vulcanized rubber surfaces from their liability to adhere when folded together; and it appears also to render them proof against a degree of radiant heat they could not otherwise stand; no doubt by its reflective power. If this article could be made with a durable surface, and proof against the heat of India, it would be invaluable for our purpose; especially as the moderate cost at which, by a right application of means, it might be manufactured, would allow of its being renewed every season at a cost of small moment, when measured by its valuable action. It has to be borne in mind that, hanging vertically, such a curtain, however resplendently it was protecting its wearer from the solar rays, would reflect none of them upon the faces of his comrades, but would send them all downwards to the earth.

With a metallic curtain then, of this description, we might, by merely suspending its slight medium between the sun and the soldier's back, at a few inches from the latter, intercept so large a portion of the sun's rays, as to render the proportion of them, which stole their way into his clothes, comparatively innocuous.

Curtain of the thinnest sheet tin.

We have then the strongest reasons for seeking perseveringly such metallic armour, in some form or other. If a metal-faced cloth of adequate durability should prove unattainable, we are not left without other resources. The cheap, familiar, and resplendent article "sheet tin," which is plates of soft iron tinned, offers its aid. The reader may perhaps know it only in the comparatively weighty substance of tin ware, or of ordinary tin sheets; but there is a manufacture of these, already referred to, named "Taggers," of such tenuity, as to weigh under two and a half ounces per square foot, and withal of much strength and toughness. A surface of this, of five square feet—an ample size for a back-curtain—would weigh twelve ounces only; and when it was finished, little above a pound: whereas a very light cloak weighs twice as much. To give this armour adequate flexibility, all that is necessary is to cut the sheets up into small rectangles, oblong or square, to turn over and seal their edges to fine wires, drawn through a fusible solder and forming eyes at the four angles of each piece, and to connect the pieces together by means of small rings passing through these eyes. This may be done in such a manner, as to leave between the plates only inappreciable fissures for the intrusion of rays. This curtain, when not used, might be folded one way like a map, and if it were made in two detached halves, meeting and overlapping each other along the middle of the back, each half might be folded separately; and when the two were laid together, they would form a small parcel a foot long and three or four inches broad, and two thick, which might be lodged on the knapsack, or strapped to the back.

A curtain for the front of the body also needed.

But though the spine demands, next to the head, especial consideration, why should not protection be also afforded to the front of the body, with its expanse of nervous skin overlying an upper and lower conclave of vitals, the latter so especially sensitive to the various impressions of the skin from tropical influences? Why let the sun batter upon the skin over the stomach through the poor protection of clothing lying right against it, with no intervening space for the play of *convection*, until the man beginning to retch, the *mephitis* of cholera prowling about catches the sound, and finds its victim a ready pupil in actual practice!

Where is the army surgeon of experience in the Tropics, who has not at times heard men say they had felt the sun "take the pit of the stomach" before they were attacked? Can there be a doubt that that which is destructive to some must be injurious to all?

While it is manifest that a back-curtain may be worn, without in any way incommoding the soldier, it is freely admitted that a question may be raised whether a front apron can be so suspended, as not in the smallest degree to impede his evolutions with his musket. But if the shoulders remain quite free, and the steel or cane arch, as in Fig. 11, which suspends the curtain free of the body, shall abut against the chest at the sides, and not spring more than three inches in front of it at the middle, it would perhaps offer no obstruction to his movements; and if it did, it might be readily shifted round over his back in a moment.

Concluding observations inviting every effort for the improvement of the Soldier's Dress.

Such then are the modifications of, and additions to the soldiers' dress in the Tropics, which, after an anxious consideration of the question in all its bearings, and after applying to it no little observation and experience, I have to offer. It is with no presumptuous confidence in their perfection that I do so. On the contrary, I do most sincerely desire that any means which would prove really superior, should be *promptly* devised and brought into action.

The subject commends itself to the attention of every one who is moved by feelings of duty, humanity, or gratitude, to further the object of neutralizing to the utmost extent, which the advanced state of science shall render possible, the effects of the climate of India upon the gallant men of all ranks, who, oblivious of any hope or prospect of personal advantage, are devoting, and it is to be feared, sacrificing themselves to the maintenance of British supremacy in the East.

To appreciate fully the importance of a sun-proof armour, a man ought, doubtless, to be a tropical pathologist. He ought to have watched the destruction, rapid in some instances, gradual in others, nearly universal in all, of the vitals of *the Portal Circle*, from the battering of the sun on the body, especially on the head. He will not be deceived into imagining an army of Englishmen to have become possessed of tropical constitutions, because under the elating excitement of war, the effects of exposure being postponed, there is a flattering promise of immunity from them. And if his thoughts are not too exclusively confined to the hospital, he will direct them anxiously to *prophylactics* as well as *therapeutics*. Seeing that men under the shelter of well-constructed roofs do not suffer eventual damage to anything like the same extent, he will look to the character of the clothing in which they are launched into the flood of solar heat; whether it be, at all points, as proof as is possible against the streams of liquid glare which beat upon it; whether, at the same time that simple and confiding recruits are being enlisted, every principle in science and property of matter available, are being as sedulously enlisted for their protection.

The question of a trial of improvements in India prior to their adoption considered.

With respect to the different descriptions of helmets, and the body tunics which have been proposed, or to any others that can be devised really better, although it might appear prudent to claim the evidence of a practical demonstration of the value of each by trial on a sufficient scale in India, before any general adoption of them was made, a higher prudence would perhaps array before the mind the sixty thousand British troops who may have to pass through great exposure next hot season as best they may; and the fact that, however jauntily they to whom it is the first year of great exposure may seem to endure it for the time, the lives of thousands, and the constitutions of tens of thousands of them will be sacrificed to the climate, unless they can, in the interim, be provided with protective clothing far more efficient than any yet in use.

Since, at any rate, no loss of effect, but greater or less advantage must accrue from the adoption of carefully devised improvements, and the question, therefore, can scarcely be in fairness viewed as even a mere risk of the expense (a point not to be named in connexion with the object sought), it would appear no great matter for a wealthy nation to incur the cost at once, of supplying her gallant sons with the very best sun-proof armour at command; if it were only to evince to them her conscientiousness and humanity. It would be a telling *fact* in the mouths of the recruiting sergeants, whose deficiency in inviting *facts* leads to practices painful indeed to every honourable mind to contemplate.

The trial of ray-proof dress easily made in England.

But happily, it is not necessary either to wait for a comparative trial made in India, or to adopt any plans untried. It would be easy to produce an artificial solar effect, which, so far as the various non-transparent *media*, we have to do with, are concerned, would be abundantly parallel to the radiation of heat from the sun itself. By means of two planished tin or other metallic mirrors, the rays of a large open fire might be reflected first upwards towards the ceiling of the room, and thence downwards, with varying degrees of obliquity. These rays may, for a *crucial* trial, be given a power threefold that of any solar rays, at the distance of our earth from the mystic luminary. Under the influence of these rays, two men may be placed side by side, so as to be subjected to them equally. One of them may be clad in the usual way, his shako or cap encased in the cotton covering supplied to the troops in India; and the other may be dressed in the manner proposed. It will soon appear which of them is first driven away from his post, and how many times longer the other is able to remain in his without inconvenience. The men may then be dressed, in succession, in the different kinds of helmets and tunics proposed in the preceding pages, to decide which of the several descriptions is most effective and otherwise comfortable. It is probable, that unless a fire of unusual dimensions were employed, it would be difficult to displace either of them. Presuming that any such result were obtained, it would surely be unnecessary to send such armour to India* to be tested! The trial might be made at once, for it is my belief, that a man caparisoned in the manner proposed might, according to which of the dresses was adopted, be enabled to sit out from five to eight men in succession in the ordinary dress of the soldier; and that, if our troops in India were clad in solar armour of this description, strokes of the sun would become of very rare occurrence, while the great accession given to epidemics through its action would cease. The simple heat of the atmosphere might then remain almost the only source of inconvenience from exposure during the day—an inconvenience not trifling indeed, nor to be lightly incurred, but of small account when compared with the assaults of the sun.

In concluding this division of my task, I may truly say that it has proved a source of no small anxiety and trouble, and that it would not have been undertaken but under deep and painful convictions, not the smallest of which has been the consciousness of wrong in my having allowed many years to elapse and many an earnest conviction to be suppressed

* If the trial were made there on a small scale, and ith imperfect patterus, such as these *first* constructions necessarily are, prejudice against an unaccustomed, though absolutely necessary bulk or weight, or want of familiarity with the simplest adaptations, wonld, too probably, lead to the rejection of them, though they shonld be the very best constructions which could be contrived. Such a rejection of the helmets in question would be of no importance—nay, it would be most desirable—if it could be followed by a prompt devising and adopting of plans *really superior*. Otherwise TENS OF THOUSANDS of soldiers who were in vigorous health in England last year, will, in India, suffer, some of them CONSTITUTIONAL DESTRUCTION, others DEATH, before the close of the present!

through a hesitation to intrude upon a field in which I had long ceased to hold any official position, and in which, according to report, such intrusion would prove unacceptable and unavailing.

ON THE HOUSING OF BRITISH TROOPS IN INDIA.

UPON this very important question the Company's government has been in nowise wanting in solicitous care. But as no small number of the barracks throughout Hindostan have been destroyed by the rebels, and a large increase of accommodation will be needed for the future, the present is the moment for taking into consideration any modifications in their reconstruction, since they would be attended with a double cost if made hereafter.

The lodgment of soldiers on a ground-floor undesirable.

To be as brief as possible. Many reasons may be adduced against the lodgment of European soldiers on a ground floor; which was universal when I was in India, and I believe is so still, and many and great advantages demonstrated in favour of an upper-floor housing of them. In the first place, every person who has studied the habitudes of malaria well knows how exceedingly more rife it is, especially the malaria generating the fevers of India, near the surface of the ground. The *natives*, though as such they ought to be more exempt, are much more prone to attacks of fever, owing to their sleeping close to the ground, than the Europeans, who lie at a somewhat higher level, even where both are equally under shelter. Other causes no doubt are also in operation, but this is a main one. In some countries the inhabitants sleeping on an upper floor are almost exempt from the effects of malaria which is decimating ground-sleepers. The wealthier inhabitants of Calcutta live entirely on the upper floors of their houses. Moreover, the glare from the ground, and from the walls enclosing premises which are not spacious, aggravates the heat of a ground floor materially, and renders it painful to keep venetians open, and to look out even towards the shady side of a house; and the look-out upon an ever-present and glaring mud wall, often enclosing a barrack-ground, is but a dull and dispiriting sight for the soldier. Yet, near a town, with his present habits, he cannot with safety be trusted in unenclosed barracks. Again, wind, which is so much longed for, and so necessary during the hotter seasons, meets with many impediments near the ground which do not exist ten or twenty feet up. A refreshing breeze may often be felt at an upstairs window when a dead calm prevails below. Moreover, if quartered upstairs, the soldier could not be constantly truanting into the sun and glare of the barrack-yard, nor would he feel tempted to do so when he had spacious upstairs verandahs to walk and lounge in, with an open and cheerful view over the cantonments.

The importance of a double roof.

Above his head he ought by all means to have a double roof,—the outer may be a high-pitched one of grass, such as is usual, and the inner a roof parallel to it at a distance of a yard, or it might be, though not so well, a ceiling of mats simply overlaid with grass or straw, and suspended from the rafters and tie-beams of the outer roof. Between them a free way should be given for a current of air to pass horizontally when pressed by wind, or vertically, through chimneys in the upper roof, when relying on its own buoyancy for motion. This current is needed as an ever-watchful *convector* of the heat, which *will* steal its way in treacherous quantity through every single roof, and, if not thus carried away by convection, come radiated down by the willing roof (the material of which is so adept a radiator) to mar the coolness below. The same amount of material that is often put into the present roof would suffice for both, though more ought to be allowed, and would prove doubly effective.

The importance of a double roof is shown in the fact that a ground floor, where there is an upper floor above it, is in general much the cooler of the two, although there are causes, already referred to, which render it, when it has only a single roof above it, much hotter than an upper floor with a similar roof. To secure the best effect, the heat and stagnation of the atmosphere on the ground-level should be avoided by residing on a well-raised first floor; and the solar heat from above should be arrested by two roofs well apart, as described above, and by an upward current of ventilation through openings in the ceilings and roofs at all times when the set from below can be commanded, as will be described presently.

Now all these advantages would cost next to nothing. If the white ants were kept from the under roof, only the outer one would, as now, require frequent repair. Also quite as large an area of shelter must, I presume, be wanted for a due protection of the inanimate as of the living instruments of war. Might not then all the contents of arsenals which need shelter, and of magazines, excepting the powder, be lodged not only as well, but with much advantage, in the ground floor below the soldiers, thus saving extra buildings for them, and needing no extra guard to protect them? There would be much less chance of fire, than in barracks at present, when the eaves of the thatch were so far above the ground. With respect to the lower roof or straw ceiling, it might be well to stretch a whitewashed cloth over it: it would prevent a hot wind, which was blowing through above it, from penetrating the loose texture of the straw, and thus overruling its slow-conductive virtue. If there were a cloth, also covering the under surface, it would of course be an additional though minor advantage.

In thus venturing to discuss the question of barrack construction, though my experience in building in India was not small, it is upon sanitary and philosophical points only I would be understood as presuming to give an opinion—the engineers of the India service, many of them of unsurpassed ability, being the authority to determine all points connected with their own profession.

Officers' quarters should be constructed on like principles.

It is not for the soldiery only that residence at a higher level would prove advantageous. It would for like reasons, be equally so for their officers. If they, as hitherto, had to provide their own residences, at most stations their ground floors might be available for Government storehouses, where it was an object to them to be relieved of a part of their rent; and they ought assuredly to provide themselves, or be provided with, double roofs, as costing but a trifle more, and ensuring a considerable increase of effect.

At the same time the fact demands attention that bungalows and other detached dwellings are more expensive and far less effective structures for the exclusion of heat than contiguous quarters in long barracks, properly placed and constructed, would prove. The wind blows during all the warmer months so generally from the north-west and south-east that quarters open in those directions would receive every current during nine days out of ten. While, if the system of subterranean well-ventilation, presently described, were adopted, the direction of the wind would be of no moment.

Defects of an ordinary bungalow.

A detached bungalow presents four sides to the heat, and all of them slope down at so steep an angle that the roof is lofty only over the centre room. All the rest of the building is assailed by heat and glare from above, around, and below, while the single roof, though so high pitched in the middle, has elsewhere no adequate elevation. There being no ventilation in its summit the hot air of each day is pent up within the huge pyramid above the level of the doors from day to day, and keeps that mass of heated matter from the cooling action of the nightly air entering around below it. At the same time the heated air commixing with the latter, as it revolves into the house, and the heated mass of wall and roof propelling caloric downward, keep the interior of the dwelling throughout the night oppressively hotter than the outer air. Hence the house appears to require four open sides to let in air and relieve the breathless oppression of the inmates. But could it have a dozen sides they would not suffice, so faulty is the construction. In fact, the whole mass of matter—roof and walls—above the tops of the doorways is in much the same predicament as the surface of the earth, receiving and absorbing the sun's rays from day to day, and growing hotter and hotter as the season of heat advances. It becomes, in short, a magazine of heat. Straw, so valuable as a slow conductor, is even a more ready receiver of rays than the bare surface of the earth. Did it not radiate back again into the sky at night a considerable portion of the heat it takes in by day, a bungalow would soon become intolerably hot, in spite of the utmost thickness of any single roof. In addition to the following arrangement for *tapping* the roof and drawing off its heat upwards, it might be worth consideration whether an outer roof of the thinnest sheet-tin from England, nailed on boards, would not be both economical and very effective in repelling the solar rays. It might have so moderate a slope as not to reflect rays, under any position of the sun, groundward, so as to annoy persons who were not on a higher level than the roof itself.

Quarters proposed for officers,

Contrast with the ordinary bungalow the following:—Take the apex of the pyramid of a lofty bungalow as the height (not from the ground only, but from the first floor) of the extended ridge of an elongated building. Divide the building by partition walls crosswise, excepting its outer verandahs, into spacious quarters. Give it throughout its length a double roof, say a yard apart, the inner similar and parallel to the outer. Run a raised pent-shed over and along its outer ridge, and make to each set of quarters two large openings through each of the roofs at their summit, or the openings may pierce the inner roof only; in which case the ridge-shed will not be needed. These openings will be sheltered by the shed above, and during the day partially or completely closed by thickly thatched and moveable frames commanded by cords hanging down through the inner ceiling and against the wall into the centre rooms below. The ceiling also of each room should have one or more openings with covers, commanded by strings, to let air out at will; chiefly at night, but often in the day, when the cooled air is pressing in with force enough to blow upwards; especially when, there being little wind, artificial ventilation is employed by means of one or other of the instruments to be described; or when, a subterranean ventilation being enjoyed, its course may have an opposite direction to the wind above, and be entering at what is then the leeward side of the building. An upward flow of the ventilation will not only carry off all heated air otherwise stagnating in the upper part of the rooms and above the ceiling, but it will also conduct off heat from the mass of walls and roofs, and thus prevent their accumulating it day by day, and striking it downwards, as already described.

with roof ventilators.

The advantages of long verandahs as promenades.

The outer verandahs of such a building should be spacious in breadth, and run unobstructed by partitions throughout their entire length. Being fifteen or twenty feet above the ground they would, of course, be enclosed by railings, and would form a delightful place of recreation for children throughout the day for more than half the year; and that to the north-west at all times when the wind was not hot; their diminished glare from the ground at that elevation, and the glare from the sky, being kept off by "*chekes*" of "*seinta*" (rolling blinds made of a stout reed), or of bamboo. Such verandahs would also form a promenade for the adults, quadrupling the time they could remain in the outer air, and enabling them often, even in the middle of the day in the rainy months, to break the weary monotony of a livelong confinement.

Such quarters would each of them present only two sides to the heat, while the roof, inclined on two sides only, instead of being a pyramid falling on all sides, would prove far more protective than the latter. The currents from the trap-ways in the ceilings of all the rooms would, of course, flow to the main openings in the roofs; and would, with the best effect, catch and carry away upwards the heat travelling downwards by conduction through the walls and roofs.

On one side of the building a spacious garden common to all the quarters might be kept up in a much better manner and more economically, as in the case of the ice committees, under the management of those officers who had a taste for gardening, than where each family has to contend with the fraud and idleness of a class of servants, of whose charges and proper work most of them are little prepared to judge. At the same time, for those who preserved their English desire of seclusion, the ground along the other side might be divided by walls not above six feet high into spaces corresponding with the breadth, say from forty to eighty feet, of each set of quarters. Thus each family would have at its command a public and private garden or space.

Such portion of the ground-floor of the building as was not employed for public stores or other purposes, might serve for the offices of the Residents.

Officers might be sumptuously housed in such quarters at no greater, perhaps at less, expense than in their present separate dwellings. Nearly the whole of the great station of Cawnpore, in my time running some miles along the river, was so cut up into small "compounds" by high mud walls, that a bird's-eye view would have given it the appearance of a divided honey-comb. These walls, with the profusion of trees they enclosed, seemed as if designed to cut off every current of wind from the inhabitants of all those ground-floor dwellings hidden within them. Though having a profusion of thatch and wall, the heat of most of them, especially at night, was stifling, unless assailed at all available points with "tattees;" often by night as well as by day; while towards the rainy season these were unavailing.

Cawnpore and other stations defectively laid out.

In rearing such a building as has been here advocated, very little "pukka" work—brick and lime masonry—would be needed. A foundation of it for the main walls, rising not more than a yard above the ground, would suffice everywhere but in Lower Bengal. From that level unburnt bricks laid with loam might constitute the rest, and, if tolerably massive, be carried up to any desired height. I erected a storied building, even without that foundation to guard against ground damp, and though the walls were divided, like those of a church, by large arches, it stood perfectly well, and was, in fact, stronger than most of the suburban masonry of London, which is run up three or four stories a brick and a half thick. For bathing-rooms, all that is necessary is to line the walls with a thin course of masonry coated with good cement.

Engineers in India are familiar with all these facts; but I have known a disposition to contemn anything but "pukka" masonry in public buildings, the much greater expense of which might prompt to a restriction of the dimensions, which would be most undesirable. Massive timbers, so expensive in India, especially when they become the lodgment and board of white ants, would not be needed for supporting the dwelling floor. By subdividing the ground-floor by narrow walls of the same unburnt bricks, these would serve the purpose of girders, and are even better; and as their distances may be small where the ground-floor is employed only as domestic offices or compartments for stores, the joists overlying them may be of very moderate scantling. I have found a large upper floor thus supported, cheap to construct, very firm, and able to carry a great weight.

The ventilators in the roofs and ceilings ought to

The ventilators: how to be covered and employed.

be abundantly spacious, and it would be better that their covers, instead of tilting on central or side hinges, should rise and sink flat against the openings, so as not to tempt the formation of false descending as well as ascending currents through them. They ought, of course, to fit fairly, that at all times when the inner air was colder than the outer, and not being urged upwards by the ventilating pressure from below, of wind or other power, it might not gravitate downwards and be followed by hot air from above to any considerable extent. Whenever these ventilators were open in the daytime, the doors of the house to leeward ought, of course, to be closed enough to force the current upwards.

Many of these remarks apply equally to the barracks for the men and their families. They have been carried more into details than may appear to some necessary, from an earnest desire to leave nothing wanting to recommend what, I believe, would prove a great improvement in the housing of both officers and men. There are other points which might have been insisted on,—amongst them the advantage of having the quarters of young officers in one building, and not tempting them, in visiting each other, to be constantly passing backwards and forwards, ill-covered with a mere cap or shako, under a midday sun from one end to another of a straggling station—so common a cause of severe, and not unfrequently fatal, attacks of illness, as I well remember.*

* Appendix D.

ON THE VENTILATION OF BARRACKS.

Not only is it of importance to Europeans of all ranks that they should be housed within a thoroughly sun-proof roof and walls, and, as I believe, that they should dwell at as high a level above the surface of the earth as possible, in every part of the plains of India; but in the case of soldiers in barracks, more particularly, that means should be provided for a copious ventilation of them at all seasons, especially in hot weather.*

The houses of civil and military officers are, in general, so capacious, that even where tatties, as in Lower Bengal, are not employed, the doors and windows may be closed throughout the day, in the hot season to shut out the heat, and in the winter months the cold, without injury to the occupants, the wants of whose lungs and skin bear a limited proportion to the cubic contents of such dwellings.

Free ventilation for soldiers' barracks especially needful.

But for soldiers in barracks it is of great moment that the whole atmosphere of the dwelling should be at all times undergoing a rapid renewal. The defectiveness of many barracks in respect to ventilation was very serious when I was in India; especially of some at Cawnpore and in Fort William. But even where the ventilation is not obstructed by walls and trees, in the western provinces the intense

* The importance in India of free ventilation has been at various times urged by both medical and military officers; especially by Mr. Ranald Martin, who has devoted so much attention to sanitary questions in India as well as in England.

heat of the day in the summer and the sharp cold of the air in the winter, in the early morning and during the night, present no small obstacle to an unlimited admission of air.

The Government has, in many instances, supplied the soldiers' barracks with "*tattees*" in the hot months, and in doing so have acted wisely as well as humanely. But "*tattees,*" valuable as they are, and effective while the wind is steady and in the west and therefore dry, are not without serious drawbacks. Even with a large and costly establishment of bullocks to draw water, of *bheesties* to carry it, and of *coolies* to splash it upon the tattees, constant vigilance is necessary to keep them from becoming dry through the insatiable thirst of the hot wind and the lassitude or indolence of the purveyors of water to it. We may then find the air within the tattee rise in a quarter of an hour from a temperature of seventy-eight or eighty degrees to one hundred degrees or more, and from a humid to a very arid state. These transitions are liable to be repeated in a barrack several times a day, and are unquestionably very trying; yet not equal to the uninterrupted play of the hot and arid wind upon the skin. Another defect of tattees is that they are of little or no use at night without the aid of blowing-machines; and of less use still during the terrific *hiatus* of a fortnight or month between the hot and rainy seasons, and during the oppressive intervals between the rainy days after the monsoon has set in, and towards its close.

The value and defects of tattees.

Again, in the cold season, the body, habituated to a copious ventilation throughout the rest of the year, yearns for fresh air far more than it does in England in weather equally cold to the feelings; and a confined atmosphere is absolutely more injurious in a climate where the skin and frame, generally, is in much lower tone, and is surrounded by prejudicial influences. In short, barrack ventilation in India is a subject demanding a close and active attention. Looking merely to the economy of expensive lives, it will abundantly repay any outlay necessary for commanding it in perfection.

The earth affords a boundless source of coolness in hot and warmth in cold weather.

Happily, we have at command a boundless source from which to draw coolness in the hot, and warmth in the cold season. When those properties of matter in relation to HEAT, through which it operates, and is to be resisted, were being considered in the preceding pages, *the subterranean absorption of heat* claimed attention, and was briefly examined. It was there stated that this property, rightly employed, was available, with great advantage, for the ventilation of buildings.

While we are wont to look to the soil of the uppermost few inches only of the earth's surface, as that in which, for the most part, we have any interest; while, if we dig deeper into it, we do so only for water or for minerals; we are prone to overlook altogether, or to employ in an unreflecting and defective manner its capabilities as an equalizer of climatic temperaments. *Equatorial* climates are, for the most part, equable more than enough;—hot at all times. But near to and beyond the Tropics, and therefore over nearly all India, we may view the uppermost fifty feet of the surface of that continent,—

or as many feet down as we can reach without the intrusion of water,—as one vast equalizing reservoir; ready to absorb, from any amount of air we may choose to subject to its action, a large proportion of its summer heat, even if we do not aid our reservoir in its annual emptying itself of such heat in the cold season, but leave it to conduct back, spontaneously, such heat tardily upwards to the surface during the winter months. But if we adopt proper measures for cooling thoroughly, in the winter, the mass of earth we select for our absorbing reservoir, we may have it emptied of more than the accumulated summer heat before the ensuing hot season, and brought down nearly to the *winter mean*, and ready, therefore, to absorb again much more heat than when it had to cool itself by the tardy spontaneous process of upward conduction through its whole mass.

It will temper the winter cold.

Furthermore, since it is by the agency of the *cold* air of the winter that we must empty our reservoir of heat, that air will become warmed by the process, and available for a tempered ventilation throughout the very season when the air is more sharp than is suitable to bodily frames more or less relaxed, and at rest; especially during sleep.

The means available in India at a small cost.

In looking around for means by which to command such valuable results, we find them offered to us at once, if we will but exercise a little thought, in the facility and cheapness with which wells are made throughout India. In the whole of the western provinces, and I believe, throughout *Hindostan* generally, wells about three feet six inches in diameter may be dug down to the water level at a cost of from eighteen pence to half-a-crown, where the depth does not exceed fifty feet. In most soils these wells are available without being guarded by any masonry lining, excepting under the water level, for the drawing of water throughout the whole day for many months, during several years. And in soils even to a considerable extent sandy, they can be dug, and will last as they are, *if not used*, for a great length of time.

Fig. 12.

The plan for cooling by subterranean action.

Now if we select, contiguous to a barrack of the largest size, a plot of ground, A, B, C, D, Fig. 12, only a hundred yards square, or a hundred and twenty yards long by eighty yards wide, less might do, and prick it over with wells about seven yards apart, the cost of digging them all will be only twenty pounds, and we shall possess two hundred to operate upon a cubic block of earth a hundred yards square,* and say fifty feet deep. There are numerous parts of India, in which the water being forty or fifty feet or more from the surface, dry wells to that depth

* The plot of ground may with preference be oblong, as 200 yards by 50, according to the length of the barrack or barracks.

may be dug; but on the other hand, in many localities, as at Meerut, Bareilly, and Delhi, the depth is much less, in some not one-half as much. In such places the number of the wells would have to be multiplied; and evaporation from the water's surface and the humid sides of the wells would make up for the effect of their inferior depth. Upon the plan proving effective, it might form an important object in the choice of a station, to select localities in which the refrigerative well ventilation could be given the best effect—whether with deep wells and a drier air, or of shallow and a more humid. At Futtehgurh, Cawnpore, Agra, and in Bundelcund, etc., dry wells from forty to seventy feet deep may be dug.

To put the wells in action we may proceed thus. Let E, F, G, etc., be successive rows of wells; the first of each row E 1, F 1, G 1, being sunk in the lower verandah of the barrack, throughout its length, though this is not necessary, and the mouths of this row being covered with wooden or bamboo gratings to guard against accidents. All the wells exterior to the building, excepting the furthermost of each row, E 10, F 10, etc., must have their mouths closed and plugged for some feet down by straw resting on a simple bamboo frame propped across the well, as at O O O, etc. If the ground is wanted for exercising the men, the mouths of the wells must be arched over with brickwork, and covered level with the ground around; but as this would be expensive, and the ground on one side of a barrack can generally be spared to that moderate extent, the simplest course would be to raise a common mud wall a foot or two high round each well, and to cover the straw, plugging its mouth, with matting or a thin thatch. The earth dug from the wells would raise the level of the surface about a foot, and would in general yield, if the lower sand were not put uppermost, a fertile virgin soil. The whole area between the wells might form a productive garden, with its surface kept cool by frequent watering from a few wells reserved and deepened for the purpose, and by being covered with vegetation; but it must not be such vegetation as could be a source of malaria. This use of the surface would appreciably check the travelling of heat downwards into our cubic reservoir below.

The wells of each row must be made to communicate with each other, thus: from the bottom of E 1, a horizontal passage P, about two and a half feet high and fifteen or eighteen inches wide, must be cut to the bottom of the next well of the row E 2, and from near the top of this well, below the straw, about ten feet beneath the surface of the earth, a similar horizontal passage must proceed to the next well, E 3, and from the bottom of this well a passage to E 4, and so on to the last well, E 10, according to the number of wells in the row. This last well being surmounted by a large cowl, S (turned to the wind by a fan-tail, or a lever moved by hand), and acting as a wind-sail, the wind will blow down it and through the passage at bottom to the next well, then up it and through its upper passage to the third well, and pursuing this course through all the wells, will make its exit through the grating of the well E 1, and into the verandah T, which should be well enclosed. As in each row of wells the last would be similarly surmounted with a cowl, every first well of each row would pour forth air into the verandah.

Supposing the barracks to be built, as has been urgently recommended in the preceding pages, with an upper floor for the residence of the men, the verandah above that in which the wells are may have its floor grated throughout, being laid with battens say one inch and a quarter wide, and three quarters of an inch apart. This should be an enclosed verandah, of course.

We shall now have an abundant ventilation of cooled air in the hot season, and of warmed air in the cold, at all times when there is any wind. In a calm state of the atmosphere the ventilation may be easily maintained by mechanical aid; the moderate amount of labour required for which may be readily afforded when the army of *bheesties*, and *coolies*, and bullocks, otherwise needed for tatties, is, with them, superseded by our subterranean refrigeration. The machinery by which an *artificial* current may with best effect be maintained will receive some notice presently.

Estimate of the capability of the terrene reservoir for cooling.

Of the capability of such a heat-absorbing and heat-exhaling reservoir as the block of earth with its cavernous surfaces would form, we may obtain some conception by a little calculation. First, as to the whole earthy surface holding a commerce in caloric with the air sweeping against it down and up the wells and through the transverse passages. Each well, where there are forty perpendicular feet available, and ten peripheral, will possess a surface of four hundred square feet, to which must be added one hundred feet more as the surface of one-half of the two transverse passages connecting it with the next wells. The acting surfaces of each well may then be taken at five hundred square feet; and of the two hundred wells at no less than one hundred thousand feet; which immense surface would be constantly acting upon the ventilating currents. These, while traversing it, being repeatedly inverted and changed in their direction, could not fail to have every part of them brought into contact with the earthy surface. With respect to the capacity, as a reservoir for heat, of our block of earth of one hundred *yards* square and fifty *feet* deep, forty of which may be assumed available, it will be found on calculation to contain, deducting the wells' space, no less than three million six hundred thousand cubic feet, weighing about five hundred and fifty million pounds. Estimating the *specific* heat of earth and of air as about the same, supposing the surfaces of the wells to be at the commencement of the hot season at the temperature of sixty degrees, one hundred millions of pounds of hot air might pass through them during the ensuing hot months, and be cooled down thirty degrees, without raising the temperature of the mass of earth six degrees, by the time the cooling process ceased to be needed at the close of the warm months. Any warming of the mass by heat that struck down from the surface of the soil would, of course, be separate, but not such as to affect materially the calculation; since, if the quautity to be cooled were doubled, the earthy mass would only be heated by twelve degrees.

Supposing the cooling to be employed about two hundred days, or about seven months, this would allow no less than half a million pounds of ventilating air daily, or upwards of twenty thousand pounds of air per hour, day and night. In bulk this would amount to more than two hundred and fifty thousand cubic feet; which would renew every hour the entire atmosphere of a barrack two hundred and forty feet long, sixty feet wide, and about twenty feet of *mean* height. Such a ventilation would be redundant, and could only take place in strong winds, since it would require a current of air through the wells of six miles per hour, and through their connecting passages of twenty. Of course the surfaces of the outermost wells first entered by the hot air would soon lose much of their coolness; but then the nearer wells would have theirs less reduced in proportion.

In the cold season, during the warmth of the day the action of the wells would not be needed, the barrack doors being thrown open. At such times the warmish current should not be allowed to blow through the wells, as it would stop the progressive cooling of their surfaces. To prevent this the cowls should be turned with their backs to the wind, and perhaps a mat laid over each of the outer wells. At night probably not a fourth of the wells might be needed for the temperate ventilation they supplied, in lieu of the sharp night-air of the cold season; but while the air was cold, *i. e.* from soon after sunset till an hour after sunrise, the wind should be allowed to blow through all the wells, the rows not in use being made to blow their current out of doors. The air of the wells being the warmer of the two, the ventilation would proceed almost spontaneously. By such management, especially if mechanical aid were employed when the weather was calm, the terrene mass surrounding the wells would be brought down to a temperature much below the *mean* annual temperature of the climate, which annual mean would be the utmost cooling to which even its deepest stratum could be reduced if the process were left to the natural action of conduction upwards through the whole mass.

Since the natural cooling and warming of the earth extends in India forty or fifty feet down in six months, while the *mean* distance of any part of our block of earth from the nearest well surface would be only five feet, the *extreme* from each, or midway distance between two wells, being under ten feet (there being six yards between the wells), there can be little doubt that the whole of the block would be effective as a heat-absorbing and heat-imparting reservoir.

Moreover, had we the making of it on purpose, we could not, perhaps, select more suitable materials. Were our terrene block a mass of metal, it would be far too quick a conductor of heat, which it would absorb down from the surface until it was saturated, shortly after the hot season set in. On the other hand, were our terrene reservoir composed of wood or charcoal, it would be useless. It would be as much too slow a conductor of heat as metal would be too quick.

Again, the earthy mass would not only cool the hot air by absorbing its heat, but also by exhaling into it much water, and this effect might be materially increased if the wells were carried down a little below the water level. This would give, besides the damp sides of the wells, two hundred circular yards of evaporating water surface, the effect of which would be much increased by the perpendicular descent of the air pressing it upon the water in every second well. The cooling process aided by evaporation.

VENTILATING MACHINES.

The blowing-machine, introduced first by Dr. Dessaguiller, I believe, to ventilate the House of Commons, more than a hundred years ago, in which the air is propelled by passing off at a tangent through a centrifugal force imparted to it by rotation, by means of fans revolving in a barrel, requires, on account of the levity of air, a great velocity to give the current any absolute force. It is a favourite blower for "cupola" and other furnaces; where the great velocity given to it causes a stunning noise. With a view to ensure more certain force in a ventilating current than this principle, acting slowly, can give, I was led, in the year 1824,

The Refrigerator a ventilating pump.

to contrive the following machine. It was a kind of pendulum pump, Figs. 13 and 14. A A is a frame

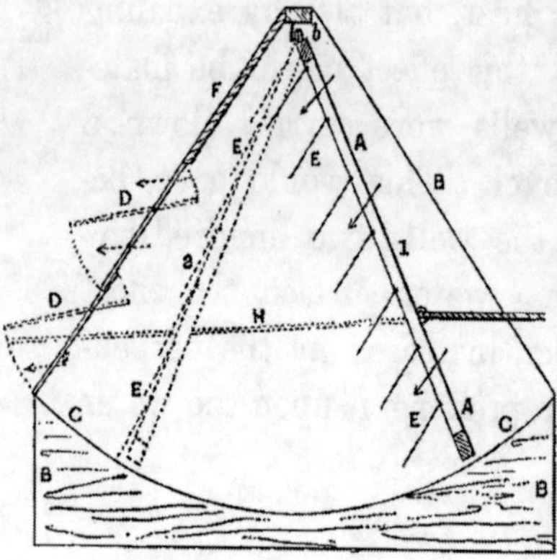

Fig. 13. Side view in section.

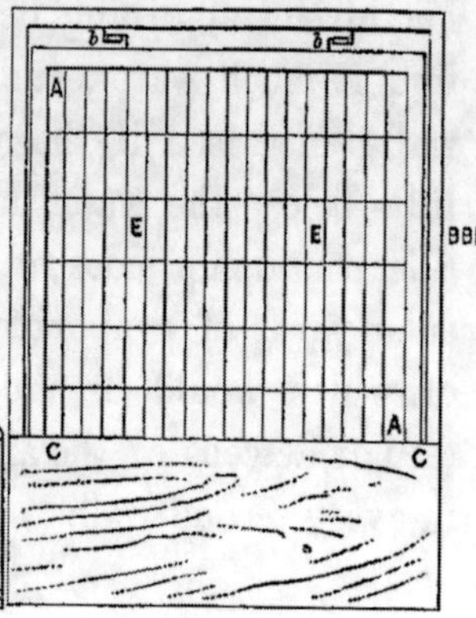

Fig. 14. Back view.

about eight feet square, hanging upon knife-edge hinges *b b*, between and close to two parallel walls of masonry or wood, B B, and oscillating between them and over a concave arch, C C, of masonry or planking. The frame on one side was laced over with tape; over which surface were stretched across, from top to bottom, lappets, E E E, of fine cotton cloth, overlying each other like venetians. When the pendulum frame, which was well weighted at bottom, was drawn back, as in position 1, the lappets flew up and the air passed through them. When the pendulum oscillated forwards, towards its position 2, the lappets fell close, and the whole volume of air in the machine was driven through the valve-doors D D, in the front enclosing frame F F, which being very light, and nicely poised, opened readily to the pressure. The frame, as seen in the dotted position 2, has nearly finished its course forwards.

Directly it commences its oscillation backwards, the valve-doors in the front enclosing frame fall, and the lappets in the pendulum rise again.

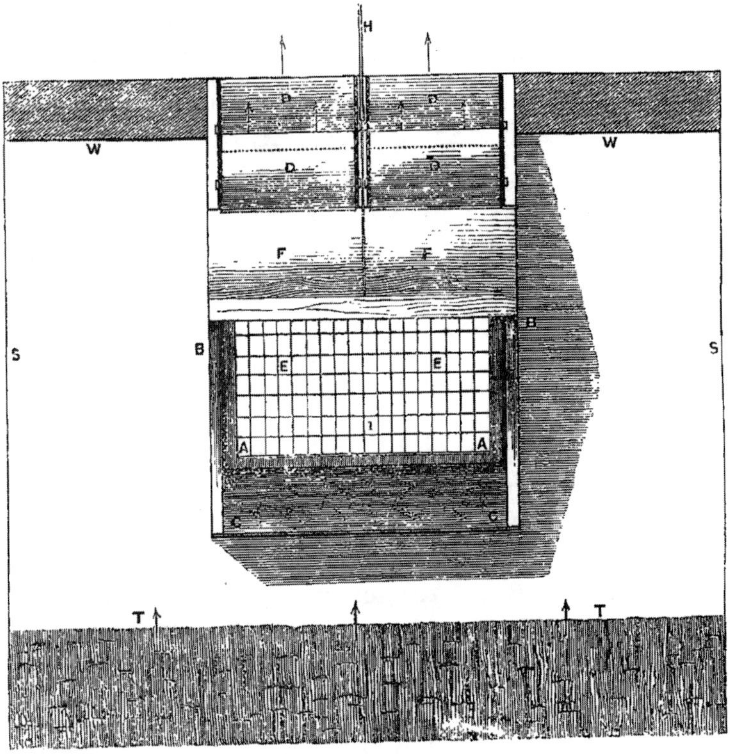

Fig. 15. Bird's-eye view.

This machine was made to cool the atmosphere as well as to ventilate, by having stretched over it a cotton netting made on purpose, the warp or threads of which were composed of cotton wick a third of an inch thick. This netting covered both sides of the frame, and had its upper edges extended into a water trough above. By capillary action it kept itself thoroughly wetted. Though the cooling power of this machine was great, and rendered the employer of it independent of coolies to sprinkle tatties, and though there was no waste of water as with these, it is not advisable that the evaporating surface should form part of the ventilating machine. It is preferable to employ tatties of three or four times the area of the pendulum fan, and enclosing the verandah space in which it stands, as seen in the plan, Fig. 15. In the former case, the greater part of the power employed was expended in forcing the wetted network hurriedly through the air. In the latter, the large area of the wetted tatty-surface, and the continuous flow through it, greatly diminished the consumption of labour in the machines fitted up in this manner.

The peculiarities of this air-pump are,—1st. The entire absence of friction in the piston, it being a pendulous frame hung on knife-edge hinges, and not touching the sides of its chamber. 2nd. Its requiring the force to act in one direction only; being a pendulum, and weighted, it oscillates freely to nearly the same height as that to which it has been drawn. 3rd. The capacious free-way for the air, the whole surface of the frame being valvular, and the formation of the valves light and nearly air-tight, if close wove cloth is used, or oiled silk.

The fissure at the hinges *b b* has leather or soft oil-cloth nailed over it, from the supporting bar to the upper edge of the frame. Where it is not inconvenient to let the man working the fan remain in the room in front of it, it is preferable to let the pulling force act in the direction of the resistance, as that of the dotted line H H, being a cane fixed to the pendulum fan, and working through a slit in the middle bar, between the lower valves D, of the enclosing canvassed frame F F.

Dr. Rankin's Thermantidote.

The ventilating fan of Dessaguiller, already noticed, which in England is now chiefly employed of a small size, but revolving with great rapidity, was successfully introduced into India by Dr. Rankin, of the Bengal Medical Service, accompanied with jets of water, or with a tattee-surface, for cooling the air. Revolving slowly by means of a winch-handle fixed on the fan-axis itself, and turned by one or more men, the fans and machine had to be given, as when first invented by Dessaguiller, a much larger size than is now common for blast purposes in England. Where there are no blank walls or other obstructions opposite the course of the current, and too near to the machine, its action is very satisfactory, being accompanied with scarcely any sound, owing to its gentle motion; whereas, it was not possible to make the "Refrigerator" equally silent; though by not allowing the valves to strike, the sound was reduced to merely the "whiff" of the lappets.

Its advantages,

and defects.

But a large portion of the power employed in the "Thermantidote" (the name given by Dr. Rankin to his useful adaptation of the blowing machine), is liable to be wasted, if any impediment is offered to the current flowing from it. The centrifugal force of so light a fluid as air revolving with little speed, is too feeble to throw it off at a tangent, especially within one quadrant only of the circle, if the exit is not perfectly free. The contained air, instead of flowing out at each revolution, is liable to continue revolving round in the drum like milk in a barrel-churn. Oftentimes, a portion only of the contents of the drum are evolved at each revolution. While the coolies working the fans may be considered at fault, the defect is intrinsic in the principle of Dessaguiller's machine, which requires great velocity to give it power. Otherwise, there is much in its silent action to recommend it. As it is of importance that employers of the "Thermantidote" should be on their guard not to stifle the current, it may be of use to cite an instance of this. One of large size was, in 1834, fixed in such a manner as to blow air through an opening in the wall of a room in Calcutta, which being not more than twelve feet wide, presented a blank wall opposite the current. This impeded it so much, that the greater portion of the air revolved repeatedly round in the drum before it made its exit. It had been placed there by the gentleman whose "office" it was intended to ventilate, contrary to the advice of the late Colonel Forbes,* who had recommended in that position the employment of the Refrigerator, of the principles of which he frequently expressed a favourable opinion, as giving to the power employed a maximum effect.

In the many cases, as in the ventilation of mines, where a powerful current has to be forced through many obstructive channels, and where it is not of importance that the process should be absolutely silent, I think the entire absence of friction, and the extensive valve-way of the pendulum pump, would

* The distinguished engineer and constructor of the Calcutta mint.

be found to render it a very effective instrument. This opinion rests not on theory only, but upon the trial of more than half a dozen, constructed for friends and myself.

A modification of Dessaguiller's machine proposed.

With a view to command the noiseless action of the centrifugal blower, without its defects, it occurred to me to suggest to the late Mr. Watson, magistrate of Allyghur, the following modification of it for trial. It is probable that the recent convulsion in India, and the death of that active officer, have taken place before it has been carried into effect.

Let W W, Fig. 15, represent the wall between R,

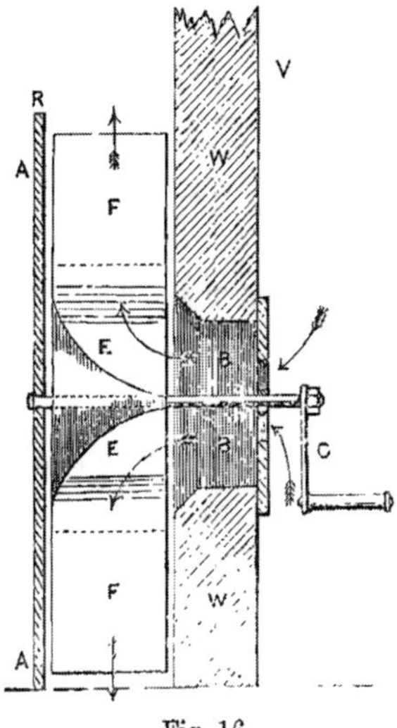

Fig. 16.
Edge view.

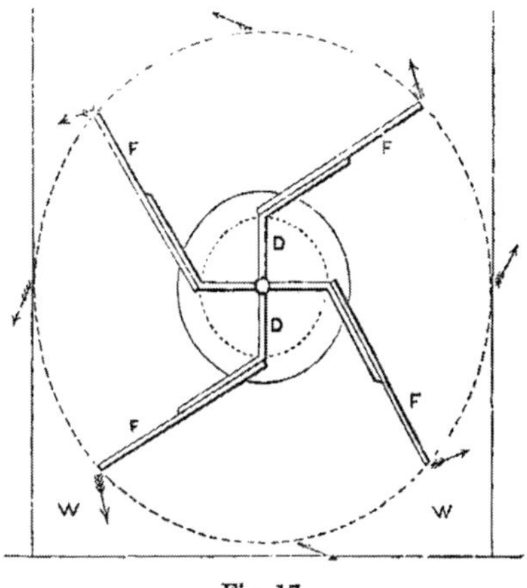

Fig. 17.
Front view, the frame being removed.

a room, and V, a verandah ; B B is a circular opening, two feet or more in diameter, either through the wall or in a doorway boarded up. A A, Figs. 16 and 17, is a boarded frame about nine feet high, which may be square or round at top. It stands parallel with the walls, at a distance of one foot and a half or two feet, and opposite the opening B. F F, etc., are four fanners carried on an axis, and four iron cross-arms, D D, etc. These fanners fit the space between the wall and the boarded frame A, without touching the sides, and are each about a yard long, the diameter of the machine being about eight feet; and they are set in revolution by means of the crank-handle C. The current of air is admitted at one side only, B B, of the machine, and impinging against a curved cone E E, is given at once a centrifugal direction, with little loss of its momentum. By this arrangement the machine, being placed with its diameter parallel to the wall, which may form one of its enclosing sides, occupies little space. The fanners are not enclosed in a drum, open only in one quadrant, as in all other forms of the centrifugal blower, but are open round the whole circumference. The air is thus permitted to flow out at tangents the whole way round, as shown by the arrows.

Ventilating machines ought not to be employed to create wind.

It should be borne in mind that when employed for ventilation the centrifugal machine should not act as a *blowing*, but as a ventilating instrument. Under no circumstances can any one sit prudently throughout the day in an *unintermitting* current blowing against one side of his person; especially if the temperature of that current is lower than of the air around him. A fan, or punkah, blows air alternately against the opposite sides of the person, and each puff is transient, and followed by an equal lull, during which the skin has time to prepare itself for the next impression. Hence most persons may safely sleep under punkahs oscillating over them all night; but, though often practised, it is with questionable prudence that persons sleep in an *uninterrupted* current of wind.

The machine now described is proposed as an effective ventilator, throwing off the entering air copiously in all directions, and giving to the centrifugal action its maximum of effect. Probably where the diameter is so considerable and the motion not rapid, six fans might be employed with advantage instead of four.

Such a ventilating-machine would have the advantage of simplicity and cheapness in a high degree, and might be employed to draw air through the wells when the atmosphere was too calm for a spontaneous current through them. The labour required to work the machines, from half a dozen to a dozen of which would probably suffice for the largest barrack, would cost but a small part of that which has to be devoted continuously to the watering of tattees. Indeed, the expense of tattees for two or three seasons would pay for the construction of the wells and machines, which, once made, would last many years. It is to be hoped that a plan promising so much comfort to our soldiery and their families, and resting upon principles so unquestionably sound, as would a system of wells for subterranean action, will receive a due attention and trial.

Objections to the system of well-ventilation anticipated.

It may be well, in concluding this subject, to anticipate an objection which might be hastily raised to the system of wells—that the resistance offered to the current by having its direction repeatedly changed perpendicularly to its course, in traversing the wells, may be such as to prevent any copious ventilation taking place through them. But they who know through how long and tortuous a course air may be pressed by no greater force than an ordinary breeze, provided the passage-way be large enough, will not apprehend failure on this account. It is true that an extravagant reliance on the mobility of air and a neglect of the resistance from its friction against a great length of rough surfaces, have, in certain instances, proved to mining engineers that there is a limit to which it can with effect be driven underground; but such are extreme cases, having no parallel with the present. Residents in towns, especially those situated on broad rivers or the sea-shore, where sewers open upon a tide-way with imperfectly trapped mouths, are painfully assured of the facility with which air can be blown up drains a quarter of a mile from the shore, and *that*, little in virtue of its levity as drain air impregnated with compounds of hydrogen, but whenever even a moderate breeze may set against the mouths of the sewers.

The effect of friction considered,

Let it be borne in mind that the length of a row of ten wells with their connecting passages will not exceed two hundred yards; while the free way of the wells is eight square feet, and of the passages nearly four. At the same time, the wind-sails, or cowls, over each of the last wells, may be given large dimensions, and be made duly conical, to receive the pressure of a large surface of wind; and this at a trifling cost, by constructing them of bamboo frame-work covered with country matting.

It is questionable whether the resistance offered by friction, in the passage of air through the small interstices of tattees, does not much exceed any that the well surfaces could offer.

Again, should any one imagine that the greater specific gravity of the air, when cooled in the wells, would offer too considerable a resistance to its displacement, he is requested to bear in mind that any force thus acting adversely is that only of the difference between the weight of the column of air pressed down the first, or cowled wells, and that pressed up the last, or verandah wells; for the intervening eight wells form—every two of them—syphons in which the columns balance each other. Now, on calculation he will find that, supposing the difference in the temperature of the two columns of air in question—that in the first and that in the last of each row of wells—should amount to thirty degrees; it will not, in a height of forty feet, produce a difference of weight exceeding a pressure per square foot of 0·18 of a pound, or that of a gentle breeze between five and six miles an hour. So that, as far as this obstruction is concerned, a current of wind at the latter pace would maintain a ventilation, and a breeze at eight miles an hour a rapid one. When the wind was too feeble, if the pendulum pump, "the Refrigerator," just described, were employed to draw air through the wells, the current must flow, however slowly it was oscillated, and the hydrostatic pressure (if the term may be

and of the density of the cooled air.

used) would only amount to eleven pounds upon the whole surface of a pendulum-frame eight feet each way.

In this calculation the obstruction to the motion of the current, arising from its density, has been given credit for the whole condensing effect of a fall of thirty degrees in the temperature, but this is more than is due to it, for the air in passing the wells will receive no small addition of aqueous vapour. Now every pneumatician is aware that the addition of aqueous vapour expands air so much as to lessen its density appreciably. Since ten or fifteen out of the thirty degrees of cooling may easily result from evaporation in the wells, a portion of the density due to this part of the cooling will be reduced by the expanding action of the vapour introduced. Indeed, the subject may be placed in another and striking aspect. Leaving out of the question the main value of the well system—that of bringing into play the heat-absorbing power of our terrene mass, and viewing it as one of cooling by evaporation only, it may be worthy of inquiry whether it would not be better to send our air down to cool itself spontaneously by the evaporation of moisture from the bottom and sides of wells, than to hoist up the water to be thrown into air, passing tatties; since the former may be generally effected by the wind alone, or somewhat aided by human or other labour; while the latter, viz., both the raising and the sprinkling of the water, must at all times be entirely effected by a large amount of labour and vigilance. If desirable, when ventilating-machines were needed, they might be worked by animal (brute) power by means of "rigger" wheels exterior to the barracks, or in their ground-floor; bullocks or "tattoos" (ponies) driving them, as horses do thrashing-machines in England. But the labour of coolies would be an expense too moderate to merit any consideration.

As before stated, the wells would require no casing with masonry, and below the water-level, only a few circles of the baked clay made for the purpose, and procurable everywhere in Hindostan. The horizontal passages between the wells, especially the lower ones, where the soil was damp, would have to be thus lined, but the cost would be trifling, and would scarcely ever have to be renewed. It may appear, at first sight, that wells only eighteen feet apart would riddle the land too much for security; but there is no real ground for such an apprehension. Nothing is more common throughout the well-irrigated districts, *i. e.*, over three-fourths of Hindostan, than to see several wells grouped together much nearer than that; and not closed at top and unused as those proposed for ventilating purposes, but open to the weather, and with large leathern bags of more than half their diameter—and often squirting water against their earthy sides—passing up and down them the whole day long.

The wells easy of construction and not too near to each other.

The cheerful and healthy housing of troops, which has been so earnestly advocated and so fully detailed, would prove conducive to the preservation of their health, not only directly, but to, perhaps, an equal degree indirectly, by diminishing some of the

The valuable indirect effects of a cheerful and healthy housing of troops.

chief incentives to intemperance—exhaustion, thirst, discomfort, and sleeplessness. While in the still more important question of their morals, and moral example, any diminution in a debauchery which at present appears to have no limits but those set by coercion, would be cheaply purchased at any price.

ON THE LOCATING OF BRITISH TROOPS IN INDIA.

THE first desire which naturally suggests itself to the mind is, that the choicest climates which that continent affords, should, as far as political and military considerations will permit it, be rendered available for the residence of the European forces maintained in India.

Importance of an early removal of convalescents to a temperate climate.

From my first landing in India I became, from peculiar circumstances, so extensively engaged in the charge of European troops, that it required but little discernment to perceive, in numerous instances, that were an immediate removal to a temperate and readily accessible climate practicable, before organic disease was established through relapses, many a constitution might not only be saved from destruction, but become as well fitted to endure any necessary residence in the plains of India, as if previous illness had not occurred.

Availing myself of the opportunity, in medical charge of the European troops at Kurnaul, I obtained leave early in 1824, a year after my entering the country, to visit the Himalayas, with the object of studying the character of the climate. From different causes the climate at that time by no means enjoyed the repute it merited. Of the invalids who had visited it, most of them, instead of remaining stationary at certain heights, had travelled through the lower ranges, and had, in two or three instances, visited the higher. They had not, therefore, derived the benefit they might. More than one instance had occurred of injury instead of benefit having resulted from a visit to the Hills. There also existed, against a residence at any height above four thousand feet in the Gurwall Hills during the rainy season, a prejudice in which officers resident there partook so strongly, that for a time they dissuaded some mutual friends from attempting it. We remained, however, throughout a heavy rainy season at Simla, at which spot there was then but one house, and that never occupied in the rains. Having made meteorological observations at various heights and in valleys, from a low level up to more than sixteen thousand feet, and having experienced in the Hills a rainy season (undoubtedly the least favourable part of the year) certain peculiar properties of the climate at suitable elevations presented themselves to my view, which promised to give them, as a temporary residence, a superiority, in some respects, even over the climate of England; and not to interfere with their great comparative salubrity for permanent residence.

The author's visit to the Himalayas for climatic observations.

Impressed with the peculiarity, the great interest,

Advantages of the climate long neglected.

and the importance of these properties of the climate in their relation to medical philosophy, and with the high claims with which they endowed it, instead of the dubious reputation which had kept it neglected for nine years since our acquisition of the territory, I was led to condense my observations and to publish them in an Essay,* which was circulated in all quarters in which the hope might be entertained that a useful influence might be exerted. A correspondence on the formation of military sanitary stations on the hills ensued with the different medical and other authorities. Mr. Sandham, a medical officer in H.M.'s service, of great ability, was directed to select localities for stations, and visited me on the subject. The opinion I ventured was that for sanitary stations the height should not be less than 6000 feet, and should not materially exceed 7000. Simla appeared to me in several respects a choice locality,—though, on account of the structure of the mountain, and the effect of one of its spurs in catching clouds and causing them to roll over the ridge, I was not sure that even a better might not have been selected. On the other hand, I thought Landour higher than was desirable for a principal station. Subsequent information confirmed my opinion as to the best heights for chief stations; but led to the belief that for some cases of disease, and for different stages of convalescence, in certain instances, the climate of both less and greater altitudes would be desirable.

The formation of sanitary stations recommended in an essay by the author in 1824.

Not only were sanitary stations formed shortly

* Appendix E.

afterwards at desirable elevations, but in process of time the Government was led to perceive, I believe through the judicious recommendations of Mr. Martin, that a portion of the troops in health might with advantage be quartered in the hills, which has been done for some years.

Reasons for increasing the proportion of Europeans stationed in the hills.

With convictions of thirty-four years' standing respecting the character of the climates of *well-selected* spots in the mountain ranges of India deeply impressed on my mind, both by an early theoretical view, which I believe to be sound, and by the subsequent experience of thousands which has confirmed it, it was impossible not to feel alarmed at a recent report that hereafter the whole British force would have to be stationed in the plains. I trust, therefore, to be excused an intrusion into political and military considerations which is unavoidable in the endeavour to prove that a sanitary measure of the greatest importance is not seriously opposed to them.*

The experience of the recent rebellion not unfavourable to it.

It is evident that if these considerations would permit it, it would be indeed a happy measure for all concerned, could the whole of the British soldiery be stationed at elevations above five or six thousand feet. Although this would be obviously inadmissible,

* Since this sheet was written I have heard with great satisfaction that Mr. Martin has, with the merited weight of his authority in sanitary affairs, brought the question prominently before the Court of Directors; and has shown, by elaborate proofs, that the advantages both in a financial and political, as well as a humane point of view, of stationing even the great bulk of the British forces at due elevations available in different parts of India, would be signally great. I trust the light in which the question is placed in these pages may afford additional confirmation to this important recommendation.

have the results of the rebellion been such as to lead to the conclusion that not only an equal but even a larger proportion of the European troops than hitherto could not with safety be stationed on hill eminences? Surely not. Even in the recent unparalleled case of the totally unexpected mutiny of the entire native army of Hindostan Proper, and that at stations with, for the most part, open cantonments, the rebels have not had nerve to move with any such concert and rapidity as would have prevented any station in the western provinces from receiving succour in good time, but for the disastrous seizure of Delhi by them.

The detention of the British force before Delhi.

Had that misfortune not overtaken the Government, or had the Government, as in the case of Bhurtpoor in 1825, issued an announcement to the effect that, to avoid an exposure of its troops in the worst season, the recapture would be postponed for some months (whether such a decision would have been politically sound or not; whether or not the postponement would have exercised a worse influence than remaining in front of the city several months before capturing it), this at least is certain, that the force there detained might in a few days have rescued the Europeans of Futtehghur and Cawnpore, disarming the troops; and in a few more Lucknow also, before any large adverse force was assembled there: while smaller columns might have visited the stations in Rohilcund and the north of Oude, and thus have prevented the occurrence of nearly all the massacres in that part of India, so dreadful in themselves, and so damaging to the respect observed towards the persons of European officers, civil and military, and their families.

It is not here proposed to raise the question whether or not such would have been the more desirable course, and whether the repeatedly occurring defeats sustained by the rebels under the walls of Delhi, in which they not only had a boundless supply of artillery, but could always shelter their guns, were comparable in effect with defeats where they are drawn away from cover and invariably lose their artillery and their baggage, but the question is simply raised, whether it is not plain that a reserve of British troops quartered in the nearest hills could have arrived in aid of those distributed over the subjacent plains in ample time to have rescued the several stations in the late disaster, had circumstances not led to the detention of the whole of the available force before Delhi?

Temporary security of any British force behind defences.

Again; without presuming to hazard a judgment on a military question, it is impossible for any observer of late events to be blind to the fact, that a small British force within a fortification of moderate strength, and well provisioned, may set at defiance the efforts of any number of natives during an indefinite period, and certainly until relief shall arrive from the distance at which Hill residence may be obtained from any part of the plains, especially if such fortifications shall stand clear of buildings and ravines which could give cover to an enemy near enough to do injury by its missiles.

Cause of the unhealthiness of forts to British troops.

This leads us to an important sanitary inquiry. The practice hitherto observed has been in general, to destroy, and often to level to the ground, native earth fortifications; and in the case of the masonry forts, majestic and venerable masses, while retaining them, to quarter in them as few Europeans as possible, experience having proved them to be much more unhealthy than open plains. Has not this, however, arisen from quartering troops in forts, according to rule, as low as possible under the cover of the ramparts? Were war in India the usual condition, and peace the exception, the necessity of this would be manifest; but the objects for which India is held, and the ability to hold it, require that a state of defence, though a contingency it is of importance to provide for, should be of very rare occurrence—so rare that it should not enter as an element interfering in the smallest degree with a sanitary housing of the troops.

Remediable by a suitable method of housing them.

Now, if common mud walls, reared similarly to the ramparts themselves, and of massive thickness, were run inwards from them as spurs parallel to each other, at a distance of twenty feet or upwards apart, and then connected by massive arches of burnt or even of unburnt brick, they would afford over them an extensive surface, which, being made level, might form the floor of barracks on a level with the rampart or wall of the fort. Were properly solid barracks of unburnt brick, solid against the climate, but left to their fate in a siege from their exposed position, erected on that base, and given a double roof and the various other provisions for ventilation and cooling already described, there would seem to be no assignable reason why so well-raised and airy a habitation might not be as healthy as if it were without, instead of within, the defences. If an open plain were preserved for a mile around, in a state of wholesome cultivation, the main bazaar which grows up round large stations being kept beyond that distance; if only barrack and domestic servants were allowed to reside within the fort, the various shopkeepers and labourers coming in for the day to their stores and occupations; and if proper measures were taken to guard against offensive matter accumulating in or near the fort, there would be good reason for expecting that it would offer a far more healthy residence for troops than most of such cantonments as I have known in India.

The spacious arches below the barracks might serve various important purposes. In the ordinary times of peace, some of them might be reserved for use as military storehouses, others for granaries; the "bunniahs" who supplied the forces being required to keep their grain stores in them. These corndealers have the neighbouring "Zumeendars" commonly in their debt for advances, and get possession of their grain, which they bury in "*khuttees*," large pits dug in the earth ten or twenty feet deep and lined with straw and chaff. The corn is often seized, reaped, and stored before it is fully dry, and is then not easily brought up from the pits to be turned and aired as often as it ought. Moreover, as these pits are commonly in the open air, though they are dug in the form of a dome, with small mouths like a kiln, which are closed up with earth, there can be no doubt that damp must often get into them.

Provision for wholesome granaries in garrisons.

The grain in military bazaars often inferior.

From such causes as these the wheat in military bazaars, when ground into all its forms of "atta," "mieda," and "soojee,"—coarse and fine flour, and granulated wheat—is frequently of an inferior description. I have known it in military bazaars, musty or sour for weeks together; so much so, that even the high fermentation it undergoes under the influence of the "tarree" in being made into bread will often fail to hide its defects. It is doubtless at times sold in the military bazaars of a quality which the Zumeendars would not themselves employ.

The importance of a control over its storing and selection.

But if the corn for the troops were stored in public warehouses, under the eye of the authorities, it would be easy to see that none was housed in an improper state. If instead of being buried under ground in "khuttees" it were laid on mats raised on a thick bed of straw in such warehouses; and were shut in by thick partitions lined with mats and straw, and outside of these, by well fitted wooden doors, so that it could be easily turned and aired in dry weather, can there be a doubt that the staff of a garrison would be enabled to exercise much more control than at present over the staff of life which fed it? When it is considered upon how delicate a balance life hangs at times, how small a cause will often turn the scale in favour of an epidemic influence from which a body of men might otherwise escape, and especially if, the epidemic being cholera or dysentery, that cause entering in the food acts upon the very organs prominently obnoxious to attack, can there be a question that of all things the wheat consumed should be known and watched from its reaping, if not also its planting, to its housing? Having been drawn into a digression upon food, I am unwilling to omit an impression which may be thought worthy of attention. The assessment paid to collectors of revenue, especially at a distance from the seats of chief consumption, is the product from grain of which a portion is purchased again by the government of the storing bunneahs, doubtless often at double the price it yielded as revenue. Indeed, it is often sold by the Zumeendar to the money-lender under circumstances of extortion, at a depreciation which is ruinous to him. To be ready with his rent for the collector, he has often (doubtless from a prevalent improvidence and parsimony combined) to borrow the means from the "bunneah" at an interest varying from thirty to sixty per cent. per annum, or more, and, besides this, to sell his produce to him in the unequal relative position of the debtor to the creditor, who can, too often, almost make his own terms. But this is not all; to make sure of his advances and usurious gains, the "*bunneah*," in the dread lest some other claimant (perhaps the collector's native agent seeking to recover some outstanding arrears of revenue) may step in and secure the crop before him, will enforce its being reaped before it is fully ripe, and will carry it off and house it in his khuttees before it has been properly dried.

Superior grain procurable direct from the "Zumeendars."

Now, if the collector of revenue of a neighbouring district were authorized to receive part of his assessments in produce required for the troops of a garrison, he could obtain it at a price far below that paid for it in the military bazaar, and would at the

Through the Collectors of Revenue.

same time relieve from a tyrannical oppression many an unfortunate Zumeendar who would rejoice if he could but pay his rent in produce, and be then under no compulsion to hurry it immatured off the ground. The collector would be welcomed with proffers of the choicest wheat in his district, to be selected by the commissariat officer. Whatever other obstacles may exist to such a measure, to argue that it would be an interference with trade, opposed to economical laws, would be one of those absurd objections, in reality meant only as stumbling-blocks, which politicians of a certain stamp are ready to throw in the way of every proposed deviation from accustomed routine.

Advantages of the preceding arrangements in a state of siege.

Under the next head, the "Employment of Troops," the subject of their food may again be touched upon, when recreative and experimental farms and gardens are mentioned; but while here advocating the *locating* of some of the British troops at all European stations, within fortifications to secure the possession of them, and thus to permit as large a proportion of the European forces of the country as possible to be stationed on mountain heights, on the best elevations at command in the different presidencies, it may be well to follow out the advantages of the measures, here suggested, to a state of siege. On the sudden occurrence of any outbreak, a fort being possessed of granaries stocked at all times with the choicest wheat, would only require coolies and women enough to be detained with their "*chuckees*," hand mills, for grinding it; while the greater part of the arched spaces would offer shelter to the garrison—quarters for them to descend into from the exposed barrack above, which would be left to suffer whatever it might from the enemy's projectiles. The inmates of the arches below would suffer nothing, though its thatch, and all else that was combustible, should be burnt, and though its walls should be battered down piecemeal and fall as ruins upon the massive arches at their base. Indeed, they would conduce to their protection by breaking the fall of shot.

Troops quartered in such forts should enjoy sanitary advantages superior to those in most cantonments.

Recollecting the position of some of the European barracks at Cawnpore, buried behind walls, and in the neighbourhood of fœtid ravines and bazaars, and also the interminable succession in all directions of mud walls from eight to twelve feet high, I cannot believe that troops, quartered in the manner described above, would not be much less subject to epidemic cholera and other diseases than those in some barracks at Cawnpore were. Were there at every European station a mere earthwork fortification of such a description as to offer to a garrison as salubrious a residence as the plains admit of, and were it preserved in readiness against a siege, a small proportion of the whole European force of the country might suffice for the temporary protection of the plains. Recent experience would seem to place this beyond a question, even if implicit reliance should not be placed on the railway system, when completed, for the rapid conveyance of troops. The importance of railways to the government and country at large is so great that the expenditure on main lines is justifiably guaranteed by the State,

Railways, their importance.

even though none but those in the vicinity of the Presidencies should pay as commercial undertakings. The expenditure they involve is also, to a considerable extent, of such a character that, if it were incurred by a government which retained a control over the productive industry of a country, in the state of India, would prove in reality an insignificant burden on it, and altogether trifling when compared with the apparent amount. This truth may be established, I believe, on the soundest principles of fiscal and economical science. As it is one of paramount importance towards Indian progression, and is closely connected with the question of transport and locomotion, I have republished in the Appendix* portions of papers in which it is fully discussed.

An entire dependence on them not necessary.

The invincibility by natives of small bodies of British troops under any good cover behind a rampart, and fairly provisioned, does happily relieve the question of stationing the bulk of our countrymen on Hill eminences, of any absolute dependence on railways; for, most valuable as these must prove on all ordinary occasions, the fact has to be kept in view, that when the natives have become familiar with them, it is impossible they should not in time discern how easily communication by them may be cut off. With a few bags of gunpowder sprung under a line in half a dozen or a dozen places, damage might be done in a few hours which it would occupy weeks to repair. Moreover, not only might large obstacles be laid in the way of trains throughout a line, and be replaced as fast as they

Their liability to injury.

* Appendix F.

were cleared away, but an obstacle of a certain description which could scarcely be observed might be employed which would throw over a whole train moving with any considerable speed. Entertaining the highest opinion of railways for main lines, I cannot but think, apart from political considerations, that more encouragement than hitherto should be also afforded to tramways. In a paper on the construction of roads throughout India, published in Calcutta in 1833, and signed "*Philodus*," I took occasion to draw attention to means for producing artificial "metalling" for common roads, materials for them being offered by nature but scantily in most parts of the country. The cheapness of English bar iron in India, which, carried out as ballast, might at all times be obtained in Calcutta or Bombay at its price in London, offers the means for laying tramways which would greatly aid the transport of produce, and would be available for military purposes. If they were broken up by an enemy at certain places, the vehicles on them would be available on the surface of the land, and could be drawn by extra aid round the damaged places on to the trams again; or they might be independent of them altogether. At present, on all the *country* roads, bullocks are the cattle employed; the jolting of the poles of the carts from the irregularity of the surface being such as would destroy horses. But if good tramways abounded, mules and "tattoos" (ponies) would be more largely bred, as well as horses, and could easily be exercised to a pace double that of bullocks.

Certain advantages of tramways.

Conceding then the objections which may be raised against too absolute a reliance on "locomotive" railways, passing through a hostile country, not only are the chances much in favour of the movement of troops being affected before hostile combinations have advanced to the pitch of damaging them, but even by the ordinary means of road travelling succour could not fail to arrive before any such garrisons had to capitulate, or were much straitened.

Ravines near Stations very objectionable, Having mentioned the vicinity of ravines, it is, I believe, considered, in a military point of view, undesirable, since they afford shelter to an enemy. It certainly is in a sanitary. The natives not using privies, and having an aversion to them, always speak of visiting the "*maidan*," the open plain, for a natural purpose. On such a plain they ought by their religion, following the example of some animals, to bury their dejections. But they are glad to avail themselves of ravines which, near a populous bazaar and the rendezvous of both sexes, become the depositories of what more refined communities are at such pains to carry off by sewers.

from the putreseent matter accumulating in them. There can be no doubt that, under the action of the weather, a decomposition of such matters *viâ siccâ*, and modified by earthy action, goes on, of a character by no means so injurious in its products, as that which takes place *viâ humidâ*, and in the confinement of cesspools and sewers. Nevertheless, in calm weather, the body of stagnant air, entangled in the recesses of a large ravine throughout a hot day, becomes charged with the gaseous products of putrefaction in all its stages. As the night advances it is liable to be displaced by a colder and denser air from an adjacent cultivated plain, which has cooled its incumbent atmosphere much more by radiation, or to be pressed upwards by a current of wind setting upon the mouth of the ravine. This stratum of contaminated air, sometimes perceptibly so to the senses, will then be rolled through the open doors of ground-floor buildings to leeward and over the unconscious sleepers they are filled with. In a struggle between the *vis vitæ* and any epidemic poison enjoying the *curriculum* of the station at the time, which side such contaminated air is likely to take can scarcely be a matter of doubt, even with those who are prompt to argue from their own "experience,"—their own merciful exemption,—in favour of tempting Providence by all manner of neglects.

Were vicinity to ravines as desirable for military purposes as might be supposed from the position of many stations, instead of being the contrary, as we are informed, their lodgment of stagnant and often very impure air, ready in store to be purveyed to sleeping breathers around, would be quite enough to demand the rejection of such localities where it was practicable. Where ravines are found near existing stations, and cannot be filled up, a preservation of them in a state of cleanliness should be a point of watchful attention. Any illicit deposits ought to be immediately and scrupulously buried; while "*khuteets*," pig-breeders, ought not to be permitted to drive their filthy swine into them to exhume, partially devour, and leave exposed noxious matter that ought to have remained subjected to the disinfecting

Bazaar pork, its abominable character.

power of earth. Neither should the pork of such swine be vendible to European troops or their families. It is true that, neglected as ravines now are, these creatures surpass jackalls as scavengers, and mitigate the evil in no small degree; but it is to be feared that, as neither Mussulmans nor Hindoos except of the lowest castes will touch pork of any kind, European soldiers are ignorantly amongst the chief customers for this unwholesome and most disgusting food.

On every account then, amongst others to cut oft facilities for intemperance, as few other native residences as possible, besides those of servants, should be permitted near European cantonments or forts. Workmen, labourers, and dealers of all kinds should live at some distance, though they might have shops in an airy station bazaar, in each of which one person only should remain at night.

It is pleasant to pass on from so uninviting a subject; though on this account to neglect it, while convinced of its importance, or to treat it lightly, would be an unpardonable affectation.

Land under a wholesome cultivation desirable round a station.

The character and state of the land round a station is of more importance than is by many supposed. Not only are swamps and low jungles in general unhealthy, as is well known, but barren land becomes in the hot season, arid and intensely hot, materially increasing the heat of places to leeward of it; while in the rains it is commonly covered with pools of water, rank with a transient vegetation which decays on the spot afterwards. Whereas a soil levelled, ploughed, and irrigated moderately from wells, bearing a "rubbee" grain cultivation in the cooler months, which is cropped and carried off the ground when it is ripe, and in the rains not allowed to be planted with a "khurreef" crop of too high and rank a growth (there being no want of plants of a suitable character available and equally profitable), will be found, I believe, so far as my opportunities of judging authorize an opinion, not only the most refreshing to the sight, but also the most salubrious condition for land surrounding a station.

River-side localities, their advantages and defects.

A high bank upon a large river is not an undesirable situation for a station, but much the contrary under certain conditions. Such a river ensures some motion in the atmosphere and certainly tempers its heat; but unfortunately rivers in India are so capricious in their course, and often diverted from their accustomed channel by such trifling causes, that the largest river will not unfrequently desert a bank under which it had flowed through successive generations, and cast up under it an extensive marshy plain, sometimes of mud as well as sand, which may, in that case, give growth to a vegetation causing its vicinity to be very insalubrious. Such an island lay off Patna, and is probably still there, rendering it, doubtless, much less healthy than in earlier times when the whole body of the river flowed by it. An extensive plain of the same kind was also deposited under Futtehgurh, which but a few years before had the main stream of the Ganges always flowing by it. Fortunately that deposit was chiefly sand, and did not therefore form so unwholesome a "teraie" (low marshy ground) as one of mud. Since the sinking of a boat, or of a tree, will in certain positions suffice to produce a set in a portion of the current which by degrees will cause a shifting of sand and formation of a bank, ending in a lateral displacement of the whole river, it is probable that by a watchful attention to the current above a station, at the rise and fall of the river, much might be done to prevent its departure from a desired course, and even to invite it back where it has gone off, if aided by a skilful imitation of such fortuitous causes of disturbance.

The vicinity of Canals objectionable.

Convenient as is a canal passing a station, observations made upon the effect of the Kurnal Canal, while in charge of European troops there, and the known effect of canals in all countries, have long convinced me that they should not in India be brought too near stations at which any Europeans reside. This is, I believe, the opinion of medical officers generally; and I supposed, until lately, it had been of late years generally acted upon by the government. Having been amongst the earliest and most strenuous advocates of canals in India, jointly for irrigation and navigation—for the latter both for the economical transport of produce and merchandise, and to ensure their not being drained low for irrigating purposes, and thereby aggravating their unavoidable unwholesomeness by exposing humid and weedy banks to the sun and air—I would regret to appear indifferent to their importance. They who may have favoured with a perusal papers published by me in different journals, between twenty and thirty years ago, on the improvement of the resources and industry of India, in which the subjects of irrigation and means of

Although they are of great value to the country.

transport were especially discussed, and the results of certain experiments and inquiries detailed, will not imagine that in deprecating the approach of canals, and especially of canal basins, to European stations, I would depreciate their great, nay indispensable advantages. It is, on the contrary, a cause of satisfaction to me to think that in putting before the authorities in India and at home, more especially before Lord William Bentinck, who paid much attention to them, the result of inquiries from time to time, I may have taken some part in paving the way towards the reception of Sir Proby Cautly's plans for the construction of the Dooab and other canals, which have been perfected with an ability and success which must place his name in a high position amongst those whose deeds prove the inestimable advantage to India of her connexion with Britain.

THE PRESERVATION OF THE SOLDIER'S CHILD.

Whether the Government shall decide upon adopting the humane and well-considered recommendation of Mr. Martin, that the great bulk of the European forces in India should henceforth be stationed on the hill eminences most accessible from the subjacent plains to be protected or overawed, or whether the expediency of keeping the troops on the spot shall be viewed as the paramount consideration, the preservation of the children of the soldiery, by rearing them in a congenial climate, is a question which cannot longer remain in its present position. *A question that cannot be longer delayed.*

The opportunity of pleading the claims of these

The rearing of children in a healthy climate an indispensable duty.

hapless children cannot be neglected by one who, from the first hour he had to witness their sufferings and fate, has felt deeply and painfully impressed with the existence of a solemn duty in relation to them, unrecognized and therefore unfulfilled. The children of the soldiery of European blood, if retained in India, ought all of them to be reared on the Himala, Neilgherry, and similar hills affording elevations not under five thousand, and where available of six or seven thousand, feet. The children might be brought down once a year, during the two coldest months, to visit their parents. Should anyone object that such care of their children would entail too heavy an expense on the Government; the proper reply to him would commence with the generous old English maxim, sadly ignored by economists in these days, "live and let live." "Your objection, if valid, would prove India indeed not worth its tenure; a due preservation of the families of those without whom you could not hold it a day forming a claim upon its revenues anterior in moral right to every other." Few children of pure English blood can be reared in the plains of India, and of that few the majority have constitutions which might cause them to envy the lot of those who die in their childhood. The mortality of barrack-children is appalling, especially in the months of June, September, and October. At Cawnpore from twenty to thirty have died in one month. In short the soldiery leave no descendants of unmixed blood. Of the half million of soldiers who have gone out to India, where are all their legitimate descendants of pure English blood, who by this time would have multiplied into a

Ungenerous objections to it answered.

Soldiers' children all swept away by death.

numerous population if born in New Zealand, Canada, or Oregon, reciprocating industrial advantages with the mother country of their parents, how much more secure and durable than the military tenure of India can ever yield? Let myriads of feeble voices from little graves scattered throughout her arid plains supply the melancholy answer—"*here!*"

Other objections answered.

But there are those who will further object—"If we do rear these families into adults, what are we then to do with them?" Were it allowable to rest a reply upon so low a moral ground, it might be argued that the males might all be employed with advantage in the service by enlistment into the army, and admission into subordinate posts in the civil departments of the government; while the females would be provided for as wives to them and to soldiers who have not brought out wives from England." But the more rightful reply is—"If that be your objection, it ought to have been weighed before their parents were invited out to a climate in which the *Creator* manifestly never intended their offspring should be reared; the physical laws He has established, and will not, to destroy human responsibility, enact a miracle to counteract, being *fatally* opposed to it!" "If that be an objection, it ought to have been weighed before we took upon ourselves to hold sway over the country." "If that be an objection, it is more valid in the mouth of the Hindoo, far poorer than the government, who, by the law against infanticide, has been restrained from a summary corrective in his own case, of this trouble of providing for children—a corrective which, though awful to contemplate, is, when

The infanticide of the Hindoo not more indefensible.

viewed in the light of humanity and reason and not of custom, scarcely more indefensible than the *protracted liquidation*, equally certain in the result, of each generation of the infant life in question—than the accumulation of suffering entailed on each victim and on its sorrowing parents (where they have not grown callous in their hopelessness) by the detention of these little ones in the plains of India, *in the face of all experience!!*"* Is there a "commissioned" or "covenanted" parent in India who could tolerate his position if he were compelled to keep his children there to sicken, to decline, and to die before his eyes, excepting here and there one with a tenacity to life or a natural vigour enabling him to be reared into a miserable representative of the parent stock?

The path of duty plain.

The case is clear. All difficulty in the question will vanish directly it is perceived that to question the practicability of doing that which is necessary for preserving the lives of the *European* offspring of soldiers in India is to question the expediency of retaining possession of the country; directly it is perceived that this is in all right and duty amongst the very first charges upon the revenues of India; most assuredly prior to the payment of the second moiety of the

* Since these pages were written for the press, public attention has been drawn, at the recent meeting to do homage to the character of that great and good man, Sir Henry Lawrence, to his humane and munificent effort to provide for rearing the children of European soldiers in the climate of the Hills. Were no other act associated with his memory this alone should immortalize it. Scarcely less grateful was the announcement that the Court of Directors had, in the midst of the present straits, afforded the maintenance of the institution founded by him their attention and support. The pecuniary vote in aid of it is most gratifying; not on account of the amount, for that is trifling, but as an incipient recognition of a duty, the complete fulfilment of which it is impossible should long be delayed.

salaries of the "covenanted" servants of the Government, from the supreme functionary down to all above subalterns at the least; not that a charge amounting to less than one per cent. on the revenue would involve with it any such necessity.

In a word, it were better *for themselves* these hapless children were passed through the fire to MOLOCH, at their birth, than left, as at present, immolated in the furnace of India to MAMMON.*

THE RECREATIVE EMPLOYMENT OF THE SOLDIER.

THE opportunity is not to be neglected of saying something on this important question, which may prove a seed dropped by a chance hand, but in a kindly soil, —a hint acceptable to authorities so desirous of the soldier's welfare as are those severally charged with the care of Her Majesty's forces. For the present, indeed, the contention and fatigues of war are affording them occupation more than enough, and of a kind which every one must lament. But it is to be hoped that all active ebullitions of the natives will be quenched by two years of chilling defeats; and then will recommence the dull routine of barrack imprisonment, objectless and hopeless, with its *ennui*, intemperance and, at times, even despair! If any one would see a picture of the gnome *Ennui* reigning absolute, not even the descriptive power of the poet Spenser will so well supply it, as the scenes within a barrack-compound in India, surrounded or not by

The disheartening character of barrack life in India.

* Appendix G.

a hot and dull mud wall. There is life there truly, for there is respiration, and perspiration enough; but life—a blank! Eyes looking upon nothing—minds caring for little and hoping less—thoughts of home long suppressed!

Regimental libraries, their value but inadequacy;

In its solicitous care the Indian Government has supplied its European troops with reading-rooms, and, I believe, very suitable libraries (and a great boon they are to some). But no small portion of the soldiery are drawn from the *village labourers* of England, who are barely fed up to the working-point, and, working as they do, not to the reading-point also.*

owing to the scanty diet and hard work of the English labourer.

If any one should weigh the English village labourer's bread and cheese for the day (he gets nothing else), and, estimating it as fuel, should set against it his daily work, valued in numbers of pounds raised one foot high per pound of fuel consumed by him, it will, I think, be found that his food, measured only as a driving power to his muscles, beats the work done by the fuel in the best steam-engine altogether. Measured by the price of food in each country, his is perhaps the cheapest human labour in the world—cheaper than most labour in India even. Again, the primary function of the human brain corresponds with the whole duty nearly of the brain of animals—that of giving nervous action to the organs and muscles; and how large a share nervous energy has to do with muscular action may be seen by comparing together the slender muscle of the

The brain occupied primarily in maintaining the animal functions.

* If my reader should demur to the following views on account of their apparent peculiarity, he is invited to bring them to the test of physiology and experience.

blood-horse, with its amazing strength, and the bulky muscle of the cart-horse, so far inferior in comparison.

And mainly so occupied in the ill-fed labourer of England.

Now the food of the English labourer is so scanty for the work done, that, after the waste and wear of his muscles and the rest of his system have been replaced, together with his animal heat, the portion available for generating nervous energy or matter (which you will), or both, is well nigh used up in maintaining the animal function of driving his muscles. The poor labourer has *inherited* a brain *for some generations* fed barely enough to support one class of functions only, either the intellectual or the animal, while it has been trained entirely into the latter; it has therefore naturally acquired by degrees more of a caballine nature. A great deal of diet has to be broken up by the digestive organs to supply the vital electricity * of the brain. With a *limited supply* of food, or a *limited digestive power*, you may have an Anglo-Saxon hedger and ditcher with a dull intellect, or you may have a *feeble-bodied* philosopher with a powerful one. You may, by training either an animal or an intellectual organization of brain through successive generations, or by searching out a brain spontaneously organized either one way or the other, command either much muscular or much intellectual action, supported on a *restricted* amount of food or of digestive power. But you cannot take it out both ways. Where you have exercised, for any length of time, both large muscular and large intel-

Intellectual and muscular power when combined require proportional diet.

* Accept the term hypothetically or supply a better.

lectual power in the same person, you must have a proportional diet well digested.

An undergraduate reading for honours must, even though sedentary, be a fair eater, or he will ere long be used up and grow consumptive. Many a strong stomach has won for its possessor high honours, and a weak one lost them. If a man pursues hard reading and athletic exercises at the same time, he must eat as much as two ordinary men, or endanger the giving way of his body or his brain, or of both.

The *ill-fed* Celt, so long as he is too lazy even to enclose his cabbage-garden and improve his cabin, is wondrously sharp in his intellect.

Muscular indolence frequent with intellectual sharpness.

Place in a school together a certain number of such *Celtic* boys, an equal number of still lazier *Bengallees*, and of our village youth of England, with their hereditary muscle-driving brains, and you may predict for a certainty that the Bengallees will be at the top, the Celts next, and the laborious Angles at the bottom. Tempt the Celt to change his occasional outbursts of exertion into the unremitted daily toil of the navigator or hodman, and within a generation or two the shine will be taken out of his intellect, especially if it is not polished up with plenty of strong food.

Cause of the dullness of English village boys.

Hence the general dullness of their village boys, especially of the strong ones, which perplexes and sorely tries the worthy country clergymen and schoolmasters of England. If they could persuade the landlords and the farmers, between them, to spare the labourer such a reasonable share of the fruits of the earth as to feed the intellectual as well as the animal functions of his brain, he would in a few generations be unsurpassed amongst races in vigour both of body and of mind. At present he and his children have not diet enough to support the *animal* functions alone in any degree of vigour. Since his vocation—labour—appropriates for their sustentation his scanty diet, his intellect is well nigh starved.

A hereditary organization not readily changed.

Enlisted as a soldier, there are, during times of peace, both an end of the labourer's toil, and an improvement in his diet in India; but a hereditary organization cannot be changed in a day. So given to muscular action had he been by nature, that at the end of a long day of toil, as a labourer in England, you might have seen him of an evening, *by way of relaxation*—lying at his length and reading a book? No, but playing at bowls, skittles, or even cricket! When you shut him up in a barrack in India and give him books, treat him however kindly you may, he chafes from inaction. He would be happy to learn to make the paper of your books, to print them, press them, bind them, pack them, carry them, and *do anything* but read them. Exceptions of course there are; men whose brains would not generate toil-energy alone, but were apter for intellectual. Some of these have sought the greater leisure of military life. Invite in more of such minds by promising them full play, and your ranks will be greatly improved, and will supply you with mighty commanders, if you will love war.

But it is not the mere labourers only to whom mus-

Manual as well as mental occupations desirable for the soldier.

cular action is as their second nature. Artizans, for the most part, love such exercises of the intellect as have their expression in manual ones. Such being the case, would it not prove greatly conducive to the happiness, contentment, orderly conduct, sobriety, and health of the soldiery, to offer them manual occupations of all such kinds in the hotter months as could be pursued under shelter, and did not require the use of fuel, and in the cold season invigorating occupations out of doors, together with such as had to be conducted with open fires or with furnace heat?

Workshops proposed.

Supposing the barracks to be built in the manner already suggested, and the ground-floors not used for government stores, they might then be employed as workshops for the men, and their verandahs as tennis-courts and bathing-rooms; but the latter opened only for bathing at stated times. Most workshops it would however be preferable to place on a raised floor in all parts of India where malaria prevails, especially in all East of Chunar.

The profit from them to be laid by for the soldier.

From the value of the articles the soldier produced, the Government might deduct the cost of the materials and tools, and give him credit for the balance, which might be *laid by* for him as an addition to his future pension. Few *English* soldiers would sit idle with such opportunities for action before them. But, even if the materials had to be charged at less than their cost, or at a nominal price, in order to produce a balance encouraging habits of occupation, contentment, and sobriety, what would it matter? India may well be charged a trumpery burden of a few lacs a year to render life in her sweltering lap tolerable to the brave fellows whose presence is her only safeguard from intestine commotions and from being racked by an ill-bred progeny, gnawing out the vitals of their mother country!

But if the occupations were beneficial to the soldiery themselves they might be rendered no less so to the country, provided some such measures were adopted as those laid by me before the Governor-General in 1833 and 1834.

Measures for rendering such occupations beneficial also to the country, proposed in 1833 and 1834.

I had had opportunities of noting that a considerable proportion of the soldiery had, through apprenticeship, a practical acquaintance with the ordinary chemical, mechanical, and rural arts of England—information which, if it could be imparted to the natives, could scarcely fail, by improving their processes, to increase employment and wealth, and thus to relieve the *land* of multitudes teeming upon it unproductively, and thereby leave a wider rent-margin for the state.* It was evident that for one soldier who would sit all day in a regimental library there were five who would rejoice in the instinctive union of hand with head work, in amusing themselves with processes which reminded them of home, and in the honest pride of imparting

* In the autumn of 1835 a series of papers by the author was published in the Asiatic Journal for that year. It is believed that a perusal of them would not be without interest to the reader who is desirous of studying the resources of industry in India, and of penetrating somewhat more deeply into the land revenue question than the many (even amongst the friends of the Government) who imagine that one-third or even one-half of the produce is absorbed as rent. That 10 or 15 per cent. is the outside that is, or can be, taken throughout the Bengal presidency, is in those papers proved, it is believed, incontestably.

instruction to others. I had twice obtained soldiers on leave of absence for experiments, and shall never forget the enjoyment they manifested at a return to familiar thoughts and actions. After having devoted attention to the native arts with a view to their improvement, I became convinced that excellent results would flow from blending European and native processes in the arts, and from sending forth thousands of lads of those *low*-castes (by far the most hopeful portion of the population) well instructed, and deeply indebted to the " *Ferringhee.*"

The following is a copy of one of the papers submitted to the Governor-General in Calcutta upon this subject. The proposal has reference to such mechanical and chemical arts as could be conducted on the small scale suited to native resources, and by the aid of soldiers and Chinamen of certain trades who would bring European and some Chinese experence to bear upon them under the guidance of men of science.

Paper on Schools of Useful Arts, presented to Government in 1834.

A Proposal for the Establishment of Schools of the Useful Arts at all the larger Stations of the Army; as a recreative employment for the British Soldiery, and for the training and instruction of Native Youths in the path of industrial progress.

Fort William, Calcutta, March 8th, 1834.

It is said, and the estimate I fear is a low one, that the mortality of our European Corps *during peace* amounts in ten years to the whole strength of the regiment upon its landing in India, and that amongst men in the prime of life. So that if the corps landed 1000 strong, 1000 men will die or be constitutionally destroyed in ten years. At 100*l.* per man, the lowest assumed rate, this amounts to one lack of rupees, in each corps per annum. In two months at Cawnpore a corps has I believe lost 100 men.*

* 100 by death, in two months, out of about 600, in the quiet times of peace! Not a usual occurrence, of course.

The mortality amongst the European soldiery has hitherto been the most grievous contingency upon the tenure of India, and it is too well known that it is greatly aggravated by drunkenness, which, although our nation's vice, would not prevail to so serious an extent were the active spirits and energy of Englishmen afforded a field for their exercise. It is a life of absolute idleness, worse to a spirited Englishman than the prospect of death, which makes any extremity often preferred by a soldier to a continuance in his present state. They who have the most mind and spirit, who are the farthest removed from Eastern apathy, can least endure that dormant state which is one of bliss to the native.

In its desire to meliorate their condition, the government has given libraries to most corps, and built reading rooms, finished in an inviting manner. All the good perhaps has resulted from this measure which could in reason be expected from it. But it has always appeared to me that far more would have resulted from employments more suited to the habits and condition in life of the men—so as to put the limbs in motion as well as the mind. At Cawnpore in 1825, I hoped to have persuaded the General Officer commanding there to propose the trial of a regimental workshop for the amusement of the soldiers; all the money realized by the sale of the products of their labour being laid up for the supply of reasonable wants for them and for their families.

I would now propose the following plan. In order to commence with every advantage, let the one of the European corps at Meerut, Agra, or Cawnpore, be selected which, upon inquiry, should be found to contain the largest number of artizans—so recently from England as to retain their dexterity in their respective arts. A common "kutcher" but spacious building, with a double tiled roof, should be erected sufficiently near to the barracks. The building should afford a large empty space divided into portions, one for each trade, and each man should have his own space.

As ingenuity and originality do not prevail more among artizans than amongst other men, most of them would be puzzled how to apply the means of the country to their arts, and how to reduce the processes they have practised on a large, to the small scale, upon which they ought to work. They would therefore require the guidance of science and original resources; and since the Chinese, though altogether far behind the artizans of England, are habituated to a style and scale of work which would suit well the natives of India, the aid of their experience would be very desirable. Expert Chinamen, one for each art, ought to be procured, selected from amongst a number on account of their intelligence.

The arts which would soon spring up from the combination of such means, ought to form a school admirably calculated for working a considerable change in the native arts of industry. Each European should have from 6 to 12 boys to assist him as apprentices, of the castes corresponding with their respective trades. The uneducated native is of so childish and suspicious a disposition, that some *finesse* would be required at the commencement to induce parents to view the employment for their children in the light of a favour. At the same time it might be well to allow the smaller boys two pice a day, and the larger ones three, for their support, to be paid out of the proceeds of their labour. Of the money realized by the sales of the manufactures, after deducting the price of the materials, the net proceeds should be lodged in a savings' bank. Two thirds might be placed at the credit of the soldier, and the other third should also accumulate as stock from which to supply the youths whose period of apprenticeship was completed, with tools, and means for commencing at their homes the new arts they had learnt. It might be well to make it a matter of some little trouble to get a child into the establishment, by requiring that evidence should be given of the parents' good character, &c. &c. And, for effect, he might hold an admission ticket bearing some imposing device and inscription, to give it a character of importance. Upon the first school promising to answer, one at least should be established at all stations where there are European corps. Thus, in time, into every province would be introduced new arts, and improvements in existing ones, conducted in a manner eminently calculated for developing the resources and increasing the wealth of India.

Let me particularly remark upon the great advantage of placing boys under an active European. The natives have not many opportunities of witnessing activity, or of learning what may be effected by steady exertion, and the ease with which it is acquired by habit. There can be little doubt that the soldiers would take much interest in the workshops, and it is a fact that they and the natives, after an intimacy is formed, agree remarkably well with each other. It would not be too much to hope, that amongst the soldiers who thus acquired steady habits from the time of their landing in India, the mortality might be greatly reduced; perhaps by one half. Should any saving of life approaching to this be effected—waiving the much higher consideration of humanity, there can be little doubt that the money saved by lives preserved, would go far to pay the cost of the establishment. A few lives saved per annum in a regiment might repay all the balance of expenses over proceeds of a large polytechnic school established in this manner. If in time a great work were not done in India by these means, under scientific guidance well applied, I would despair of any important change being effected by any other that could be proposed, except indeed by a certain system of economical policy on an extended scale, which might work a change in India so vast and so rapid that at present it would appear to most persons folly even to imagine it.

JULIUS JEFFREYS.

The art of turning: its important advantages to the soldier

Without entering into any detail of the various mechanical, and of certain chemical arts which might with advantage be practised as an interesting occupation for the soldiers, there is one art in particular, which is of such general application, and affords such healthy and entertaining exercise, that to omit to specify it would seem an oversight. That art is turning. It is an art which any man may learn, and at which by practice many would acquire a dexterity which would render it fascinating to them. It has the great advantage of giving exercise of a moderate kind to the whole body without progression, and therefore of requiring but little space. The useful products of even the simple lathe of one movement, are various; and when other "movements" are added, and the tools handled with any skill, the lathe becomes the universal agent and type of mechanical progress in a country.

and the public service.

The soldiery, imprisoned by the sun, would soon learn tō produce, and rejoice to produce, almost everything, not weighty, required for the public service. Though its apparent cost, on their being paid liberally for the work, should be double the trade prices of England, the virtual cost would be nothing, or rather a negative charge through the mere saving of human waste, resulting from their improved health and habits. Railways could give employment to an army of turners, the nicest and most expensive part of the "rolling stock" being the product of the lathe. For all heavy turning, the revolution might be given by prisoners (always abounding) at treadmills; or by coolies, or through shafts from steam-engines placed at a sufficient distance to prevent any communication of heat from them.

Also to railways;

and especially to the natives.

To native art, the sending forth of lads—the soldiers' native apprentices,—trained in the use of the lathe would be invaluable. All native turning is performed in the rudest manner by a cord wound round the suspended matter to be turned, and pulled backwards and forwards, giving it a reciprocating motion like a drill. Half the time, therefore, it is rotating backwards, during which the tool is not acting on it; while there is a constantly repeated loss of power in stopping and restoring its momentum. When a heavy mass has to be turned, even of the working stroke one half of the run is lost before it has sufficient momentum to admit of the tool being applied to it with any effect. Hence the *turning* of the "*girrees*," large pulleys, used at the wells for irrigation, is a serious matter, and is seldom done with any accuracy. These pulleys continue to be used as long as they will hang upon the spindle, be-

Native turning very defective.

coming often at last a ring of wood, with a bore worn to three or four inches, grating round a fixed spindle of three-fourths of an inch! The power wasted through imperfect well-pulleys, throughout Hindostan, would probably be much under-estimated at a cost of 100,000*l.* a-year. As to native iron turning, the Englishman who would discipline his mind to patient endurance could not do better than put himself in a position to witness, pay, and wait for the process and its product.

The government works in India have diffused skill amongst the workmen in their vicinity; but apprentice lads sent forth annually from every station, who had never fallen into the rude and indolent practices of the country, and who carried out with them lathes of their own making, and other tools, would establish an improved system throughout the country with a hundred-fold greater rapidity.

Serviceable lathes can be obtained by contract at so moderate a price, that if they were supplied from England, the cost of providing every willing soldier with one ought to prove no obstacle whatever. But through the aid of a few skilled turners at a station, each good lathe could soon be made to generate a dozen like itself; so that eventually all the lathes used by the soldiers and their apprentices might be made on the spot; the mere castings being sent from England.

The punching press next in importance.

Next to the lathe, the fly* press is an instrument most needed in India. Riveted spheroidal boilers of various sizes are employed in numbers to be estimated in all India by myriads, or even

Native boilers worthless through bad punching.

millions. The punching and riveting of the scales of which they are formed, leave to native iron turning even, the palm of comparative excellence. The waste of the liquor in sugar, salt, and salt-petre making, and the delays attending the removal of the "*keraees*," boilers, for a repeated plugging of the irregular holes with a cement of almond, sugar, flour, and clay, which is soon burnt out again, forms a serious part of the cost of these manufactures * as conducted by the natives.

Since a perfectly serviceable fly press may be made with a framing of wood,† only a little nice metal turning and drilling—all lathe work—would be needed for introducing into India generally, the instrument, second in importance to the progress of mechanical art.

Experimental farms; their value and interest

Other proposals submitted to the Government about the same time related to the establishment of experimental farms near to large stations. These might likewise with great advantage be, partly at least, conducted by the soldiers. The chief crops are the "*Rubbee*." The tillage commences in October, and the crops are reaped in March. During several hours of a morning and evening the soldiers could occupy themselves with benefit to their health upon the farms. The "*Khureef*," or crops of the rainy season, which are of an inferior description, would be raised by natives chiefly, though the soldiers not on duty might at suitable times superintend even them.

The question of raising cotton in the best manner,

* Appendix II. † Ibid.

and other commercial produce, would soon be decided on such farms. At present, owing to the heavy expenses of irrigation in the finest cotton districts, those of Bundelkund, cotton is not in general planted at the season for the best crops, October, but in the commencement of the rains. It is not a "Rubbee" but a "Khureef" crop I believe in most places. This alone would account for its inferiority.* In the papers at the conclusion of this work will be found information connected with irrigation collected with no little pains, and showing the extent to which irrigation by wells is practised, and the defectiveness of the means employed, as established by my own experiments.† When the water is raised but a small height and from open reservoirs, it is commonly tossed up in baskets by men. From the circumstances of the case, the labour in this operation is employed with better effect. But throughout the greater part of Hindostan wells supply the water, and generally from a greater depth than twenty feet. Experimental farms for the recreative employment of European soldiers should all lie in such positions. Wells cannot be a source of malaria, but tanks, jheels, and canals are inevitably injurious in this respect, though of great, and in many localities indispensable, value to native tillage.

for deciding the question of cotton cultivation.

That the method of raising water from wells ad-

* The late Dr. Royle, in his able researches into the cultivation of cotton, remarks upon the too hurried growth and maturation of the plant in India. In papers published in India and in others on irrigation addressed to the Government of Calcutta twenty-four years ago, I mentioned this fact as referable to the cultivation of cotton too commonly in the rainy season, instead of in the cold and preferable season, on account of the expense of the irrigation needful during the latter.

† Appendix F.

Irrigation by wells: machines for improving it.

mits of great improvement, and would in time receive it on farms under scientific guidance, there can be little doubt. Did the space and character of this work invite it, it might be desirable, with a view to promote these objects, to detail the experiments which were made, and to give plans of certain economical hydraulic instruments, the contriving of which they prompted. Two of these were tried on a large scale, and one in a model. They were adapted to the means of the natives, and had for their design, to be as cheap in construction, and as economical of labour, as possible. How far they would fulfil these conditions it is for others to say. Having no manner of pecuniary or other personal interest in the introduction of them, it was not to be expected that I could incur expense upon them. On news of the occurrence of a grievous famine in Western India reaching this country, I brought the subject again before the Court of Directors, but their established system and policy did not admit of even a trifling demonstrative outlay upon one.

Windmills of a simple construction.

As a "power" to work either of these apparatus, a windmill of a very simple construction, and without cogged wheels, though of the vertical kind, was also contrived. It answered thoroughly, and could in India be made of a large size for about 20*l.* and by the natives eventually for less; but even that sum a Zumeendar would not at present be willing to lay out upon the most effective apparatus. It may be a question also whether during the season of the "*Rubbee*" growth, there is a sufficiency of wind. From a table kept from October to March, 1833, at

Wind uncertain in force in the cold season.

Futtehgurh, there appeared to be in each month a sufficient number of days of strong wind, of velocities ranging from 10 to 20 or more miles an hour; though on the majority of days the wind was light, and not a few were quite calm. But whether wind were employed or not, as a power, assuredly the endeavour should be made that the *hydraulic* apparatus in use should itself combine efficiency and economy in the utmost degree.

No real ploughing in India.

Ploughing in India is in a worse state still than irrigation.* Persons who extol the simplicity of the process must either be superficial observers or indifferent mechanicians. It is true their opinions have appeared to receive confirmation from the imperfect success which has attended the attempt to introduce the heavy English plough; but that is nothing to the point. Doubtless, in the hardened soil, and with the feeble cattle of India, the massive English plough might not answer. But that is not a reason why a plough should not be employed and the land therefore not be ploughed. The native instrument is not a plough. A plough consists mainly of a wrest, sock, coulter, mould-board, and share. The native article lacks the two last altogether, and in general the coulter. The sock also is often merely pointed wood instead of iron. Hence the breaking up of the surface of the land which it is a misnomer to dignify by the name of "ploughing," has to be repeated many times, often from *ten to twenty*, and, after all, the husbandman has not unfrequently to cover his field with women and children to break

Character of a true plough.

* Appendix F.

to pieces with clubs of wood the hardened clods which his so-called plough set loose without crushing.

Ploughs to be made and used demonstratively by the soldiers.

In the cold season, the smiths amongst the soldiers having made ploughs fitted especially for the light ploughing suited for India, but complete with their coulter, share, and mould-board, with how jocund exultation would the ploughmen amongst the soldiers exhibit upon the neighbouring fields an art which would indeed astonish the native, who has no conception of what a proper furrow is, with the soil pierced by the sock, slit by the coulter, underrent by the share, and inverted and shivered by the mould-board, ready to be pulverized by a little harrowing! Any objection to a proper ploughing of the land, taken from the fact that the seed has to be sowed more shallow in India, is without foundation. It is not in the plough furrow that the seed is sown, but in the harrow furrow, which may be as shallow as the cultivator pleases. The fact is, the natives are well aware that a deeper ploughing than theirs would be especially desirable, not only as giving them a larger command of fresh soil, but also as forming a deeper sponge to hold the water of irrigation, so much of which now evaporates to waste at the surface.

That the bulk of the soldiers who were not reading men, and probably most of these also, would rejoice in such occupations as a recreation, especially all who had not acquired habits of indolence and hopeless dissipation, might, I think, be confidently anticipated.

Remarkable match of one English against ten native sawyers.

I once at Agra tried an English artilleryman, who had been a sawyer, with a good-sized hand-saw, against *ten* native carpenters together, with their poor implements and squatting attitude. Though he was out of practice, and not in English health, and they in daily practice, he beat the ten hollow by the evening; having done more work than the whole of them together, and won the prize for which they had unitedly and keenly contended with him. The poor fellow spoke of the occupation as the greatest treat, and exhorted me to get him leave to come again.

It was this incident which led me to inquire into the previous callings of the soldiery, and into contemplating amusing employments for their abundant leisure. Having on two subsequent occasions obtained soldiers on leave for several days at Cawnpore and Futtehgurh, after I had become acquainted with the state of many of the native arts, it struck me forcibly that employments interesting to the soldiers might, at the same time, be made to render incalculable benefit to native industry.

Racket-courts, their defects in India.

In addition to such industrial occupations, recreative games, which do not call for violent exertion, might be offered in greater variety than at present to the men. Rackets are not perhaps well suited for men who have been several years in the country, and have lost the elasticity of youth; and the racket-courts built for them at the different stations, though spacious and substantial, are scarcely the places for Europeans to be found in, even of an evening, during any of the warmer months. Even when built with their backs to the south they are not protected from a sun which travels in an arc nearly through the zenith. The floor and the side-walls are in succession, during the day, subjected to the whole of its power, and become magazines of heat to be radiated forth upon the persons of those who, when the sun is declining, commence their game heedless of the excessive heat of the massive oven they are in. Exercise in it brings forth at once a copious perspiration, which the quick movements subject to the evaporative power of the air, and then no doubt all sense of heat vanishes; but such profuse exhalation is very exhausting. It is trying to the constitutions even of the young, who, "feeling all the better for it," are not very ready to believe that it tends to use them up prematurely. Surely all such courts requiring massive walls should be placed under shelter, as has been proposed in the preceding pages. Surely the heat of the earth's surface in India during seven or eight months of the year is quite enough for European endurance without catching a double supply of it, by means of lofty walls acting as sun-traps, to be projected upon the body, right and left, after the sun itself is got rid of!

Golf and billiards suitable games.

The Scotch game of golf is, for an out-door exercise, better suited for evenings during three-fourths of the year in India than the more athletic exercise of cricket. Within-doors, billiards and similar games, but under strict conditions against gambling, might be more encouraged. When I was in India I never heard of billiard-tables being supplied to European regiments. A few to each regiment would offer the men an interesting recreation during the tedious hours of midday confinement.

That the measures recommended in the preceding

pages would not, all of them together, eradicate drunkenness entirely may be true. Before that desirable end could be consummated the men must bring with them better notions, and habits, from England. Our whole nation has yet to learn the unquestionable physiological truth, that if any alcoholic drinks are taken habitually, it should most assuredly never be done upon an empty stomach. The temporary stimulation, if very moderate and turned to account *at the moment* to digest solid food entering the stomach at the same time, may produce no injury in the generality of constitutions; nay, in some cases of weak, or absent, nervous power, the stimulation may invite a digestive action which shall lead to the production of more nervous matter or power than was wasted by stimulating the nerves—so that there may be a balance in favour of the moderate stimulant. Such cases are to be found amongst sedentary and intellectual labourers, and amongst persons weakened below their natural average by temporary illness; but never perhaps amongst bodily labourers in the open air, who will perform their labour for the greatest number of years and with the greatest ease in proportion as they disuse fermented liquors, and especially distilled forms of alcohol. Innocent, however, as a pint of beer may be, *taken with a full meal*, it is never perfectly innocent taken upon an empty stomach, more particularly when taken to support labour.

Intemperance mitigated, but not to be eradicated by these provisions.

Stimulants: the only right use of them.

Give to the great Spirit of Evil the possession of this delusion over the mind of a nation, namely—that men must have "something to drink" (that something meaning an alcoholic fluid) from time to time,

Error and injurious results of English opinions on the subject.

taken on an empty stomach, to support labour, and he will bind the labouring portion of that population either in the fetters of drunkenness, or in a constant, and in many cases agonizing struggle against it. Labour soon induces some little languor and thirst. A draught of water will relieve the latter, but a draught of "good beer" will relieve both. After the beer, however, the langour and thirst return all the sooner from its use,—the former from the waste of nervous energy by the stimulation, unrestored by any attendant and large process of digestion, and the latter, the thirst, from the slight febrile action which always accompanies stimulation of an empty stomach. The desire for more beer increases with every hour of labour and every repetition of the draught, and by the daily evening becomes, in the case of many men, urgent—by the Saturday evening irresistibly great. Then comes in the aid of the absurd convivialities of toasts and healths, as an excuse for satisfying a craving which is the necessary physical consequence of the delusion of taking "something to drink" on a more or less empty stomach day by day to support labour. "*Adh' seer attah*," "a lb. of meal" to eat, is the sensible request of the Hindoo Cooly in return for a job done, and that in a thirsty land. "Something to drink" is the infatuated request of the English labourer, and gift of the English gentleman, and that in our cold moist climate, when the recipient is often neither exhausted nor perspiring, and would be the worse for it if he were! *

* The severest labour I ever witnessed is that performed by the human beasts of burden, who carry ore from the iron mines in the Poondur district

So long as this notion and practice continue, many of our soldiers will go out to India ready to take in liquor as instinctively as aquatic animals. When remonstrated with, they will, as I have often heard them, plead the *drought and heat* of the climate as their excuse, just as in England men plead the need of "keeping out the *damp and cold!*" while in our colonies, with intermediate climates, men drink as much as or worse than in England. Could any one undertake to deliver our nation from the two delusions *of associating drink with labour, and of taking liquors on an empty stomach* (or with the illusive meal of a crust or a biscuit), and, it must be added, of the Saxonism of drinking toasts and healths (substituting, if they must be retained, the more reasonable eating of them)—could any one effect all this, or even the former, leaving the toasts, the benefit conferred on our dear country would be cheaply purchased at more than one India* given as a return for it! It would reduce by one half the outlay on strong drink in Britain; that, worse than wasted, half† exceeding in amount by some millions the total revenue of India, exceeding five years of British interests in it, and being the instrumental cause, directly and indirectly, of much more than one half of the lamentable and costly amount of crime which disgraces our

of the Himalayas—labour that no whiskey-drinking Highlander could, within many degrees, perform. The "something to drink" of the former is obtained from the rills on the mountain sides. Alcohol, in fermented or distilled forms, most of them scarcely know the taste of.

* Appendix N.

† The consumption of alcoholic liquors in Britain is nowhere I believe estimated under a cost of 50,000,000*l.* annually, and it is said to cause a loss of time and health costing nearly as much more; besides the greater part of the charges attendant on crime and its punishment!

country!—a truth which could be reduced to a demonstration were this the place for doing so!

ON THE HOPEFUL ENCOURAGEMENT OF BRITISH SOLDIERS SERVING IN INDIA.

It is not without grave consideration this subject is approached. It is the character of the ground which must be trodden in treating it with any measure of faithfulness which has alone prevented an urging of the following appeal many years ago.

The position and remuneration of the British soldier in India a serious question.

So long as the British force in India was kept at the lowest scale which appeared safe, and was not often in the field, and was reinforced gradually both by recruiting on the part of the Company as far as they were able to induce men to accept of their service, and by only one or two of her Majesty's regiments going out at a time to take their turn of service there; and also so long as communication with England was comparatively tardy and expensive, it was possible that the existing system should continue for some years to come, without precipitating that inquiry which is alone necessary to convince every high-minded statesman and every wary politician of its very questionable character. But when the bulk of the British army has now been thrown into India, when education is making progress at home (though too slowly) amongst the poor, when the press of the people is having its attention drawn to the heroic deeds and sufferings of the soldier of all ranks; and when the electric telegraph* has brought the recesses of the country into contact with the Presidencies, and promises, before long, to bring these as to news into juxta-position with London, it is as morally impossible that the position of the soldier should long remain what it is as it would be morally indefensible.

The claims of the common soldier the subject; but the officer's position also anomalous.

While it is the claims of the whole European soldiery *of the ranks, serving in India*, both those of her Majesty's service and those of the East India Company's, which are here advocated; while it is not proposed to take any such liberty as to discuss the claims of men of equal and superior rank and influence to the author; it is nevertheless difficult to deal with the case of the former without a remark upon the anomalous position of the latter. If the force of custom and of established order is of inestimable value in giving permanency to that which is right, it is scarcely less powerful in maintaining that which is often absurdly wrong. India is a dependency of the Crown in trust for the benefit of the people of England and of the natives of that continent. The Crown feels itself bound to administer the reciprocated benefits impartially, but to such a length has it carried this conscientious desire that it has dealt hardly with the less influential of its own immediate servants. Not satisfied with a

* It is not possible, when naming the Indian telegraph, for one who well knows the vigilance and perseverance requisite for carrying ont novel undertakings in the climate and with the natives of India, not to pay a tribute of admiration to the extraordinary rapidity and success, and scientific ingenuity with which Sir William O'Shaughnessy has laid all India under ties of obligation to him, more lasting even than the ferreous bands which are of them at once the instrument and type.

most proper and constitutional forbearance from converting the Indian services into a magazine of imperial patronage, it has actually, while its own servants have been *ordered out*,—while their presence in India has been required for the security of the country, allowed them to remain in the following anomalous position.

An officer *ordered* out from the Horse Guards may have, and many a one has, remained twenty-two years in India in the onerous charge of European troops, and having thus spent the best of his strength in the protection of the country and its government, he is permitted to leave it without even the thankful and rightful acknowledgment of his services in the form of an adequate pension out of its revenues, or even any pension from them whatever. Yet he meets there another officer in charge of native troops, who at the end of a similar term retires with a reasonable and handsome pension.

A long expatriation in the service of India, in which every year may generally be reckoned as two in an officer's constitution, in the one case terminates unrequited, in the other fairly remunerated. Yet the services of the former, to say the least, have not been a whit inferior to those of the latter. Whence is this? simply through the accident of the one having started from the Horse-Guards and the other from the India House! From the commencement of sublunary rule men have been familiar with that wilfulness of patronage which ofttimes gives lucrative employment to inferior men; but who ever heard of men of equal rank and merit, of similar occupations, of like duration of service, and both serving in the same field, finding themselves at the end of their career in opposite positions as to requital?

Military claims on India.

Grand estimates are made of the value of India, which some describe as the richest jewel in the Crown of England. Let us accept the figure. Few have endeavoured more than the writer, by practical efforts and ratiocination, to prosecute the inquiry with such care as to arrive at some definite conclusions as to the resources of India and the means for drawing them forth. Her resources no doubt are great, and it is high time that efforts should be made for the development of them. But however men may differ as to the means by which this may best be effected, upon two points all must be agreed: firstly, that internal peace and security are the basis on which alone can be rested any attempts towards it; and secondly, that that peace and security must have for their main foundation the presence of a large body of British troops. If then the resources of India are indeed great; if she has any right to the high pretensions accorded to her of being of first value to this great empire; let her, before assuming so much, at least pay what is due to her protectors, and let her recognize the fact that in all equity *theirs* stand as the first claim upon her resources. Let her hereafter requite, as far as money will do it, brave survivors of all ranks who, having spent their best years in serving her, would fain return to their homes to rest from toil, upon the pensions she has always owed but never paid them! To the presence and merits of the British soldier she owes her pre-

The native owes to the British soldier personal safety and opportunity of wealth.

servation from anarchy and ruin. To them also does every sleek effeminate baboo owe his personal safety and to him blissful opportunities of gathering riches year by year; while his brave protectors are accumulating,—not wealth, but disease!—are not adding to their substance, not fattening like him in purse and in person,* but wasting away; many of them leaking out their very blood; when not from wounds in the field, from their bowels in dysentery! It would be no heavy charge on the baboos of the Presidencies had they alone to provide all that is yet required to render service in India acceptable to the British soldier. Every such requital put together would not increase the military charges to an extent amounting to five, probably not to two, per cent. on the present revenue of India. The politician who has given the question that deliberate investigation which has been attempted in the preceding and following pages, and who is yet of opinion that the revenues of India cannot be made chargeable with these the first claims upon them, does virtually place himself, most assuredly, amongst those who pronounce the possession of India to be no blessing, but a curse to the people of England at large. But the right, though loyally unclaimed, is in its very nature absolute, and India is bound in honesty and gratitude to acknowledge it.

It is not however the cause of the well-informed, the exalted, and the free, that a private individual can venture to advocate. If a reference has been made

* A baboo's growth in wealth is generally indicated by an increasing rotundity of person.

to the position of the commissioned officer it is because, having some points of similarity with the soldier's, were all reference to it abstained from, the indubitable claims of the former might be instanced in a high tone, but by no means fairly, as a reason for ignoring the claims of the latter.

Responsibility of the nation.

Our subject then is that *hopeful encouragement* of the British soldier, serving in the ranks in India, which will, with the measures proposed under the preceding heads, ensure such an improvement in his moral habits, his health, his contentment, and worldly happiness, at the least, as will prove an inestimable blessing to himself and his friends; and remove a reproach from the nation which gave him birth, and which is answerable to his MAKER, and in the sight of humanity, for the influence of its treatment upon him.

The introduction of Africans early recommended as a highly politic measure.

Before entering upon this subject the question presents itself at the outset—What is to be the numerical strength of the British force maintained in India? Some Indian statesmen have spoken of eighty or a hundred thousand! To any one who has made himself acquainted with the real condition of the soldier in India, especially his mental, it must afford no small satisfaction to observe that a more moderate force of European troops is now spoken of as that necessary to be maintained in the country. Everything connected with that force has ever appeared to me the saddest subject, but one,* connected with the tenure of India; and has led me to contemplate a large introduction of Africans for a tropical soldiery as on

* Appendix I.

this, and other accounts, a most desirable measure. So fixed was this impression, that on the arrival of the first notice of the outbreak, I could not refrain from expressing it in a letter to the Court of Directors.

It was gratifying to observe that shortly afterwards, the introduction of Africans was advocated in the columns of the 'Times' by an able military correspondent, who appears to have also well considered the question, and with a professional ability to which I could not pretend. To avoid a lavish expenditure of British life, aggravated by moral degradation of the victims, and to impress the natives with the fact that it is vain for them to rest their hopes on the sickliness of Europeans, by showing them that England had abundant *ethnic* resources elsewhere, and superior to those of Hindoostan, were the objects which in my own case had prompted the thought.*

Broad distinction between military service in India and elsewhere.

Alike in justice and in policy, the broadest distinction should be made between military service in India, and in England or any healthy colony, properly so called. In India the casualties amongst the troops have *during peace* amounted *per annum* to at least 1000 in every 10,000! In England and her healthy colonies they have ranged from about 90 to a little above 200; while the latter proportion, being more than double that in the adult population of this country generally, has with good reason raised a cry of astonishment, although amounting to only *one-fifth* of the casualties in

* Appendix K.

the European army in India in ordinary times of peace!

In India extensive war has occurred eight or ten times in the last forty years with casualties exceeding the rate of *fifty* per cent. per annum! In Europe it has occurred but once during that period; and though the mortality, that in the Crimea, was unparalleled, it fell short of the rate in most Indian campaigns.

In India the climate during the quiet times of peace imprisons the soldier completely, for three quarters of the year, and causes, unceasingly, more or less of bodily distress and mental depression. In England and her colonies the soldier experiences no such confinement, distress and depression, excepting where he has made himself a criminal; and it is then temporary only, not perennial

In India the soldier is surrounded by a population with whom he can hold but little intercourse, and enjoy no kind of sympathy or friendly association; while the burial ground is the public place of his constant resort over the funeral of his comrades, and the '*Dead march in Saul*' the gloomy music ever ringing in his ears. In England and her colonies* he is surrounded by fellow men having the same fair complexion of body and mind, the same language and tastes, and the same hopes for time and eternity, with himself. He is free to enjoy the open air under a genial sky, playing at healthy athletic games with his comrades on the bowling-green or cricket-ground, enlivened with merry tunes by some fiddler, in place of following all those comrades one by one, perhaps

* India is not a colony, and never can become one.

within the year, to sultry graves and to the depressing music of death; and with the expectation always before him of being himself followed ere long in turn!

Lastly, and not least; if he is a parent in India, his children, if not hybrids, have hitherto nearly all perished before his eyes in their infancy or early years; whereas in England and her colonies the soldier's children being born and bred in climates congenial to them, are no such cause of heart-rending anxiety as they invariably are in India, to the parent whose natural affection has not been cruelly blunted by *avoidable* bereavements which his loyal subordination constrains him patiently to endure!

Service in India should be free.

From such a comparison as this, which does not indeed represent the whole strength of the contrast, it is manifest that the soldier expatriated to India is to be viewed as altogether in an exceptional position. Our constitutional principles, and political rights, place it beyond controversy that employment in India ought to be made as attractive to every man whose services are required there, as is service at home, or in a colony. So that his service, like that of his superior's, might be at all times the willing service of a free man, not the constrained service of a bondsman who had allowed his fetters to be slipped on him *while he was in the dark*.* As to any charges this might entail upon the revenues of India, even though it might be shown that they would be counterbalanced by the pecuniary saving resulting from the larger proportion of men left effective and of lives preserved, that would be a mean unrighteous ground

* Appendix L.

to take! If the dominion of Britain is, as politicians affirm, a blessing to India, it behoves her to pay the due price for that blessing. What! is she to be blessed by the protection of Englishmen, and those Englishmen to be ruined, and their children to perish, in return for the protection they afford her!

All classes of Britain have their claims on India.

It is said that India is of inestimable value to English parents of the upper and middle classes, as offering a handsome provision for their sons. But do these or the sons of the poorer classes form the great numerical majority of Britons in India? Did the ancestors of the latter play a whit less active and self-sacrificing part in gaining possession of the country than those of the former? Upon what rightful ground then should India be the making of the one, and beyond all question the marring of the other? Who gave, or had any constitutional right to give, India to the upper and middle classes for them to serve themselves of it—to appropriate to the advantage of their own classes exclusively the beneficial interests Britain may have in the connexion with her? If the British Constitution is not a mockery, and the rights conferred by it a delusion, can any or all the estates of the realm, without doing violence to its whole spirit and authority, confer on these classes any rightful power, to make use of the humbler classes of their countrymen—numerically the nation—as the cat's-paw to be destroyed in obtaining chestnuts for them out of the furnace of India? Whence in common reason and justice does it happen, that while a cadetship to India has such value that the lady-mother, seeking one for her son, has to haunt

Inequitable character of the present system.

the India House from day to day and practise all the arts of pathetic imploration in that *pantheon*, until the blessing is bestowed by one of the dignities enshrined there, a rank-and-fileship is not only valueless, but of such negative value, that in the case of the village mother the tables are turned; that it is not she at the Director's door, but the Company's serjeant at hers, who has to practise all the wiles of seductive persuasion with a rank-and-fileship ready in his hand in the form of smart money? Whence is it that while the one mother is all anxiety lest her son should fail of a cadetship to India, the other mother is "all of a tremble" lest hers should accept a rank-and-file one? No such thing is here claimed as that the latter should stand on an equal footing with the former—no impossibilities, no levelling. On the contrary, we contend for that just recognition of the claims of all, which alone can ensure permanency to that gradative order—to those broad steps in the social structure which are needful for its stability, and of which the everlasting pyramids of Egypt are the type—types set up, as under a blind impulse, by her despots—as if, by contrast, to mark and to mock the misproportions of political systems like their own, and of those convulsive products of reaction no less, which are their proportionate reciprocals, and to stand as the enduring prototypes of the constitution of Britain, in which every order, from the extended base to her crowning top stone, was to have its rightful existence, importance, position, dimension, and solidity! We ask for no such unreasonable absurdity as that the remuneration of the uneducated

No levelling, but a just admission of claims sought.

and unrefined should equal that of the educated and refined; but we do ask that they shall be proportionate—that life in India shall be as acceptable to the one as to the other, in comparison with what each leaves behind him in England. Surely when we consider what is the cottage life here, with its bread and cheese, and alternations of hard labour, and of hungry inaction, this is not much to require!

Volunteering in India no proof of the attractiveness of life there.

But it is said by some that life in India is desirable and attractive to the soldier, and that this is proved by the fact that upon a regiment's having completed its time there the soldiers very generally volunteer to remain in other corps in preference to returning to England. No doubt, after many years of such lives as soldiers lead in India, few that are prudent will venture upon what England then offers them. The impressions of a colder climate, though less felt by those who are in circumstances to watch each deviation from health, than might, without a close observation of the cause, be anticipated, are for a long time very trying to the soldier, whose skin and liver are in general in a much more exhausted state than theirs, and who has none of those protective resources on retiring, which his superiors can command. It takes some years of cherishing care, such as poor men cannot have, before the benefit of a bracing climate is felt. Without the command of such care a man had better remain an exotic in India, with his sluggish liver and skin kept in action artificially by heat. The officer returning can look forward, however small his means, to, at all events, a warm bed and fireside in some small home or lodging, in which he can snuggle, while the wind is howling without. The soldier discharged after a ten years' service, if he returns to England, has to be thankful if he can find occupation which will require him to be out with his cart horses before day-break in the snow. An occupation to which he looked back with pining recollections when first he went out (which he so often expresses), he now, after years of inaction, lassitude, and exhaustion, looks forward to with dread. Men who repeatedly in hospitals have had such extensive dealings with the Potentate of the lymphatics, MERCURY, insinuating himself in his form of *mild sublimity*,* into their every tissue, that their spirits have ofttimes been on the point of borrowing from the god his wings, and leaving their earthly tenements to his undisputed possession, must feel themselves no longer simple Englishmen, but *hydrarguretted calcinations* of Englishmen. Every surgeon of an European corps in India must know that the men after a few years are quite unfitted to struggle with life in a cold climate,† supporting themselves.

Furthermore the adage, "use is second nature," applies to no habits more forcibly than to those of inaction and confinement within doors, when once they are thoroughly confirmed. It is true that, in

* The "mild sublimate," or chloride of mercury—calomel.

† It is not long since I met a soldier who showed me his medal for good service, and discharge order, and who stated that he had been ten years in the Company's service, and had returned within the year; and he added that he had received some months of advanced pay on his discharge, but that he was now in such straits he feared he would be compelled to sell his medal; that he had been so ill in India, especially in Burmah, that he was quite unable to do work here which would support him, as stronger men had the preference. It would have been better for him to have remained in India at all hazards.

India, a large proportion of the soldiers chafe, and drink themselves to death, under a condition so opposed to the habits of out-door life and labour in which they had been reared. But the very fact of some men outliving the feelings entertained by nearly all for a time, proves the establishment in their case of that mental habituation which amounts often to an entire change of nature, but proves nothing to the present issue. If it were true that soldiers on becoming personally acquainted with life in India give it the preference over a return to England, then might the recruiting serjeants be, without apprehension, provided with a persuasive argument of the greatest force—that men disappointed with their lot after a year's trial would be replaced again at their homes in England. But do not our Indian authorities know perfectly well that such an engagement would lead to the return of three-fourths of the soldiery? If the Government cannot venture to make any such an engagement, can it be truthfully said that the contract on the soldier's part was made voluntarily and with his eyes open?

The expense requisite small compared with the duty.

It will be found that an additional charge upon the revenues of India, absolutely trifling in comparison with the urgency and solemnity of the duty, would suffice to supply the recruiting serjeants with *attractive truths* which would draw an abundant supply of men after every *repulsive truth* had also been plainly and fairly put before them; as in all honesty it ought. Thus they would find the service equal to their expectations, and if not in all cases satisfied, be, at least, no more mortified at their experience of it than are their commissioned superiors who, though free to retire at any time, upon the whole find reason to remain in the country.

It is even probable that the measures necessary for this righteous consummation would lead in the end to no charge at all upon the public revenue; nay, it would conduce to the happiness and contentment of the men, and consequently to their efficiency and the prolongation of their lives, to an extent which might more than repay the apparent charge, and might effect a considerable annual saving. But if instead of the unimportant pecuniary charge, which the necessary measures would at the most involve, their costliness were such as to press with serious weight on the revenues of India, it ought to be borne as a necessary tribute *to justice and to honour*, or the tenure of the country ought most assuredly to be relinquished.

The poverty of our peasantry no apology for the system.

The ignorance and impoverished condition of our peasantry are not very creditable to the social state of a country into whose lap Providence has poured the riches of the world; but, that advantage should be taken of their want of knowledge, credulity, adversity, and sensuality, to ply them with all manner of fictions and the beer-pot to enter upon a life the discomfort and hopelessness of which they afterwards constantly endeavour to drown in intemperance, ill becomes the country which has assumed to be the exemplar of freedom and honour, and the protectress of injured races! In this matter England may well take up the words, put by inspiration into other mouths, and exclaim: "thou hast set me to keep another's vineyard, mine own vineyard have I not kept."

Were a similar course adopted in Africa or upon any other ethnic coast, of inducing natives of a tropical climate, by means of utterly false representations and libations of alcohol, to accept conditions binding them to serve as coolies in some bitterly cold one, where they and their children rapidly perished, may we not confidently hope that Exeter Hall would ring with denunciations of the practice? Yet there are few to examine into, and question the propriety of, doings in England, of which this is but an imperfect picture! Is it, as the roguish serenaders in our streets appear to have discovered, that a goodly supply of plumbago and grease are needful as an emollient for the British heart; or that there is some occult psycho-physical affinity, some elective attraction between British philanthropy and a black complexion?

Grievous moral condition of the soldiery in India.

Do the people of England know the amount, and the causes, of the appalling drunkenness which prevails in British regiments in India as soon as peace returns, and patriotism and prowess cease their sway? Do they know that men in despair are constantly committing serious crimes,* that they may be transported even as felons out of the country—that one instance, if not more, has occurred of the murder of a native for that object alone; that they have gone so far as to assault their officers, and that repeatedly, that they might get themselves removed from India on any terms; that an illicit connexion with black women is absolutely preferable to marriage with

* Appendix M.

fellow country-women to all who have not become callous to the fate of a legitimate offspring by the latter; that to the feeling parent, who is not under the protection of strong religious impressions, the pining away of his children is a foremost one amongst the many incentives to seek oblivion in intemperance; that the mere sense of having been thoroughly taken in by the recruiting serjeant rankles in the minds of many?* Let inquiry be made in a candid spirit, and these and many other facts will be established, which (as a banker would say) form heavy items standing at the debit of the tenure of India!

Notable "general order" against mutinous conduct.

The reader will find in the Appendix† a copy of that notable document, speaking volumes as to the mental condition of the soldiery—the "*general order*," which an excellent nobleman considered it necessary, when Commander-in-Chief in India, to issue, in order to suppress the growing crime of assault on officers with the view to transportation, in which the perpetrators are promised death as their reward, and their minds relieved of the illusion of hoping to find, in transportation for life as felons, a preferable alternative to vegetating hopelessly and sickly like endive, gloomily immured in India. The "order" may have been quite right and necessary, but it involved in it the severest condemnation of the system which, as a *rank* soil, could only bring forth evil fruit. Men, who *with their eyes open* enter the *ranks* in India, are too commonly the damaged characters at home, which the system having nothing reformatory in it, but the contrary, cannot reclaim,

* Appendix N. † Appendix M.

but must render lost *for ever* there: while the great bulk who go out knowing nothing true of the life they are undertaking, nay having their minds filled with false impressions, are, for the most part, no worse men than the generality of their countrymen of all ranks; but in proportion as they have active and sanguine temperaments do they also become ruined by the system—by the hopelessness and disappointment it involves them in. Let not any who, favoured by birth, education, and outward advantages, feel not the evil of their own hearts; who consider not that the respectability of their character is mainly due to providential circumstances; who never ask themselves the humbling question, "what hast thou that thou didst not receive?" be too ready to apply hard epithets to these reckless ones of either class. Is it becoming that men who in the field exhibit prompt obedience and devoted valour, who are ready at any moment to risk their own lives to save their officers', should be spoken of only in the most opprobrious terms, when, the excitement of war being over, the blank hopelessness of their position, staring them in the face, drives them into dissipation and too often into crime? The man, whatever his rank, who is least disposed to feel for, and meliorate, their condition, and most ready to revile them indiscriminately, may rest assured there is, in this his present disposition, too much evidence that had he been as adversely trained and placed as they, he might have been found not a whit better in moral rectitude, patience, and self-command than any of them.

Moral superiority of the fortunate due to a *Providential* position.

What is to be said of the following extraordinary

oversight in the public mind; for it can be nothing else than an oversight? A soldier, in the Crimea, grounded his arms and refused to serve any longer. This was unquestionably a military offence meriting the severest punishment which in these days of reasoning humanity could with propriety be inflicted. He was sentenced to transportation as a felon. If a soldier ordered to India, dreading the life there, were to follow that example, he would, *having made himself a felon to escape being sent to a tropical climate*, be the only man in the regiment whom the public would from that moment shrink from transporting to one! All his former comrades would continue to be ordered there without any adequate or acceptable inducement, while he and his new compeers, burglars, garotters, &c., would, if transported at all, have the finest climates in the world selected for them! And any one who, with the author, should argue that the dangers of a tropical climate offer natural instruments of punishment especially suited to deter men from the commission of heinous offences, and *under a rightly managed system* to be instrumental to the reformation of those transported to them, would run the risk of being charged with inhumanity!* Marvellous inconsistency!

Extraordinary inconsistency in British polity.

In England, when a man is condemned to death society will, if he is not reprieved, as a matter of course, and with scarce a month's notice, subject him to the extremity of mental alarm and bodily injury—it will hang him outright. If he is reprieved, it will in-

* It is not, of course, meant to be suggested that felons should be sent to India.

stantly shrink from subjecting him to the minor alarm and injury of a transportation to a tropical climate. At the same time it will not hesitate to inflict on loyal subjects a transportation practically similar to sending felons to the Tropics, in being accompanied with a *climatic* imprisonment equally and necessarily absolute in both cases, in being equally irrevocable for many years, and in terminating for the most part in death; but dissimilar, in that it could not be said of the felon that the conditions on his part were not voluntary if he chose to commit the crime in the face of the tropical penalty, of the serious nature of which he would of course have been carefully apprized before hand, by authorities *whose object it was to deter him from getting sent out.* Whereas it cannot be said of the recruit that the conditions on his part are voluntary, when the serjeant, so far from taking any pains to apprize him of the true character of the tropical life he was about to incur, and of its real hopes and prospects, does his best to sophisticate him by his statements, and to weaken his judgment by the beer-pot!

India no blessing to our working classes.

Whatever may be the imagined value of India to England,* it is beyond a question true, that that value interests at present the minority only. With respect to the bulk of the nation, from whom the common soldiers are drawn, what prayer is there that poor parents throughout the land have to offer up with greater fervour than that India might become early qualified to take care of herself, or her guardianship be transferred to other hands? Let any one who will question this ascertain the feelings of most

* Appendix O.

of those parents who have had sons in India; or let him go out there, and when the war shall be over, and the soldier's honour, therefore, shall not interfere with it, let him simply offer to purchase the discharge and bring back every man who is anxious to leave the country. His purse would soon convince him of the truth of the position he had questioned. Were he a millionaire and true to his word, he would reduce regiments which had not been long in the country to "skeletons," by drawing away nearly all their men.

Unsound arguments respecting the soldiery and their conduct.

To argue that the great bulk of the soldiery are unreasonable, and unworthy of consideration, because a certain proportion of them are so far superior to the average of men, in contentment, endurance, and self-control, as to influence the mass sufficiently to maintain order and keep the system from breaking down altogether, and because the service offers a certain number of posts for such men in the "warrant staff," which are "prizes any steady man may in time secure," is to argue neither soundly nor fairly.

It is to argue unsoundly, because you have no right to expect more from a body of men, under any given circumstances, than you find by long experience to be the moral result of those circumstances acting upon the average of men; especially when the men are those of your own voluntary seeking. If you offer terms acceptable only to hoodwinked men, or to men of damaged character, it is not reasonable that you should lose consideration for and condemn those whom you obtain on such terms, because they do not prove as satisfied and meritorious as you would like. It is to argue unfairly, also, because it is the very rarity itself of steadiness which your system begets which leaves to each "deserving man" the prize of becoming a "warrant officer" in process of time; because it is the terms you offer *to all*, and not to a few only, upon which depends your right to faithful and satisfactory service from *the whole body*.

The only just and safe position for military service in India.

Military service in the ranks in India can never be in a just and safe position until its fundamental condition shall be an engagement, in the name of India, that the recruit shall be replaced at the home from which he was invited out, should he at the end of a year or two's trial find the service unacceptable or disappointing to him. Until this is conceded it is mockery, and something worse, to tell him that he entered upon the engagement voluntarily with his eyes open. With his eyes open! Did you, or could you, give him any correct notion of the life he was invited to enter upon? Had he been placed, even for one whole day, in the atmosphere of a forcing-house amongst pines and cactuses, and forewarned that that at least would be the temperature in which he would have to live night and day more than half the year? Had he been placed with his head before some open furnace, covered withal by such a headdress as you have as yet provided for him, and just at the distance where a thermometer would rise, from the radiance alone, to the same point that it does in the sun in India; and was he kept there for one day only, and then informed that that was a specimen, and an imperfect one, of the solar action he would be subjected to day by day while in the field? Was he led through the gloomy wards of a hospital, with cases of dysentery and cholera on the right hand and on the left, and then informed from statistical tables of the exact chance he woud have of occupying one of those beds—how many times temporarily, and when fatally? Was he informed that, according to the well-established chances of life in the ranks in India, he must not flatter himself that, after the ten years he was being bound for were terminated, his reasonable prospect would be a wending homeward to his native village whistling the tune of "Home, sweet Home!" for that, in all probability, he would before that time have been carried to his long home by martial steps treading to the tune of "The Dead March in Saul!"

Otherwise the bondage worse than African slavery.

Unless all this information at the least has been afforded him, let it not be pretended that, after having rightly understood the nature of his engagement, he has entered upon it voluntarily. Since this is not possible—since the life he undertakes can not be fairly placed before him—since from the nature of the case the peasant of England must, in going out to India, proceed there very much in the dark—it is manifest that to engage him in England to an absolute term of service in the Tropics becomes a one-sided bond. Let it ever be borne in mind that he is transported to a hostile climate, with unavoidable imprisonment during peace and destructive exposure to it during war; that his case bears no parallel to that of coolies taken from one tropical climate to another at least as favouable to them, with healthful industry in the fields of cultivation, not destructive exposure in those of war. Let it also be borne in mind that the charges attendant upon his expatriation were incurred not with any view to his benefit, but to serve the objects of his employers alone. To require him to refund those charges, or any part of them, before he can release himself from an engagement to serve in such a climate, whether entered upon in blindness or not, while he is not afforded a pay from which it is possible he could ever save the means, is to place him in a state of absolute bondage many degrees worse than African slavery, bating the middle passage, as it existed under the generality of British planters in the West Indies. Many degrees worse, inasmuch as the *African* is not conveyed to *Siberia*, *Hudson's Bay*, or some other clime as hostile to him as India to the poor Briton, but to one quite as congenial as his own;*—inasmuch as, under British planters at least, the average duration of the slave's life in the West Indies far surpassed that of the British soldier in India;—inasmuch as the children of the African did not, one by one, sicken and die in their parents' arms, like all, but illegitimate hybrids, in India; but grew up around them in health, and, for the most part, well treated;—inasmuch as the climate, and service, the African was transported to did not, either imprison him throughout his life in a state of inaction, tolerable it might have proved to him but

* It is not to justify African slavery that this unanswerable comparison is instituted, for a more zealous opponent to slavery does not exist than the writer; but he would feel it to be a maudlin and insincere emotion, were it not consistent; were it not directed, at least as much against bonds upon white limbs in the East, as against bonds upon black in the West.

intolerable to the muscle-vibrating Briton, or subject him when in the field to an exposure reducing from sickness alone, his chance of life to a few months' duration;—inasmuch as the number per cent. of slaves flogged, and the suffering from each flogging, could not have amounted to a tithe of the cases amongst soldiers of the two diseases, dysentery and cholera alone, or of the agony which in a few hours transforms a robust man into a corpse from simple torture! Should any one protest against this comparison on account of the greater indignity of slavery and the lash, he is reminded that the soldier is not altogether exempt from a liability to the latter indignity, as the author too well remembers;* and as to the former, it is in name only that its absolute subjection differs from his, so long as an engagement, entered upon not only in unavoidable ignorance but under a practised deception, shall place him for many years in irrevocable bondage in the climate of India!

Argument from the poverty of the English labourer, its worth.

To argue that the condition of the labourer in England is so abject, that service in India, such as it is, ought to be preferable to him, would not only be presumptuous, exhibit little of generosity or patriotism, and reflect severely upon our social state, but it would prove too much. It proves the soldier's life in India to be sad indeed, if it cannot be fairly laid before men in so depressed a condition lest they should decline to enter upon it—if after they have gone out, the option cannot be safely afforded them of returning

* Appendix N.

to England should they, after a fair trial of the service, prefer life at home though so "abject." In proportion as the peasant's life in England is one of trying depression, must his expatriation to India be deplorable for him, since disappointment at the change drives so large a proportion of the soldiers into a reckless indifference to life, intemperance, and despair!

The ignorance and the appetite of the clown, plied by the wiles and the beer-pot of the recruiting serjeant, together with the extreme irksomeness of unremitting toil to some of better powers, might possibly prolong for a time a supply of men for India; and the loyalty of discipline, so perfect and so admirable in the British army, might possibly perpetuate a respectful endurance of a helpless life, convenient enough to those, if any there are, who may heedlessly regard the soldier, much as they do cattle,—as an animal without a mind or soul, to be sought for at the lowest possible rate, and cherished only upon principles of economy; but, to take the lowest ground, such a state of things cannot be otherwise than dangerous. Glaring anomalies, to use the mildest term, cannot last for ever. Each British soldier in India secures the command of 500*l.* per annum of revenue to the government, and to India does his part in saving her from anarchy of the worst kind. Did he cost the double of what he does he would be the most productive of labourers,—the cheapest of agents.

Service in India altogether exceptional.

His position, like that of his "commissioned" and "covenanted" superiors, is altogether exceptional. The case of the soldier entering the army here to defend its shores, and those of its *colonies properly so called*, its congenial climes peopled with his own race, is, we repeat, and should be seen to be, totally different from an expatriation for the defence of the great *Tropical* dependency—India. Is it not manifest that India should be called upon to make life in her swarthy bosom as nearly as is possible as attractive to the soldier as it is in New Zealand or Canada? Now the difference in the pay and prospects of the soldier in India does no such thing. During the excitement of war, enlistment may possibly be spontaneous. Pugnacious spirits will rush through fire and water to take a part in conflicts. But in the quieter times of peace, it is beyond a question that the liability to serve in India proves a daily increasing drawback to enlistment into Her Majesty's Army; and that it may be expected, as communication with the country is shortened, to prove a serious obstacle to it—an obstacle which may become insurmountable when, in addition to this, public opinion is directed, as sooner or later it must be, to the unutterably dishonourable* arts practised to induce the simple clown to enlist; arts which if similar could be practised towards the sons of the gentry, for any public object, would indeed raise a storm from one end of the kingdom to the other!

The simple remedy for the humiliating evil.

Now for all this humiliating amount of evil, the simple remedy is to make India chargeable *in the first instance* with the measures necessary for rendering her non-commissioned defenders as happy and

* Appendix N.

contented as her commissioned. Few will then desire to avail themselves of the right, which the legislature ought to have required of the holders of India, from the first, as the fundamental condition of service in that climate—as the *Magna Charta* of those entering it—as the touchstone of their freedom—as their sole guarantee against lapsing into a bondage as abject, and much more grievous than West Indian slavery—a right, respecting which it is none too strong to affirm, that every day during which it is deferred is a day of disgrace to our pretensions, as a freedom-loving, and freedom-protecting people—namely the option of leaving India, excepting, of course, during war, if, after experience, service in that climate shall prove an unacceptable constraint. Freedom: the right of service in India.

Should the number of those availing themselves of the right exceed a very small proportion of those selected for the service in England, it would simply prove that the service is not duly inviting to Englishmen—that the terms it offers must be improved To say that India cannot afford it, is to pronounce her bankrupt. To entrap our countrymen into serving her as bondsmen is something worse than would be a like act on the part of a white-lead, or arsenic manufacturer, who should entice operatives intohi s mill, and detain them there by force, to serve him upon terms unacceptable to them, and for the very pretty reason, real or pretended, that he could not afford to pay them better! Of the two cases his would be the less unjustifiable, inasmuch as his employment would not be destructive to their children as well as to themselves.

Its cost but small.

But the truth is that to do all that is necessary for changing the aspect of the service altogether, and rendering it acceptable to the soldier in every way, would not absorb three, perhaps not one per cent. more of the public revenue of India. The reader who will look through the Appendix, will not think the author indifferent to the claims of India. He might perhaps be able to prove that he has *worked*, as many hours as some eloquent declaimers have *talked*, about developing the resources of India and meliorating the condition of the natives. Yet with all feeling for them, especially for the low caste men of India, *the workers*, increased by many friendly recollections of *them*, it is impossible for him not to wish that some of the concern felt for the landholders and ryots of India, and of the eloquence expended on their behalf, were transferred to the claims of the fine fellows whose presence there alone keeps those *protegés* of British *philethnicy*, from robbing, mutilating, and murdering their fellows of neighbouring villages!

For the "*hopeful encouragement*" of the soldier serving in India, each and every point dwelt upon under the former heads demands an earnest attention in the first instance, but in addition to these provisions for the protection of his body, for the occupation of his mind, and the solace of his parental feelings, he must have *a future* for him to look forward to, held up before his view.

Were it possible to station the whole of the British force in India on hill elevations, and to keep them there permanently, the objects of a large part of our requirements would be fulfilled. Even though the service were not in other respects rendered more promising than it is, very few men, probably not one in a hundred, would then avail themselves of the power to return to labour in England, from a healthy and easy life amongst their comrades in the Himalayas or Neilgherries; although that right ought, most certainly, to exist, and to be available whenever the arrival of recruits would permit men to retire without lowering the numerical standard of a regiment.

One-third of the British force may be in the hills.

But though the whole European force could not of course be afforded a climatic advantage which would totally alter the character of service in India, which would change what is a living death to some, and a dying life to others, into as enjoyable an existence as their sublunary condition admitted of, yet sufficient evidence has surely been produced, especially by Mr. Martin, to induce the government to decide upon stationing one-third of such force on hill elevations.

If men arrived at that privilege by a previous residence during a certain period in the plains, so hopeful a prospect would act beneficially upon the whole body. It would, with the other provisions set forth under the former heads, tend to keep them more temperate and contented than it is possible they should be at present. But to complete the fulfilment of India's obligations to her protectors, and to render the future duly hopeful to them, a suitable provision for their declining years must be held out to them. If to every man who had served twenty years in India a pension of not less than forty or fifty pounds

40,000 effective men might suffice.

a year were secured, a force of forty thousand men in the improved spirits and health of an army so well protected and hopefully circumstanced might prove ample for the whole of India, especially when the main lines of railway were completed. They would, in fact, be more effective than double the number of men tortured by solar heat in the field from imperfect protection, after enduring a barrack life, with their bodies parboiled and their minds gloomy, without occupation, and without a future in prospect for themselves or their children. It is the rapid melting away of an European army in the field in India which renders so large an apparent force and such great reserves necessary.

Pension proposed.

But supposing fifty thousand men to be the force kept up, the number of survivors at the end of twenty years who sought the pension in preference to remaining in the hills, could not exceed two thousand, or at most two thousand five hundred. A pension of forty pounds to each of these, with a suitable addition to those amongst them who were non-commissioned officers, would only amount to a gross total of, say, 150,000*l*. a year, supposing the average of them enjoyed it as much as twenty years; while it would fill with hope and contentment fifty thousand breasts!*

It is not uncommon to hear the "heavy expenses" of the European force in India spoken of in a tone which the complainers would themselves perceive to be utterly unreasonable would they but take the trouble to view the question in its proper light. Were a shipowner, who had charged himself with

* Appendix P.

conveying emigrants across the ocean, to commence drawing a comparison between the walls of the cottages they had to be contented with in England, and the greater costliness of the walls of trusty ships; and were he consequently to employ frail vessels which caused the loss of many lives, he would not, in neglecting to provide the utmost protection against the aqueous element by which his emigrant passengers were surrounded, be acting a part in anywise more unreasonable than they who, comparing the expenses of a man as a labourer or as a soldier in England with what he costs in India, would dole out with a niggard hand the rupees necessary for protecting him *completely* against the calorific element into which he had been enticed and immersed to serve other interests—European and Native, not his own.

The British soldier the guard of the opulent native.

As to the interests the natives have in the presence of the British soldier, however much *a jealousy for class privileges*, folly, bigotry, and other causes may have rendered many of them blind to the fact, there cannot be a question that the comparative security with which "zumeendars" and "shroffs," throughout India, have rested upon their pillows during the present century has been due to that presence. The opulent baboos of the Presidencies, the progressive filling out of whose *cellular tissue* with sebaceous deposits may be taken as the symbol and measure of the progressive filling up of their cellars with Company's tissue and bullion deposits, would view with quaking hearts the departure of the last British soldier from India. They know very well that it would be the signal for the descent upon them of armed bands from the interior, compared with whose tenderest mercies the ferocity of their own Bengal tiger would be gentleness itself; that, to have the dagger of Ehud buried in their obese persons would be more considerate treatment than they could hope for from beings whose minds, filled to the brim with thoughts of rapine, had no space left for any other; and who could not give them credit for having surrendered their last hoard until *torture* had done its worst upon their bodies.

When we consider how great is the interest which these gentlemen have in the presence of a British army, how they owe to it everything they have in life and their lives besides, how great is their collective wealth, and how admirable and unparalleled their munificence (which contrasts remarkably with the tenacity of many a professor of a more self-denying faith), it is fair to presume that they would be happy to see devised some fiscal measure by which their class might bear a more reasonable share than it does of the charges of an army under whose wing they are thus protected and cherished.

The sepoy better paid than the British soldier.

Any fair comparison instituted between the expenses, pay and pension of the British soldier in India, and of the sepoy, would show the latter to be out of all equitable proportion higher than the former. In the first place, every expense connected with the conveyance of the soldier to India and his protection there from the effects of a climate in which he is an exotic, has of course to be deducted. Compare then his bare pay (from which there are serious deductions) and rations with the sepoy's. The latter is fully three times that of able-bodied coolies or labourers in India, who are hired everywhere by natives for two or three rupees a month. Hence the sepoy can save an additional income to his pension, which, expended in his native country, will enable him to support a family in much comfort. Whereas the British soldier's pay and rations in India, far from amounting to three times an able bodied labourer's wages in England, scarcely equal them, low as they are; yet if his military merits are but equal* to the sepoy's, he is not placed in an equal position with him, unless he has the means afforded him for laying by an income which would provide equal comfort for him in his native country. If the pensions of the two are compared, the disproportion will be found greater still. The sepoy in his native climate has a reasonable prospect of living to enjoy a pension, which is in itself a handsome retiring provision with Indian wants and Indian prices. The British soldier's chance is to be dead some years before he could claim any pension; and it would not place him in England in a position admitting of any comparison with the retired sepoy's.

When therefore all these considerations are duly weighed, it cannot but appear no great matter to claim for the soldier, the best of whose days and constitution have been expended in India, a pension of 50*l.* a year, amounting annually to the small aggregate charge of 150,000*l.* or so, on the revenues

* Recent events would prove them of tenfold worth, even could the fidelity of the latter be implicitly relied on.

of India, especially when it is borne in mind that the anomalous possession of that dependency is either in itself utterly unjustifiable, or, so far as British rights in it are concerned, is upon all constitutional principle, to be held for the equal benefit of all classes. Any other view is one of rapacity, opposed to the spirit of our constitution. A British parliament, which justifies its present constitution upon the ground that it represents as effectually the interests of all classes as if the suffrages on which it rests were more general, can take no other view than this; for it is manifest that upon an extension of the suffrage to the classes whence the soldiers are drawn, that which is now a constitutional right would become *law*.

Recapitulation.

In conclusion; to recapitulate. It cannot be too strongly impressed upon the mind, that whatever may be the state and terms of enlistment and the remuneration of the British soldier serving in Europe, or in our colonies, properly so called, service in India should be held to be altogether exceptional. It is not possible that the recruit should obtain beforehand any correct knowledge of life in India, nor can he, or the soldier ordered out, be contented, or have reason for contentment there, unless the depressive effects of so hostile and imprisoning a climate are counteracted by cherishing treatment and encouraging prospects. Tempered by their beneficial influence, military discipline would make service in India eminently reformatory of those whom circumstances, and a feeble morality, may have rendered lost to society and driven out to India; and no less protec-

The service might be reformatory.

tive of the morals of the larger number who have been tempted to enlist at a time of confiding simplicity and of temporary need. It may even operate as an instrument in aid of that teaching which assures them that "religion has the promise of the life that now is as well as that which is to come." Just and generous towards them in things temporal, its tendency must be to soften their hearts towards things spiritual.

The soldier's habits caused by his position chiefly.

Of those who know the soldier in India only as the subject of unhappy influences, in incessant strife with himself and his circumstances, and in frequent strife with good order and his officers, ever searching after oblivion in intemperance, and the scandal of Christianity among the heathen, there may be few who can bring themselves to view all this moral difference which exists between him and his more fortunate superiors as mainly the effect of his untoward position, and, in a certain sense, as the measure of it. Yet such beyond doubt it is. Say not until a trial, complete in all particulars, has been persevered in and failed, that he might not, like some of his superiors, have proved as unflinching an exemplar of Christian morality in peace, as of soldier-like valour in war!

All interests, but his, have their advocates.

While volumes have been written to advocate what have been called British interests in connexion with India—the interests of the Company and their nominees on the one hand, and of merchants and manufacturers on the other; and while pamphlets have been showered, thick as leaves in Valombrosa, to advocate the cause of the natives against the Company,—while all these interests have been most ably defended by every sound fact and argument which could be collated, and by a great many more besides,—there is one very important interest which has at least equal rights to any of these, but in support of whose claims on India not a single volume has yet been written. It is that of the people, numerical, of England—of all those classes who are called upon to supply the soldiery, without whose presence and aid every other British interest in India would undergo *a rapid tropical evaporation*, and every native interest, save those of marauders, a sanguineous *liquidation*. British rule in India as it might be, and even as it is, is a blessing to its people. It may be a blessing also to the educated classes of England, if they like, weighing blessings by bullion, to think it so; but as yet it is no blessing, but verily a curse, to the people of England at large. The utmost that can *at present* be said of it, is, that it absorbs a portion of the population temporarily in want and not able to get out to a healthy colony—absorbs them much as the sea does the population of a foundering ship, the absorbing element being water in the one case, heat in the other.

It would be distressing beyond measure, and not a little alarming, were it impossible to satisfy claims so equitable in themselves and of such pressing importance as those here advocated, since it would point to the only proper alternative—an early abandonment of the country; but happily the measures necessary in order to place the British soldier and his offspring in India in the position which is their due, are not such as would exhaust either the intellect or the means at the command of the State.

The first duty.

In the first place, the *Clothing, Housing, Locating,* and *Recreative Employment* of the Soldiery, having received a thorough and scientific investigation by a suitable number of qualified minds conscientiously selected for the duty, no pitiful question of expence should be allowed to interfere with the determination to render them as beneficial as was possible.

The second.

In the second place, the legitimate children of the soldiers should be cherished and reared in a healthy climate by the Government, as has under a former head* been fully and plainly set forth.

The third.

In the third place, after a service of twenty years, jointly in the Plains and Hills, they should be entitled to a pension of 40*l.* or 50*l.* per annum. A common labourer's and porter's wages in England varies from a pitiful 25*l.* a year in the country to 50*l.* in towns, and a mechanic's from 70*l.* to 100*l.* a year or more. Surely then men drawn from these several classes are entitled, if they survive long service in India, to the above pension, since officers, when entitled to theirs, have commonly reached their majority and enjoy a pension of 270*l.* or, fully double the salary which a young man of education, even of average university education, can hope to receive as a tutor, professional assistant, &c., or in the church as a curate; while, if the officer remains a few more years in the service, his pension mounts up to much more than that. The pension of 1000*l.* per annum which the civilian receives is *twenty times* what is

A comparison of pensions.

* Page 171.

here sought for the soldier; whereas *the generality* of civilians, even as now appointed by merit, would, without the aid of capital or interest, have found it difficult, in their early prime, to secure any permanent occupation yielding a salary of more than 200*l.* a year, only equal *to eight times* the miserable pay of a Suffolk labourer, *four times* the pound a week of a London porter, *or double* the wages of a London mechanic of any skill. That there are some of these educated classes, civil and military, who combine with real merit the talent of making their way to fortune at once, which would have availed them had they not entered the service, is true; but it is equally true of many a soldier, could he but have escaped his position and started anew in life. If it be contended that a large part of the civilian's pension is the fruit of stoppages from his pay, the friend of the soldier may reply that he will be well satisfied bya similar arrangement of a pension "stop'd" out of pay made so handsome as to admit of it, and to leave at the same time a proportional current affluence. It is not with any the smallest intention of criticising their amount, as if they were not fairly earned by long and faithful services to India, that a reference is here made to the pensions of the civil and military services; but solely with the view of showing, by a fair comparison of the money-value of the time of men of each class, how very moderate is the pension here claimed for the soldier; since it does not exceed the mean of the wages of the several classes from which he is drawn, while a major's pension is double and a civilian's at least five times the salary which could have been calculated upon from employments open to men of education unaided by interest or capital. If the soldier has been here supposed to enjoy the advantage of serving during a portion of his time in the hills, so would also a portion of the officers, while the rest have the great privilege of a furlough to Europe after ten years' service, or at any time in the case of sickness, during which they receive pay quite adequate to their support.

An army of Britons maintained in tropical India must of necessity be costly. India has no right to expect, any more than individual employers of Englishmen, that she is to command their unequalled services at any but a proportional cost; especially since, in enticing them from the pure and wholesome bosom of their mother country, she, their stepdame, has no better rest to offer them, excepting in certain spots, but on her huge brown carcass, steaming with heat, fretting with "prickly-heat," infested with parasitic insects, and oozing noxious vapours at every pore! India has no right to expect cheap defence.

Costly to India as a large British force must necessarily be, it is the most profitable investment she has ever made, and it is not at present quite costly enough to satisfy the demands of justice and sound policy. The outlay upon it is stopped short of the last tithe or two requisite. The main charges which more immediately concern the interest of the Government, but do not conduce to the happiness or contentment of the soldier, are incurred, but the small increase necessary to ensure these most important ends remains yet to be added. It is this addition which will make all the difference possible in the social position of the soldier, and in his hopes and therefore habits. It will make all the difference between his existence being one of bondage the most abject and hopeless, however much longer loyalty and discipline might cause the majority to struggle against and drown in liquor the sense of it,—or one of free and willing service at all times, such as England should alone permit her sons to be bound to in any tropical clime.

An acknowledgment of the right, or its alternative.

If India is to remain a dependency of England,—a blessing many think—a burden some,—let her revenues be chargeable, as a first claim upon them, to the extent necessary to render the protection of her *a willing service at all times* on the part of the humblest of her gallant defenders, and thus to ensure also the services of well-disposed men. To continue to withhold this right, would be to proclaim by acts, more forcibly than any democratic orator could by words, the necessity of that extension of our parliamentary franchise to the classes from whom they are drawn, which would very soon ensure for the non-commissioned protectors of India this their birthright as freemen, and the rightful charge upon her revenues which it involves.

APPENDIX.

(A. and B.)

NOTES to these letters have been deferred, and fall under advanced letters in the latter part of the Work.

(C.—Page 98.)

It is true that in the Crimean and former wars frequent complaints were made of the *weight* of the soldier's head-dress; even of the shako weighing but a pound. When we consider what was the common weight of the casque and helmets, both of ancient times, and of the days of heavy armour in the middle ages, when men were encumbered with so heavy a body-dress in addition to the head; or when we turn to native women and children *running for many hours*, day by day without intermission, with a weight exceeding that of twenty shakos on their heads (I have occasionally seen lads carrying eight "*goomma*" bricks, a cubic foot, weighing 100 shakos!); to suppose that the oppression caused by one shako was due simply to its weight, would imply that its wearer had degenerated into the feeblest of human beings. The oppression is doubtless occasioned by the pressure round the brows, of a hard inelastic and impervious substance clipping and heating them; and by confined heat and perspiration; there being no ventilation, or at best a mere semblance of it. My own solar hat in India weighed certainly above two pounds, and was often worn for many consecutive hours. There cannot be a doubt that the oppressiveness of the ordinary head-dress of the soldier is not due to its weight, as is imagined; but to its imperfect poising, its pressure and its want of porosity. It is absurd to suppose that the soldier cannot learn to carry a hat of a weight to which any healthy girl might readily be accustomed; and not a twentieth of what many a girl, both here and in India, carries easily for many hours a day. Complaints of the weight of the head-dress.

(D.—Page 127.)

Mistaken advice respecting exposure.

"Let it be the fashion to be English. It is a fallacy to suppose that the climate compels to be otherwise. Let the young man never enter a palkee, but go about on the back of his poney. Let him not fear the sun—it may tan his cheeks but it will not hurt him. It is your effeminate gentlefolks who live in dark houses artificially cooled, with a dozen Hindoos at work with fans and flappers to beat the flies off them, who suffer by exposure; not the hardy young Englishman who, if not intemperate, soon becomes acclimated; and the more readily so the less he regards the sunshine, which is healthy enough in moderation."

This is the advice of a most gallant and able officer, Brigadier Jacob, whose personal experience has no doubt confirmed it hitherto. He therefore possesses the semi-tropical constitution referred to in page 40 in the body of the work. That in the Presidency of Bombay, so many stations of which are maritime or within the influence of a marine atmosphere, while others on table-lands are materially affected by their elevation, and that in Madras to a certain extent, for the same reason, exposure to the sun is not deleterious to an equal degree to what it is in the more continental Presidency of Bengal, is no doubt true; but that on land in any part of the Tropics the natives of our climes can habitually expose themselves is a fallacy it is most dangerous to propagate. Just as a man recently from Europe can endure exposure, not without danger but with less suffering and danger than the same man after some years residence in India, so also is it true almost without an exception that in proportion as that man is able to keep up his English tone by surrounding himself as nearly as he can with an English climate, will he, when the necessity arises, be best able to endure exposure. To the truth of this fact every physiologist of experience in India will bear testimony. It is indeed a truth not necessarily resting for its evidence on tropical experience, but predicable upon physiological law. The more nearly the animal body is in its normal state, the better is it able to endure extremes of either heat or cold. To treat as effeminate an avoidance of the sun of India, and to recommend men to harden themselves to it by exposure, is even something less prudent than to urge men proceeding to Russia or Hudson's Bay to go about unprotected by suitable covering and not effeminately to fear the cold. In our own country, even our soldiers would not be rendered hardier, but much the contrary, if they mounted guard in snowy winter nights in a light summer dress. It is a curious fact that, on first emigrating to Canada, Englishmen feel the cold much less than afterwards; less even than those born there. In the opposite extreme, in the Tropics, the case is much stronger. The man who habitually exposes himself may rely upon it that, whatever may be the apparent impunity with which he does so, he is weakening his constitution, and laying for himself the foundation of visceral disease.

But where is the need for so much argumentation? Do not the records of the wilfulness of stern commanding officers show in the fatal results how grievously they have erred in imagining they could harden their soldiers in India by sufficient exposure? In the preceding pages instances of this have been adduced occurring many years ago. Within a few years a notable case has occurred, which occupied the attention of the whole press in India, and was rightly and strongly denounced by it. An officer commanding one of H. M. regiments in India thought to acclimate his men by marching and drilling them in the forenoon; but the result very soon belied his expectations. The sickness and mortality induced were such as to attract the attention of the government. It was natural that the officer himself should lay the disaster upon the unhealthiness of the barracks. But these, though faulty enough, as has been stated in the preceding pages, had been previously long occupied by different corps which did not suffer in like manner.

In the unavoidable exposure of the troops now in the field there is too abundant evidence that exposure to an Indian sun is in every degree more or less injurious, and that as a rule, they endure it on an emergency best who have most carefully avoided its influence, either by keeping habitually under shelter, excepting when it was low, or by clothing themselves in the best way they could against the power of its rays.

(E.—Locating of Troops. Page 154.)

Interesting character of the climate of the Hills.

The climate of the Himalaya Provinces (though the subject has lost the novelty it possessed when the Essay, from which the following are extracts, was written at SIMLA in 1824) has acquired an increasing interest and importance now that it has become not unfrequently the refuge of the government, and of a portion of the European troops; and this interest and importance will greatly increase should the bulk of these forces be hereafter quartered under its benign influence. If the matter of that Essay has been in a measure merged in the more recent writings of those who from time to time have recorded the results of their own and others' observations through the large amount of experience, which has since been afforded, it is believed there will yet be found in the original form, in which certain leading views connected with the effect of a mountain climate on the human body were put forth, an interest which may repay the perusal of these extracts. With respect to one point—*dampness;* if the *theoretical view* on which, in the absence of all the subsequent experience, an opinion had to be grounded, may appear to have placed the effect of *mists* and rain on lofty mountain heights in too favourable a light, as being much less humid and injurious than rain and fogs on the plain surface of the earth, I would beg the reader to bear in mind, that the convenience of vicinity to the plains has led to the selection of elevations the climate of which is by no means purely mountainous. Even SIMLA, which in a direct line is perhaps twenty miles from the plains, has to bear much of the brunt of the monsoon, charged with vapour exhaled from the hot and watery world below. Darjeling overhanging Bengal, and Nyne Tal overhanging Rohilkund, are doubtless most faulty in this respect. They and their mountain fellows in line, right and left, receive the brunt, and are the first *precipitants* of torrents which would never have risen as vapour from a cool mountain surface into its rare circumambient atmosphere. Each rank, behind, catches and brings down vapours that burst through them, until, at a certain distance, we have fully exemplified in nature the truth theoretically maintained in this Essay, that a lofty mountain air, even when opaque with mist, cannot have a like suppressive effect on the skin with an atmosphere of an equal, apparent, opacity on the earth's low level.

EXTRACTS from an ESSAY ON THE CLIMATE OF THE HILL PROVINCES (of the Himalayas), AND ITS CONNEXION WITH PATHOLOGY.*

"Oftentimes reflecting on the great difference in the properties of the atmosphere of these elevations, and that on the plain surface of the earth, and the necessary effect of a change to the former on the human constitution, certain pathological views have presented themselves to me, which, if just, must be of some importance. Of their truth, the arguments contained in the following pages will, I trust, induce conviction in the minds of those who favour them with a perusal. They have been corroborated by such experience and observation as my own residence has afforded, and by such information as I have been able to acquire. Another inducement arises from the fact, that, although nine years have elapsed, since the British protection has been extended to these States, their climate has gained as yet little of the celebrity it merits. More than merely occasional reports is necessary, to give rise to full conviction in the public mind of the certainty of facts, not a little extraordinary in themselves.

"Much prejudice and uncertainty not unreasonably exist on this subject; the minute attention requisite to explain all facts connected with it, and to remove all causes liable to create deception, not having as yet been afforded.

"The evidence necessary is, either that of an extensive experiment, or of strict pathological reasoning on the question. Neither has hitherto been afforded. It is on the latter evidence chiefly, that an institution of this nature would be commenced, since the former evidence, namely that of an extensive and well conducted experiment, must itself be the result of the institution in question.

"There are many reasons, sufficient to account for this climate's having obtained but little of the celebrity it merits. It is not easy, without actual experience, or a study of the philosophy of the atmosphere, to be impressed with a firm conviction, that places nearly of the same latitude can differ very greatly in climate; and that the summits of hills can possess very equable climates; although a person may not doubt of the

* Written at Simla, in the only house then existing there, and published in Calcutta, in 1824.

summits of lofty mountains being covered with perpetual snow. Hence the climate of the hills is often confounded with that of the adjoining valleys, and hence it is even supposed by some to be subject to sudden extremes of heat and cold. From the known unhealthiness of the neighbouring *jungly Terais*, and from the reported luxuriance of the wood on the hills, doubts naturally arise as to the purity of the air. Added to these are very general suspicions of its being unhealthy from dampness. Distrust has also arisen from too low situations (not higher than 3000 or 4000 feet) having been chosen for residence by invalids. All these groundless apprehensions will, I trust, ere long be entirely removed.

Mountain summits in Europe not inviting.

"Although the climate of mountainous summits, owing to peculiarities in the barometric properties of their atmosphere, has of late years commanded the attention of philosophers, the effects of such climates on the human constitution have hitherto scarcely attracted the inquiries of the physician. This is not to be wondered at, since the climate of mountainous summits in Europe, where alone such inquiries could hitherto have been expected, must have afforded, owing to its inclemency, little prospect of interest to the physician; especially as the diseases prevalent in those latitudes are not in general such as to be benefited by the properties of the climate of mountains. In India, however, it is far otherwise. The inclemency here is not as in Europe in the climate of the hills, but in that of the plains; and it will be my endeavour to prove clearly, that the peculiarities of the air of the former are well calculated to remove the injurious effects arising from the latter. . . . .

"Before entering on this question, I will venture to state, that most of the diseases in India, namely, those arising from heat, are chiefly, if not entirely, induced through injury of the functions of the skin. The truth of this will become manifest by considering, that there are no means by which the interior of the body can be affected from without, but through the medium of the skin—either that of the surface, or of the lungs; that the skin is endowed with various functions, which while vigorous, entirely preserve the internal parts from atmospheric injuries;* and therefore that the internal parts cannot suffer

* In evidence of the truth of this statement I will instance the following fact, than which nothing can more strongly corroborate it. It is well

from the effects of heat, till the functions of the skin are either suddenly or gradually deranged. It will be proper therefore, in the first place to inquire into the changes, effected by heat, in the functions of this membrane. Some effects of climate on the functions of the skin are too manifest to escape the notice of any individual; but there are several, which being more intricate, though not less important, have commonly passed unobserved. . . . ."

"In Britain, where the air is generally in the former state, viz., cold, somewhat damp, and of full weight, the removal of heat must be effected in a great measure by direct conduction. And as these states of the air exist during the greater part of the year, much heat is generated in the body, in order to supply so rapid an abstraction by conduction.

"On visiting India, the action of the skin is quickly altered. The sudden change in its functions, and the stimulus of heat, are among the chief dangers to which a person on first arriving is exposed.

Effect of a Tropical climate on the skin,

"The temperature of the air during a great part of the year, being but a few degrees under that of the body, little heat can now be removed by conduction. The internal heat accumulates, and would soon give rise to fatal disease; but that its stimulus rapidly excites an active perspiration, which, in evaporating, absorbs much of the heat that excited it; and the heat and dryness of the air greatly increase this evaporation; so that the quantity of fluid exhaled from the surface in a healthy person who has lately arrived in the country is very great. For some time the excited skin has strength to supply the exhalation required, and during this time the heat being thus moderated, is not much complained of. Excitement so unnatural cannot long be endured by many; nor can such unaccustomed action be long supported. The functions of the skin become gradually weakened, and in some cases ultimately exhausted.

known to philosophers, that certain gentlemen, desirous of ascertaining what degree of heated air could temporarily be borne, had the resolution to enter a chamber, or oven, the air in which was heated to a temperature far above that of boiling water; and that they remained in this atmosphere for a considerable time with impunity. Here the power of the cutaneous functions was strikingly evinced. They guarded, for a time, the skin and vitals from a degree of heat, which otherwise would have even altered their structure, coagulating or producing incipient decomposition in all the soft parts.

"The first channel for the egress of heat, conduction, carries off little heat in India, during the greater part of the year. When the second channel for its egress—active perspiration—is much weakend by exhaustion, heat internally accumulates, oftentimes increased by diet too free in animal and vinous stumuli.

and through it on vital organs.

"Several internal functions, those of the liver and stomach especially, are at first excited, then ultimately exhausted, partly through their sympathy with affected skin, and partly by the stimulus of accumulated heat. Hence diseases, varying with circumstances* and predisposition, are induced and renewed by a continuing cause. . . . ."

"We have then to inquire into the properties of a climate, calculated for the restoration of the injured functions, and the removal therefore of diseases incurred by a residence in Hindostan. Functions which have long been overpowered by the action of stimuli, cannot, by the continuance of stimuli, be forced into healthy action. Neither the stimulus therefore of heat nor of cold can force those of the exhausted skin to their proper action, for the former has already enfeebled, and the latter may paralyze the nearly exhausted vessels.

"It is no doubt true, that the severity of a British winter is oftentimes less felt at first by persons just returned from long residence in India, than by those who have always resided in Britain. It would be absurd to attribute this to superior vigour in the former. May not the following be the true explanation? That there are two kinds of insensibility to cold. The one resulting from hardiness, the consequence of frequent exposure in a vigorous constitution, by which the *whole* system becomes, through habit, insusceptible of feeling and suffering from cold. The other arising from exhaustion of that cutaneous sensibility, which urges a person in health (though not perhaps hardy) to guard by exercise, or by artificial means, against greater cold than the constitution is habituated to. Hence it is probable many persons on returning from India, are indifferent towards an extreme degree of cold, which is at the same time injuring them.

* Exposure, excesses, and miasmata, which last, though they may operate alone, are rendered far worse in their action when occurring with functions previously diseased.

"The restoration of these functions must be effected by soliciting the cutaneous vessels, for it is impossible to force them, to regain their healthy action,—I. By carefully avoiding the stimulus of extreme heat or cold. II. By lessening, if possible, those powers, which tend directly to check their action.

Properties of a restorative climate.

"I. To the end that extremes may be avoided, it is highly advisable that a mild and regular climate be visited in the summer, in order that by its gradual and regular approach a mild winter may be found salutary to functions partly renovated.

Barometric pressure — its effects on the skin.

"II. The great utility of lessening those powers, which, though natural in a healthy state, materially oppress the action of the enfeebled vessels, will be rendered manifest by a clear but brief inquiry into their nature and force. The chief power which moderates the perspiration in health, but must check it in a diseased state of the skin, is the pressure of the air. This great force, at the level of the sea, is nearly equal to fifteen pounds on every square inch of the skin, and its tendency to prevent exhalation from the surface may be judged of by the fact, that, if the whole atmospheric pressure were removed, the vessels of the skin would immediately give way, and all the animal fluids would evaporate away, leaving the shrivelled body drier than a mummy. Now, although an entire removal of pressure would, on many accounts, prove instantly fatal, yet it will be readily understood, that the other extreme of great pressure, though natural in health, may be too much for a feeble constitution and exhausted skin. Were not this reasoning sufficient to confirm the fact, experience would bring conviction of the truth of it. By a partial removal of this oppressing power, the skin is, as it were, solicited to resume a free action. Hence perhaps the exhilarating and free sensation, independently of coolness, enjoyed on ascending from low situations to a moderate height in all countries, commonly, but incorrectly, attributed to greater purity of the air. The other opponent force to the perspiratory action is moisture in the air. This prevents the action, not so much by pressure, as the former does, but by pre-occupying the interstices of the air, and thus resisting the evaporation. Moisture has much greater effect in obstructing the action of the skin, when the air is dense and heavy, as on the level surface of the earth, than when rarefied. For, since dense air can hold more water in solution than rare air, before it becomes damp (*i. e.* oversaturated), it must be far more loaded with moisture, than damp rarefied air.

Fogs on high elevations less oppressive than below.

"Hence fogs or mist in elevated situations produce much less oppression and deposit much less moisture, than in low situations; a fact which is unquestionably and necessarily true; either on the theory of the diminished *solvent* power of the air, owing to its rarefaction, or on that of the great rarity of the vapour, arising from the superincumbent column of vapour being much less in quantity than at the plain surface of the earth. The true *theory* perhaps includes a combination of the two. The *fact*, however, is certain. This absence of oppression also arises in great measure form the fact that damp rarefied air (though its interstices are occupied by as much vapour as the temperature will admit of) allows, owing to its lessened density, of a ready expansion of the perspired fluid from the *warm* surface.

"It is a fact of some importance, that the mists which must occasionally be met with in those situations, where the advantages of moderately rarefied air can be experienced, have not the oppressing effects of fogs in heavy air.

"It follows, therefore, from what has been above said, that the same measures required for obviating great atmospheric pressure, lessen also the effects arising from dampness; for the oppression arising from moisture, and that from atmospheric weight, are both diminished at the same time by elevation.

"The conclusion, which results from the inquiry into the properties of a climate, calculated for the removal of diseases in European constitutions, incurred by a residence in Hindostan, is plainly this—that a temperate and regular climate should be visited in a situation sufficiently elevated for the atmosphere to be rarefied, and its pressure moderated.

Advantage of Tropical over European mountain heights.

"The former of these requisites is met with in many parts of Europe, and were the distance from India less, these advantages of climate would in general be sufficient; but the latter requisite, which is of no small importance, cannot be possessed in Europe. In countries where the climate of the plains is temperate, that of mountains of adequate loftiness is very rigorous. The inclemency of mountainous heights in Europe altogether precludes the advantages which would arise from the levity of their atmosphere.

"It is not to be regretted that Europe does not present climes, possessed of all the requisite properties, for they are afforded at a small distance. In these mountainous districts are numerous spots possessing all the advantages in question.

"First,—As to climate. At altitudes between six thousand five hundred and seven thousand feet, climates will be met with approaching very nearly to that of the temperate parts of Europe. The temperature of these elevated situations possesses also the great advantage of being more equable than that of the plains, the annual variations being less. It may be admitted as established, with regard to the climate of mountains, that much less difference exists between the seasons than at the plain surface of the earth. This may be shown to be evident on various accounts, among which are the following:—The atmosphere, it is well known, does not derive its heat directly from the sun's rays, for very few of them are intercepted in their passage, by it—most reach the earth. Hence during the hot season the rays are accumulated on the plain surface of the earth, or in valleys; and from their concentration they keep the incumbent air at a forced temperature; and also are radiated and reflected to all contiguous bodies in great intensity. But in the cold weather, when the rays travel obliquely to the earth, many more are intercepted in their passage through the upper regions of the atmosphere, the greater part still however reaching the earth. From the obliquity and lessened intensity of the rays that fall upon the earth, far less accumulation of heat occurs beyond the Tropics at that season. Hence the reason of the great difference near the earth's surface between the seasons. On the other hand, on the summit and sides of mountains, little accumulation of heat takes place at any season. The sun's rays, falling on very inclined planes, have little intensity from their being spread over a great surface, and from many for the same reason being reflected off to the valleys. Lastly,—A very small portion of the earth's surface being occupied by lofty mountains, it is plain that the rays, which fall on them, can but little affect the general temperature of the widely extended mass of atmosphere of the same altitude which surrounds and is continually passing over them; and the *absolute* quantity of heat in the atmosphere being chiefly derived from the earth's surface, is not, at a distance from the surface,

Equability of climate on mountains.

liable to so great or so sudden variations. The permanent lowness in the temperature of the high regions of atmosphere has been well shown by Sir H. Davy to arise chiefly from the increase of *capacity* for heat, the consequence of rarefaction.

Remarkable equability of the Indian Hill climates.

"The difference between the summer and winter is less, as the distance from the plain surface of the earth increases. Hence at those heights, where the summer is far colder than that of neighbouring plains, the winter, though of course colder than below, is by no means cold in proportion. This statement, of which the above is the theory, will be proved by the following comparison of the extremes of last year (one of perhaps less variation than common) near London, and of the extreme temperature of this year at Kurnal (about a degree south of the hills), noticed in January by myself, and in July by a gentleman resident there, with the extreme of this year also at Kot Gurh in the hills (altitude 6660 feet), the hottest season being now passed, observed in January by Lieutenant Gerard and in June by myself.

1823—*near London.*	*Fahts. Scale.*
Lowest in January	4°
Highest in May	78
Extreme difference of the year	—74°
1824—*Kurnal.*	
Lowest (observed) in January	31
Highest in July	122
Extreme difference of the year	—91
1824—*Kot Gurh* (*altitude of* 6660 *feet*).	
Lowest in January	23
Highest in June	82
Extreme difference of the year	—59

"It is true the temperature of the air at Kot Gurh and similar elevations is at times above 82°, and it appears to have risen once last year to 89°, according to the tables of Lieut. Gerard. The same occurs at times in England, but the thermometer at the former elevation has not been noticed during several years below 22°, whereas in England it often falls below Zero of Fahts. scale; and it has been observed at Hurdwar (in the plains), a few miles north of Kurnal, at only 26°, giving to each place greater annual extremes than the above, which may therefore be considered a fair general comparison.

"The equality in temperature for a long period is very striking in this climate. For the space of a month the extreme *diurnal* change in the open air is often under 15 degrees, and often under 5 degrees for many consecutive days and nights. The air at these elevations has not only a temperature for many months very mild, and at all times more equable than that of the plains, but it also is very pure.

"From the universal declivity of the surface, all superfluous rain runs off to the valleys as it falls, whence it is quickly carried to the plains. The soil, lying on the rock, is dry; hence little evaporation takes place from the ground, and hence the air during rains is not, as in the plains, constantly saturated with watery exhalations. Hence also vegetation, though luxuriant, is not rank. There is no sudden destruction and putrefaction of vegetables from excess of moisture on the one hand, nor a rapid transition of their elements into revegetation by excess of heat on the other. During such hurried and incomplete vegetation of succulent weeds, many elements are perhaps lost* which assume in combination the forms of various gases. These, if inhaled in a concentrated state, prove fatal, and, indeed, under any circumstances, are highly injurious.

and purity of the air.

"Owing to the nature and declivity of the soil and other causes already mentioned, the air of these hills is never so far replete with moisture, and does not even in the rains, when occasionally misty, deposit such humidity on clothes and furniture as in the plains.† Neither is it ever exhausting from dryness. It is not at any time rendered arid from excess of heat, as during the hot season below.‡ In respect of climate, therefore, this atmosphere has every advantage: it is mild, equable both in its heat and moisture, and of unusual purity. In winter also, though at times keen and bracing, it will not prove cold in proportion to the temperature of the summer.

"Secondly,—The great superiority of this atmosphere is its levity and its diminished pressure. At these altitudes of six

* The nature of the climates in which miasmata are most abundantly generated, and of the vegetation from which they appear to arise, will, I think, authorize such an explanation. At all events, the truth of the preceding statement itself is unquestionable.

† ‡ These facts I have also ascertained by repeated hygrometric observations, sufficient to prove the truth of these statements.

At Simla, &c., barometric pressure reduced by one-fifth at least. The effect of this.

thousand five hundred or seven thousand feet, the weight of the superincumbent atmosphere is diminished by one-fifth at least. A weight of three pounds is removed from every square inch of the surface of the skin. It is then necessary to inquire into the effect of such an important change on the body.

"1. As to the functions of the skin. The beneficial effects of diminished pressure in their derangements I have already pointed out. In these situations, where one-fifth of the whole pressure from the surface of the body is removed, how suitable must a residence be to Indian invalids generally, for the derangements in question are common to all, injury or exhaustion of the skin being attendant on all the diseases of India! How desirable to an invalid must be the easy change from that climate, in which the functions of the skin and viscera, already weakened by the stimulus of excessive heat, are by its continuance suffering insuperable exhaustion under too great atmospheric pressure, to a climate, in which not only is all such stimulus removed, but pressure—the great opponent force to their action—moderated! In short, as it were from a state of compulsion to one of solicitation!

"2. The effect of diminished pressure on the organs and circulation. Upon a reduction of the external pressure, the solids, all of which are more or less elastic, except the bones, expand, the solids and liquids are less severely pressed against and into each other, and the circulation is freer. By these means internal parts, if formerly in a state of irritation, oppression, or congestion, are relieved. . . . ."

"For the removal therefore of derangements of the more important viscera, the peculiarities of this climate are especially adapted. By its temperate coolness it conducts off with sufficient quickness superfluous heat, so as to prevent accumulation and irritation; and its equability both in temperature and moisture guard against any sudden chilling or paralyzing effects. By its gradual and regular approach the cold season will, it may be presumed, have in most cases a bracing effect, giving tone to the cutaneous vessels, whereas, were it very rigorous and variable, as in Britain, it might have a contrary effect.

"The moderate rarity and levity of this atmosphere are especially favourable. By these states of the air encouraging a return of proper action in all the cutaneous functions, through their intimate sympathy, those of the viscera will be indirectly benefited; and by their inducing a free circulation in, and flow of the blood to superficial parts, the viscera will in a direct manner be relieved from its internal redundance and irritation.

Its effect on the *brain*.

"Next to these parts the brain is that most frequently injured; its sufferings indeed are generally complicated with theirs. In all cases of cerebral irritation or plethora, whether from fever, visceral disease, apoplexy, or the direct influence of the solar rays, as in a stroke of the sun, the same causes *generally* operate in India, viz., acute sympathy with the skin and viscera, and accumulation of heat. The connexion between these parts and the brain is so inseparable, that a climate, which is admirably adapted to the restoration of their functions, must on this account alone act very beneficially on the cerebral functions. Hence a climate mild, equable, and regular in its seasons is in all cases desirable for affections of the brain.

"The diminished pressure of this atmosphere, owing to the peculiar structure of the head, must add great additional efficacy to this climate in its affections. The brain being the only part contained within a firm covering of unalterable dimensions, an increase or diminution of atmospheric pressure on the head itself can have little or no direct effect on its contents; but on a removal of a considerable pressure from the rest of the body, a general expansion of the elastic solids must take place; their dimensions are increased, while the head remains unaltered. This increase of dimension in the body must partly be supplied by fluids, gravitating from the head, and urged downwards by the elasticity of its contents; and hence the quantity of fluid circulating in the brain is lessened.* This change,

* That a diminution of one-fifth of the atmospheric pressure must have considerable effect in lessening the determination of blood to the brain, may be judged of by the fact, that on a further removal of one and a half-fifth more (*i.e.* diminishing the weight of the air by one-half), even considerable suffering and severe headache is produced, and it is said that at greater heights blood oozes from the nose and ears. It may at first appear curious that nearly similar symptoms are induced by an opposite cause. By subjection to great and unaccustomed pressure, as in a diving-bell, headache and flowing of blood from the nose and ears is often produced. From this similarity of symptoms I have heard it urged as an objection to these elevated situations, that from diminished pressure a fulness in the head and its consequences are likely to ensue. Careful

though not mensurable from its being divided throughout the body, undoubtedly occurs, and must of necessity have an important effect in diminishing the fullness of the cerebral vessels, and therefore the oppression or irritation. Most of our efficacious remedies for these very numerous and frequent affections of the brain have this end in view. How advantageous then must that climate be, where natural causes gently but continually operate most favourably for their removal!

"In concluding this subject, it is of importance to observe, that in order to secure all the benefits of climate above specified, it is highly necessary the situation chosen for residence be not of less altitude than six thousand five hundred feet, as otherwise much of the benefit afforded by these climes will be lost. As it is very desirable the minds of all invalids should be impressed with the importance of this, that they may derive all the advantages of a temperate and rarefied atmosphere, I present the

reflection will soon evince the incorrectness of such a supposition. In the case of greatly increased pressure all the soft parts are somewhat diminished in volume, but not the head. Hence by the general compression more blood than natural is forced into the head, of which the necessary consequence is headache from plethora; also by the increase of blood in the head, and the irritation consequent upon it, the small vessels are distended till the weakest give way, and blood flows forth, as for instance, from the extreme vessels of the nose and ears, which are covered with very delicate membranes. On the other hand, when the pressure is *diminished*, the manifest inference is that the effects must be directly opposite; and this may be plainly shown thus:—at great altitudes the quantity of blood sent to the head is suddenly diminished, which together with its not being properly oxygenated (owing to imperfect respiration in such rarefied air) gives rise to severe *nervous* headache. Such headaches are often relieved *by laying the head low*, and thus favouring the flow of blood to the brain—a measure which would aggravate the headache from plethora; also on this great removal of pressure the most delicate extreme vessels (*viz.* those of the nose and ears) give way, and blood flows out, not from increased internal force, as above, arising from irritation and plethora in the brain, but from diminished external force. It is plain when vessels contain a fluid, the elasticity of the gases in which exceeds the strength of their coats, but is kept down by external pressure, that either by *increasing* sufficiently the *internal* force of the fluid, or *by lessening* the *external* force, the weakest of such vessels will give way, and the fluids be effused. I have been induced to enter into such a length, lest the symptoms attending imprudent visits to very extreme heights being misunderstood, the very salubrious climate at the moderate altitude of 7,000 feet should be suspected of increasing that irritation and fulness in the brain, which it is especially calculated to lessen.

following extremes of July this year, noticed at Sabathoo by J. Gerard, Esq., Surgeon, and at Simla by myself:—

Sabathoo, altitude 4,200 *feet.*		*Simla, altitude* 7,200 *feet.*
Highest, 78° to 89°	Extremes of temperature during July, 1824.	Highest, 61° to 74½°
Lowest, 65 to 78		Lowest, 56 to 65

"On the 24th of June the thermometer rose to 96° at Sabathoo, whereas it was not at that time above 81° at the highest at Simla. From this statement the superiority of the latter altitude, both as to mildness and equability, is sufficiently evident, and in regard to levity its atmosphere is greatly superior.

"If the preceding Dissertation has been conducted with correct and sufficient reasoning; if the nature of disease incurred by a residence in India has been justly considered; if the qualities which must render a climate well calculated for the restoration of invalids have been properly investigated; and lastly, if on careful examination the climate of many lofty situations in the Hill-Provinces has been shown to possess all the requisite qualities, sufficient has surely been exhibited to justify a hope that the knowledge of such truths becoming general, many invalids may hereafter be directed to this interesting country, where a most salubrious climate is afforded, in some properties unequalled, and accessible to all from its situation on the confines of Hindostan."

(F.—Page 164.)

Fiscal questions of immediate importance.

Though having little direct connexion with the main subject of this volume, the following papers relate to questions of especial importance and interest at the present time. The facts and arguments have all the force they had when first published—equally inviting attention now as then. To the fiscal and economical views the reader's attention is particularly requested. If they are sound, may it not be contended that if the Government is determined upon, or involved in, permanent settlements, it would be wise as well as perfectly equitable, in districts in which, from an increased expenditure purposed on its part, or from other causes, a rise in prices is to be expected, that the denomination of the contract should be modified—that estimating the revenue in maunds of wheat, &c., at the present low prices, the condition should be that the Government may claim the rent either in money at the fixed rate, or in the specified number of maunds of grain? When, through the effect of canals, railways, or an increased local expenditure, the price of produce rose greatly, as it often would to double its former amount, the Government, *without taking any larger share of the produce*, might then fairly claim a proportional money increase. If no such provision has yet been made, it would surely be well that the step should be taken now, when an advance of prices may be expected from the above causes in so many districts; since, though the claim might appear equitable without such provision, it could be made with a far better grace with it in possession, before the rise had commenced.

On the Resources and Industrial State of India. Extracted from the *Asiatic Journal* for October, 1835.*

"A former paper † on the subject of the natural resources of India closed with an intimation that an inquiry would be made into various departments of labour in that country, by which would be established the fact that little or none of the economy and ingenuity, the natives have credit for, is to be met with in the processes in use in their several arts.

State of agriculture in India.

"Agriculture, the widest and most important field of Indian labour, may be first subjected to such an inquiry as the limits of this paper will admit of, which will compel the writer to confine his observations to the chief processes of husbandry. The first of these is the preservation and renewal of the soil. It is well that the fertilising power of the climate is so great in India, as to cause land, the soil of which is wholly neglected, to yield crops which repay the labourer's toil. Such is the neglect of the people, that most lands do little more in reality than support the families connected with them; while vast tracts, solely upon this account, are out of cultivation; and of others, not the surface soil alone, but the land itself, is destroyed by rain, which, had the level of the land been preserved, might have been kept from acquiring destructive velocity, until conducted off by suitable channels.

* The following facts, arguments, and views have now, in 1858, whatever force they possessed in 1835. Time indeed will be found to have confirmed it.

† In which the proportion of the produce available and taken as rent, and the distribution of the population, were discussed, and in which it was shown that the Government rents could not in general much exceed 10 per cent. of the gross produce.

"The consequence of this neglect of preservative measures is everywhere manifested. In Upper India, all the lands are scoured; their alluvium is annually carried away by torrents, whose collective body forms the vast waters of the Ganges, in the rainy season loaded with the best riches of the country. Of these, enough are bestowed upon certain low lands in Bengal, in a deposit of excellent soil, to tell of the value of the far larger portion carried off to the ocean. Few, perhaps, who look upon that volume of turbid waters, reflect that they are rendered yellow by treasure, more valuable far than the gold of the richest stream; that, did they bring down to the sea instead, an annual tribute of the precious metals, exceeding all that is drawn yearly from the mines of Peru, its worth would be small in comparison with the spoils they are allowed to collect from Upper India by an infatuated people, who appear never to have possessed energy for resisting this, or any other species of plunder. It is not supposed, indeed, that all removal of the alluvium could be prevented; but it cannot be doubted that much of the land under cultivation might be protected by a more complete system of the field embankments already employed where the necessity is too urgent for them to be neglected. Easily as the embanking such lands might be effected, the people find the other occupations of husbandry too engrossing of their time to permit them to attend to this. At the same time the undertaking appears to be too expensive; and the cost of the work is always pleaded in excuse of the neglect of it. What does all this indicate, but some extensive mismanagement of labour, in a country where there are hands enough, if well employed, to carry into effect every work of improvement that the most enterprising nation could desire?

"Where the preservation of the soil is so generally neglected, it is not surprising that little attention is bestowed upon its renewal. Hence, the manuring of land is practised on so small a scale, and in so few places, that it can scarcely be said to exist. Refuse matters, which might form the basis of manure beds, are consumed as fuel; and no straw can be spared for the purpose by the half-starved cattle. The scanty supply of artificial food is one reason of this. Another cause is the multitude of the cattle, rendered necessary by an universal waste of

The renewal of the soil neglected.

their power, which has to be compensated for by numbers.* Under a powerful sun and an arid wind the soil of all the higher lands is either bound into an almost stony hardness, or reduced to loose sand, according as its aluminous or siliceous particles abound; whereas a mould, rich in the organic matter it is at present annually deprived of, would have the firm cohesion of its parts prevented in the one case, and its substance become retentive of moisture in the other.

Ploughing unknown in India.

"Ploughing does now express an operation upon the soil in England, which the Indian husbandman has no knowledge of. He knows not how multifarious and complete a work the parts of a plough properly constructed may be made to perform. His idea of ploughing embraces not the uplifting, inverting, and at the same time shivering throughout, of the soil, which the modern English plough so admirably performs. Small as is the depth, to which the native plough acts upon the soil, it fails of effecting, even upon that portion, a suitable division of the parts. Nor do the four ploughings, allowed before each sowing, suffice to prepare the land; not less than eight and often a dozen are practised, and the land remains ill-divided still. The land side of the pitiful furrow is as much broken by the plough as the other. The plough has no firm surface to re-act against, and cannot throw the soil over, nor effect that peculiar crushing of it which the English plough performs, and in default of which the Indian husbandman has to dodge down the loose clods upon his land, by repeatedly traversing it with his plough. It hence happens that the expense of ploughing in India, estimated in prices of the produce, is greater than that of ploughing in England; and it consumes much more than double the labour! So false is the economy of working with a rude instrument. It may well be termed expensive simplicity. The plough consists of too few parts to do the work, though they should have the best form given them; but they are formed apparently with no knowledge of the peculiar principles concerned. The English plough is not, indeed, an instrument suited to the feeble strength of the ill-fed cattle of India; but its form might be so modified, in the wrest and mould-board especially, as to render

* The ruminant ox, too, whose manure is of much less worth, is bred, chiefly on account of the needless roughness of the work in the field and on the road, instead of the horse species whose manure is so valuable.

it an invaluable acquisition to Indian agriculture. By diminishing the labour employed, it would diminish the consumption of the produce reserved to command this labour. More produce would then be available for rent, and the rent ought to be raised accordingly; but returned to the people in working their civilization. Great, in saving labour, as would be the direct benefit resulting from the introduction of a plough suited to the means of the people, there would be added a resulting benefit of no small amount, when, by bringing to the surface a deeper stratum, the powers of a double quantity of soil were commanded, and the crops rendered heavier and more certain. Thus, also, it is probable, the expenses of irrigation would be diminished. Less of the water diffused over the surface would be lost by evaporation, than at present. Absorbed by the earth of a deeper ploughing, it would be retained until drawn gradually upwards by the sun's rays; during which time it would nourish the plant as effectually as the larger quantity lying in the surface soil, so much of which is lost at present by exhalation, through the free action of the air and sun.

Irrigation, its state in Western India.

"Defectively as the important operation of ploughing is conducted in India, that of irrigation will be found still more defective. In Upper India the cost is such as must appear incredible to those who are uninformed on the subject. It will be found to range, in all parts of Hindostan watered by wells, from about 8*s.* to 1*l.* 10*s.* the acre per annum, according to local circumstances, and the nature of the crop. This, in a country where grain produce bears less than one-fourth of its price in England! Owing to the expense of the process many tracts of land cannot be watered, and consequently yield only one, and that the uncertain and coarse crop of the rainy season. Few lands are adequately supplied with water, which, in a tropical climate, in such a soil as that of India especially, appears to give unlimited fertility to the land. The writer will here take the opportunity of remarking that the expense of irrigating many of the best lands places in an absurd light the notion that one-third of the crop is, or can be, on an average, the amount yielded up for the government rent. There are vast tracts of the best land, in provinces where the settlements are not permanent, yielding two rupees per bigah of revenue, the expense of irrigating which is four rupees. If the former represented the value of one-third of the produce, the latter must be that of two-thirds. Thus, between the government and *one single operation of husbandry*, would be swallowed up the whole crop! The ploughing, already shown to be so expensive, would have to be performed for nothing; nothing would remain for seed-corn, or harrowing, for reaping, or threshing; and nothing for the support of the people during the rest of the year! But there are many other lands, the expense of irrigating which is not less than four times the rent, and in some it is eight times.

Cotton and other produce not irrigated.

"Connected with this process is a curious fact, pointing out the small local value of all the commercial plant of India, in comparison with that of the grain-crops of the country. The prices of indigo and cotton do not admit, in general, of their respective plants being watered. The process is too expensive to be borne by them. Hence, for the former, the low lands of Bengal are preferred, although the plant upon them is ever liable to be destroyed by inundation; and the latter is entrusted for its watering to the uncertain showers of the rainy season in the Upper Provinces.

Irrigation by wells; its cost.

"Of the various methods by which irrigation is practised in India, nearly all are attended with so great a waste of labour that the cultivation could not bear the expense were not the labourers habituated to the fewest wants of life. The method in most extensive use may be selected for exemplifying the truth of this. In the method alluded to, the power of bullocks is employed. Two bullocks and two men are occupied at one well or reservoir, and it will be found that upon an average they do not raise a greater quantity of water than 5000 pounds one foot high per minute. The bag it is raised in contains usually from 250 to 300 pounds, and is raised from a depth of from 30 to 50 feet in from two to three minutes. A pair of bullocks, such as are employed by the ryots, cannot work at this rate more than half the day. Now, the labour of one Englishman has been estimated so high as 6000 pounds raised one foot high per minute; allowing this to be too high, and that in general it cannot be rated higher than 5000 pounds raised one foot per minute, the man working only six hours, it does still appear that the work of the two bullocks and two men in India cannot be valued above that which an Englishman can perform when his labour is most advantageously applied. It would be absurd to estimate the power of a pair of the feeblest bullocks at less than that of three men; so that there is here a triple loss of power, to which is to be added the total loss of the power of the men employed with the bullocks, since their strength is not engaged in the work. Were not their wants as contracted as their ingenuity, the expense of labour here noticed would be attended with a consumption of a large part of the crop. Until the processes for raising water for irrigation shall be improved in India, a great improvement in the condition of the labourers cannot be hoped for. It already costs 8*d.* in India to raise 1000 cubic feet of water 30 feet high, which is prodigiously more expensive than the raising of water by steam power in England, and nearly as much so as it would prove were human labour employed on the work *at its present rate in England.*

"The reader will not be detained by a mechanical examination of the several methods in use in India. Any person, disposed to afford them such an examination, will find in most of them errors against right principles abundantly numerous to account for the defective result. There is one instrument, the general principle of which is perhaps the best that could be employed. The instrument alluded to is that which has been confounded with the Persian wheel, and in which the water is raised by an endless chain of buckets. But the invention has never been completed. Even in Holland and in the German mines, where it has been employed, the delivery of the water from the buckets does not appear to have been effected in the best manner. In India its action is impeded by construction so rude, as to deprive it of all the advantage it ought to have over the simpler methods, worse in their principle.

"Such is the state of the chief processes in Indian agriculture. An examination in detail of the minor operations, though for the most part equally faulty, is not requisite to establish a point sufficiently proved, that the oppression under which Indian agriculture really lies is a system of labour generally misapplied. The writer will presume that he need not occupy the reader's attention by an examination of the several mechanical and chemical arts of India. He has, on former occasions, treated the subject, and may now briefly remark, that in the whole circle of them he could hardly point out one in which labour is not greatly misapplied. What then is all this universal waste of labour but extravagance of the worst kind? The people of India are, indeed, to all appearance, a very parsimonious people. Theirs is extravagance without enjoyment. The luxurious man

Extravagance, as elsewhere, results in the poverty of the people.

wastes labour in the form of its products, but he has the enjoyment of these products. The native of India wastes labour without production. His terminal condition is no better than the former's, while his intermediate state as to enjoyment is worse. His is not, indeed, luxurious, but it is parsimonious extravagance. It is not a wasteful consumption of things produced, but of the labour which might produce them. What is true of each individual is true of the whole country. The things of wealth are not truly enjoyed; but the expense of them is incurred. The labour of the country is expended, but expended unproductively. That very system of labour throughout India, which wears so seductive an aspect of economy and simplicity, is in reality extravagantly wasteful of means, and is the main cause of the poverty of the people. General poverty is the natural result of such general extravagance, whether that extravagance be accompanied by enjoyment or not.

Greatness of the natural resources of India.

"From all that has been said flows evidence which renders unnecessary any detailed inquiry to establish the fact, that the natural resources of India are prodigiously great. Whence does it arise that such extravagance of means does not cause an utter impoverishment of the people, but from the boundless natural resources of the country, which not only supports such a system of extravagance, but yields them some funds with which to pay the revenue of the state?

What are the instruments for working improvements in India?

"The question now presents itself—By what means can a great work of improvement be wrought in the system of labour in India, of agricultural labour especially? The agency, it is by all agreed, must be European. The parties then are private individuals and the government. The writer believes that much might be done by gratuitous efforts on the part of the former, whether settlers or members of the service. If such efforts were general, natives would be found in many places willing to adopt improvements, the benefit of which had been made evident to them. Members of the service, if prepared for the work, and not readily disheartened by the apathy of the people, would find in it a highly gratifying and useful occupation for their leisure hours, and settlers in India might spare some, though in general less, time to the purpose. The current expectations of politicians appear to assign to these last the drawing forth the resources of India and the civilization of the people, not by gratuitous efforts but in the search of gain. By whichever means effected, the writer would rejoice to witness the success, and is of opinion that the utmost encouragement ought to be afforded to enterprizing settlers by the government; but he is unable, from any experience or opportunities of observation he has possessed (and they have not been small), to entertain the hope that capitalists, unassisted by the government, will find much gain from such undertakings in India.* Exorbitant profits, such as indigo once afforded, can alone counterbalance the losses inevitable, at all times and in all places, from the fraud and negligence of the people. The system of labour in India must undergo a wide improvement before the people will work productively as hired labourers, or before they will do work by contract without advances of money; and of such advances, a large part is almost invariably lost. The peculiar advantages possessed by Bengal, for the production of silk and indigo, make these, to a certain extent, an exception; but, in general, little gain is to be expected on the part of Europeans, from undertakings dependent upon field-labour in India, whether it be hired or working upon contract. In all such cases, the apparently low price of labour is a fictitious advantage, as almost every individual who has relied upon it has found to his cost. There are other difficulties also, scarcely less formidable, in the way of settlers in the interior of the country, which it is not the purpose of the writer here to touch upon.†

Individual settlers can effect little.

It has long become manifest to him, that the only party which can, with benefit to itself, undertake the great work of improving the agriculture and arts of India, and of facilitating the means of transport‡ throughout the country, is the Government. There are many persons not unwilling to admit that it would be the duty of the Government, if the funds were forthcoming, but who contend that it does not lie in the power of the Government to do any great work of improvement in India, owing to its straitened means; and others oppose as an objection the lavish expenditure said to attend all works constructed by a Government. In examining into the weight of these objections, the writer is led to ask a question which may imply an opinion apparently para-

In India the fit agent for improvement is the Government, as the commander of the rent, and increase.

Objections to this, and the answer to them.

* ‡ This anticipation is proved correct in the need of guarantees, for railways. Permanent works for irrigation on an extensive scale, may perhaps form an exception, and answer to shareholders without guarantees; but, *both for the people and the State they ought to be the property of the latter.*

† The author now does so, unreservedly, in the sequel.

doxical, but which he fears the event will prove correct; namely, whether it is possible for the Government of India to make any rapid accumulations of money through retrenchment, to however large an extent, in its expenses? In India, where the adjusting powers which might be supposed to operate in England do not exist, it is unintelligible how local revenue should fail to decline with local retrenchments, unless the funds arising from such retrenchments are returned to each district yielding them, in expenditure of some other kind, such as the construction of works of public utility. If the revenue were taken in kind, if the Government could make any use of the stores of grain, &c., then, indeed, these might annually be collected, whether stocked in granaries afterwards or lavished among its servants. The cultivator would in no way be concerned in the use made of revenue taken in kind. Whatever might be done with it, his ability to yield up an equal quantity next year would remain the same. But it is not *produce* that the Government will receive. The cultivator has another duty, besides the raising of the produce, to perform; he has to sell it; and to whom can he sell it but to the consumers of the rent? The produce in question is the rent, and they who consume it must be consumers of the rent. To say that it is paid for by any other persons, is to imagine it at once to be rent and not rent: it is to raise up an imaginary class of customers who have no existence. The customers who buy the rent-produce (or, which is the same thing, employ those who consume it) are all the persons who receive the means from the Government. The same money circulates annually as the token of the connexion between the three parties—the Government, the parties it employs, and the landholders. If the Government diminish its expenditure among those it employs, these again have less to expend, directly or indirectly, among the landholders. The price of produce then must fall. The same quantity of rent-produce brings less money, and less rent can be paid to the Government.

Government savings can only be realized by previous expenditure on improvements.

"This seems to be the inevitable consequence in India of diminished expenditure. It is true, that could the production of *exportable* produce be increased at the same time, and the promised surplus from retrenchments be converted into this produce and exported, the revenue might perhaps be kept up; for this would in reality be no money-retrenchment, but merely a transfer of outlay from the payment of one kind of labourers, the servants of the state, to another kind, those preparing produce for exportation. But the remittances in produce cannot be so rapidly increased, and if they were, the prices of produce would for a time fall so much in Europe as to check purchases, and production, in India. Again: money carried away from a distant province to pay off a debt at the presidency, does not return to purchase produce in the district in the same way that most of that from local salaries and wages does. The former has to make a long and circuitous route, during which it becomes greatly diminished before it can, if ever, return to the district which yielded it. The money is long in coming back to the produce of which it is the token; and, as will presently be shown, the produce in India cannot, instead, follow the token so far. In any given district, then, in which expenditure is greatly lessened, it appears inevitable that the revenue must fall off; any considerable diminution of local expenditure in India appears to amount, while the means of transportation are so bad, to a virtual abandonment of part of the revenue of the district.

Local works costless to a government in India.

"The object, then, of the writer is to show, that, to whatever extent the revenues of any district shall have declined, consequent to the diminution of expenditure in it,* to just such an extent, whether great or small, might outlay have been made on works of public benefit, in every such district, at no cost to the government; what might be laid out thus, being otherwise lost by a fall of revenue. The government, by endeavouring to carry away its savings, being no richer than if it had liberally laid out with one hand what, in its wisdom, it had saved by the other.

"It would appear, that a public debt in India can only be paid off very gradually in the present state of the country, however great may be the promised surplus from retrenchments. It may be possible, indeed, to do it more rapidly, but it will cause a serious decline in the revenue; for the revenue if kept up, will press much more heavily on the people. If any one doubts this, let him explain how it is possible to carry away

* It is remarkable to how great an extent the revenue of Bundelkund, and some other districts, falls short of what it was in ancient times; manifestly, the author would say, from this very cause.

the revenue-money of a district without causing a fall of prices in the district, and with it a fall in the value of the revenue-produce. It is no other than an aggravation of the evil, which in a former paper was shown to occasion so scanty returns of revenue from certain districts. The coining of money in the neighbourhood would avail nothing; it would not at all enable the landholders to command money, when the real purchasers of the produce were transferred elsewhere. Whithersoever the revenue-money is carried, thither must the produce, of which it is the token, follow it; or if it goes so far, that the latter cannot follow it, the former will henceforth, like a shadow, cease. The mind may be so confused by contemplating the dealings of the different industrious classes with each other, and with the raisers of produce, as to lose sight of this connexion; but the connexion nevertheless will remain the same, and with a result disappointing to any statesman who should lose sight of it.

The effect of carrying away from a district its rent.

"The importance of not overlooking the thing signified, when employing its sign,—of not forgetting the revenue-produce, when dealing about the revenue-money, is immense, where, as in India, so much of the revenue of a province is sometimes carried out of it.* Thus, it is true, that roads can hardly be so bad as materially to affect the expense of carrying money or bills out of a district. A hundred well-made money-carts require, at the most, 200 pair of oxen, which will convey away fifty lacs of rupees at no great expense; and by the

* In here speaking of money, as the *sign* of the rent-produce, the writer will not, he hopes, be suspected of falling into the exploded error of supposing that money is of no other worth than as a sign and measure of value. Inasmuch as a rupee may be supposed to have cost as much of labour and capital (*i.e.* reserved labour) to produce it, as a rupee's worth of grain; and as it will readily command as much of any commodity as the latter, the two are of equal worth, of course. In the present question, however, we are not concerned with the intrinsic value of the money, which might be great or small. It might have a fictitious value, as paper-money. The present business of the writer is to remind the reader, that money, in the case in question, is only the representative, or, sign of the rent; for what the land yields annually is produce, not money. The money (though it may be changed for other money) cannot be renewed. It must circulate annually between the parties concerned, and therefore must be kept, as near as possible, to the source of the produce; every step it recedes from the source being attended with loss to the government, *in exact proportion to the difficulty with which the produce is conveyed after it.*

statesman who shall mistake the *token* for the *thing*, it may therefore be thought of little consequence to the government that the province is without roads, or that what are called its roads are its least passable parts; but he who shall view his object through a correct statistical eye-piece, will see far off innumerable hackeries and bullocks, with an army of drivers, creeping over all parts of the province, and striving to follow the money, with thousands of tons of produce, over mechanical obstacles almost insuperable. He will see fifty carts, with their drivers and cattle, detained a week by the side of a brook, until it shall subside so as to be fordable; others, even in the best season, delayed by sloughs. He will cast his sight over those parts of the province where wheeled vehicles cannot move. There he will see droves of bullocks, loaded with grain, employing often a man a-piece to urge them on their weary way. He will know that *this* is the real movement of the revenue out of the district: that the other—that of the money—was merely the sign of this movement. Thus fixing his sight, not on the *sign*, but on the *thing signified*, he will perceive that the party to whom the revenue belongs, and who is pleased to carry it away from the province, is the one of all others whose interests are most affected by this excessive difficulty in the transportation of the produce * He will not doubt that the quantity annually consumed in this laborious removal of the remainder, would, being saved by a well-made canal,† yield, though there should be no toll upon it, an usurious interest on the capital laid out; for he would anticipate with confidence an improvement in the resources of the province, which would bring the poorest up to the present condition of the richest part of it. On the other hand, he will know that if, after the produce has followed its token as far as it can over the present obstacles, an attempt is made to carry this token still further, the connexion between the two will give way; the token may be forced away to the presidency, this year, instead of being expended in the neighbouring province; but the produce cannot follow it. Whatever revenue

The party most interested in facilitating means of transport.

* At the very time this paper was in manuscript in Calcutta, in 1834, one of the ablest acting governors Bengal has possessed, remarked in the author's hearing that the Government had little interest in roads. "Roads!" he said, "what has the Government to do with roads? If the people want roads let them make them."

† Or tramway, or perhaps even railway.

had not been carried away is all that it will fetch; and this, or little more, will, in time, be all the revenue forthcoming. From all such observations, it will become plain to him, that *the remittance of revenue to a distance from its source ought to be deferred until the means for the transportation of produce are complete.*

Importance of canals.

In the first instance, a large canal, running the whole length of the Dooab,* and others branching off to the verge of the Jumna, opposite Agra and Delhi, might be made by the revenue saved by retrenchments, but in danger of being swamped by economy; so that these canals might, in reality, cost perhaps nothing. The same might be said of a canal through Rohilkund, and one through Bundelkund. The difficulties, excessive delay, and danger, of the navigation of the rivers above Allahabad, are so great, that it would be well if the traffic could all be transferred to canals. It might not be advisable to attempt to carry the navigation of canals into such impetuous and shifting rivers as those of India; and this would be of no moment, as, in any case, boats of a different form would be required for the navigation of canals from those upon the rivers; and the canals might terminate in basins on the verge of the rivers, in suitable places; so that the canal and river-boats might have their contents removed readily from one to the other. No other connexion with rivers would be needed, than channels enough to insure the supply of water at the heads of the canals, and outlets for superfluous water in their course. The former should proceed from such parts of rivers as maintained a permanent course, and should be cut through a bank naturally hard and durable. The latter, for some distance from the canals, it would be requisite to make of masonry, and with gently-inclined shoots. It is by quickly-running water only, that land in India is so rapidly cut into ravines. By allowing it nowhere in a canal a current of more than a mile or a mile and a half an hour, and guarding the channel of each waste-way as above, there is no part of the plain country of India, not liable to inundation, through which canals might not be carried with ordinary judgment.

Roads.

"Next to canals, roads are most needed in India. Short, well-made roads, connecting canals with the country on either side, would confer the benefit of the former to the whole of the pro-

* Projected and completed now with great ability by Sir Proby Cautley, and with these anticipated results.

vinces they traversed. But land-carriage, of the best kind, from great distances, is so expensive for bulky produce, of which the chief wealth of the country is composed, and roads are made with so great difficulty in India, and require such incessant repair, that canals ought to be preferred wherever it is possible to make them, though at any apparently heavy expense. At the same time, where canals cannot be more advantageously used, no obstacles ought to be allowed to stand in the way of the construction of roads.

Canals jointly for irrigation and navigation.

"Digging and embanking are among the few operations in which the cheapness of Indian labour does manifest itself. The quantity of labour misapplied every season in the process of irrigation in the Dooab alone would suffice to dig from one end to the other of that province a canal of the largest size. The penning-up of the water of canals, by means of locks every few miles, according to the descent of the country, which would be necessary for navigation, would form heads elevated above each fall of the country, from which water might be drawn off, over the lands around, so as to irrigate them spontaneously, with the trifling aid of water-courses. The dispensing with the necessity of raising the water at all would add greatly to the value of all the lands so benefited. The quantity required in the more arid parts of the country cannot be raised a few feet at a less expense than the whole rent of any but lands of the first quality. Such canals could only afford water, of course, to the country within two or three miles of the banks; but this would be an extensive and greatly enriched tract throughout their course. Lands more distant from canals might, in some cases of late crops, be watered by means of windmills, upon wells and tanks; and on the banks of the great rivers, in many places, the force of the stream might, with the utmost advantage, be employed to raise water out of the river, by acting upon floating mills. Upon a sufficient number of mills of each sort being set up by the government, to serve as models for the people around, and to demonstrate to them the advantage to be expected from their use, the landholders, upon being satisfied that they would answer might easily be induced to have recourse to them, provided the construction of them were sufficiently simple, and a readiness to instruct the people in the making of them manifested by the government. They even express the greatest readiness to pay the price of any instruments made for them which should answer; and this is the utmost enterprize that can be expected of a native landholder. There are numerous other improvements in the agriculture and arts of the country, which the government might thus be instrumental in introducing, and which would become productive of incalculable benefit, not less to the government than to the people.

Further objections answered.

"With regard to the objection, that funds are always wasted in works conducted by a government; the writer may observe, that this is by no means true, where a government can employ superintending officers of the first ability, and of high principle, such as that of India has at command from other departments, and where, in many cases, establishments and materials, not otherwise employed, would be available. But the objection itself is not sound, where the government is the only party who could recover funds so laid out for the good of a province, by raising the taxation, as the money became diffused. There is no province which could not easily supply the labourers, and the produce for their support. As the government created a demand for the produce, its price would rise, and more would be raised to meet the demand; and these together would create a rise in the revenue of the district, just in the same manner as land around one of the larger stations, though by nature no better, is made to yield much more produce, and can be assessed at double, often quadruple, the rate it can bear in the heart of the country. Every district contains abundant means for such works, if the people were but judiciously distributed. Owing to the revenue-produce having to be conveyed out of a district in which there are neither roads nor canals, but trenches, which employed as roads would often answer almost as well as canals, the depreciation of produce is so great, that even the best lands are ill-cultivated. In many places, as already noticed, produce can only be carried on the backs of bullocks, and by way of employment, there will be a man to each. Oftentimes, men are employed in work which ought to be performed by cattle; and any one acquainted with the state of such districts must know that, crowded together for want of employment, no small portion of the people sit at the homes of their friends half the year, doing little or nothing. With such abundant means as are now misemployed in each district, any works might be executed;

but they never will spontaneously by a people so improvident and wanting in energy. What in England were best done by joint-stock associations, in India, if done at all, must be executed by the government. Where the government has the power of recovering the sums it expends in a district by raising the taxation afterwards, where these sums could be made with certainty to flow back into the public treasury, the government would merely have to act the part of a beneficent agent, directing the people towards the most advantageous employment of their labour. Any person who doubts whether the funds expended could be made to return, can have little insight into the causes of the present impoverishment of the people, and into the natural resources of the country.

Permanent revenue settlements, a hindrance to improvement.

"Where the land-revenue has been permanently settled, the means of working the good of the people are more limited, unless, indeed, they be rightly taxed for the express purpose of carrying into execution works of benefit to themselves. A permanent revenue-settlement in Upper India would be a measure deeply to be regretted.* Any improvements in the condition of the landholders of Bengal, in general, is to be traced, not to the settlement of the revenue, but to the stimulus of commercial advances to a prodigious amount.† By a permanent revenue settlement, a gratuitous sacrifice, with no substantial benefit to the people, is made of the resources at the command of the government, for working out the problem of Indian improvement within any reasonable period. Instead of stimulating them to improve their husbandry, it cannot fail of an opposite effect upon a people of the native temperament. But its worst feature is, that it involves in it the yielding up of the only, and the great, instrument in the hands of the government, by which it could work that change in the distribution and productiveness of agricultural labour in India, which must be effected before the people can make any great advancement towards a state of prosperity, and our tenure of the country can rest upon any secure foundation. Among a people of so little general enterprize as the natives of India, the greater part of the public revenue ought to be, as indeed it is, drawn directly from

* Such is still the Author's conviction, though that measure has been now carried into effect.

† Owing to its peculiar advantages in the growth of indigo.

the soil; neither the transfer of taxation from the land to the products of commerce and manufacturing industry, as by some urgently recommended, nor a diminution of taxation, as by others contended for, would afford any substantial relief to the people now, supposing either were practicable; and ultimately they would rather depress their condition, by lessening the expenditure of the government. The current opinion, that the natives of India are too obstinately prejudiced in favour of their ancient habits; to alter them if required, is by no means correct. Their prejudices (their religious superstitions excepted) do not greatly exceed those of any other ignorant people. With them it is more indifference than obstinacy. They are habituated to seek comfort in inaction, and to confine their wants to the primary necessaries of life. Hence a general want of enterprize prevails. So far from being an obstinate, they are a remarkably tractable people. It is upon this valuable quality in their character the writer would ground the hope of their labour being rendered more productive. *By acting upon the ready tractability of the natives* measures of improvement must first be brought about. Good-will, on their part, and a sense of dependence on the government, would certainly follow upon the success of such measures being made manifest to them. Such a policy as has been recommended, the writer believes, could not fail, in time, of adding prodigiously to the revenues of the state, and at the same time to the comfort of the people.

The great and self-imposed responsibilities of Britain!

"In her Eastern conquests, Britain has assumed, unasked, the position and responsibilities of the political guardianship of India, the duties of which, being those of highly-civilized rulers towards a half-civilized peopled, are far more extensive than the functions of any European government. Although the word "government" may be the only term applicable to the supreme power in each case, it must not be supposed that, by employing the same term, the greater moral responsibilities of that of India can be escaped. The interests of the government, as well as of the people, do indeed call for the commencement of a system of suitable interference and paternal guidance, on its part, in which no measures need be had recourse to at all offensive to the people. On the contrary, the very measures suited to the objects in view would have an air of benevolence on the part of the government, at present incredible by the people, and would by degrees transform a fearful disaffection in the hearts of millions into a self-interested and loyal attachment to the government, desirable for the security and happiness of all! As the agriculture of the country became relieved of a large part of the crowd resting upon it, a portion should receive instruction in the various useful arts of life, while a portion of them, and that not a small one, together with their sustenance (no longer needing their aid in raising it), might then, most justly, be claimed by a government so beneficent, as the means of strengthening its arm in the country, and of supplying produce for paying its charges without. With their fertility increased, the heaviest of the expenses of cultivation reduced, and the readiest means afforded for the exportation of their produce, the rent of the distant provinces of the country might, after leaving to the landholders half of the benefits, be raised to an amount almost incredible at present. What are now among the poorest parts of the country, would become the richest, and could not fail of yielding many times the rent now obtained from them.

"The period of retrenchment in the public expenses is remarkably favourable for commencing great works, especially such as will facilitate the transportation of produce; for, in order to recover the funds expended, the taxation need not then be raised; since what would have been lost by the revenue declining from retrenchment, without other local expenditure, is saved by expenditure on such works, which is sure to keep the revenue up to its full standard. Such appears to be the legitimate purpose to which to devote, *at present*, funds resulting from retrenchments. To employ them towards liquidating the debt of India, payable at a vast distance from the source of much of them, and thus to divert them from the prior object of enabling the produce of the provinces to follow its money-representative, and of increasing the quantity of produce, does not appear expedient. It is like attempting with seed-corn to satisfy a demand, which would prove trifling after the harvest.

"It is to be feared that, at present, no considerable part of the revenues of India is likely to be devoted to the purposes recommended. So long, however, as the government shall not again, like an Indian devotee, tie its own hands up with a permanent settlement in Western India,* the means will still remain in its

* That settlement has been made in several districts. It is to be hoped it will not be extended throughout India.

power for commencing that movement, to which alone we can look for any advancement of the people towards a state of prosperity, and any increase in the revenues of the government:—not a movement, indeed, of armies for the territorial enlargement of British India, but of mind for the enlargement of her resources:—not an increase of superficies, but of solidity:—not an acquisition of more land, but a deeper cultivation of that we possess; a drawing of more produce from the surface of India and more minerals from its bowels:—not a heaping of people upon people, but a judicious distribution of those we have; a transfer of millions at present jammed in the agrarian crowd to all other pursuits of civilized men; a portion of them to the service of the state."

The Laws of Economical Science in Europe inapplicable to the Mental Constitution, Habits, and Tastes of the People of India.

"The responsibility of a Statesman is not requisite for inducing any reflecting person, at the present moment, to contemplate the amount of good, which has been wrought in India, under the Government granted her by the late Charter; and the prospects she has of being able to meet the increased demands upon her by the provisions of the new.

Slow progress of useful knowledge in India.

"He is no sincere friend of the government of India who, founding his remarks upon former days, would tender to it, either a retrospective flattery, or prospective hopes. He must be a bold Statesman who could affirm that India has made an advancement in useful knowledge, and temporal prosperity, at all commensurate with England's moral and pecuniary obligations, and ability to assist her. And he an ingenious one, indeed, whose art has such attenuative power as, with the handful of literary spangles about the metropolis, of India and the sister Presidencies, to gild over the mass of leaden torpor and ignorance, which lies, at this moment, as heavy over the whole country as ever.

"The benefits, reciprocating between Great Britain and India, fall very far short of their mutual obligations.

"The former, having assumed the position and responsibilities of a political guardian to the latter, was bound to have afforded her a course of instruction, such as would, at the least, have whispered of the lofty attainments of her tutor. And in return for such a connexion, India might have been enabled to purchase, annually, from Britain, an amount of manufactures fourfold that at present imported; and to afford, without distress to her people, sufficiently rewarded employment, for the thousands of Englishmen, whose services the state must command for effecting the vast improvements in its power.

"The system of non-interference with the pursuits of the people, so rigidly maintained hitherto, has been attended on their part by as rigid a refraining from all improvement; and the abundant examples afforded them of the advantages of civilization, have been almost as unproductive of good.

"It was to be expected, that politicians, who are disciples in the modern school of economists, and students of the *motives* now actuating men in Europe, in the concerns of life, should calculate upon the presence of the same *motives* in India; and expect that people to make advancement in civilization, and of consequence in prosperity, through the influence of example and opportunity alone. It was to be expected, that they should pronounce 'a man's self-interest'—'his emulation'—'his desire of improving his condition'—'his love of enjoyment'—'his wants'—'tastes,' in short, his natural desire of attaining to the 'greatest happiness,' to be imperious motives, which must force the natives to burst the ties of prejudice, and, rising from their apathy, to press forward to a state of reasonable existence; upon their being afforded evidence, exemplifying the vast increase of moral and domestic happiness, which civilization brings forth to the nations wooing her.

Civilized example of little effect.

"It was to be expected that many also in India would be fascinated by doctrines promising so much at so little cost—by the satisfactory notion, that, in proportion as they multiplied their own enjoyments, they were doing good by the force of their comfortable example; and that others should suppose, that, by bringing the products of the industry of England into the market of India, they would excite new tastes and a desire of improvement among the natives, acquiring wealth themselves the while.

"If it shall be proved that all these hopes are fallacious, being founded on an erroneous estimate of the native character, let not the reader doubt that many, whose duties have led them to a daily intercourse with natives for twenty years, labour under this ignorance; nor let surprise at this excite him to proportionate censure, until a reasonable allowance has been made for the difficulty they experience in drawing aside the veil which native duplicity unremittingly places, and reduplicates around men in office. Truths, frankly admitted to a private individual, the utmost shrewdness on the part of the former often fails to discover. With every allowance, however, on this account, there is no small ignorance of the native character still to be accounted for, and to be regretted.

"Whether it has resulted from principle, from a persuasion founded as above, or from neglect, it must be admitted that, while the people of England have been subjected to legislative interference which, in various ways, controlled or modified, not their pursuits only, but their social, domestic and personal habits even—the people of India have been hitherto unincumbered by any interference; excepting some very cautious interference in the way of education, and any amount requisite for fiscal and political purposes.

The state of India in general stationary.

"With the exception of the scanty fruits of the very limited interference in the way of education afforded them, the natives of India have assuredly undergone in no one respect any the least improvement. The little that has been effected has resulted from what little interference has been practised towards them. The general impression of the natives, and indeed of many observant Europeans, appears to be, that the extension of the British Rule over the Provinces, and especially of its system of judicature, has induced, not only no moral improvement in the people, but even that some demoralization has resulted from it. It is conceded, that the natives in general are sorry judges in questions of morality, and that any demoralization is questionable, since the diminution of a non-entity is impossible. But no candid person, qualified to form a judgment, will affirm, that any moral improvement is traceable among the people of India generally, beyond the limits of the influence of a few Missionaries. In their habits, the writer will affirm there is none whatever—neither in their tastes. In their arts, it has been already shown they are rather retrograding than otherwise.

"The generalizing spirit of modern philosophy,—of that portion especially which has been termed Political Economy, and honoured by the title of a Science,—has tended in no small degree to involve India's question in perplexity. So fascinating prove its doctrines, so imperative its laws, as to close the sight of many a politician to the sad realities of India, to the mountains of facts opposed to them; from which turning aside, he builds his castle on a molehill; upon the case of the few hundreds in Calcutta whose "prejudices are plainly giving way" after all the "motives" of the economist, and all the example of Europeans ought to have been working good for a century. Do such persons forget, that in every large community there may be expected some, from a spirit of singularity, some from a love of novelty, and some few from superior intelligence, ready to desert the customs of the multitude? And is it upon this small number, not yet filled up to the proportion in other countries, they rest their hopes that, without any other appliances, the whole mass will, within any period of human calculation, be aroused from their torpor, and occupy themselves in the rational pursuits of intelligent men? Let not the writer be accused of undervaluing the study of the most interesting, and important—of any, but divine subjects—those treated of in 'Political Economy.' He must be allowed, however, to maintain the opinion, that, in the present state of our knowledge, it would be well to designate it the *study*, rather than the *science* of Political Economy. If it be called a science, it must be given *laws;* and to the mind of every statesman the term *law* conveys the impression of all that is absolute and irresistible; whereas the very foundations upon which this study is grounded are ever liable to change, even in the same land; and they differ in every differing soil.

Economical laws of Europe inapplicable to India.

"In the same people and climate the motives for human action upon which this study is built, are so liable to change, that what may be predicated of one generation of men, often cannot of another. But of countries, climates, and people, differing from each other in a degree as vast as is the geographical distance of India, from England, little can be affirmed in common.

"It is very possible to show that, what to an Englishman would be a motive for exertion, is a motive to the Indian for

Contrast between English

and Indian temperament. sleeping—that, what the former would propose as an interesting amusement for the leisure of the day, is put off by the latter as a burdensome duty to an indefinite 'to-morrow,'—that, what the former values as the first of earthly comforts, worthy of soul-wearying efforts for their attainment, are viewed by the latter with a calm indifference, as undeserving of a thought—that while 'to better his condition' is an ever powerful motive to an Englishman, infatuating hundreds, for a visionary prospect, into entering on a life of excitement and disease, while it is inducing hundreds to traverse the world for wealth—wealth is very rarely sought by the native with the ultimate object of improving his condition.

"The following picture of the family of a Hindoo, whose industry and wealth give him a high place of usefulness in the native community, may be taken as a very fair standard for comparing the habit of industry, wants, tastes, desire of improvement, &c., of the two nations; or the motives which determine man to produce and enjoy wealth in England and India.

"A Hindoo, whose income is on the advance, does, at the most, add a little ghee to his meal of pease, and change his body-dress for one of finer texture. As far as his means permit, he supports even distant relations; sometimes allowing his dependents to increase to a large number; unless the prospect of wealth and of its security tempt him to hoard.

Native hospitality.

"Let full justice be done to a remnant of the best feelings of Patriarchal times, when every member had a claim on his tribe—feelings affording a moral lesson to the increasing pride and selfishness of domestic society in England. Upon an inquiry, however, into the motives in operation, the truth will afford some explanation of this paradox in the morality of the two nations.

Its causes.

"The Native has a far less personal use for his money than an Englishman, beyond a very humble subsistence. Hence his indifference, if a servant, at a threatened discharge. Hence also the difficulty of persuading him to leave his own neighbourhood. It is on this account that recruiting in the Native Regular Army is attended with difficulty, where, as in the Company's territory, the people can obtain the means of subsistence at home; while the applicants for service in the Provincial

Corps often greatly exceed the vacancies; although the pay and respectability of the former are much superior. A native, whose income can do more than sustain him in his accustomed style, has little motive for withholding support from connexions, for whom he can feel but little attachment. With his increasing means the number of idlers among his relatives increases. He will often allow an able-bodied fellow to hang upon him for months; a man, for whom his affection is in reality so slight, that, for an inducement of the smallest scale, he would, too often, alas, be guilty of his death! Frequently, though his desire to hoard is great, he is alone prevented by fear, lest his wealth, exciting their cupidity, he should be poisoned by these very relations. So indifferent is he about 'improving his condition,' that, instead of expending his gains as he acquires them, for this purpose, he supports the very parties from whom he is sometimes in fear of his life; and the life of any of whom, excepting perhaps his own child, he would sacrifice for a trifle. The whole tribe lives together, with a *lota*,* *kuttora*, *dhotee*, and *half a seer of atta* a-piece, but without a thought. This is no rare case; it is most common. It is the case of most natives of substance who are not hoarders.

"Where the parties are not so lawless, and the prospect of hoarding is greater, as in the case of Sepoys and in towns, the only *strong motive* of the native for the acquirement of money has its play.

"The steady, persevering industry of the Shroff, Bunniah, and Mahajun, may then be observed. But its fruits can scarcely be perceived, except perhaps in the *suwarree*,†—in a gay *palkee*, with a small retinue of *chobdars*,‡ for show and protection. Their wealth is acquired to be hoarded, until accumulated to an amount corresponding with their ambition.

Wealth not acquired for personal enjoyment.

"A portion is then squandered in a marriage or other ceremony, rupees being thrown in thousands to the populace indiscriminately, which the Englishman would have long since thrown into circulation among the industrious of the community, while he added their products to the comfort of his family, but which the hoarder had no reasonable way of employing. The

* A brass pot, and dish, a body cloth, and a pound of meal.

† Equipage.

‡ Club-bearers.

rest of his wealth, if not left to a family, is equally unproductive; immured, first for years in a chest, and then for ever in a ghat or temple—where, irreclaimable for any purpose of adequate use, it serves only to gratify the hoarder's religious ambition. Such is the condition in mind and body of the superior orders of the whole Hindoo population, even in Calcutta itself; where the exception, of not one in the hundred, but marks the general rule. A relaxation of prejudices, and a modification of customs is to be observed in a number just sufficient to encourage the philanthropic statesman to the utmost exertion. They fail in their compliment to the judgment, taste, and readiness to improve, in this people, who speak with admiration of certain natives of respectability having availed themselves, at last, of the opportunities afforded by European enterprize, and begun to purchase some of the instruments of comfort, invariably required by gentlemen in civilized life. The writer can only find cause for unceasing surprise, that a people, of intellectual powers, equal to those of the generality of mankind, should be so far behind all other people in appreciating the excellence of all the products of English skill, which any intelligent savage, even, would value and desire.

Errors respecting the demand for British manufactures.

"So erroneous have been the opinions circulated regarding the native character, and so illusive the reliance on 'The general laws of human action;' 'The universal desire of man to improve his condition;' 'His desire of enjoyment,' &c. &c., as to lead to the exportation to India of vast quantities of the products of civilized labour, in the form of prepared metals and manufactures, with the confident hope, that the natives would purchase them readily. The result proved that, with the exception of cotton goods, sheet copper, and some iron and zinc, no demand worthy of notice could be excited even by sales at a ruinous discount on prime cost. Nor have twenty years' persevering enterprize, on the part of English merchants, established any satisfactory demand of other manufactures; nothing amounting to one-tenth part of what such a population ought readily to take. The extent to which the delusions prevailed, will be proved by a reference to the speeches of some of the leading members of the trading community of England, at public meetings in London, and some of the commercial towns. Before the Charter of 1814, one person is found to hold out an unlimited demand for glass, window-glass especially; as soon as the obstacles to its introduction were removed. About ten years after, a city politician at a London meeting, exhorted his fellow dealers not to contract their trading in blankets, for that the demand, *as soon as the barriers were thrown down, and British goods could find their way into the heart of India*, would no doubt become enormous, 'for,' said he, 'if we allow only one of the cheapest 16-shilling blankets a-piece for each adult in India, the demand will exceed our utmost efforts of supply.'

"So long has this delusion lasted, against the inflexible evidence of glutted and falling markets, that, at the approach of the next Charter, Mr. Felkin of Nottingham addressed all persons interested in the *bobbin net* trade in these words: 'I would here observe that as no one can say *bobbin net* may not, in the event of this monopoly (The East India Company's) ceasing to stand in the way of its free export and sale, be generally adopted in India, and China, so it is a matter of easy demonstration, that if only every woman at the head of every family in India (saying nothing of China) were to use but one square of bobbin net a year, the whole of the existing machinery of the trade, full-handed, and worked eighteen hours a day, would scarcely produce a supply sufficient for that market.'

"Again at the renewal of the last Charter in 1853, and up to the present hour, many like anticipations have been expressed.

"The above are selected, as the opinions of men, influential in their respective lines of business, while many similar might be selected, were it necessary, in proof of the extent to which misconception on such important questions prevails in the minds of the people of England. Did not such opinions foster a lamentable delusion, and lead to the extension of machinery, under the vain prospect of a demand, which will never *spontaneously* arise on the part of *that* people, they would be truly ludicrous to those who have been eye-witnesses of the habits and condition of the natives. Who but must smile at imagining one of these many Hindoo mothers of families—her sable neck adorned with a flowing collar of English bobbin net; and her head with a basket of recent cow-dung to be kneaded into fire-cakes with fingers which our glovers of Woodstock would protect with their softest kid-skin! or at fancying her husband, who can barely allow himself a coarse horse blanket at 10 annas, wrapt in one of English lambs-wool costing 10 rupees—a sum collective, he perhaps never possessed in his life? Nay, it would be a strange occurrence for a wealthy Native, a few in Calcutta excepted, to allow himself any so costly a covering in bed. While out, he will draw over his shoulders a shawl valued at 500 rupees: on his cot he will cover himself with a common chintz *Russaie*, at a cost of one or two rupees.

"In addition to the illusions excited by the attempt to apply to India the laws of Political Economy founded on human motives as they are exhibited in Europe, and by very incorrect information, on the parts of authors and orators, on Indian matters, may be placed the promising demand, rapid at first, now slowly progressing, for cotton goods and sheet copper, which led to the impression in England, that, if an abundant and cheap supply of other manufactures were always in the market, the Natives would certainly and rapidly acquire a taste for the comforts of civilized life. Many years of vain efforts proved, that some other causes were overlooked in the anticipation. Excessive extortion on the part of the Company for revenue has of late years been cited as this cause, which, by impoverishing, has deprived them of the means of gratifying or acquiring a taste for the comforts of civilized life, and of becoming good customers to England. That the quantity of the agriculturist's produce taken as revenue (though little, the writer believes, if at all above, from 10 to 15 per cent. of the gross produce, after deducting the commercial plant), proves a heavy burden to the people, and that they are in general lamentably poor, are facts which it would be very imprudent to deny; but the assessment itself is not the main cause of their poverty, nor is their present poverty the chief obstacle to their acquiring the habits of civilized life.

The causes of slow progress and poverty in India.

"It is not poverty in means, but poverty in taste. Moreover it is not, in India, poverty in means, which stands as the antecedent, or as it were, the cause of poverty in taste, as is commonly argued; but the reverse; universal poverty in taste occasions the universal poverty in means. The latter is not the cause, but the consequence of the former. It is of the first importance that this relation should be kept in view by the Indian Statesman. Out of many which might be adduced, the reader's attention is requested to one striking fact in illustration of this truth. In no country in the world, those in the Frigid Zone excepted, is window-glass more needed than in the upper provinces of Hindostan, by a people of the bodily constitution of the Natives. To the westward, the people suffer as much from cold and damp, as any in Europe. Few escape fever and rheumatism in the rains and cold weather. And in the hot season the dust, and parching wind, are distressing even to brutes. Again,—at any city on the banks of the Ganges, window-glass is procurable at a price, as low perhaps, as in London. Yet it is no less true than strange, that with so good reasons for its use, and so ready a supply everywhere, the houses of all, even the wealthiest Natives (with the former exception of a *few* in Calcutta), are unprovided with window-glass. The writer has watched the erection of houses, upon which half a lakh of rupees have been said to have been laid out (few indeed indulge themselves with such mansions), but not twenty rupees on window-glass. What renders this the more surprising, is the custom, not uncommon, for such wealthy Natives to glaze one or two apartments for the reception of their European guests; while scarcely any are found to do so for their own comfort. Here we have superadded some experience in its use. But the whole in vain. Wealthy Mussulmans are indeed found much more ready to avail themselves of the articles of comfortable use, offered by English enterprize at so low prices; but in their case even, it is to a limited extent, and the number of wealthy of that religion is very small. Hence window-glass, of which so large a demand was anticipated, is always at a serious discount in the Calcutta market; although it would be difficult to name any article which men, right as to their *senses*, would want more in such a climate. How different this from the rapidly increased demand for this very article, when it was once introduced into England; lamented by a Sage of those times as a mark of such degeneracy, that, in one generation it was finding its way, after glazing patrician windows, even into the cottage farmhouse of those days.

Cotton goods, the demand for them exceptional.

"The comparatively large consumption of British cotton goods, which for a time underwent a rapid increase upon the opening of the trade, has been, and is still, daily adduced by the hopeful, as an earnest of an approaching vast demand in India, for all other products of British industry.

"The writer would refrain from the endeavour to dissipate so pleasant hopes, were not too many persons, relying on a false analogy of motives, disposed to avoid any interference with so promising a course, and did not others, with full confidence in them, try the Indian market to their cost, with every possible production of art.

"The demand for cotton goods, which, up to a certain amount, underwent a rapid increase at first, was to have been expected from, and is to be attributed to, the very ancient taste of this people for cotton fabrics for dress. It was no new taste, no demand for a new article, but merely a transfer of custom from the coarser and dearer, to the finer and cheaper wares.

"So far from the quantity of English cottons, now taken by the natives, being any ground for future hope, it needs but little observation to perceive, in the fact of the amount having been for some years nearly stationary in the older provinces, that it was only an ancient demand for cloths of such kinds to a certain extent, which, being transferred to those of England, rendered saleable proportional importations; and the amount, still small in comparison with the whole clothing of the people, is but evidence of that indisposition to improve their condition of life which the writer has already sufficiently established.

No spontaneous improvement in India.

"If he has been successful in placing in their true light the deceptive appearances which this question wears, and the delusive expectations which have been founded on them; and, if he has disproved any real improvement in the people from their own spontaneous efforts, the Author will consider the proposition demonstrated,—that the system of non-interference maintained towards the natives unremittingly, with the exception of that sparingly afforded in school education, has been attended on their part, with a refraining from all spontaneous improvement.

Mere example unavailing.

"That abundant example afforded them of the advantages of civilisation has been unavailing, is manifested in the state of Calcutta itself, and of the country in general. The reader's time will not be occupied by any long demonstration of what ought to be apparent to the mind of every unprejudiced observer. But one remarkable instance may be adduced, illustrative of that peculiar trait in the native character, which proves the barrier against all spontaneous advancement. The Calcutta *hackery* is painfully eloquent in proof of the fact, that example very abundant, evidence very striking, means as ready as possible, and considerable pecuniary advantage, though all combined, fail in inducing the people to adopt of themselves a simple improvement. *Hackeries* on wooden axles have been possessed by natives of all ranks, and degrees of wealth, in Calcutta, while for a century, their English fellow citizens have used vehicles, in vast numbers, on well-turned iron axles, the easy draught of which ought daily to have been noticed by them. At the same time, English enterprise has supplied their markets abundantly, with iron of all forms and dimensions, requiring little workmanship in order to form it into axles and boxes, and at a price which would be entirely saved in work, now lost by the excessive friction, in five or six months, at an estimate on the average daily hire of a hackery. At the same time numerous accidents from the snapping of wooden axles would be avoided. With all this, the grating wooden axle is still used (the thickness and looseness of which cause this serious loss by friction, which the people entirely overlook), and it will continue to be used, until hackeries of the usual form and price, with the addition of an iron axle, are introduced by Europeans; so as to demonstrate by trial the pecuniary advantages which would result from them, and to habituate a sufficient number of the natives to their use.

"This and a hundred other instances prove that example and opportunity alone are unavailing, though supported with good pecuniary reasons for improvement. When, however, a very great and manifest saving is noticed by them, or some vast gain, the natives will occasionally exert themselves. Thus many have adopted the European method of making indigo, their own producing an unsaleable article.

"An ingenious author has drawn a parallel between the condition and habits of the people of England and India in ancient times, and has hence inferred that their present vast difference is to be attributed to certain political causes which have always operated disadvantageously towards India. He has, it may be supposed, succeeded in establishing a parity of condition at some former period, but by no means of character. A day of helpless infancy there is, during which some parallel as to feebleness may be drawn between all children; but he would err against experience, who should thence infer that any difference to be observed in after life in their strength and energy ought to be attributed to certain causes affecting the nurture and education of the parties differently; and not to the difference nature has made in the constitutions of men. To the case of nations this argument is equally applicable.

"It is affirmed, and affirmed truly, that the natives are found to have powers of understanding, adequate to the acquirement of all kinds of human knowledge; and it has hence been concluded, but concluded falsely, that the opportunity alone being afforded them they will learn *all* that it is useful for them to acquire, and *put in practice* what they learn. In proportion as the Indian mind is extolled for readiness to understand, and learn the philosophic truths discovered by others, has the philanthropist to lament its deficiency in those qualities, to which are due, much more than to the former, the advanced civilisation and greatness of England. However sincere may be their intentions, they are not India's best friends, whose desire of establishing for this people a high intellectual character would lead them to affirm that the mighty change which ought, long ago, to have commenced in their habits and condition, may be trusted to any spontaneous exertions of their own.

"The doctrines founded on what are termed the *laws* of Political Science, though far from being universally applicable in the Western World, may serve as a sufficient guidance to politicians of the present day in Europe; but, applied to India, they cannot fail to misguide the judgment, and be preventive of good.

"They, who are really acquainted with the native character, who have seen through false appearances, and, sifting well the expectations of the hopeful, have found them to be little more than chaff, to be scattered by the blast of time, cannot fail of the conviction, that a system of economical policy, suited for England, is inapplicable here. In England, a vast and efficient, though complicated machinery of motives, forms, and then rules, the active character of each generation; needing, on the part of the statesman, but little guidance, and cautious interference.

"In India no such engine is at work; nor can the people build it up of themselves. They have not the moral, mental, nor physical energy, which, in the rudest times, characterised the people of England; and which, in each successive generation, has added some movements to the machine of motives, which now, in return, determines our artificial, but highly civilized national character.

"In India, there being no such powerful instrument, capable of doing the work itself; the work must be done by the hand (like all other work here) of the statesman at present; suitable and beneficent interference must be practised towards the people; for without it there is no reasonable ground for supposing they will ever make progress in the habits of civilized life."

On the State of the Useful Arts in India.

"That the Natives of India are deplorably ignorant of that knowledge, which is of infinite importance to man, of the knowledge of all that is revealed to him in Christianity, is a fact which, in this place, it would be needless and painful to dwell upon. It is presumed, that this ignorance, on their part, is deplored by every one professing Christianity; and that, by whatsoever instruments he works, and whatsoever road he takes, though his first object, in the order of time, may be the temporal, his first object in degree, must be the spiritual advancement of the people of India.

"Let his zeal be how great soever, let his philanthropy be unbounded, man, doomed to act through a mysterious organism of matter, cannot influence or benefit the minds of his fellow-men, but through the agency of matter, subjected to a change of form or place. The forces inseparable from matter resist these changes, and will yield only to superior force applied by labour. Whether it be in an inanimate form, as books, or endued with life in the persons of delegated teachers and preachers, the agency of matter is necessary, which can be moved, combined, or supported, only by labour or its products. And this labour can be supplied only from some accumulated stock. That no such accumulation, under the form of its representative, money, is possessed by the party, with whom the duty of providing education to the people chiefly lies, would appear from the scantiness of the sums annually expended by the Government for this most important object.

"The writer has undertaken, in this Essay, a secular part, in

Erroneous views of native arts.

the general work of improvement. Upon no subject are more erroneous opinions current, than the state of the arts in India. It is indeed generally admitted, that they are rude; but it is commonly added, that they are simply and cheaply conducted, and therefore well suited to the habits and means of the people. In this manner, every process almost, in their agriculture and manufactures, meets with some European defender; a circumstance to be traced to the situations of the observers. Few of them have that personal interest in the question, which would lead them to a narrow investigation of facts. The age, at which most of them have left England, a long residence in India, and an education chiefly literary, must disqualify them for a just comparison of the relative advantages of the arts of the two countries. The great difference between the incomes of these persons, and of the natives in general, and the familiarity of the former with the prices of English finer manufactures, cause many to forget, that prices, which appear very low to them, are ruinously high to the poor native; prohibiting his use of many articles, which the former had supposed abundantly cheap. And they fail to consider, that it is the proportion the price of labour in each country bears to that of its product, which determines the relative cheapness of the processes.

"Among the few persons, who are at the pains of affording any attention to the native arts, an erroneous opinion is prevalent, that great ingenuity is evinced in the simplicity of the instruments, by which they are conducted. And they, whose taste leads them to admire every thing of an Hindostanee character, are wont to foster their predilections by dwelling upon this imaginary ingenuity.

"The pages of historians being for the most part wasted in recording the exploits and outrages of tyrants (the human beasts of prey), it is no easy matter to trace human inventions in the arts to their respective sources; a subject more worthy the contemplation of man. It would appear, however, that nearly all the nations of Europe, and the west of Asia, have excelled the natives of Hindostan in the variety and ingenuity displayed in the simple instruments, used in the dawn of their arts. And this is the case with the Chinese.

The dawn of art in Europe and Asia.

"In the commencement of the arts in any country, the primary effort must be, to obtain a result which will answer the purpose intended, with the least possible fixture of capital—with the simplest instruments; or with none, if the work can be completed by the use of the limbs alone. Hence the toes even are exercised to dexterity, and pressed into service.

"Centuries have elapsed, since in England the simple household instruments, neater far, and more effective, than those of the natives, have given place to the complicated machines of many parts, which effect so vast a saving of labour. These, occupying separate buildings, are seen only by their respective artists, or by the curious. And the manufacturers even, having known from their youth no other, forget the many elementary instruments, from which their own machinery has been formed. In England, full of arts, the arts do least display, to public view, their processes, at the present time.

"Hence few, but those, whom curiosity or business leads to the study, have any knowledge of the innumerable processes to which matter is subjected, before it is presented to view in the attractive form of the comforts and luxuries of English life. Few reflect, that they are indebted to European ingenuity, to English especially, for nearly all that they touch, taste, or handle, and that, until of late, every article, though much dearer than at present, was produced with instruments, beautiful in their accuracy and simplicity.

"It does indeed evince much ingenuity to simplify an instrument in the mechanical, or a process in the chemical arts, provided no sacrifice be made of labour, material, or certainty of result. But to adhere, without any attempt at improvement, to instruments merely because they are simple,—instruments wasteful of labour and material, and uncertain in the result, marks a very obtuse and spiritless state of mind in a people. It shows them to be deficient in *speculative and theoretical* men, without whom a people must ever grovel in hovels with the beasts of the earth. To extol an adherence to such mean instruments, and to ridicule minds directed to their improvement, is by no means creditable to the judgment of any, whose opportunities, as members of a civilized community, should have taught them better. It is an earnest of what the condition of a people would be, composed of such beings as themselves!

Simplicity in means — their advantages and defects.

"Let the unhappy Molunghee have the same wants as the English saltmaker, and let them be supplied by the sale of his labour. Its product in salt, exclusive of the high duty, already dearer than that of the Englishman's labour, would soon point out how much of ingenuity or advantage lay in the simple processes of the Molunghee—in his rude furnace of fragile and slowly-working earthen boiling pots; where the excess of earthy surface swallows up one half of the heat; in his simple employment of limbs, able, though half-starved, to raise at least thirty pounds, in baling about the liquors with a two-pound cup; in his economically dispensing with a wooden trough or drain, which he might have made in one month, perhaps week, of the many years he has expended in walking, backwards and forwards, between the source whence he dips up the salt water and his boiling pots. And where wood is his fuel, a fraction of that he has wasted in the furnace would have yielded all the planks required for the material of the trough, to be put together with wooden pegs, less acted on by salt, and therefore better for the purpose than iron nails. Where he ought to make fifty maunds, he makes but one; as would be shown by the price rising, if he were supplied with the comforts of the Englishman, perhaps to fifty rupees a maund. It would then be clear that the present price, low comparatively with that, results merely from the human labour employed being remunerated worse than the labour of beasts; falling short of the wages of the horse in England. A hovel, a strip of rag, barely defending him from the reproach of absolute nudity,—a handful of parched grain, or boiled rice, which he can scarcely afford to season with the salt he makes,—in short, a keeping on the lowest scale of existence of the labouring animal, alone prevents the price rising so high as to admit of a profitable importation of salt from England.

"In the preparation of other chemical products,—of the earthy and metallic salts especially,—they are either wholly ignorant, or so wasteful in their processes, as to raise the prices above those at which many of the articles can be supplied from Europe.

Indian dyeing. "In favour of the Indian art of dyeing much has been said, which a close inquiry will not bear out.

Of cotton. "Cotton having been for ages the fabric of dress, and coloured cotton petticoats worn by all females but those of rank, while nature has been lavish towards this country in the supply of dyes, it might have been expected that the dyeing and printing of cotton goods would have been brought to a high state of perfection in India; that every effort would, ages ago, have been made by the native dyers to fix durably the spendid dyes their country affords.

"But the same sleepy adherence to custom is marked in this as in all other trades. Their ignorance and waste of the materials they act upon, and of their own labour, is shown in almost every part of a native dye work. Their mordants are of uncertain composition, and badly applied. Black and red are their only very durable colours. Their blue dyeing of cotton is so ill performed, that a few washings reduce the colour of native blue goods from the deepest to the lightest shade. The reason is that in this, the land of indigo, its use is not thoroughly understood. The blue vat is not properly made, being more a suspension than proper solution of the dye, which does not undergo deoxidation, the apparent change upon which its solubility depends in the English blue vat. The brown colour of Boglipoor, and buff of some other cotton goods, which are of renowned durability, prove upon examination to depend upon the silk interwoven with the weft, in which the colour is chiefly seated.

"To two or three colours, therefore, the poorer native women have to confine their tastes, or to wear their gayer chintzes until so discoloured with dirt and offensive, as to render a scouring unavoidably necessary.

Dyeing of silk.

"The dyeing of silk, a luxury beyond the reach of the mass of the people, is an art of far less value to a poor people, while it is one more easy of attainment; the affinity of silk fibre for colouring matter greatly exceeding that of cotton. The splendid silk vests, which the Mahomedan chiefs must have introduced from Western Asia, the unlimited prices, which rude but luxurious courts would afford to pay in satisfying wants limited in variety, will sufficiently account for the comparatively advanced state of the art of dyeing silk in India.

"In this branch even of the art their processes are also rude and expensive, as shown by the high price of the product, and by the fact that Europeans, near the metropolis, have been able to extract some profit from the little improvements they have introduced into the business; though, acting it is presumed, under the disadvantageous use of hired labour,—the ruin of nearly all undertakings in India, in which wages form a large part of expense. Though the dyeing of silk is an art of less value to this people as consumers, it is to be encouraged as an instrument in the silk trade for increasing, though in a small degree, the commercial exports of India.

Soap making. "The very important chemical art of soap making is in the same backward state as the rest, and its product as dear in proportion. Hence the mass of the people cannot afford to make use of soap. It proves, upon the whole, a less expensive course to consume labour and apparel, in beating the latter to pieces, by degrees, upon boards and stones, than to employ soap in the washing of their linen. The soap is very bad, and, considering the price of the material, dear. A portion only of the alkali is rendered caustic, and is but imperfectly combined with the oleaginous matter; while the larger quantity of free carbonate and sulphate of soda and the chloride separate in grains, causing the soap in damp weather to grow humid and decay. The dark and offensive character of native soap indicates some damaging of the materials in the making. Where natron is employed, they do not succeed in destroying the offensive vegetable colouring matter, being unable to construct furnaces for the purpose.

Glass making. "With so abundant a supply of excellent alkali, and of siliceous earth, in the form of quartz, in all the hilly districts, and the finest material for fire-brick in many parts of the country, and, it is presumed, for glass-house pots in some place or other (though the writer has not met with what he would suppose the best), excellent glass might have been made by this people: and, from the soda earth alone, a good green glass may be manufactured. The glass of the country is quite unfitted for any important purpose, and it is very unsightly; made with a great excess of alkali, at merely an ordinary red heat, it is gradually acted on even by water in time.

"The common country 'Kaunch,' glass in mass, upon being ground to a fine powder, and macerated in water, undergoes a gradual separation into various substances; and decomposition, so long as it is kept humid, appears to be progressive. The liquor becomes strongly saline, from free carbonate and sulphate of soda, with a separation of lime and iron, setting as a fine paste on the surface of the glass sand.

"For looking-glasses, trinkets, and phials for European customers, the glass-blower is under the necessity of using English broken glass, a standard article of sale in the larger bazaars.

"The small size and unequal heat of their forges confine the efforts of the native glass-blower in general to the treatment of a few ounces of the metal. Hence any vessel, above a phial size, is blown so thin as to be of little use. And though so thin, the glass is very liable to crack from changes of temperature, owing to his inability to anneal it properly.

"In the treatment of the earths, and in the proper use of fuel, the natives are surprisingly ignorant. It were useless to introduce the manufacture of mineral acids, and of etherial liquids, and the casting of iron; for they have no vessels of a porcelainous nature for holding the former (none fitted even for the complete preservation of common oil and spirit), nor fire-bricks, for furnaces, for the latter. Without fire-bricks they can neither have works for founding glass nor iron, nor for making stone-bodied pottery. This, the basis of the chemical arts, being wanting, they are deficient in all the rest. Stone-ware and fire-bricks.

"It is hoped that the reader is now persuaded of the ignorance prevailing in some of their most important chemical arts.

"The native simple mechanical arts being within reach of the observation of most persons, the writer would presume he might treat their defectiveness as a self-evident proposition, were not a too hastily formed opinion current that excellent simplicity is manifested in all native machinery. Mechanical arts.

"It would occupy more space than the limits of this Essay admit of, to attempt an inquiry into one-fourth of the numerous mechanical arts. Out of many which might be instanced one or two remarkable cases may be selected, familiar to all European observers, regarding which they too commonly fall in with the native error of mistaking cheapness for economy.

"When remarking upon the faulty construction of native boats, the writer has often been replied to that the low rate of hire, and the small capital of the parties, did not admit of superior boats being employed; that they were in short well River boats.

adapted to their purposes. The price of food being the standard, and the poor condition of the dandies taken into account, it is a question if any river navigation in the world is so expensive; and it is very certain that none is so dangerous.

"It is not too much to affirm that more than nine out of ten of the losses on the river arise from the badness of the tackle, and from the boats not being decked, nor divided into compartments. Many boats are even supplied with a deck of loose planks, which need little more than being nailed down and caulked, so as to admit of a wave breaking over the boat, or the gunnel being occasionally dipped under water, without the swamping of the boat, as at present, being the consequence.

"The division of the boats into compartments, said to be not uncommon in China, would be an important security to native boats. It would secure against sinking, numbers which annually are lost upon trees and kunkur banks. The hole thus made is commonly circumscribed, and would not let water into more than one compartment; and the boarding of the partition would add greatly to the strength and durability of the boat.

False economy in boat sails.

"False economy in the tackling greatly adds to the tardiness of the most tedious of voyages—that up the Ganges. A native sail, made of gunny-bags, is at the best a net for allowing the wind to slip through. One advantage it has, that of allowing the helmsman to see a-head distinctly through it. This is the condition of the sails of country boats when new. But such is their state in general, that frequently more than one-half of their area is unoccupied by cloth. They seem as set up in mockery, not for use. Like worthless bags, they let fair winds, as valuable as money, slip through them; while the interest upon a costly cargo, and the wages of the boatmen, are often running on much faster than the boat. The boat, having lost the necessary wind, is invariably detained for days at some, if not all, of the many places on the river, which, not admitting of the use of the tow rope, can only be passed on a return of that fair wind, which, had it not been allowed to run through the sail, would have carried the boat past the place of detention, in a few hours.

"The reader, who is not aware of it, will be surprised when

he hears that country canvas (answering all the purposes of European though not so durable) required for a large sail of 30 feet by 20, costs only 20 or 25 rupees, while the worst sail cannot cost under 6 rupees, leaving a difference of 14 or 19 rupees, which does not even make up for the inferior durability of the latter. Let the cargo be copper, worth rupees 8000. The *weekly* interest upon this, at 6 per cent., is about 10 rupees; and the weekly wages of the men about the same. Exclusive of the expenses of the boat itself, here are current charges amounting to 20 rupees a *week*, the value of a new sail. So bad is the tackling, as is too well known, that boats are frequently upset from delay in lowering down the sails (the mode adopted by the natives). The "*sheets*" of the sails, instead of being so fastened as to be readily set loose, are tied in knots; and the halyards stick in the common loop of rope, or under the sheaf of the rickety pulley at the mast-head. Nor does this rude tackle admit of the sails being so braced, as to make the best use of a side wind. The want of a keel is but half the cause of the drifting of country boats. Wind which would slip off the properly inclined and gently concave surface of a well stretched sail, is detained in the belly of a native sail (provided the latter do not let it escape) and tends more to push the boat sideways, than onwards. And, since keels cannot well be used on the Ganges, it is strange that moveable weather-boards have not been adopted; through means of which, barges on the Thames sail very fairly, drifting far less than the boats on the Ganges, though as shallow, flat-bottomed, and keelless, as any of the latter. So dangerous and expensive is the navigation of the Ganges at present, and so wide the field for improvement, that the writer has long considered the improvement of boats to be one of the few fields open for successful enterprize on the part of Englishmen in India; since abundant employment would be afforded by their countrymen for the conveyance of stores and of merchandize.

"The difference in cost of a boat, built and rigged in a manner suited to the navigation of the Ganges, and of the rude native boat, would not exceed the amount paid for insuring one load of saltpetre or cotton, from Furrackabad or Agra, to Calcutta. One trip would pay the difference, if the boats were built at Ghats near the jungles in the Terrai; and the risk would be reduced almost to nothing. If the boats were built, so that no part projected much above the water,—the 'chopper' (thatch) being entirely removed,—the stern cut down quite to the level of the rest of the boat,—and the men given one of the compartments about mid-ship for their use; which alone should not be decked, but sheltered by a low awning, rising at most two feet above the edge of the boat, and provided with canvas curtains to let down only when the boat is moored;—there cannot be a doubt in the minds of those who have witnessed the delays occasioned by adverse and side winds, that the journey might be shortened by one third, at the least. Especially if the boat were properly formed, and provided with a weather-board moveable to either side, and a small wherry or canoe; for want of which, the delays, from the tow-men having to swim across mouths of nullahs, and to take very circuitous routes, and from the drifting of the boat in crossing channels of the river, exceed anything that could be supposed by one who has not witnessed it. Many a large boat, lost upon a lee shore in a storm, might have gained the windward shore with the aid of a little boat, at the commencement of the gale, before she drifted.*

The 'budgerow.'

"Did the subject of this Essay admit of it, it were easy to show, what indeed must be evident to all who have afforded it an examination, that a budgerow, the common travelling boat on the Ganges, is of the very worst construction possible. It is a monument of folly; of sin against every principle of science concerned in its structure.

"Who but must also be pained at observing the oblique action of the oars of a dinghee, nipping the water, as a thing to be cut between the blades of shears?

"All the above are selected, as familiar instances.

"Time would fail one, in pointing out the absurd errors against principle, and the waste of labour and material, manifested in nearly all the native arts.

The up-country hackery a favourable exception.

"It is a grateful task to seek out some exceptions. In the formation of the wheel and axle of the up-country hackery some ingenuity is apparent. The outer single bar in the *lurree*, and the oblique sticks in the *chuckra*, give such support to the extremity of the axle, as to admit of a small iron pin serving for

* After a severe storm I counted eighty wrecks in one day, while descending the Ganges.

an axle. But this, and the whole vehicle, are commonly so ill tied together with string, as to be liable to frequent accidents.

"The cross movement in the simple rope-spinning apparatus is neat; and a familiar one in the oldest machines in Europe.

"Lastly, The best instrument, as to principle, appears to be the Persian wheel, employed for raising water. But the invention is no property of India; nor perhaps of Persia. It was probably an Egyptian instrument originally. So undeserving are the natives of it, however, that they have nearly defeated its action, by bad construction. It is, therefore, rarely used, where the water has to be raised above twenty-five or thirty feet.

"An inquiry into some of the agricultural processes in use in India, has been made under a former head.

Conclusion resulting from the inquiry.

"From this inquiry we are forced to the conclusion that, as far as the arts of life are concerned, the people of India are making no considerable advancement in useful knowledge; although so long the subjects of England, the land of science and the arts.

"That they are making no great advancement in pure and natural science, or in moral science, is a fact, upon the proving of which it would be idle to expend time; a fact, which every humane person, who has observed their sufficient intellectual powers, must deeply regret.

"Let those, who are so disposed, attempt to hide the prevailing ignorance of the people, under the dazzling glitter of the infinitely small proportion, who, at the expiration of a century, have had the riches of European science made known to them."

The disappointed expectations of a century may suffice to establish the fact, that industrial and social progress in India, through European example and enterprize alone, will prove at best a very tardy process.

In addition to the obstacles to progress presented by the inertness of the people, there are moral and juridical obstacles of a more formidable character which might alone account for the fact, that the people of India at large have but little advanced in the century which has elapsed since the battle of PLASSY; nay, that in some respects they have retrograded.

On the Moral and Juridical Obstacles to Progress in India.

During the last eighty years orators and writers on Indian questions have put forth and repeated nearly the same confident expectations and promises, that in a few more years a great work of progress would begin to manifest itself. On the renewal of the Charter, which opened India to British settlers, and subsequent to which the jealousy towards missionary efforts greatly declined, the press abounded with such expectations. It likewise did prior to the Charter of 1853.

While the questions before us are the moral and judicial causes retarding secular progress in India, a few concluding remarks will be ventured upon the slow progress of religious truth in that country.

The universal pravity.

The first cause retarding the advancement of the people and development of the resources of the country will be found in a universal pravity, which defeats the efforts of the government to administer justice, rendering such a machinery as it has seen fit to employ almost abortive, and which makes it most difficult for the European settler to conduct, with integrity and security, any operations connected with the raising of produce.

Honour prevalent, but not honesty.

In England we are little prepared to note that wide distinction between *honour* and *honesty* which obtains in less civilized and heathen communities. The exigencies of a rude state of society will call forth and establish an exhibition of honour which is surprising even to members of a Christian community trained to respect and rely more upon honesty and truth for its social security. Hence nothing is more common than for persons from India to speak of the greater honesty of native than of English servants. The servant employed within doors will, as a matter of honour, not purloin things *customarily* exposed. The man *entrusted* with jewels or money will in general be faithful to the charge. Even when he has the disbursement of the money he will often content himself with overcharges limited to a certain commission upon customary purchases; but he will cheat to the utmost extent he is able when the purchase is not "customary." It is the same in business. Agents acting in a particular way will often merit respect for their honour, but place them under other circumstances and their fraud will be bounded only by opportunity. I have known the same runner-with-money carry repeatedly from 50*l.* to 100*l.* in silver—a heavy load—about his person, from one to two hundred miles through a dangerous country, with his life in constant peril and his reward the mere pay of a pound or two for the trip. Out of 3000*l.* sent out in this way none has been lost, though any of the runners might have gone off with what was a fortune for life without the possibility of capture. One of the most trustworthy was, on account of his shrewdness, taken away from his *professional calling*, and therefore from his *professional honour*, and given an agency on account of his imagined *honesty*. In the extent and audacity of his dishonesty he proved unrivalled. His honour had been as perfect as that of a shepherd's dog, and based on about as much reason and morality.

With respect to veracity, the standing rule in which every child is educated appears to be—carefully to avoid ever speaking the truth, excepting as a matter of interest or necessity. One native gentleman of rank has told me of another, in his presence, that he was lying, and always did so without causing any shame or disturbing his equanimity at all. Mendacity a part of education.

As regards humanity, there is a like deplorable shortcoming and inconsistency as in the case of honesty. Instances of liberality are frequent, even apart from an ostentatious munificence, and of compassion also occasional; but as a rule, the lives, fortunes, and happiness of their neighbours weigh nothing with them. They will compass each other's misery, ruin, and death for the smallest object. When to these are added a perfect self-command and a large amount of cunning, it may be, in some degree, imagined what must be the amount of crime, and oppression, and the difficulty of detecting them and of redressing wrongs amongst such a people; and how unequal a combat must an Englishman of integrity have to wage with them in the transactions of life and in legal disputes, if he is to be allowed none of the privileges of his race. But of this presently. Inhumanity.

Desirable as they would in themselves be, the most perfect code of laws and the profoundest learning in the administrators of them would avail next to nothing compared with *a sufficiency in the number of eyes and ears and honest minds occupied in the work.* Judiciary provisions.

I have seen a station filled with fine military youths, who have come out from England originally with a fair school education, Military men unoccupied.

and who, if duly encouraged, would soon qualify themselves up to the standard of most country magistrates here, wasting their time and too often losing their morals in absolute idleness. Since the ablest military commanders have exhibited much acquaintance with civil government, no one will contend that to occupy the minds of officers with such pursuits, instead of leaving them in idleness, would detract from their military efficiency, provided they were not removed from their sphere of regimental duty.

Judges overwhelmed with duty.

At the same station might be seen, as at every other, a judge and magistrate, functions often combined in the same person, overwhelmed with "cases" and completely mystified by the native officers of his court. The prisoners in the convicts' jail were happy beings compared with the unfortunates in the "witnesses jail," to visit which required at times some nerve. No small number of those detained as witnesses, sometimes for months, were there solely through the malice or cupidity, or often both, of some native official in power, or of some one who had bribed him to apprehend them as witnesses to a transaction, which had either never occurred, or never before been heard of by them.

Corruption and atrocity abounding.

I have known a crime of the greatest atrocity, comprising the murder of many persons and robbery of much treasure, perpetrated at the instigation of the mayor of a town, and the magistrate there decoyed off in his zeal, in the hottest season, for some days in a circuit in the opposite direction to that in which the professional robbers were despatched. I have known manufacturing works of large extent and value, and of a peculiarly interesting character, ruined through the unbounded fraud of the native agents employed to collect produce, upon the owner, an English gentleman, declining to have the prosecution of one of them conducted with the aid of perjured witnesses. The case had to be withdrawn, and with it all check to the fraud of others.

Since under a system of vigilance totally inadequate to the necessities of a country in such a moral condition, the poor or honest man has not a chance against the rich and corrupt, is it not manifest that the ends of justice would in the main be greatly promoted if the doors of the court-house were closed, and a beadle were placed in the ante-room to decide every case by the toss of a rupee? It would, at least, ensure to all an equal chance of success, and thereby place a material check upon unjust aggressions of power and wealth. Is it not plain that the first requirement towards the administration of justice *amongst the natives* of the provinces is a large increase in the number of the agents? In England nine-tenths of the disputes amongst country people are settled by magistrates. In India a still larger proportion are of a character upon which a fair decision could be pronounced by any mind of ordinary intelligence. When it is further borne in mind that to the poor, and others actively occupied, almost any prompt decision is preferable to great delay, and that in many of the local courts the causes have been two, three, and four years in arrear, it must be evident that a system which so overloads its officers with work becomes worse than useless.

An increase of European functionaries the only remedy.

If high legal attainments, and consequently proportional salaries, were required only in judges of appeal, the question of expense need no longer be urged in the way of a great increase in the number of European minds occupied in the administration of justice. Medical men form some of the best magistrates in England. At civil stations in India the surgeon who has the greater part of his time on his hands, and has a mind more disciplined by severe study and the necessity of logical and cautious deductions than the, frequently youthful, magistrate himself, might occupy the office, and would fulfil its duties thankfully, if his present comparatively pitiful salary of 30*l.* a-month were doubled. An abundance of medical officers would qualify themselves for the office of civil surgeon and magistrate. In a large proportion of criminal cases, such as wounds, murders by violence or poisoning, rapes, &c., the surgeon's evidence, as it is, is felt by the magistrate to be more reliable than all the rest together. But how much better could the former weigh the convictions of his own mind than impart them to the mind of another! Thus for 60*l.* a-month he would perform the joint duty of surgeon and magistrate, for which the present functionary receives three or four times that salary. This would leave an ample fund with which to put in requisition the honest British intelligence of all regimental officers at the station willing to qualify themselves to take a part in the work. It would not be easy for a crafty band of native officials to blind with their subtle dust so many active eyes. A prompt decision

The opportunity for, and value of medical magistrates;

and of military.

of cases would then be ensured, which is often of greater importance even than a correct decision—not that the latter would not also be greatly promoted. In short, jurisdiction partaking very much of a simple and military character would be far better suited for a people most of whom are so wanting in moral principle of every kind, and in such humble circumstances. A large majority of disputes relating to property are connected with the land, of the position and ownership of which much must be already known in the revenue department. Might not that department, strengthened by European aid from the military, of different grades of information and rank, adjudicate upon all such cases at least? In short, since the occupation of the country must presume a state of peace to be the usual condition, and therefore since three-fourths of the time of the large body of military men, necessarily maintained in it, must be usually unemployed in the duties of what at present is their sole profession, is it not manifestly a great waste of moral and intellectual resources, as well as injury to the parties themselves, not to open to every one of them the door to useful and profitable employment? Entering the service through a channel of much humbler expectations than those of the civil service, experience has proved how ready military men would be, for a moderate addition to their pay, to qualify themselves for, and to fulfil with equal efficiency, most of the duties, for the performance of which the established expectations of the sister service require a five-fold greater remuneration. Not that these would be grudged could the revenues of India support on such a scale of remuneration functionaries in number at all equal to the task.

Unless the greater part of the British morality, intelligence, and firmness, present in the country, can be put into requisition for the administration of justice, the next alternative desirable would be the decision of cases *by lot*, as upon an average securing justice in one half of them. Of the Company's *European* judicial establishment, it may be with truth predicated that integrity is almost universal, zeal very general, and learning not unfrequent; but supernatural powers would be necessary to overrule the retarding and perverting influences of native corruption. It was to be expected, but is not a little mortifying, that the people should fail to recognize in their own character the cause of the oppressions under which they groan, and should be ready to lay them at the door of the government and its alien representatives, whose qualities are misunderstood by all but the wily officers surrounding them; while these are interested in fostering such misunderstanding, if only to relieve themselves of much of the odium invited by their corruption.

The Want of Protection to Mental Property.

Not only is the insecurity of the person and of material property resulting from the insufficiency of the means employed to protect them, a bar to progress, but, as elsewhere throughout Asia, the *rights of mental property* having never been recognized in India. The government, following Eastern example and perhaps also the opinions of a certain class of politicians of the West, has I believe established no law for its security, though the importance of the question was recognized upon the Author's inviting the attention of the government of India to it in Calcutta in 1833.

Progress of invention commensurate with the protection of it.

Even the more civilized countries of Europe have not yet arrived at an equitable and politic view of the rights of mental property. In England, especially, it is oppressed with preposterous burdens; and even then defensible only at great and anxious risk. Nevertheless it is a notable fact, that if over one map of the world the countries were severally coloured and shaded according to the absence or existence of protection to mechanical and literary invention, and according to the extent of the protection; and if over another map they were coloured and shaded according to the mental and social stagnation or progress, and the degree of progress; it would be found that almost everywhere the presence of colour and the degree of shade corresponded in both. Throughout Asia, where there has never been protection, there is absolute stagnation. In the United States of America, where the encouragement given to native invention is most complete, there is its progress greatest. In England (which might and ought to stand foremost) and in France, it is next.

On suggesting and urging the adoption of certain improvements in their operations to natives in India, one of the first objections raised has been the certainty of loss from others copying them as soon as they proved successful. A people of so little enterprize stand in especial need of protection, as do likewise Europeans who venture upon novel undertakings in India.

A THIRD OBSTACLE to progress in India is the adverse influence upon European enterprize of the same native depravity which renders the administration of justice so difficult, especially in conjunction with the indolence of the people. If labour be hired, the employer's eye must be constantly upon it; if contracted for, the advances of money, always required, become consumed, and not half the products forthcoming.

The Judiciary Policy of the Government an Obstacle to European Enterprize.

The character and tendency of the judiciary policy indicated by the measure named by its opponents the "Black Act," here claims attention. The extent to which the Future of India—its progress and the stability of British rule—would be affected by that policy does not appear to have been duly considered, nor indeed the equity itself of the measure.

The "Black Act," its injurious and dangerous tendencies.

With the notion of doing equal justice to men, whether black or white, it has been hastily purposed to place Europeans, in their amenability to the local courts, precisely on the same footing with natives. Since no English gentleman of honour and self-respect would, *if he knew beforehand* what this would involve him in, trust himself and his capital in the country for any mere prospect of pecuniary gain, or if he did, would deserve and be pretty sure to lose it, the certain consequence of such a system of false equality would be to make the interior of India only tolerable to such European settlers as were on a level with the natives in morality, but in time much more formidable to authority—all of them unscrupulous, and many of them daring men of a buccaneering spirit, ready to make themselves captains over thousands and to conspire to unseat a government in a spirit of like unscrupulous ambition to that of some amongst those who founded it.

It would be easy to adduce instances proving beyond dispute the utter impossibility that Englishmen of integrity should meet natives on an equality in the local courts or before local magistrates. Were the "Black Act" to be carried into effect, the only part of the British dominions (Lord Palmerston has said, of the world), in which an Englishman could not boldly affirm "Civis Romanus sum," would be India. If Parliament were to enact that all men happening to bear a certain patronymic, or to live in some particular county in England, were, from a given date, to be deprived of their dearest civil rights because like rights cannot, under an absolute government, be conferred upon the natives of India, and they are not fitted for them, the injustice would not equal that of such a measure as the "Black Act." Neither the person nor property of an Englishman surrounded by a sea of natives is safe unless he can carry about with him some of the dignity of his race. The majority of the natives, so far as conscience is concerned, would not hesitate to take his life for half-a-crown, or to disprove the perpetration of the act by another for a shilling. Let him be dragged before a native court, especially one presided over by a native, and incarcerated in a native jail, and that prestige will be gone through which alone he can live safely and honourably. His only chance then is to have his own armed retainers and to set authority very much at defiance. As it is, more than one man of integrity has had to suffer ruin rather than to fall into the universal practice of suborning witnesses, without which it is childish simplicity to go into court. The climate being dead against him would alone make the fancied equality most unequal. He must have certain civil privileges to balance in some degree its effects, or it will very soon aid the natives to ruin and destroy him. He cannot stand by day labourers in the open field, or be smothered on the floor of a native court-house in a crowd of corrupt contractors, or lie, committed to jail by a Mahometan judge on the satisfactory evidence of oaths upon the "Koran" or Ganges water, without perishing from heat which scarcely affects the native. In fact we have, in the very complaints of the Company's civil officers against many of the planters, proofs of the moral effects of its own discouraging and repressive system towards those who, till of late years, were considered, and indeed styled, "interlopers," and who had often to slip their way into the country licensed only as free mariners, and liable at any time to expulsion.

Insecurity of a settler without some privileges of his race.

If the moral and material progress of India is to be furthered by the example and enterprise of Englishmen, encouragement must be given to men of the highest principle. The "Black Act" would render India tolerable only to men of the lowest.

Planters of high principle needed for India.

It is of the greatest importance, not only to the improvement of the commercial produce of India, the development of her great resources, and the moral as well as industrial progress of her people, but to British prestige, and to the name of Christianity itself through the example of its professors, that every possible provision should be made to invite out settlers who are above, and not below, the average of Englishmen in moral tone and feeling. To such results the fancied juridical equality proposed would be fatal; and fatal also, it is believed, eventually to the government itself. These opinions are based on close personal observation and subsequent inquiries, extending over a period of more than thirty years. In confirmation of them evidence could be adduced in quantity, quality, and strength, which would indeed surprise the reader, who may not from circumstances have been placed "behind the scenes" in India or be acquainted with those who have.

It may appear presumptuous, but the writer believes he could suggest a judicature to which the European alone should be amenable, which would at once foster, instead of wound, his integrity, sense of justice, and self-respect; and at the same time ensure to the native litigant with him more certain justice than it is possible can be obtained under the present system.

Anomalous privileges in India of the British as a government;

But there is that in the proposal which must be puzzling to the unsophisticated Englishman, who, in his resolute simplicity, imagines that wherever the dominions of his Sovereign extend he can carry about him his civil rights at least. He may feel concerned to think that his country, so properly jealous of the constitutional rights of her own citizens, should find herself the despotic ruler of a people six times her own in number, to whom she dare not confer a fraction of such rights, and is even barely able to administer civil justice at all; the basis of legal justice, *evidence*, having scarcely any available existence whatever amongst them. He may feel concerned at seeing his country levying taxes and war, confiscating property and life, and enacting laws (and all upon a grand scale), amongst a people who have not, and cannot be given, a word to say in the matter. And he may easily imagine that when this contradictory and un-English position of his race is divested of the grandeur of power and magnitude, and the contrast is not between Englishmen and Indians in the mass, but between an individual Englishman claiming all his own rights, and something of the privilege which his race has so largely assumed, in civil dispute with a native possessing only such rights as can be safely doled out to him, that such a contrast may cause his country some misgivings at the anomalous position in which she has placed herself. But if he reflects at all, what must be his surprise, not to say mortification, on hearing that, to appease her conscience and do homage to British principles, she is minded to make scapegoats of such of her own sons as venture into the region of her arbitrary rule—that, because she cannot raise the native up to the standard of their rights and privileges, she purposes to depress them down to the abject level of the native—that, while she justifies her own exceptional course and the gigantic privileges she assumes as necessary for her security in the country, she would refuse to the individual Englishman a recognition of the smallest fraction of such privilege as also necessary for his existence there, and would even deprive him of the dearest of his own—trial by a jury of his countrymen and personal security against arbitrary power, and that in a country where he cannot have the safeguard of any powerful public opinion, and where the local civil authority is unavoidably in the hands of men for the most part young enough to be the sons and sometimes even the grandsons of English judges, or even in the hands of natives whose religious bigotry is strongly against him, in spite of all their professions and possibly even desire.

but denied even their own rights as individuals.

The individual Englishman may fairly crave of his countrymen some explanation of the grounds upon which they collectively assume such boundless privileges over India, demanding absolute obedience at the peril of life and property, never dreaming of anything like equality or reciprocity of authority with the natives, and knowing that it would be incompatible with their position in the country to do so, and yet turn round upon him—one of their own privileged race—and, lecturing him upon the universal equality and rights of man, would ignore altogether his claim to clothe himself with a little fragment of such privilege—as it were, a mere *sun*-and-*knave*-proof cape of it. Nay, more, that they would actually deprive him of many of the rights he is born into as a Briton, and depress him to the low social level which the Indian has inherited from immemorial time, and in which, for his own security and that of his protectors, it is needful that he should be kept! as if the daily physical evils besetting the former, of heat, and prickly-heat, exhaustion, mosquitos, boils, and black-bile, with its more familiar mental correlative and metaphrase, "melancholy," and with heavy liabilities in reversion of cholera and fever, were not quite enough to torture him, without the maddening sense of wrong which, in spite of all casuistry, every Englishman must feel who is subjected to the operations of the *Black Act!*

In Mr. Venables, the indigo-planter, government has found a very able and *powerful* subject, who has held a district for them, after their own officers had to desert it. Let such settlers be encouraged, and it will be well, in all times, for both the governing and the governed. But let the country be rendered tolerable only to *Venables* of another stamp—to men who find it neccssary to risk a constant collision with authority in defending themselves when in the right, and thence grow unscrupulous of wrong—who surround themselves with retainers, mere goats by themselves but wolves when led by Englishmen—and let ten thousand of such leaders be spread over India, having a common cause in disaffection to the government—let this, more than probable, result issue in due course from the "Black Act," and we have evidence in what one powerful but loyal planter can do, of what might be enacted by ten thousand disloyal.

Unless India can, as formerly, be closed to Britons and British enterprise altogether, and it cannot, it would be well, not as a matter of right only, but of prudence also, that a different policy should be observed to that here earnestly deprecated. It will be well not to hold up at the threshold of India a legal civil-equality sieve through which, all substantial grains of sterling metal refusing to pass, nothing but moral dirt will go through to be spread broad-cast over the country.

On the Causes retarding the Progress of Christianity.

Christianity has not made the progress in India which the friends of missions have expected and promised. Have they not too hastily accepted the views of those who point to conquest as opening the readiest door to her entrance, and thereby subjected themselves to the taunts of such persons upon their failure to lead her in? A naval commander has recently gone so far as to speak of the British broadside as being the necessary forerunner of the Gospel; and in terms scarcely less plain have some divines, in the case of China, promised Gospel fruits from our opium wars!

Conquest not the proper precursor of conversion.

Our conquest of India is an accomplished fact, which we cannot reverse were we to desire it, and which it is our duty, as far as it lies in our power, to render beneficial to the temporal and spiritual interests of the people. But to imagine that conquest was either the legitimate or the surest course for promoting either of these interests is as wide a departure from scriptural teaching as it would be from historical fact to affirm that it was undertaken for that object. There are no truths more emphatically set forth in the word of God, and established in the history of His workings, than, first, that material power is not the instrument he has authorized or blessed as the means for conversion (where it appears to have proved so, it having only opened the way to a corrupt and worldly acceptance of Christianity)—and secondly, that a simple and confiding employment of spiritual weapons in reliance on His support has been attended with a success, which proves the continuance to this very hour of miraculous interpositions more marvellous than any performed merely upon the bodies of men, in the days of miracles addressed to the vulgar senses. "Put up thy sword into its place"—"we wrestle not with flesh and blood"—"the weapons of our warfare are not carnal," and fifty more scriptural passages, may be quoted to show the will, and as many scriptural instances to show the workings, of Providence. While miracles in abundance were performed by the apostles to attest their mission, they had little power to deliver themselves from the hands of men. Rarely was divine power employed even to set them free, and even then chiefly to produce an effect on the minds of others. In two out of three miraculous jail-deliveries, they neither needed nor attempted to escape. So far from *worldly power* being made to protect their path, it was always obstructing it, and most of them were left to suffer martyrdom at its hands. Weak unto death in the flesh, their spiritual strength was infinite: they did more than Archimedes imagined he could do—they upset the world! And it has been so ever since. Where no human sword has cleared his way with carnage—where the missionary has gone forth with his life in one hand and his

Bible in the other, he has rarely had to lay down either of them. Out of weakness he has been made strong—the very spectacle has been disarming; he has "turned to flight the armies of the alien." We speak, of course, of scriptural missions, not Romish; and whether we turn to ancient or modern times, to the one hemisphere or to the other, we have the universal result of success in close proportion to the outward weakness of the agent.

Christian teaching and example unaided by the sword irresistible.

Witness the unaided power with which a *practical* Christianity brought under its sway in ancient times the whole Roman and Barbarian world, and in modern times races savage, haughty, and bigoted in the extreme, through the agency of a few missionaries unarmed and unsupported by arms. Witness Tahiti, a people under the sway of an arrogant and crafty hierarchy, unsurpassed in cruelty and barbarism, with a religious system of human sacrifices, as it were prepared for the immolation of the missionary; brought, by half a dozen earnest men, who landed with their lives in their hands, into a state of Christian civilization more advanced in some respects than the generality of Christendom itself! Witness the Sandwich Isles, a parallel case. Witness all such parts of Africa as Christians have visited with the aspect of beneficence only. Witness New Zealand,* a people not haughty merely, but, at the time of their visitation, beasts of prey! actuated by the ferocity of the belly, to whom the battle-field was their shambles, yet so miraculously humanized by the missionary alone that it required a too abrupt assumption of sovereignty on our part, and occupation of their country, to rouse them into a temporary hostility against us; and even then they declined to combat on the Sabbath, though brave as any of ourselves! A son of the writer (who went to New Zealand upon a kindly presented cadetship to India for him having been declined),† his tent pitched by a lone wood-side, was awoke one

* If since the dynastic occupation of their country, the evil example of the countrymen of the missionary has had an adverse effect in some parts of New Zealand, it does but confirm the truth of the proposition.

† The Afghan and China wars had just then occurred. It is manifest that, since the soldier can scarcely, without a destruction of the military system altogether, decline enacting anything he is commanded to do, the parent who places him in that position shares, to some extent, with the government which employs him, the responsibility of his acts. Did rulers find that questionable wars cut off the supply of living instruments,

early sabbath morning by a sound of many voices, where he had supposed himself alone in the wilds. Hastily dressing himself in surprise, which, if it amounted to alarm would be excusable, he sought a glance of its source. As he approached it a peal of sacred song, causing the woods to resound with the name of the Prince of Peace, disarmed all fear. He found a tribe of New-Zealanders congregated spontaneously at their orisons, with, it is believed, the Liturgy of the Church of England in their hands, their missionary pastor being engaged at some distant station!

What youth, with any religion, but must have felt deeply impressed with the protection which that sacred name threw around him. The day was not long past when that very tribe might have been clamorous with strife, as to who first espied him as their prey, to be hewn limb from limb to satisfy the cravings of a diabolical appetite. Whereas now they were ready to embrace him as an unarmed brother in Christ, whose life, no doubt, they would readily protect with their own! That a reflex effect of a lasting character should, by such an incident at the savage antipodes, be produced on the mind of a youth from England may be well supposed.

At the end of a century's manifestation of British power and wisdom, and of extensive Missionary labour, the late occurrences in India do not exhibit a state of things at all contradictory to the whole tenor of Scripture, that worldly wisdom and the power of man are not the instruments of Providence for the propagation of the Gospel. It has doubtless made progress in cases where it came in accompanied by them; but the progress has been feeble compared with that where it has presented itself in the persons of its preachers alone. Idolatry and pride more rampant still than those of India have given way before it, when it appeared in the aspect of humility and love alone. It was

the military system would soon become, what it professes to be, purely and directly defensive. They would learn also that, while the direct necessity of self-defence is the only clear evidence of Divine permission to engage in war, *precautional* warfare involves in it that dangerous step into a dark abyss, which marks man's self-relying distrust of Providential care and rule; and rarely fails to disappoint him—a truth hard to learn; although the confidence with which such wars are engaged in by one generation is generally equalled by the condemnation they receive *from the next.*

then that in India itself the Southern Missions had such rapid progress. It was before we entered India as conquerors.

India converted, but for the exhibition of power.

Having enjoyed no small opportunity of studying the character of the natives, having employed them by thousands, both educated and uneducated, and well considered the obstacles to their conversion, and therefore also to their industrial and social advancement; the conclusion is forced upon my conviction that if in the inscrutable purposes of the Almighty it had so happened that no European had up to this day set foot in India, but the Protestant Missionary, she would (speaking humanly) before this have become evangelized—that is, there would have been an outward acceptance of Christianity from one end of the country to the other, and with it a moral change and social progress, which under present circumstances it will take long indeed to effect. This is not the opinion of a visionary fanatic or a book-worm; but of one who has been, even more than enough, occupied in practical dealings with man and matter—in employing the former to work upon almost every form of the latter.

In saying this, it is not of course meant that our position in India is not to be valued and maintained, so long as its tenure shall appear a Providential arrangement. If it has been an obstacle to higher influences, it has been outwardly the means of preserving order, and mitigating mutual oppression, amongst the people. But let not the Missionary accept the proposition that it is his proper pioneer and adjuvant, and that his small success is due to the feebleness of his Mission against native bigotry. Rather let him see in the domination and example of the professors of the religion he has to advocate, an influence so little in accordance with New Testament means, that what has been effected in the way of conversion in India is to be received as a gracious exception to its promise, surpassing anything that could have been rightly anticipated.

(G.—Page 175.)

The claims of the soldiers' children advocated with no personal reflections.

In giving a public expression, at last, to deeply implanted impressions on the fate of the Soldier's Child, and (under a future head) on the prospects in India of the Soldier himself, I would desire to be understood as reflecting only upon *the system* to which the minds of all of us have been enslaved by custom, until a common assent to it has become established. So far is it from my intention to cast reflections upon any *persons*, either as individuals or as members of authoritative bodies, that I feel too conscious of being myself especially chargeable with neglect in the matter. It is true that I have not failed, when the opportunity offered, in private conversation, to express my convictions on these subjects, and that I might plead the excuse of having no official responsibility in the matter. But there is the greater responsibility of observation and conviction. I have felt in such cases the choice to lie between three unsatisfactory courses—either, in touching upon evils of such magnitude that the mere naming of them may be displeasing, to smooth them down with soft and inadequate terms, which, serving only to perpetuate smooth and inadequate impressions, are worse than useless — or to refrain from any public remonstrance whatever, a course, at least not actively injurious like the former—or lastly, to give a *truthful* expression to one's impressions, employing terms and epithets neither feebler nor stronger than were due to truth. The price of such a course—the certainty of inviting displeasure, and the imputation of cavilling, with the uncertainty of any beneficial result—has been more than I have hitherto felt prepared to pay. Of the three, the middle course has been hitherto taken, as the preferable one—a course which, while open to reproof by some, others will think it would have been well to have adhered to still.

(H.—Page 188.)

Arts of Importance introduced into India.

Some apology may appear due to a record here of the following operations and their result. But they whose views are enlightened, and whose interest in Indian progress is sincere, will scarcely think so.

The Operator entered upon an Indian career, mainly as an inviting field for favourite pursuits in science, well supplied with philosophical apparatus. It became, almost on landing, his ambition to effect something towards the advancement of Indian art by the aid of European science. The furthest thought from

The successful introduction of important arts into India.

his mind was to undertake any business operations, as such, conscious of a disqualification equalling his distaste for them. A zeal and ambition, overpassing pecuniary, were necessary for carrying out to a successful completion undertakings not commonly surpassed by private works in England in the scale of the operations, and by none in the variety of them.

Absence of the fundamental means of the useful arts.

Let scientific machinists and chemists form their opinion as to the extent of the *undeveloped* industrial wealth in a country with boundless natural resources and a teeming and intelligent population, but in which the fundamental instruments of useful art are wanting to the following extent. In mechanics no lathes (worth the name), no fly, or punching presses; no proper grinding or crushing mills; wind unemployed as a power for machinery, and water nearly so; and scarcely any gear-work, and that absurdly faulty. In metallurgic art, no fire-bricks whatever; nor knowledge of real furnaces, or kilns. In chemical art, scarcely a knowledge even of the mineral acids, or of the uncombined alkalies; no ceramic ware of a "body" less pervious than a common pipkin; no glass (of Indian manufacture) deserving the name.

An inviting field for peaceful ambition.

Here was a field for any one who should be as ambitious to exhibit before the natives the ascendancy of England in the arts of peace, as her captains have been to establish her ascendancy in the art of war! Here was an opportunity to wield over matter, brute and ponderous, the powers of nature, providentially placed within call of human intelligence, until the natives should look on with amazement, and begin to think that there was nothing impossible to Englishmen! Here was an opportunity for attempting a practical solution of the wordy anticipations of politicians respecting "British skill and capital developing the resources of India," repeated almost from the days of Plassy to the present hour; but by how many attempted to be brought down from thin air and reduced to a stubborn reality?

Moved in a humble degree with such desires, it was that, at the suggestion of an officer who was acquainted with his pursuits, the Operator was led into an attempt which would at once introduce into India a variety of important manufactures, though at that time his knowledge was theoretical only; he having *no practical acquaintance whatever* with any of them.

At that period mineral waters were much in vogue for

medicinal purposes, and one of these, soda-water, as a luxury verging to a necessary in India. Artificial Harrogate water, on account of its action on the liver, was a favourite remedy with some; especially with the late Mr. Sandham, a medical officer of great ability, in H. M. service, at whose request it was included in the products of the mineral-water manufactory which was established.

The reader must know that a place more barren of resources from art, and at first sight from nature, could scarcely be found than the interior of India more than a thousand miles up the Ganges from Calcutta. At one time the very screws and nails used, and some of the implements necessary for the workmen, had to be made on the spot. A large part of the machinery and prepared metals had of course to be obtained from England. Nevertheless, in the course of three years, after almost incredible difficulties, works were established on what might fairly be termed a grand scale. As from a large brewery in England, the products went forth to all parts of the country to those who vended them.

Determined that the works should be self-relying, the opportunity offered itself to attempt the manufacture of oil of vitriol (sulphuric acid), vitreous stone pottery, and eventually glass, which form the necessary basis of the chemical arts in a country, and of fire-brick and furnaces of the metallurgic—also of soda, potash, compressed citrate of lime, &c. For the vitriol chamber, which was of considerable dimensions, a large boat-load of English sheet lead had to be procured from Calcutta, a journey more tedious than that from England.*

Grossness of the native taste. Remarkable incidents.

* On the arrival of the large rolls of lead, which the natives took for "*lead roots*," which they fancied to be a natural production in coils, the following incident occurred, worthy of note as showing the influence of caste upon the tastes as well as the prejudices of the people; and how wide is that social separation between the different castes which rightly handled might be converted into as wide a religious and political one. To remove on to a bank of sand, without dropping them into the river, the rolls of lead weighing a ton each, the thatch of the boat had to be thrust up, when a large nest of stinking rats was upset into the river. The captain of the boat leaped into the water, as he was, and swimming into the eddy in which the creatures were struggling, he caught them up one by one by the tail, and chucked them old and young upon the thatch again. Upon the object being inquired: what led him to reverse what had been supposed a good service and riddance, he replied,

Oil of vitriol manufacture.

Preliminary experiments, proving the expediency, led to the construction of the chamber well underground, by which the heat and draught of the climate, which would have stopped the generation of the acid or greatly reduced the product, were obviated.

With the exception of a small chamber at Calcutta this was the only sulphuric acid work, not in India only, but probably in all Asia. There is a miniature and empirical production of the acid by native alchemists—an article they sell at about three shillings the ounce, while this cost about the English price of a penny or two-pence a pound—only one hundred and fortieth part the cost of the native acid! When it is considered that the corrosiveness of the acid is such a bar to its shipment from England that the freight and insurance by the time it reached the heart of India would multiply its price many fold, and that the

Its importance to India.

"Pardon your servant; when any of us boatmen are not well, and our stomachs too weak to relish our ordinary fare, we treat ourselves to a rat or two, which we breed in the thatch!" On another occasion, while travelling by water, having towed to land the huge carcase of a putrid alligator with the vain hope of extricating, without the aid of thorough decomposition, its skeleton from the almost ferreous bands of ligament and sinew, upon my abandoning it, after notching and blunting every hatchet at command, the boatmen petitioned for the eggs. Ripping the creature up, they took out bushels full of the blue and putrid shelless spheroids, which the men of all the half-dozen boats devoured day by day, keeping them in baskets in the sun, until a gust from the roof of the boat on which they were, no "spicy gale from Araby the blest," bringing to mind their existence, now in the last stage of cohesion, I ordered them to be thrown overboard. Yielding however to a request that they might be finished off that evening, it was no small trial to the stomach, when some men and boys entering our boat to bale out the water, the exudations trickling down their skins were rank with the odour distilled from within. Taxing one almost naked boy with the cause of the visible rotundity of his stomach, he replied, patting it complacently, "*Hān khodawun unde se bhurguya*," "Yes, your worship, it is brimfull of the eggs."

Contrast with these men, many of them fine enduring fellows though at present so disgustingly coarse in their tastes, the affected and fastidious Brahmin, who may be seen to walk about with a gauze veil before his mouth, lest animal life and matter in the form of animalculæ should chance to enter it; and then reflect what an opportunity the former, and all that division of abject castes immediately above and below them, offer, if skilfully taken by the hand, to be relieved of their social depression and oppression under Brahminism, and raised into an independent antagonism to the Brahmin and Rajpoot.

chief ingredient, sulphur, is cheaply obtained of the purest kind in the East, and the other, nitre, is actually supplied to England *from India;* and when it is further considered that sulphuric acid forms the root of the chemical arts of a country from which they branch out into the magnificent growth they have attained in Europe—in England especially; and further, that this acid would render available much Indian produce, citric acid for instance, which cannot in the form of lime-juice come with advantage to England; the indispensability of the manufacture of this acid to the progress of India in chemical arts will be manifest. No little perseverance in experiments, and contrivance, were required to enable one who had never seen any acid work before to bring the production, in a climate particularly adverse to it, up to the maximum attained in England—to an average exceeding two and a half times the sulphur consumed. To makers of this acid in England it may be useful to know, that experiment proved pure *shell-lac* to be nearly proof against its action, even when of considerably greater density than it ever attains in the chamber. Hence beams and planks coated with lac, which were placed within it, were preserved many years, and secure "joints" could be formed with lac at all seams.

Manufacture of fire-bricks, furnaces, ceramic ware, and glass.

The manufacture of fire-bricks, furnaces, and especially of vitreous pottery, left every other difficulty in the shade. The mineral resources of the country within a radius of two hundred miles had to be explored. Men were kept in all directions searching in the banks and beds of rivers and by well-diggers for earths and stones. Of the specimens brought in, hundreds had to be tested and some were closely analyzed. Eventually Bundelkund yielded three of the most important materials, and Rohilcund two others. It was not until after two years of unremitted efforts, persevered in, at one time, almost as much by night as by day, and with an expenditure on this branch alone of more than three thousand pounds, that a manufacture was perfected of vitreous stone-ware equal in quality to any in England, and on a large scale, from twenty-four to thirty thousand articles a month being produced. Upon a specimen being shown to a manufacturer here he was unwilling to credit the fact that its material was artificially compounded, affirming that for such ware a naturally compounded earth must be found. The fire-brick, which had no small share in effecting this, was brought to a refractoriness and freedom from expansion much surpassing that of any English fire-brick. The reason of this would be evident at once to the scientific reader, did space admit of the process of their manufacture being here explained. When it is considered that a good fire-brick is at the foundation of all ceramic, vitreous, and metallurgic art, and that no brick less fusible than a house-brick existed throughout India, saving fire-bricks imported all the way from England, and no ceramic ware with a better "*body*," however painted and glazed, than that of a house tile, the perfection of these arts in India will not be thought unimportant by those who admit that if we draw largely upon her revenues we owe her, in return, instruction in *practical*, as well as theoretical science. Soda, potash, and purified and compressed citrate of lime were also produced in these works; from twenty-five to thirty pipes of lime-juice having in one season been reduced into that solid form. But this product was discontinued; its novel form in cakes causing its intrinsic value to be unappreciated in the London market. Mineral waters, soda, potash, Harrogate, seltzer, and chalybeate, of which, mainly the first, from ten to twenty thousand pounds worth were at one period despatched in the year, gave the commercial support to the works. As even the wire used was in general drawn on the spot, everything—the acids, sulphuric and hydro-sulphuric, the alkalies and salts, the vitreous bottles and the wire—were all produced within the walls. The corks alone, to the annual value of about eight hundred pounds, were imported, and from France. Any full description of the various experiments, furnaces, kilns, grinding and other mills and machines, presses, "wheels," &c., devised and constructed, would form a volume of itself. At the age of twenty-eight the owner had the satisfaction of seeing his work complete; but as he had throughout the period professional duties and anxieties — to his temperament more trying than all these operations upon brute matter—he was doubtless ageing in constitution three years in one.

Its importance.

The use of saltpetre in the acid works drew his attention to the crude sources of this article, and led to the following peculiar process, and extensive and distinct works, for its refinement. The nitre of India has two distinct sources, yielding two very different kinds of crude saltpetre, though the two are often mixed in the market in various proportions. One is the result of some elective or inductive affinity which leads to the formation of nitre where other salts, common salt especially, are in existence. This article is easily cleaned by one process of solution and crystallization, but then it is poor in nitre, yielding from 15 to 30 per cent., though containing more. The other kind of nitre is largely generated in its proper native source,—the drains, ditches, and walls of villages where animal matter is undergoing decay. Its saline matter is all saltpetre amounting to 80 or 90 per cent., the rest being soluble animal impurities. But then their solubility, and the dark and greasy character they give to this article, even after two refinings, render it less marketable, though so much richer, than the former.

Varieties of crude saltpetre.

Aware of the two facts, first, that nitre suffers no injury by a heat of 500°, and secondly, that at that heat, and below it, animal matter becomes thoroughly decomposed and reduced to charcoal, which is a powerfully clarifying agent, this interesting experiment was made. A parcel of forty pounds of this fetid crude salt was taken. One half, dissolved in hot water, was poured into a capacious glass jar. The other half was carefully charred, spoonful by spoonful, on an iron plate over a chafing dish, and the jet-black product similarly dissolved and poured into a fellow jar. The former solution was of its usual dark colour of London porter, and yielded small, dark, greasy, and friable crystals. In the other solution the *charcoal*, into which the impurities had been resolved by the frying, settled rapidly, leaving the supernatant liquid as clear as crystal. It was drawn off by a syphon, and yielded beautiful prismatic crystals the size of the finger of pure saltpetre. This specimen was sent to Calcutta, and valued at two shillings the cwt. above the finest article in the market, that being four or five times the cost of the crude material in the Futtehgurh and Oude districts. So valuable a process for rendering marketable a cheap article which largely abounded, prompted, after various experiments, the following erections. A large building, standing on thirty-two timbers, as a table on its legs, one hundred and twenty feet long, one hundred wide, and fifty high at the centre, and twenty at the eaves, contained this apparatus. A reverberatory furnace, having a circular bed, bottomed with sheet iron and twelve feet in diameter, was mounted eighteen feet high over a hollow arch. Two flat iron arms set

Peculiar process for refining it.

Extensive works for the purpose.

edgeways, one of them being concave, the other convex, radiated to the circumference of the furnace bed, from a spindle in its centre which passed through its bottom into the archway. It was there mounted with a grooved wheel, round which a chain passed to a "rigger wheel" driven by bullocks. The iron arms were each six to seven feet long and six inches deep, and swept the furnace bed as they revolved. In the archway under the furnace stood a massive wooden vat twelve feet high and ten in diameter, half filled with cold water, with a wooden agitator, the axis of which could be connected above with the spindle and wheel just described, so as to be driven round by the same bullocks. Directly fires were lighted in the two large fireplaces of the reverberatory three hundredweight of the crude saltpetre were poured in through tubes in its roof, and swept round the bed by the iron arms, which were so notched below as to lay the salt alternately in a disk round the centre, and in a flat ring towards the circumference. The motion of the sweeps kept the salt from being over heated, while the constantly renewed salt kept them from becoming red-hot in the intense heat, and bending. In six or eight minutes three hundredweight of the salt were completely carbonized and thoroughly melted, when two draw-slats in the bed were opened, and the molten salt, at a temperature of 500°, fell into the water in the vat below.

Their capability and success.

In ten hours *ten tons* of the salt were thus fused and discharged into the vat; by which time the whole was in full ebullition, and the vat became a wooden boiler, the heat coming down in the saltpetre, and the same fuel performing the double duty of carbonization and solution. The liquor, being allowed to settle for ten hours, was drawn off limpid into leaden coolers twenty-four feet long, twelve feet wide, and two-and-a-half feet deep; which became a maze of beautiful crystals, the first crop weighing four or five tons, and the second about three more. As this process could be repeated every twenty-four hours with ease, the capability of the works may be estimated. The works contained also large evaporating and dissolving boilers, of iron and copper, some of the former twenty feet long.

The making of these proved impossible by native skill. After employing about sixty smiths for some weeks in the attempt, and the destruction of much English sheet-iron by their efforts to punch it, a large fly-press was contrived and erected, which could receive the sheets with the edges of each pair overlapped, so that the holes were punched through both at one time; and as the machine guided the sheets with great rapidity, three unskilled labourers could punch the plates of a large boiler in one day; and so accurately that the rivets could be dropped into all the double holes at once; whereas some sixty smiths, with their native means of punching, had attempted the work for a fortnight, or more, and failed. The whole of the framework of this press was of timber, yet it answered perfectly, and lasted well. Large punching press for boilers.

Ill health compelled the owner to leave all these undertakings; but not until they had suffered a severe shock, through the impossibility, after a time, of obtaining the crude salt, though it abounded, without advances; and of securing these without the employment of suborned witnesses and other intolerable practices.

One of the chief agents having embezzled eight thousand rupees, the *Amil*, or head of the office, undertook to prosecute him. On entering the works one morning, the proprietor had a dozen smartly dressed and shrewd men introduced to him as the witnesses against the defaulter, by the Amil, who, anticipating his objections, remarked, "These are not only very clever, but most truthful men. I have explained that master will only consent to the truth." When they all exclaimed, "As Heaven is above, so is master below; on the holy Ganges water, we will all swear to the truth, and prove it so that master shall have justice." The process was then explained with great zest on the proprietor's consenting to listen to the temptation. These men, having never seen or heard of any of the parties till that day, would take a month to get up the case, to learn the facts to be proved, to invent a variety of incidental circumstances, to vary their evidence, and contradict each other on trifling points in such a way as to avoid the appearance of collusion, and to practise themselves against all possible cross-questioning—in short, introducing one hundred lies for each truth proved, and being quite ready to prove the claim double the real amount in order to secure a large commission as well as pay. It was impossible not to admire the ingenuity, shrewdness, and cunning of these men, and to lament that they were thus prostituted. On their being paid for the day and dismissed, the head of the office remarked, "It is of no use to go into court with the real witnesses in any such cases; they are base and brutish '*goônwarees*,'* who will not only tell more lies than the skilled witnesses, but be caught in them, and their evidence will be proved good for nothing; whereas master would to a certainty have gained his cause, for I had secured the ablest company of witnesses in Furrukabad." He was right as to the issue; especially as handsome bribes to the officers of the court would also have been necessary. The attempt, without these practices, would have been vain. The impunity of one defaulter proved an example for others; between 2000*l.* and 3000*l.* of advances, though made with all apparent lateral security, vanished, and what was worse, there was no hope for the future.

Here were works most complete as a manufacturing and commercial undertaking, and employing on the spot and in the district some thousands of men on much advanced wages and earnings, exhibiting also in the peculiarly "trussed" roof alone, and the stability of a stately building against hurricanes, though standing on lofty timbers which had to support the walls of matting twenty feet high (saltpetre devouring earth and brick walls), mechanism in carpentry instructive to the people; and in the various processes and the scale of the operations, in the furnaces; in the iron, copper, lead, and wooden boilers, crystallizers, and vats; in the peculiar saline liquor pumps, and pluvial evaporating apparatus, &c., a step scarcely inferior to the works first described, towards developing the resources and industry of India,—a raised platform in the universal level of dormant ignorance, which merited better aid from an enlightened government than to be overwhelmed by a system under which success with integrity was an impossible conjunction.

A curious incident occurred when the reverberatory process was first tried, which was at midnight owing to delays in completing the preparations. The sudden descent of four hundred pounds weight (the quantity tried) of the salt at the heat of 500°

* Clowns.

† In a hurricane which blew down some trees and buildings, its constructor was up at daybreak, watching in some alarm, from the shelter of a tree, the springing of the large and elastic structure to each heavy gust; when a number of the workmen made their appearance an hour before the time, certain, as they confessed, that they should witness the ruins of their occupation.

or more into water at 80°, in a hollow covered vat under an archway, gave rise to such hideous noises, followed by moaning sounds, and that at midnight, that the whole of the men on the process screamed out, took flight, and reported in Furrukabad, that "master" had at last gone too far, and had revolted against nature by putting heated salt into cold water instead of cold salt into heated water; that the heat of the salt was past the endurance of the water-spirits, who shrieked with pain; and that they saw their master carried up into the clouds. However, finding on the following morning this ascent a mistake, and encouraged by the light of day, the process was again attempted, and though some again decamped, the rest held on under the eye of an assistant, and became in time familiar with the roar and outlandish plaints repeated every ten minutes or so.

(I.—Page 203.)

The Traffic in Opium in the East.

The saddest subject connected with India and China, beyond all question is Opium. Would that it were possible to be silent upon it, lest the remarks which an anxious study of the question for many years constrains me to offer should in any measure prejudice, in some minds, the interest which may have been excited upon the main subject of this volume!

I would fain startle the reader who cannot afford even the following condensed view of the question his attention, with a few preliminary facts and arguments!

Striking illustration of the quantity of opium consumed in China.

The opium consumed in China, three-fourths of which are imported, and one-fourth, or one-third, now grown in that country, and every ounce of which is chargeable at our door, amounts *annually* to 100,000 chests or more, and was *rapidly increasing* at the time of the late outbreak. That would make about 20 million gallons* of *laudanum*, which placed in nine-gallon casks end to end would extend 400 or 500 miles!—*a quantity sufficient to poison to death in one dose averaging five drachms each, old, young, and infantile, four times the whole population of the world!* Were that laudanum from a single year's opium deposited in a gigantic, tower-shaped, vat, standing 500 feet high, either before the Houses of Parliament or before the India House,

* Calculated in wine measure of four quarts to the gallon.

and were that vat to suffer a judicial bursting, such would prove the quantity and the force of its contents, that the Eastern building in the city would, almost in the twinkling of an eye, be washed down amongst the ruins of the neighbouring streets; or the western, with all its titled and learned councillors, with their many virtues and not unfrequent errors, voting at the time perhaps a resolution in favour of the traffic, would be swept away into the Thames in fewer seconds than Sir Charles Barry was years in rearing it, by a cataract of laudanum 500 feet high and 70 in diameter; as liberated from the dissolving vat!

Its comparison with the spirit consumed in the British Isles.

Awful as would be such a catastrophe, and deplorable as a national loss, it would be small in comparison with the annual injury done to China by our opium; little as casual observers may be disposed to notice it. The reader who may question these effects is invited to a perusal of the following remarks; and he is implored not to draw a comparison between our nation's shame in the West—the spirit debauchery of Britain, and our greater shame in the East—the opium debauchery of our own planting in China; unless it be to remonstrate from the homefelt injury of the minor though gigantic evil of Spirit, against the terrible effects and prospects to China of the greater evil of Opium.—Unless it be to institute such a comparison as *this*—the total production of spirits in Great Britain and Ireland, both for home consumption and for exportation, exceeds *twenty millions of gallons!*—a quantity alarming to contemplate. The opium consumed in China, if dissolved in that spirit, would just about suffice to convert it all into laudanum;* and then, in the physician's estimate of its powers, *all that solvent spirit present would be nearly as so much water compared with the* OPIUM! Moreover, opium acts, not less, but more powerfully upon the *Mongolian*—the Chinese, than on *the Caucasian*—the European race; and not less, but more, when smoked, or rather deeply inhaled, than when taken into the stomach. Spirit debauchery is indeed our great domestic vice and shame; but it has crept in upon us unawares from the day when distillation first made spirit known in Europe under the illusive belief that it was the elixir of life—

* Taking it as wine measure.

and obtained for it the credit, and name, of "*aqua vitæ*," "*eau de vie*," &c. It is the same agent, also, as that which gives attractiveness, whether right or wrongly, to wine and other fermented liquors: so that, if we are ensnared by alcohol, we have become entangled unwittingly in its meshes. But not so with opium. Is there one member sitting in the British or Indo-British Council Chambers, who could refrain from denouncing as a felon, deserving transportation, the chemist whom he found teaching his household for gain to consume laudanum as an agent of vicious excitement? And would that chemist better his position, would he not rather drive the injured parent or husband frantic, by proving that his family, by use, could now consume it by spoonfuls with apparent impunity, or by arguing that, if he did not entice them, some other chemist would? or by coolly calculating how insignificant a proportion, and therefore loss, his family was to the whole population? Yet such, nay in many respects worse than this, have been our doings in China!

The comparison deprecated as reprehensible.

Oh! do not parade before the world our nation's drunkenness—"publish it not in the streets of Askelon," unless it be to serve some beneficent and sacred object! Do not think to better our shameful doings abroad by a shameless exhibition of our state at home! What would be said of the apologist, and his apology, who, upon being remonstrated with for debauching his neighbours' wives, should reply, "Why make such a pother about that? I can tell you what is just as bad. Only come to my home, and you shall see how abandoned my wife and sisters are"? Yet wherein is the difference between his argument, and the common apology for the debauching of China with opium—that it has its parallel in the spirit debauchery at home—which finds its way into the mouths of even able and excellent men, who have accepted it from others, and circulated it, as opium-defence currency, without duly reflecting upon its extraordinary character?

Without for one moment admitting, that the necessity, supposing it existed, of bolstering up the revenues of India by opium, could justify a continuance of the traffic, it may be shown that the necessity does not exist, and could only end in ruin if it did.

We have at last well nigh succeeded in breaking down all *Local* and *Imperial* opposition in China to the entry of opium, having long and easily corrupted all the former authorities,* and now intimidated the latter. But, with our evil success we have equally destroyed the ground of opposition to the cultivation of opium in China, which, according to the best information to be obtained, has grown up with such rapidity since the opium war of 1842, as already to equal nearly one-third of the importations.

Facilities for the production of the drug in China.

The reader may not be aware that China possesses, in a greater degree than India, the facilities for a cheap production of the drug,—quite equalling it in climate and soil, and surpassing it in that density of the population, and difference in their habits, which lead to the excretion and preservation of an immense quantity of highly *nitrogenous* manure, so favourable to the plant, and which also supply, for wounding its matured capsules and collecting the juices, perverted fingers innumerable of women and children, unfettered by castes from a general co-operation. Let it not be imagined that the requirement of the land for grain would form any obstacle. It would even less than it does in England to the production of hops, in which the land rent is a small consideration. The price of opium in China would pay for the import of food from any part of the world, though raised at English prices. In the remarkable facilities for the production of the drug in China, and the rapid growth of it now, we have, in fact, painful and irrefragable proof, both of the self-denial of the supreme government of China, which, under severe edicts, and against the recommendation of certain of its financiers, restrained the production to its utmost, during the two hundred years, at least, in which we have evidence of their being familiar with its properties and dangerous use ; and we have proof also of the influence of our doings,—and what must they issue in ! Having established the most extensive and deeply rooted debauchery the world has known, and while relying upon it, as forming a large and increasing proportion

* Strange! that the facility with which opium is now introduced through our too successful corruption of the local functionaries, which is a serious aggravation of our offence, should be constantly cited by the upholders of the traffic as an apology for it!

of the revenue of India, we have thus started an opium cultivation in China, which in the nature of things must increase, and leave the opium revenue of India stranded; and when gone, that opium traffic will leave the government of India "poor indeed,"—not through the loss of its opium purse only, that were "something, nothing," but by filching from it its "*good name*" throughout this nether world, and amongst the hosts in heaven.

Far better were it now, and at once, to look to the legitimate sources of revenue in India, in affirming which to be abundant for all needful requirements of good and secure government, we are not indulging in the mere speculative opinions of politicians, or in secondhand information.

Growth of the traffic in the hands of England.

Again, so far is the British government in India from having merely inherited the traffic in opium from the Mahometan, and from having used any endeavours to limit it, that the latter are said to have resolutely repressed a deleterious cultivation of the poppy. Ninety years ago no regular trade in it existed; but a vicious propensity for opium was discernible amongst the Chinese on the coast sufficient to stimulate the cupidity of the Company's functionaries in Bengal, who commenced, after a minor trial or two, with a venture of a thousand chests, which they had *to smuggle* into Canton in an armed vessel. And so far is it from being true that any endeavours were employed to repress the traffic at any time, that, though the Company proved their knowledge of its character by once expressing a wish that for "the good of Humanity" this could be done (as if the whole was not entirely in their power), they warned their Bengal government against any such steps as would injure their revenue from it. The traffic, having, like a poisonous reptile, crept along the shores of China, took forty years of *fostering care* to nurse it up to four thousand chests, after which it grew rapidly, and in ten more years had so far advanced as to excite the envy of the native governments of India, whose cupidity, at last, over-ruled their better professions, enticed on as it was by the example of the leviathan parent of the creature. Onwards it grew, breathing forth as it were a moral *aura morphiana* which has affected merchants and political functionaries, Christian and Bhudist, as fast as they have approached it, until in 1840, when Commissioner Lin with tears declared that every chest of opium imported was the death-warrant of numbers of his countrymen, the quantity upon which he proved his sincerity by a most righteous destruction of it was no less than twenty thousand chests, present at one time; the importation then being nearly forty thousand chests a year; and now, since every barrier set up by the supreme government of China has been practically broken down by the former war, the amount has risen to upwards of seventy thousand chests, while the cultivation in China, the restriction of which has for the same reason been relaxed in despair, appears to have brought the total consumption up to an increasing one of one hundred thousand chests; and it is in the very nature of such a debauchery to continue to progress until it has reduced to impoverishment and ruin any nation falling under it, how numerous soever it may be!

It can only terminate in the ruin of China.

Ready means for the suppression of the traffic.

Let not then truth be abashed by the mistaken assertion that England, acting either through her Imperial government at home or local of India, endeavours to restrain the production of opium. She holds the monopoly, absolute within her own territory, and it is most desirable that she should continue to do so, and with it the responsibility and odium of all excess in production beyond a mere medicinal supply for the East. This might authorize a cultivation to the extent of two or three thousand chests a year. Her rule is also despotic. Thus doubly armed, she held an entire command of the production in her own territories for many years when it amounted to no more than that quantity; and she could of course bring it down to that amount again; and would very shortly, could she see it to be her interest to do so. Possessing an entire command over the ports of India, she has a nearly equal hold upon the opium from Native States, the distance of most of which from the coast would increase her ability to restrict the passage of it, to any extent she desired. It is indeed sad to think that her example has brought some of them into that anomalous position of depending, like herself, upon this odious traffic for a considerable portion of their revenue. But now that she will little desire subsidiary aid from them in the form of any more "contingents," there is afforded a favourable opportunity for commencing a restriction on their export of opium.

To such a course she is bound, as having been herself the exemplar of EVIL instead of the GOOD for which she was placed in her privileged position in the East.

The path of duty plain.

The path for England is surely plain enough. Let her fulfil her late treaty both in its spirit and letter. As in the case of Africa, let her make amends for a long course of wrong-doing by protecting the coast of China, who is as unable to guard herself from the intrusion of the opium clippers as Africa from that of slavers; and let steps be taken for reducing without delay the production of opium in British India and of checking that in the Native States by warning the merchants that it will to a certainty be seized and confiscated when caught in the Chinese seas. Happily there is so little chance of an opium revenue having any permanency, that Indian financiers may be anxious to turn at once to other and legitimate sources before the production of the drug in China has run to an irrepressible length, and our nation shall lie under utter condemnation as the cause of it. They who contend that India cannot be ruled without the aid of a revenue from opium, proclaim, in other words, the duty of our retiring from the country; but it is not so. Her resources properly husbanded are ample. She may not indeed afford *at present* the double charge of a full civil and military establishment—the latter employed only during war—but she can afford a machinery quite as effective as she has yet had, and much less costly; and she may, assuredly, be made to yield a larger revenue than she does.

The monopoly of production must not be relinquished by the government of India.

With respect to the production of opium, it would be a mistake indeed for the government to relinquish the monopoly of it. In no other way can the growth be limited to the small amount which will suffice for a medicinal supply for India. But, as absolute in power, and the sole producer, the government can as formerly restrain the production with no great difficulty to the quantity made thirty or forty years ago. Then may we hope for that Divine blessing upon our rule in India, which, at present, who that is not blind or bold, indeed, could venture to invoke?

Incident causing the author to become acquainted with the traffic.

My own acquaintance with the subject dates from the year 1831, when, in passing by water the chief opium magazine of the East India Company at Patna, I paid a visit to a friend who had charge of the scientific department of it. After he had led me through story after story, and gallery after gallery of the factory, with opium balls right and left tiered in shelves to the ceiling; upon my expressing amazement at an exhibition of opium, enough to supply the medical wants of the world for years, he replied, nearly in these words: "I see you are very innocent; these stores of opium have no such beneficent destination. It is all going to debauch the Chinese, and my duty is to maintain its smack as attractive to them as possible. Come to my laboratory." There I saw broken balls of opium procured from China, by the Bengal government, as approved musters for imitation, by the cultivators. Though I had been several years in India, this was the first I knew of the nature of the traffic, and thankful was I for the accidental visit, and the painful impression it left, and that the next person, whom the Governor-general did the honour of selecting for the office upon the death of my friend, felt bound to decline it.

Upon looking around for information, I heard that the natives, where they ventured an opinion, the Mahomedans especially, were equally scandalized at the engagement of the Company in such a traffic.*

Independent action of the medical profession of England.

That the medical profession of England is prepared to form its own independent judgment on so grave a question, uninfluenced by any party considerations, we have an exemplary proof in the fact, that in the year 1843, at the moment when the opium question was coming before the House of Commons, having undertaken to obtain an authoritative opinion against any use of opium as a luxury, I found men in the first position most ready to pronounce against it; and it was gratifying to notice the weight of their opinion on the House, and the force with which the Earl of Shaftesbury (then Lord Ashley) wielded it in the resolution he moved. It is true that an opponent in the House inquired for a medical opinion from China itself, and named Dr. Parker as a highly qualified authority on the spot; but then he did so with every deferential expression towards the collective opinion of the heads of the profession in London; and it is curious that, expecting such opposition, I had placed

The Earl of Shaftesbury's motion in 1843.

* A pamphlet, published in 1842, entitled 'England and China, by an Englishman,' of which between 2000 and 3000 copies were circulated, was written under the deep impression first produced by this incident.

amongst papers for his Lordship, an extract, I had received from America, of a report recently forwarded to the Missionary Society there by *Dr. Parker himself*, in which be expresses amazement that a country, occupying the position amongst Christian nations of England, should be found implicated in a traffic not only destructive to health and life, but frequently unseating the intellect, and driving to furious madness its unhappy victims. Had his Lordship not been induced by the Minister to withdraw his motion (at a moment when he appeared in the arms of victory), upon the grounds that negotiations for peace were progressing in China, this remarkable remonstrance from Dr. Parker, while it would doubtless have proved a more satisfactory answer than its seeker expected or desired, would have shown that learned and conscientious minds, though separated by the globe, would pronounce but one opinion upon such a question.

Opium as an Article of Luxury, and a Comparison of it with Spirit.

While statesmen, financiers, and traders, though abundantly wary of it as far as their families are concerned, are trifling with this dangerous agent, and speak of its properties as if it were an article of modern experience, to the physician it is known in the writings of the ancients; its very patronymic, "*Thebaicum*," reminding him that it dates back to its preparation in *Thebes*. Its more familiar name, "Opium," having doubtless been derived, as the Greek "*Opion*," from the Arabic name "*Ufyon*" or "Ufeem" (rather than from the Greek "οπος," juice), shows it to have been very anciently known in Asia. In Persia, as far back as the ninth century, it is described by the physician Rhazes,* who also dwells upon its injurious effects as an article of luxury. In the different parts of India we found, in the various dialects, *Khush-khash*, *Koaknar*, &c., and more generally the Hindee "*Poast*," to be the familiar names of the plant from which opium was being prepared at the time we obtained possession of the country. In China, according to Sir William Ainslie,† we have no earlier notice of opium than in a work entitled *Puntsaou*, written

Historical notice of opium.

* Op. Rhaz. de re Med., lib. i., p. 198.

† Ainslie's Materia Medica, vol. i., p. 621.

in 1600, in which it is recommended for the cure of dysentery. But it appears improbable that that ancient people, familiar with most natural agents before Europeans, should not have known one so important and so obtrusive to the senses as the mephitic exudation, frequently spontaneous, of the poppy-head.

Oversight respecting its action.

The action of opium upon the human system, and its admissibility or not as a luxury, is one of the many questions upon which certain moralists and physicists, by creating in them divisions, do little credit to their respective bodies,—a sure result of allowing the judgment to be warped by partial evidence, and of neglecting to keep prominently in view a dispensation of the Almighty which determines the whole condition of man. It being a prominent part of His great design to exercise the higher faculties of man, his moral especially, the relation to him of every material agent is made such as to keep him at all times in a state of probation. Many of the direst agencies are in their operation sufficiently uncertain to qualify his fears, and sufficiently inviting to tempt him to brave them. If every bullet entered a heart, there would be an end of war and of the virtue of refraining from it; if fatal disease followed every licentious act, there would be an end of incontinence and of the virtue of chastity; were every approach to drunkenness fatal, men would be shy of alcohol and sobriety would be no virtue. So also, if every use of opium, as a luxury, were lethal, there could never have entered into the Supreme Councils of Bengal the hope of debauching China with it.

The danger of a luxurious use of opium rests in the very facts adduced by its promoters in defence of it—namely, that while opium is beyond all comparison the most fascinating and destructive of narcotic stimulants to a people falling into its snare, a proportion of its devotees, sufficient to be a lure to others, are able for many years to restrain themselves to an apparently moderate use of the drug, while, here and there, instances of longevity occur, and of constitutions able to carry the consumption to an extraordinary extent. Such instances are not wanting in England. Doctor Christison, of Edinburgh, cites several which had been scraped together to defend the claims of the executors of an opium-eater of rank upon a repudiating insurance-office.

In a similar manner the Imperial Opium Trade Interest has

had little difficulty in bolstering up its cause with *quasi* medical evidence from India and China of a like character—the isolated facts of which may no doubt be true: and some residents in China may truly testify that they have seen little evidence to the contrary. Their opium transactions being with active men of business, the capable, and not the debauched, all who pass into the latter stage cease to cross *their* path. But to bring forward as evidence prosperous indulgers in opium, is merely to exhibit the *decoy-ducks*, but for whose existence and example the traffic would very soon come to an end.

For evidence from China worthy of reliance we must turn to the disinterested and the devoted, especially to the medical missionaries. The picture they exhibit is appalling indeed, yet such only as might be predicated by any one acquainted with the properties of opium and the present magnitude of the traffic.

Opinion of the medical profession of England.

But not to anticipate our subject we must turn, as first in authority, to the voice of the Profession in England expressed in the opinion of a sufficient number of its most sagacious and learned members, who had no need to wander to China nor pore over interested evidence to settle the question. A profound study of the living man, that wondrous assemblage of organs for repair and waste, kept in harmony by a *sensorium commune*, with its spiritual functions also, more wondrous still, cannot but enable them at once, and *ex cathedrâ*, to pronounce against his employing as a luxury an agent, the action of which is so powerful upon his system in its normal condition, unviolated by the drug; however nature, when compelled to submit to its intrusions, may struggle on to save appearances and put off the hour of her bankruptcy.

The following then is the opinion already referred to. Its force is increased by the fact that, having submitted to the distinguished physiologist and surgeon who worded it, one drawn up by myself, he did me the favour of substituting this more emphatic opinion:—

"However valuable opium may be when employed as an article of medicine, it is impossible for any one who is acquainted with the subject to doubt that the habitual use of it is productive of the most pernicious consequences, destroying the healthy action of the digestive organs, weakening the powers of the mind as well as those of the body, and rendering the individual who indulges himself in it a worse than useless member of society.

"I cannot but regard those who promote the use of opium as an article of luxury as inflicting a most serious injury on the human race.

(Signed) "B. C. Brodie."

Signed also by—

Dr. R. Bright, F.R.S.	Dr. P. Latham.
Dr. Chambers, F.R.S.	Mr. R. Liston, F.R.S.
Dr. Ferguson, F.R.S.	Sir C. Locock, Bart.
Sir J. Forbes, F.R.S.	Dr. Macleod.
Dr. Glendinning, F.R.S.	Mr. J. C. Moore.
Dr. Gregory.	Dr. Paris, F.R.S.
Sir H. Halford, Bart., F.R.S.	Dr. A. T. Thompson.
Dr. Hodgkin, F.R.S.	Mr. F. Tyrrell.
Mr. Cæsar Hawkins, F.R.S.	Dr. B. Travers, F.R.S.
Sir H. Holland, Bart., F.R.S.	Dr. Thos. Watson, F.R.S.
Mr. Aston Key.	Mr. Anthony White.
Dr. Jas. Johnson.	Dr. J. C. B. Williams, F.R.S.

Before adducing direct evidence from the East as to the effects on the Chinese of the gigantic importations of opium, it may be well to examine some of the palliating arguments current.

1. It has been said that the Chinese waste much of the opium by reducing it into an extract.

2. That as they smoke it in general, and do not eat it, the deleterious effects must be less.

3. That the spirit debauchery of England is as injurious as the opium of China.

Upon the character of this apology, even supposing the assertion were correct, it has been felt necessary to remark already, and to deprecate the parading of our nation's shame as a vindication of our wrongdoings elsewhere.

Erroneous opinion as to the waste of the drug in

As to the waste of opium by the Chinese in preparing the extract, were it true, it would only affect the main question as lessening the rapidity of the evil progress. But it has been too hastily caught up from an unfortunate passage in the writings of a late worthy missionary who had long and loudly proclaimed the ill-doings of opium in China, and who might, under particular circumstances, be pardoned for the qualified tone of appeals which he felt still constrained to make. In preparing their extract the Chinese adepts treat the drug by successive processes, obtaining extracts of different degrees of strength. A glance at their processes will satisfy any qualified judge, as might be expected, that they do not leave in the bulky refuse a particle of any active principle. That writer's estimating the refuse as part of the drug resulted merely from a want of acquaintance with toxicological chemistry. The other portion of the passage referred to, which has been circulated with an effect its author would, if alive, lament as much as any one, gives a conjectural estimate of the extent of the mischief in China which is still more incorrect, as has been abundantly shown.

its preparation in China.

By erroneously imagining a large portion of the opium to be wasted, and then allotting to each smoker a quantity so large as would prove how great was the decay of nature in all of them, he lowered the estimate of their number to two millions. As the opium imported, and produced in the country, has doubled since even that recent estimate, that would raise the number to four millions; but the estimate is quite erroneous. If the number of smokers does not exceed ten millions* the extent and rapidity of decay in each must be great indeed. Moreover, what is to be said of attempting, as has been done by some, to palliate the evil by comparing its extent with the whole population of China? Such an apologist would be little disposed to accept as an excuse for the ruin of a daughter that she was but an unit in the millions of England.

With respect to the comparison between the smoking and eating of opium, the evidence of all disinterested and close observers confirms what might be physiologically predicated, that opium, when smoked, or rather *deeply inhaled* in the peculiar manner practised, so far from being less, is far more active than when eaten.

The process of smoking opium examined physiologically.

For a clear perception of the process it is necessary to advert

* This would allow 5 grains of opium a day to novices, 20 to habitual smokers, 40 to the more advanced, and 80 a day to the debauched.

to the ordinary condition of the human chest, in which it is about two-thirds inflated, there being below the region of the breath, which consists of only from 20 to 30 cubic inches, a large volume of air from which about 140 cubic inches can be expelled, and which may be termed the supplementary air,* and above the region of the breath another volume or space, into which 100 or more cubic inches may be drawn, and for which the name complementary air appears suitable.† Thus, then, there is, including the space of the breath, room for no less than about 280 cubic inches. Now it must be plain that when the opium smoker, or rather inspirer, empties his chest to this large extent by a strained expiration, and then makes a long and deep draught of air through the subliming fumes of morphia and the other mephitic principles in the opium pipe, until his lungs are inflated with not merely 30 cubic inches of returning breath, but also with 240 cubic inches or more of supplementary and complementary air, that the fumes so carried in must visit nearly all the extensive and highly sensitive pulmonary surfaces. If the indraught be not checked at the onset by spasm in the larynx, that portal of custodiary sensitiveness, as happens on the intrusion of many irritants, the vapour cannot but be carried in it throughout the lungs, and have an opportunity of acting upon their whole expanded surfaces as long as the distension continues. Now, Chinese opium smoking, as it has been described to me by those who have watched the process, is just such an action. The chest having been inflated through the pipe to the utmost, the indraught is detained in it as long as the breath can be held. It is then slowly expelled by the *nostrils*, in a long-continued expiration; and any of the mephitis not absorbed by the lungs has an opportunity, in visiting the frontal and maxillary sinuses and olfactory membrane, of acting upon their expanded nervous surfaces in close proximity to the brain. Having heard the fact of the narcotic vapour entering the air cells questioned, I have thought it necessary to dwell upon the structural and pneumatic conditions rendering this result inevitable. It may be the case that the vapour of morphia at first acts as an irritant on the *glottis*, but directly any has found entrance to, and gratified the system

*† In a work entitled 'Statics of the Chest,' 1843, I have adopted these terms in the absence of any previously accepted names.

by way of the lungs, there must be a sympathetic announcement against further interference communicated to the larynx. It will soon grow accustomed to what gratifies the *sensorium*.

Dr. Nathan Allan, an American physician, who has paid much attention to the question, in writing upon opium smoking,* brings conclusive proof, both from fact and from physiology, of the more powerful and deleterious effects of opium imbibed in that manner than by way of the stomach.

With respect to the comparison between opium smoking and spirit drinking in England, it is to be lamented that this argument is put in a specious form by a popular writer on China. Into the morality of this argument we have already entered. Viewed simply in a physical light such an assertion must put the patience of any unprejudiced physician to no little trial.

In the year 1839, having been much thrown in the way of the working classes in our manufacturing towns as well as in the metropolis, and pained at the unfavourable contrast their habits presented to the temperance of the Hindoos and other Indian races, I obtained the opinion of a large number of the leading members of the profession upon the use of alcoholic drinks, many of them the same who denounced the use of opium as a luxury, but the utmost extent to which their opinion went, and with which my own observation equally accorded, was that such beverages were unnecessary for persons in health, and not conducive to support strength to labour. No such opinion against them could, or would, have been expressed as the above notable one against opium.

Mistaken course of the friends of temperance.

It is to be regretted that the friends of temperance have in their zeal, on some occasions, given a countenance to the argument of those whom they suddenly found so alive to the evils of spirit drinking in England, as to compare favourably with it the opium smoking of China. But the friends of the British temperance cause have taken nothing by this acquiescence. The argument being attempted as an apologetic, and not a moral one, evinces no especial desire on the part of its employers to take part in any way in the temperance movement here, but would be equally or indeed more applicable against it, *mutatis mutandis*, had the spirit interest of Britain to be defended;

* Church Missionary Intelligencer, April, 1857.

thus, "If the opium trade in China is not interfered with, how much less can the smaller evil, the spirit, in England!"

Without enthusiasm in a good cause the hands of the most feeling must soon hang down in a cold and selfish world; but enthusiasm is ever endangering an unintentional departure beyond the strict limits of truth; always to the injury of the cause in hand. It would be well for England, as well as China, if the friends of temperance would denounce every comparison of Spirit with Opium debauchery appearing to qualify the latter. The following fact will show the danger, while endeavouring to steer the social vessel out of the Charybdis—Spirit, of trifling near the Scylla—Opium, upon which it would be shipwrecked indeed! Since the last opium war, when power and wealth were combined to defend the luxurious use of opium by every specious argument, in Parliament, by pamphleteers, by the press, by Indian statesmen, and by opium smugglers; by all of whom it was repeatedly set forth as no worse than the use of spirit, nay by some as positively beneficial; the growth of an improper use of the drug in England has made more rapid strides than it did in China for the first thirty years of the East India Company's fostering efforts. The reason of this is sufficiently plain. Alcohol having no such sway over China as over England, there were few there with debauched appetites ready to lend their ears, while there was no misguided press there to pour into them the moral poison qualifying a use of opium, of which there have been such reckless instances here. On the contrary; every *unbribed* statesman in China, from the Emperor downwards, every moralist, poet, and satirist, united with one voice to check the growing evil, and did for a time retard it. In England, as we have seen, the pen of Protestants has been otherwise employed; and nothing has been wanting to send our reckless classes along the fascinating road to opium ruin, but instruction in the practice of smoking the drug!

Teetotalers unjustly charged with opium eating.

The increasing consumption of opium in England led to a report, which, though a further digression from our subject, I cannot, in justice, refrain from noticing, viz., that the abstainers from alcohol, the teetotalers, had taken to the use of the drug. Though placing no credit in it, I thought it right inquiries should be set on foot throughout the kingdom. Not finding a single instance of a teetotal opium eater, I traced the report, which had been circulated in every newspaper throughout the kingdom, and authoritatively stated in Parliament, and even, I believe, from the pulpit, to its original source—a journal of wide circulation, the avowed organ of the liquor trade. Upon applying to the editor for his authority for it, all the reply I could obtain was, that the statement was highly credible, since, with a general decrease in the consumption of spirit, there had been an increase in that of opium: and that if it were an incorrect explanation of the fact it could be readily contradicted! No. The abstainer upon principle from alcohol will hardly take to opium. It is the *intemperate* craver after new excitement, and the fashionable seeker after a stimulant in *its bulk* and *effects* more disguiseable than alcohol, who, under the teaching of the Imperial opium interest, are spreading the habit in England!

Opium far worse than even spirit as an agent of debauchery.

Much as truth will readily aver against spirit, it is of opium only she is prepared to affirm that the great majority of those who indulge in it at all, especially its smokers, are, with different degrees of speed, indeed, but irresistibly drawn on, both by its fascinating presence and by its agonizing absence, to their utter destruction; its dire effects on body and mind surpassing those of every other excess to which the depraved appetite of man prompts him. The reader who should think any further evidence necessary to confirm so authoritative and emphatic an opinion as that of the Medical Profession of England, might be supplied with bitter facts enough to fill a volume.

Testimony from India of the destructive effects of opium.

The following are a few: First from India, where the drug, when taken, is chiefly eaten, and its use repressed as far as possible by the British government within its own territory. In the villages where the Company's opium is produced, even the Hindoos, the most temperate of people, have caught the mania. Mr. A. Sym, an opium agent of the Company, writes in a letter dated 13th March, 1840,—

"The health and morals of the people suffer from the production of opium. Wherever opium is grown, it is eaten, and the more it is grown the more it is eaten; this is one of the worst features of the opium question. We are demoralizing our own subjects in India; one-half of the crime in the opium districts, murders, rapes, and affrays, have their origin in opium-eating.

"Both Hindoos and Mussulmans eat the drug; and its

pernicious effects are visible on the population of the opium districts, particularly in the neighbourhood of the depôts."

And to a friend he remarked — "One opium cultivator demoralizes a whole village!"

Of the outlying province of Assam, then more recently under the East India Company's control, Mr. C. A. Bruce, superintendent of their tea plantations, addressing the government, gives the following frightful picture:—

"I might here observe, that the British Government would confer a lasting blessing on the Assamese and the New Settlers, if immediate and active measures were taken to put down the cultivation of opium in Assam, and afterwards to stop its importation, by levying high duties on opium land. If something of this kind is not done, and done quickly too, the thousands that are about to emigrate from the plains into Assam will soon be infected with the opium mania; *that dreadful plague* which has depopulated this beautiful country, turned it into a land of wild beasts, with which it is overrun, and has degenerated the Assamese from a fine race of people, to the most abject, servile, crafty, and demoralized race in India." .... "This vile drug has kept, and does now keep, down the population; the women have fewer children compared with those of other countries, and the children seldom live to become old men, but in general die at manhood; very few old men being seen in this unfortunate country in comparison with others. Few but those who have resided long in this unhappy country know the dreadful and immoral effects which the use of opium produces on the native. He will steal, sell his property, his children, the mother of his children, and finally even commit murder for it."

Another gentleman holding an official situation under the East India Company in Assam has written thus in a private letter to a friend:—

"The cultivation of opium is free in Assam; the fearful results from its use, which every day present themselves to notice, are very painful to witness."

A strange attempt was made in parliament, by an opponent of Lord Ashley's motion, to refute these statements by charging the effects described to the unhealthiness of the climate, as if officers selected for their ability, and long resident in the province, could commit themselves to such statements ignorantly. I have always understood the climate of "this beautiful country," Assam, excepting where overrun with jungle—*the consequence*, as Mr. Bruce says, of the depopulation—to be much less unhealthy than that of Bengal. That a climate which had fostered a numerous and "fine race" of Indians should afterwards sweep them away would be strange indeed.

In the free state of Rajpootanah in the west of India, with its more arid climate, opium has also seriously injured its once remarkably fine race. Hence one East India Director, when addressing his parliamentary constituents, rightly protested against the wresting of the opium monopoly out of the hands of the Indian Government, as threatening India with a desolation by the drug; and hence another Director of the Company rightly argues in the same strain, in a pamphlet known to proceed from his pen; though in their zealous remonstrance to save India they prove too much, as we shall see on turning to unhappy China for evidence of the effects of opium there.

Testimony from China of the destructive effects of opium.

Turning to China we may indeed multiply evidence in accordance with the Profession's opinion, from the havoc of opium there. One remonstrative statement of Dr. Parker's has been already referred to, in which, if I remember right, he adds that the unhappy victims of opium mania have in their frenzy to suffer death at the hands of their own relations. This proverbial occurrence amongst the Malays, of "running a muck," appears to prove that opium exercises *not a milder but a worse effect on the Mongolian race.*

"Thus Charvet ascribes to this circumstance (race) the different effects of opium on the Javanese and Malays (both belonging to the Mongolian race) as compared with those produced on Europeans, Turks, and Persians (the Caucasian race)." *

"The Javanese," says Lord Macartney also, "under the influence of an extraordinary dose of opium, becoming frantic as well as desperate, not only stab the objects of their hate, but sally forth to attack in like manner every person they meet, till self-preservation renders it necessary to destroy them."

In another report of Dr. Parker's, dated December 31st, 1838, when the evil was not the fourth of what it now is, he

* Pereira's Mat. Medica. Ed. 3. Vol. i. p. 118.

says, "comparatively few victims of the opium mania have moral resolution remaining sufficient to attempt an emancipation from its most deplorable effects. Personal observation has furnished abundant evidence of the appalling extent of the evil."

Another medical missionary of judgment and experience, the Rev. W. Welton, lately returned from China, after a residence of seven years in Fou Chou, a city of 600,000 inhabitants, informs me that the injury inflicted on that city by opium almost baffles computation. He estimates its victims at more than half the adult males, and says that Chinese statists and men of letters estimate the smokers of opium higher still. He says that in the case of the poor the habit is almost universally destructive, though, according to his observation there, the effects of opium are more commonly narcotic than phrenitic. He states that it greatly impairs their ability to work from the first, and kills them on an average in ten years from the commencement of the use of it;—that the loss of productive labour and destitution of the families of the poor threaten to become general. It is not its fascinating effects only which tempt the poor onwards in the use of it, but its effect also of lessening the activity of the organs of nutrition and change, by which the appetite is lowered and life maintained on less than the natural amount of food; and want, from the superinduced indolence, is little felt. But this hastens on their destruction. In the case of the rich the effects are not so rapid, as long as they are able to partake freely of some highly sustaining diet; though with them also any permanent moderation is altogether uncommon.

Beyond comparison more alluring than dram-drinking, opium-smoking soon brings the whole system, the nervous system and mucous surfaces especially, into a condition rendering every temporary withdrawal of the narcotic agonizing. Mr. Welton, from whom I received the above account of his own observations, elsewhere remarks:—"The Chinese enumerate among the evils of opium-smoking the following—the whole body pervaded by aches and pains; hands and feet enfeebled; headache and colicky pains; can neither sit nor sleep; cannot travel nor work; when meal-time arrives, loathe their food; frequent and incessant discharges from the nose and eyes. These symptoms are but premonitory to others far more serious, including a diarrhœa which it is most difficult, if not impossible, to remedy. After the habit is once formed, and cannot be kept up by a needful supply of the drug, which requires increase, the preceding category of evils ensue, and are so distressing and insupportable, that the victims of it will even sell their wives and children to get a supply. This is the invariable testimony of the Chinese themselves, which I am well able, from my medical practice among them, to corroborate and confirm. The natives themselves are most anxious to devise means to relinquish the habit, without suffering the dreadful and distressing bodily ailments and symptoms already detailed. In proof of this, at the time I write this, numerous handbills are posted in every direction in the streets, pretending to have discovered some such precious antidotes to the evil effects of the drug. Empirics, as in England and America, avail themselves of the credulity and urgent necessities of their countrymen, by advertising a nostrum for the evils of this vice, pretending to be derived from America, Spain, India, the Red-haired country, Western Ocean country, &c." *

Dr. Ball, long resident in China gives this frightful picture: "Throughout these" (maritime) "districts and in all the towns may be seen walking skeletons, and families wretched and beggared by drugged fathers and husbands, multitudes who have lost house and home, dying in the streets, in the fields, on the banks of the rivers, without even a stranger to care for them when alive, and when dead exposed to view till they become offensive masses!"

Evidence of a like character might be indefinitely multiplied. The Rev. W. C. Burns, who has been more than eight years in China, writes from the vicinity of Namou, 16th July 1856,—"The ravages of opium we meet with here on every hand, and the deterioration of the morals of the people generally I cannot but ascribe in great part to the use of this ensnaring and destructive drug. When will measures be taken by those in power to lay an arrest on the opium traffic, which is inflicting such indescribable injury on this people, and which threatens in its progress, by its direct, and by its indirect effects—*poverty* and anarchy—to sweep away a great part of this nation from the face of the earth?" †

* Church Missionary Intelligencer, 1857.

† "What is the Opium-trade?" by Donald Matheson, Esq., p. 11.

Poverty no doubt!

> "Side and back go bare, go bare; foot and hand go cold—
> But belly, God send thee ale enough, let it be new or old!"

In this brutish old distich substitute "opium" for "ale," and the men of Lancashire, Yorkshire, and Lanarkshire will find a ten-fold reason why the masses of China receive so little of their useful fabrics.

On the Moral and Religious Aspect of the Traffic.

With respect to the heavy responsibility attending this erroneous course, as might be expected no one party has been prepared to accept it, nor does it, as has been supposed, lie exclusively at the door of the India House and of the merchants.

A full share of blame rests with successive Parliaments and Governments of England from the commencement of the century and earlier; for parliamentary Committees have from time to time discussed the subject, and even admitted its grave aspect, but have advised, as expedient, silence and non-interference; while of the different Cabinets during this period some have adopted a course the least defensible of all. And with respect to the nation at large; in a parliament returned especially upon the Chinese Question, what is the proportion of the electors of England who have given the history of our relations with that country any independent inquiry? Moreover, amongst those who have long had not only an acquaintance with its facts, but a moral sense also of their character, the writer of these pages is one who has to confess a sluggishness and faint-heartedness in remonstrance which would not have existed had those related to him been involved in the ruin. When therefore the imperial opium traffic has the inevitable effect of blunting, as with an *aura morphiana*, the moral sense of merchants and of every official in the East and West, so that the honourable and humane consent to connive at it, and at the ramified system of immoralities it necessitates, the whole thing must be denounced as a NATIONAL sin, every one of us, according to the light and influence he possesses, having to bear his share of the guilt, as he will of the judgment which in some form or other never fails to be visited on offending nations.

Let no one then rashly appeal to the antecedents and

presumed moral inflexibility of any individual officials to justify an indolent confidence that all is right, and a neglect of impartial inquiry. Such a course compels the expostulator who would be faithful to adduce facts and even personal motives he would gladly submerge under the general inquiry. If then the *aura morphiana* extends its influence to the far west, dulling the moral sense of imperial Statesmen here, what must be its effect upon those who are unfortunately placed in the centre of its intensity—upon traders and functionaries, especially where these are, through near relations, closely interested in the traffic? One of two consequences is inevitable. They must either sink into an insensibility as complete as the effect of the drug itself on the smoker, or break away from their ensnaring position, at whatever sacrifice to their pecuniary interests; as has been done in certain exemplary instances. Let our supine nation take to itself the blame, and not lay it all upon those whom she allowed to lapse into a position from which none of them can individually extricate themselves without a sacrifice few have moral strength to make.

England's privileged opportunities for good in the East.

GRAND and extensive to human appearance were England's opportunities for good when she invested herself with the moral guardianship of the East,—when, the Almighty, by not restraining her arms, allowed her to assume power there with all its responsibilities. In her sway over India and her command over thetrade with China great was her secular gain, but great also the return which she was bound, and ought to have rejoiced, to make.

She found India and China—one half of the world's population —through the protective restraint of a *Mahomedan* Government over the former, and a *Bhuddist* over the latter (such was the gracious intervention of Providence)—under the sway neither of that scourge Spirit, nor of that greater scourge Opium. Knowing the obstruction offered by the former agent to the moral improvement of her own Saxon race, deeply impressed ought she to have been with the responsible privilege devolving upon her, as mistress of a boundless field unensnared by these agents, for plying the vaunted influence of her Christian civilization—as mistress of the plains and people of India, and mistress of a position in China second only to that, in moral and religious opportunities!

Placing herself uninvited on the coast of China, she found her an immense and ancient Empire far removed from all the benign influences of Christianity with which she herself had for centuries been favoured, and therefore possessed of the faults of our common nature due to the circumstances of her position. She found her people as proud, contemptuous, fraudulent, and vain, as with like disadvantages her own would assuredly have been; and also (looking to the fate of India) reasonably distrustful and exclusive.

Did she, as THE REPRESENTATIVE OF PROTESTANT MORALITY IN THE EAST—*a privilege and responsibility from which she cannot escape*—bring even the ordinary influences of a *practical* Christianity to bear upon that people—of integrity, honour, generosity, benevolence, and humanity—influences which when honestly and perseveringly applied are irresistible?

No one mindful of the power with which *a practical* Christianity brought under its sway in ancient times the whole Roman and Barbarian world, and in modern times the most savage and haughty races through the agency of a few unarmed missionaries, can for a moment doubt that by the exhibition of some Christian principle, some little generosity, some little nobility of soul, the distrust of the Chinese, with their puerile vanity and arrogance, would have long since given way, and our relations with her been placed upon a reasonable footing, without the employment of any such means as we have been, and are now adopting. To deny this were to run in the face of all experience; to which the case of China itself is no exception.

In permitting England to occupy the highest position of influence on the coast of China, the Almighty has laid upon her an obligation from which she cannot escape—that of being the EXEMPLAR OF PROTESTANT MORALITY in the sight of that people. That of this trust He will sooner or later demand an account, no one who has studied his ways in history, or His announcements in Scripture, can for one moment doubt. Did she then use endeavours, by a consistent and elevated bearing towards that people, to improve their morals, and subdue their prejudices?

Her depraved course.

The very contrary. *She did not even leave them in their existing demoralization!* Finding them, like her own race, prone to, but under the bondage of no especial agent of, drunken debauchery, the cultivation of their snare, OPIUM, being thoroughly repressed in China, she plied them for the sake of gain with this lethal agent from without!

Opium debauchery in China, thĕ nursling of *England* (for her parliamentary committees and government have been accessary to it from the first), was fed the first year, as we have said, with one thousand chests of the drug, and required fifty years of fostering care, on the part of the government of India and the merchants, to enlarge its powers of consumption up to an annual demand for four thousand chests; but in the last thirty years it has been acquiring a giant growth.

The nine months' supply destroyed by the Chinese Commissioner Lin, in 1840, would have made *laudanum* enough to fill about forty thousand hogsheads, or a vat seventy feet in diameter and 100 high! In 1855 the quantity exported from India rose to seventy-seven thousand four hundred and thirty-five chests,* while the whole growth of China (the efforts of the government having been paralyzed by the former war, and our subsequent breach of solemn engagements to check the import of the drug) has now risen to probably thirty thousand chests annually, making a total of more than one hundred thousand; and in the nature of things the quantity must increase, to the utter decay and impoverishment of the people, unless it be arrested by Divine intervention in some form or other:—let it be our prayer, through a gracious influence upon the hearts of our rulers, and not through a destructive judgment upon the nation.

THERE ARE FOUR CONTINGENCIES OF THIS TRAFFIC WHICH GREATLY AGGRAVATE ITS CHARACTER. Homage perseveringly done to one evil principle is sure to involve with it homage to many.

Ruin to China, or repeated collision with us, inevitable.

1. In the first place. The opium traffic must either override all opposition in China, or bring us into repeated collision with the government and people. Hitherto the latter has been the case. Let any one acquaint himself with the tenor of all that has been said and done by the Chinese government and its councillors, and all that has been urged by the moralists, poets, and satirists of China, and his surprise must be, not that so insolent and exclusive a spirit towards white men has been exhibited at Canton, but that it has not been greater at other

* Of about 120 lbs. each, nearly all of which entered China.

places. In a word, what would be the feelings and conduct of every Englishman who had a spark of patriotism towards a people too powerful and crafty to be excluded from our shores, and whose main occupation was spreading this very opium ruin throughout our land! Do we not find in the Chinese that very inconsistency which is to be expected from a people long taught by their leaders and teachers to hate and despise us for the prominent exhibition of our character, and at the same time disposed to respect the better part of our character, and avail themselves of the advantages it offers them of protection and gain?

The traffic in opium scandalizing the religion of the Gospel.

2. The effect of the traffic in dishonouring the name of Christianity is a second evil of greater magnitude still. After a hundred years of the contact of *Protestant civilization*, the doors of China remained unopened to us. There were indeed faithful men who sent, and more faithful who went as, missionaries, from the hour that England sent her opium; but could she invoke a Divine blessing upon such double dealing? The influence of the devoted missionary is doubtless marvellous, but then he must be untrammelled by obstacles from his own side. The more he has to combat trouble and danger from those to whom he brings his message, the more is his singleness of purpose manifested, the more his self-devotion; and the greater therefore is his success. But if his fellow Christians are on all hands exhibiting their Christianity in a moral aspect which makes the heathen themselves shudder, what can be his success? What but such as we have seen after a century of labour!

To charge this failure to peculiarities in the Chinese character, and to their pride, is indeed a pitiful admission of the weakness of our influence! To have to batter open their doors by the force of brute matter, to have to run at them with the momentum and moral worth of a buffalo or rhinoceros, is to exhibit no strength to boast of, but weakness most abject! To find on our entry, that, after a hundred years of our *example and exhibition of Christianity* at their gate, the darkness, depravity, and cruelty of idolatry, have not been in the smallest degree mitigated by it, but are, apparently, all the more rampant from its vicinity, is humbling indeed! but it is not to be wondered at. It is not the words of the missionary, or the printed book in his hand, to which the heathen will or can give heed. For the value of their message of peace on earth, goodwill, and love, he looks of course for an exhibition of them in the lives and actions of its influential professors.

Every missionary informs us that the people point in scorn to the opium chest, and tell him to carry it away before he brings his Bible. When the Emperor warned his subjects against Christianity as "a religion which all men knew to be one which corrupts," he said, "the pure natural heart of man, and makes him willing for gain to destroy his fellow creatures," he drew but a reasonable inference, whilst he spoke, in a few words, volumes as to the effect of our in-thrust of opium. Here is a palpable proof that it would have been well for the message of the missionary could he have proceeded from some foreign land and have presented himself as of another race and faith from the opium purveyors; while England, if she insists on exhibiting herself reeking with opium, should at least come forward as the avouched high priestess of demonolatry! If she will deepen the depravity of the heathen for gain, let her not scandalize Christianity by assuming before them the white robe of the Saviour, her skirts foul with opium!

3. A third contingent evil flowing from this deplorable traffic is that it has involved us in a breach of faith which may challenge the history of human improbity for its parallel. Upon what ground can England hereafter with any face bind nations to their treaties?

Breach by England of the solemn treaty with China.

At the close of the last war it was notorious that, determined not to legalize the traffic nor make a revenue out of it, the Emperor, even in the hour of his prostration, rejected all proffers and temptations to that course.* At the same time he conceded an admission into five ports, and a cession of Hong Kong, we stipulating aid to our utmost for the suppression of smuggling. Saving admission *into* Canton, and the local dispute of the *lorcha*, whatever its merits, his part was fulfilled to the letter—say, if you will, on account of his weakness.

The reader is exhorted to ponder over the following treaty, and proclamation by Her Majesty's Plenipotentiary, and then say if it would be possible by the force of words to impart greater solemnity and distinctness to a promise!

In all the treaties and proclamations which have been promul-

* The recent admission of opium into *Shanghai* and *Amoy*, under a duty, appears to be a *local* act to raise a revenue for suppressing the insurgents. If it were an *imperial*, it would but prove the fatal growth of our evil influence.

gated since the Conquest, it would not perhaps be possible to find one in which all the power of our language has been put into requisition to an extent equal to that with which China is promised and the world assured, in these documents, of our determination to root out the smuggling, and our shame that British subjects should be engaged in it! *

Supplementary Treaty, signed in English and Chinese at Hoonan Chae, 8th October, 1843.

Supplementary Treaty of 1843.

" *Article XII.*—A fair and regular tariff of duties and other dues having now been established, it is to be hoped that the system of smuggling which has hitherto been carried on between English and Chinese merchants, in many cases with the open connivance and collusion of the Chinese custom-house officers, will entirely cease, and the most peremptory proclamation to all English merchants has been already issued on the subject by the British Plenipotentiary, who will also instruct the different Consuls to strictly watch over and carefully scrutinize the conduct of all persons, being British subjects, trading under his superintendence. In any positive instance of smuggling transactions coming to the Consul's knowledge, he will instantly apprize the Chinese authorities of the fact, and they will proceed to seize and confiscate all goods, whatever their value or nature, that may have been so smuggled, and will also be at liberty, if they see fit, to prohibit the ship from which the smuggled goods were landed from trading farther, and to send her away as soon as her accounts are adjusted and paid."

"PROCLAMATION.

"*British Plenipotentiary, Hong-Kong, Sir H. Pottinger, G.C.B.*, 22 *July*, 1843.

Proclamation of the British Plenipotentiary.

"Her Britannic Majesty's Plenipotentiary trusts that the provisions of the Commercial Treaty will be found in practice mutually advantageous, beneficial, and just, as regards the

* Her Majesty's Plenipotentiary must have felt that to particularize by name the grand subject of the smuggling—*Opium*—would, in connexion with so many invectives, have cast a stigma upon the great purveyor of it in India, and the merchant-prince conveyors of it into China. To suspect that the omission was made with any *sinister* object, in the midst of so many solemn appeals, would be unjustifiable.

interests, the honour, and the future augmented prosperity of the governments of the two mighty contracting empires, and their subjects, and His Excellency most solemnly and urgently calls upon all subjects of the British Crown, individually and collectively, by their allegiance to their Sovereign, by their duty to their country, by their own personal reputation, respect, and good name, and by the integrity and honesty which is due from them as men to the imperial rights of the Emperor of China, not only to strictly conform and act up to the said provisions of the Commercial Treaty, but to spurn, decry, and make known to the world any base, unprincipled, and traitorous proposals which they, or their agents or *employés*, may receive from, or which may be in any shape made to them by any subject of China, whether officially connected with the Government or not, towards entering into any collusion or scheme for the purpose of evading or acting in contravention of the said provisions of the Commercial Treaty.

"Her Britannic Majesty's Plenipotentiary will not allow himself to anticipate or suppose that the appeal which he now makes to all Her Majesty's subjects will be unheeded or overlooked by even a single individual, but at the same time it is his duty, in the responsible and unprecedented situation in which he has been placed by the course of events, to distinctly intimate that he is *determined*, by every means at his disposal, to see the provisions of the Commercial Treaty fulfilled by all who choose to engage in future commerce with China, and that, in any case when he may receive well-grounded representations from her Majesty's Consuls, or from the Chinese authorities, that such provisions of the Commercial Treaty have been evaded (or have been attempted to be so), he will adopt the most stringent and decided measures against the offending parties; and where his present powers may not fully authorise and sanction such measures as may seem to him fitting, he will respectfully trust that the legislature of Great Britain will hold him indemnified for adopting them in an emergency directly compromising the national honour, dignity, and good faith, in the estimation of the government of China, and in the eyes of all other nations.

"God save the Queen!

(Signed) "HENRY POTTINGER."

Solemnity of these documents.

In these notable documents what moral expression is wanting, what sacred and lofty sentiment omitted, which could serve to pledge England most deeply to sincerity?—England, the Exemplar of Protestant Christianity, pledged by the Plenipotentiary of Her Most Gracious Majesty—"*the Defender of the Faith!*" The language is apparently that of patriots as sensible of their country's wrong-doing towards China, as were those good men of her wrong-doing to Africa, who stirred her up to remorse and a suppression of the great but lesser moral evil of the two—the slave-trade.

What must be the trammelling and embarrassing character of a traffic which has placed men of high honour and principle—the nation's choicest statesmen and other functionaries—in the following anomalous position!

Their promise made to be utterly broken.

Pray let the reader note the force of every line of this promise to the ear of China—this outburst of remorseful indignation—this homage to justice, honour, and humanity! Is there an Englishman who will not blush to know that from the commencement of the traffic up to the date of the signature of these documents, and ever since, there never has been the smallest effort on the part of Her Majesty's Government to check the trade? On the contrary, the production of the drug in India by the Company has been encouraged by the Board of Control; it has been defended repeatedly by members of different governments; every effort made in parliament to check it has been thwarted; parliamentary committees have repeatedly recommended silence upon it; the Earl of Shaftesbury's motion against opium that very year (1843) was withdrawn at the request of the Minister; the Company have gone on increasing the supply with an extraordinary rapidity; the Consuls in China have done nothing to check the smuggling, or take any of the fine steps promised, and could not, as one of them significantly stated. Moreover, that the threats held out, in an honest heart no doubt, by Her Majesty's Plenipotentiary, ended in nothing. "Every means at the disposal" of Her Majesty's Representatives—a powerful naval force, and "the most stringent measures"—its broadsides—were never once heard, nor threatened, against the opium craft; excepting in a solitary instance in which an officer, Captain Hope, of the 'Thalia,' committed the mistake of supposing some meaning to be attached to treaties and promises, and diverted from their course some opium ships, not, indeed, as such, but as proceeding beyond the prescribed limit of thirty-two degrees of latitude: while this small effort is said to have been balked by his removal to another station!

The consummation of the improbity.

If all this shall appear incredible in history, still less credible will be the following consummation of it—the actors being men of such high honour, that his self-confidence must be great who would lightly occupy their embarrassing position. After we had for many years totally neglected to fulfil our treaty and promise against smuggling; nay, had in the interim *doubled our introduction* of opium—while it was notorious that our traders continued, as always, to bribe the local officials of China;—that the great Government of India was pushing increasing quantities of opium every year into the smugglers' hands, ready put up in packages of Chinese weight (though refraining of course from itself smuggling, but having even indemnified losers of seized opium);—that the smugglers' ships were perfect sloops-of-war in their armament and "slavers" in their speed; —that not only they carried the British flag, but it was mounted also by licensed Chinese craft to secure immunity on the coast, —while it was notorious also that the Supreme Government of China, especially since the war, was utterly powerless to prevent the opium ships from breaking bulk, though unquestionably sincere, and the local government equally powerless and at the same time corrupt;—while the very terms of our promise proved our knowledge of her weakness—will it be believed, after all this, that our Government, when about to charge China with *her laches* in not admitting us as stipulated into Canton, instead of first making some amends for the past by setting to work at once to fulfil *our* very solemn stipulations, actually found themselves to have drifted into a position in which they felt compelled to save appearances by giving the Emperor notice that England would consider herself relieved of her obligations to him on account of his failing to do his part in the suppression of the traffic?—Relieved of obligations, the very terms of which had implied his inability to oppose the power and craft by which the smuggling was supported!—*relieved* at the eleventh hour of obligations which, from the very first hour, not one of the parties bound by them had manifested the smallest intention of observing!

Let the reader compare a breach of treaty on our part so solemn in its reiterated assurances, and in its importance to China, as promising to save her from the breaking in of many million pounds weight of opium annually, with the breach she has committed (if breach it is with such justification) in refusing to our traders the convenience and recreation of a free entry into Canton, and then let him in candour say which party, in this realized parallel of the fable, is the wolf and which the lamb—or goat, if you will.

England tempting heathen rulers to sin.

4. The fourth, and perhaps the saddest contingency of all, connected with the traffic in opium, has been the constant endeavour on the part of our government to induce the Emperor to legalize its introduction. A recommendation to that effect on the part of a *heathen* councillor about the year 1838 was not to be wondered at, but it must be to *us* surprising that his tempting arguments were unheeded and he degraded. More than one *British* councillor, fearing no degradation in *Christian* England as the advocate of that policy, has prompted the effort to persuade the Emperor to take off the contraband and to make a revenue out of the drug!

In this proposal there was no real parallel whatever to our spirit duties. The same active principle pervades beer, wine, and spirit, which the large majority of our nation having long consumed, and, being their own rulers under a constitutional government, have not made up their minds to disuse and suppress. All that a British government can do is to tax spirits highly; and if the country countenances any Chancellor of the Exchequer in such expressions as that he looks with satisfaction to an increased consumption of spirits, the fault is its own. But even in England, were opium inhaling to be introduced here with destructive and rapidly increasing effect, there cannot be a doubt that its importation and sale would, by the most stringent measures, be reduced again to a medicinal amount.

To our persuasive arguments the Emperor Tuou Kwang replied: "It is true I cannot prevent the introduction of the flowing poison; gain-seeking and corrupt men will for profit and sensuality defeat my wishes; but nothing will induce me to derive a revenue from the vice and misery of my people!" Here was a *heathen* ruler reading a lesson in morality to a *Christian* government!—a severe and courageous sarcasm after his having recently felt the power of "civilization" in arguments of lead and iron.

Thus does England, with her Bibles all over the world, and her shelves breaking down under her endless accumulations of *stereotyped* religion and morality, find herself the failing and rebuked TEMPTER of one heathen ruler, and now again (as is too well known) at the same work with his successor!—the corruptor of the morals of heathen rulers—*the tempter* of them to desert their people, and give up repressive measures which had for generations been thoroughly successful, until ruined by *her* cupidity and power! Let her succeed, and he will then wash his hands of the blood of his people, he will leave them free to grow opium for themselves, and England will have the satisfaction to know that she has consummated the greatest crime that one nation could commit towards another!

We read, in history, of lawless subjugations—of cruel exterminations by the sword—of bigotry and ambition doing their worst in the hands of a Cortez and Pizarro; but we do not read of one nation besetting another, for filthy lucre's sake, until she has laid both people and ruler prostrate under the debauching impetus of a poison, to the growing force of which human judgment can assign no limit! Many are the dark pages in history, but that, it is to be feared, will bear the deepest shade which shall faithfully record the doings of England towards China! Many are the attributes of the Great Spirit of Evil; but to *tempt* has been ever esteemed his arch-attribute, from the time, as the sacred poet sings,—

> "When first this *Tempter* cross'd the gulf from hell,"
> "Brought death into the world, and all our woe," *

and has acquired emphatically this designation of THE TEMPTER. *The Tempter* has had his agents at work in all ages and countries; but it is reserved for the nineteenth century, and for England—Protestant England!—to perform this agency on the most gigantic scale. It is England, alas! who, breaking in upon one-third of the world's population with a flood, the end of whose desolating course she neither knows nor heeds, is found, from time to time, when she has alarmed them with her arms, at the ear of their heathen ruler, whispering into it

* 'Paradise Lost,' Books X. and I.

temptation to desert his people and do violence to his conscience—to such natural light as has been vouchsafed him from on High! The first great temptation was that of the mother of a future world: the last is that of the father, in responsibility, of one third of *its now living, breathing millions!* We would not, and dare not, compare this with the former greatest crime on earth of the greatest of criminals. At the same time, while utterly unfitted to attempt such casuistry, we dread to think how near, in the sight of unerring Justice, the one crime, were it not done in blindness, would approach towards the other!

Who, with the opium traffic before his mind, but must have looked with double alarm at the late convulsion in India? If it is passing off as a severe, but not consummated, judgment, it is because the long suffering of God is great. If, in spite of this warning, the production of opium is being pushed with unabated force, it is because the perverseness of man is greater. If the declarations of Scripture and the dealings of Providence assure us that His righteous will must in the end prevail, it is because His justice and power are greater still—are infinite!

War and conversion in China.

With respect to the conversion of China, whatever may be the merits of the present war, when so many speak confidently of its importance as opening the door to the entrance of the Truth, one is prompted to ask if it is under the banners of a MAHOMET or a BAJAZET the triumphant entrance is to take place? If, in making her appeal to the *God of Battles*, England can venture at the same time to appeal to Him as the God of *Creation* and of *Mercy*, who knows that she had in vain pursued towards her enemies an undeviating course of *beneficence* and *honour*, and that she cannot escape the slaughtering of His creatures, by leaving them in their perverseness, let her lift the sword, but let no one so disregard His entire word as to propose that the Missionary shall look to the sword as his precursor, by which he may hope to reap the fruit of his labours, escaping the thorn—by which he may avoid that helplessness, self-renunciation, and reliance on Divine protection alone, which constitute the moral strength of his position. Whether, in His inscrutable purposes, the Almighty shall be pleased to make "the wrath of man to praise Him," is a secret which rests with Himself. Our guide is His written word. In it we are expressly forbidden to look to force in any way as the pioneer of the

Gospel. With that word in their hands, is it possible that any friends of missions can invoke a blessing on their work, with any such notion in their minds, as that their Missionaries should enter the gates of China marching close in the rear of *Power*,—treading to its martial sounds,—*marked* with its dust,—and mixing their hymns with the '*Io Triumphe*' of the motley and exulting train following the chariot of Victory?

(K.—Page 204.)

African troops for India raised without slavery, or much expense.

Objections to the introduction of Africans into India have been raised, on the ground of its affording a countenance to the slave trade, since the men must be purchased on the coast. Were it so, I freely confess that, with at least an equal abhorrence of slavery with my neighbours, nay, from a desire to be consistent in that abhorrence, I would prefer an appearance of it in Africa, to the reality of it in England. We may be very certain that the starving and oppressed African taken to the climate of India, congenial to him, and raised to the respectable position of a well-dressed soldier, might be safely given his liberty, and the promise of being conveyed back again to his squalid and *enslaved* life in Africa, if he were so insane as to prefer it. No such promise to the British soldier as discharge and a free return at any hour to England can be ventured upon; showing which would be most contented and free. But whatever might be the state of the recruiting in Africa at the outset, letters by thousands, as soon as they could write, or messages through one or two influential men, brought back to Africa, accompanied with substantial presents, would in no long time set whole provinces volunteering, where want and periodical famine are so frequent.

The missionaries might be able with a good conscience to aid the work with their influence, when they considered how important, on moral grounds, it would be to lessen the number of British soldiers in India, and were assured that every religious advantage would be afforded to the African recruit as a soldier in India. It is absurd to suppose that from a teeming, abject, and oppressed people recruits could not be had on about the same terms as amongst the natives of India, as soon as it ceased to be a *terra incognita* to the former. To commence with the rates of remuneration to West India corps would be to spoil the work, and to remunerate the African as absurdly as would be a recruiting in England on a scale of pay equal to that of the commission officer of the India Service.

African troops in India would possess a peculiar value. Their mere presence would trip up the confidence of the natives in their climatic advantages; but for which confidence, it is, from long past conversations with them, my conviction they would not venture on rebellion. The African could never amalgamate with them, and must at all times feel that his own existence was bound up with that of the British power. We may hope that he would become a convert to Christianity, and set a fairer example of its profession than do our unhappy fellow-countrymen in the ranks in India. After a generation or two his offspring in India might supply recruits on the spot. In the mean time there would appear no want of African tribes abundantly martial in spirit.

The Caffres themselves, who have given us so much trouble at the Cape, are said to be in such abject want as to be willing to take any service on any terms; and they certainly do not lack valour. As to any capriciousness and uncertainty of character, surely that would be corrected by discipline and education, and, after a force was once formed, by the influence and example of the older soldier upon the recruit. It would be of great importance that a rate of pay little if at all exceeding that of the native soldier in India should be, from the first, established.

(L.—Page 206.)

The enlistment Acts of 1847 an important but incomplete step.

The Acts of Parliament of 1847 were undoubtedly an important step towards a wholesome system of enlistment, as affording the recruit the opportunity of revoking, before a magistrate, a precipitate decision. But when he is enlisted for Her Majesty's service the liability to serve in India is of course kept out of his view; and when for the India service, the serjeant, as a matter of course, and of fact, cannot, and would not if he could, give him any true notion of what he is undertaking. And should any of his friends have it in their power to do so and to convince him; is he not always under some pecuniary obligation to the serjeant, before he sees the magistrate, which, however small, a village lad has no means of liquidating? and does he not in withdrawing subject himself to many taunts, and ridicule, which the least educated can least withstand, and, as he walks away, to be jeered as a renegade? In short, is it not very true that he does and can only accept service for India in the dark? Notable effects of recruiting practices will be found under the two following heads:—M and N.

(M.—Pages 213 and 214.)

Remarkable General Orders on military crime in India.

The following extracts from the General Orders of Commanders-in-Chief in India are selections from amongst the stronger specimens of what may be said to form the burden and current matter of military orders relating to European troops in that country. Coupled with the endless regimental orders and punishments, and with the condition of mind of the great majority of the men, they establish incontestibly the fact, which might without their evidence be predicated from the whole premises of the question—that military service, to the European soldier of the ranks in India, is no blessing, but an iron bondage, so irksome that men who are all that the commander could desire in the field in Europe, seem completely metamorphosed when immured in barracks in India. Such a service moreover draws in amongst them, as a matter of course, characters so undeserving that even *it* is the best life the four quarters of the globe offer them; but not a reformatory one: in its present state, or future prospects.

General Orders respecting Mutinous Conduct on the Part of British Soldiers in India.

"Head-quarters, Simla, 2nd August, 1844.

"*General Order.*

"His Excellency has more than once pointed out the very serious liability which soldiers incur who offer violence to their superiors. The present is the eighth instance in five months of soldiers in H. M. regiments in Bengal, sentenced to transportation for this offence; but without the desired effect in the prevention of the crime—and unless a more immediately exemplary punishment be adjudged by courts martial in the worst cases of violence, of which the present is one, it would appear to be impossible to look for any diminution of that insubordination which has of late become so disgracefully frequent. This Order is to be read at the head of every regiment, &c.

"By order of his Excellency the Commander-in-Chief,

"(Signed) H. C. SMITH, Major-General,

"Adjutant-General of H. M. forces in India."

"SIMLA, 27TH MAY, 1847.

"*General Order by the Commander-in-Chief*, *25th May*, 1847.

"Since the commencement of the year 1847, the General Orders have recorded no fewer than sixteen convictions by General Courts Martial against men of her Majesty's service for gross acts of insubordination and violence towards commissioned, and non-commissioned, officers. During the same period of but four months the courts martial returns of regiments record as many as *forty* convictions by inferior courts martial of men bearing the name of soldiers for similar ruffianly offences outraging the discipline of the army and disgracing the service to which they belong.

"The acts of which many of these men have been convicted rendered them liable to a sentence of DEATH; and the Commander-in-Chief therefore deems it necessary to call the attention of all concerned to the remarks contained in the General Order number seventy-nine, of 2nd of August 1844.

"Should violence to superior officers in the execution of their office continue as frequent as it has now become, Lord Gough is determined to carry into execution, in every instance, the sentence of a court martial, whatever it may be.

"His Lordship however confidently trusts that the appeal he now makes to the sense of duty of the Soldiers of H. M. Regiments serving under his command will not be in vain.

"This Order, with that of the second of 2nd August 1844, will be read at two successive parades at the head of every regiment and detachment of H. M. service in the Bengal Presidency, and afterwards at the head of every troop and company, by the officers commanding them, and a report made to the Adjutant-General of H. M. forces in India of such having been done.

"By order of the Right Honourable the Commander-in-Chief,

"(Signed) C. R. CURETON,

"Adjutant-General H. M. Forces.

"By order of His Excellency, the Right Honourable the Commander-in-Chief,

"PAT. GRANT, Lieut.-Col.,

"Adjutant-General of the Army."

EXTRACT BENGAL GENERAL ORDERS, BY HIS EXCELLENCY THE COMMANDER-IN-CHIEF, DATED HEAD-QUARTERS, SIMLA, 14TH AUGUST, 1852.

"*Remarks by His Excellency the Commander in Chief.*

"This is the fourth case of soldiers of this distinguished regiment who have been sentenced to transportation within the last six weeks. His Excellency has reason to fear that this disgrace to his regiment and to the army, Thomas Queeney, was actuated in his outrageous conduct by a desire to get himself transported. If the Court were of this opinion, it would have been well had they refrained from meeting his wishes and sentenced him to punishment of another nature. The sentence of transportation shall however now be carried out to its full extent; and at Norfolk Island, the place of the prisoner's destination, he will soon discover the vast difference between the life of a well-conducted soldier in India, and that of a convict subjected to the severe discipline and hard labour of the prisons of the penal settlement.

"The Commander-in-Chief has been given to understand that the soldiery of this army have received from the ill-intentioned an incorrect description of the life of military prisoners sentenced to transportation, and imagine that it is one of comparative ease and comfort and preferable in many respects to that of a soldier in India. His Excellency cannot perhaps do more to dissipate this erroneous idea, than to make known the following extract from the instructions given by the Secretary of State in the Colonial Department to the Lieutenant-Governor of Van Dieman's Land regarding the treatment of convicts, and which will have to be carried out in the case of the convict Queeney.

"'Arrived at Norfolk Island the convict will be employed at hard labour. *No authority except that of the Queen herself will be competent to abridge the time of his detention there.* On the other hand, the misconduct of the convict in Norfolk Island may have the effect of prolonging his detention there indefinitely.

"'Even good conduct on the part of the convict cannot abridge the duration of this part of the sentence.'

"The removal of the convict Queeney from Norfolk Island to another locality, where however he will still have to work as a felon, at hard labour, can only be obtained by a long course of continued and unvarying good conduct on his part, such as would have secured him, had he remained in the Army, certain promotion in his profession and the means of retiring eventually to his native country. He is now debarred by the sentence of the Court from the hope of ever seeing his country again.

"The above observations will show that the life of the convict is one of disgrace and toil. Let the evil-disposed soldiers therefore be warned by the fate to which this man Queeney has subjected himself: a fate to which death would be preferred by every honourable soldier.

"This order and the order of the 14th July last, publishing the trial of Private John Gill, Her Majesty's 29th Regiment, are to be read at the head of every garrison or body of troops at a general parade, and subsequently at the head of every troop, company, or detachment of Europeans of the East India Company's Service in Bengal.

"The prisoner will be sent to the Presidency under proper escort, and made over to the Town Major of Fort William, in view to his undergoing the sentence awarded, in accordance with instructions which will be communicated to the officer commanding the Meerut Division.

"By order of His Excellency the Commander in Chief,

"(Signed) H. T. Tucker, Lieut.-Col.,

"Adjutant-General of the Army."

(N.—Pages 214 and 222.)

A striking and painful — The following incident, though it occurred many years ago, has lost none of its significant importance by time. Delusive announcements by recruiting serjeants are to be seen to this day even upon the walls of the government military offices and barracks. The only but more humane difference, in the treatment of disappointed offenders in India, consists in the less severe corporal punishment now inflicted, and the greater frequency of transportation; though under another head (Appendix M) will be found evidence of so great an increase of military crime of later years in India as to have led to a General Order by the Commander-in-Chief of distressing, however necessary, severity.

incident connected with recruiting trickery.

As long ago as 1820 I saw in various parts of England and Scotland, as well as at the India House and at the Horse Guards, *a blue picture*, familiar doubtless to many, which I freely confess a youthful indignation prompted the desire to tear down had I the opportunity. It was headed by an invitation to fine young men to enter the *Honourable* Company's Horse Artillery, as if more than a small proportion enjoyed that privilege, where a fortune would soon be made; and the process was exemplified by a picture below of a horse soldier cutting a native to pieces and plundering from him a bag of treasure!

In July, 1823, Lower Bengal was a waste of waters—the inundations of the Ganges; out of which, within the whole bounds of a certain horizon, stood a solitary island, the site of a large Brahmin village, upon which were gathered in refuge the inhabitants and stock of the submerged country around. To that island had drifted in a *typhoon* one of the largest hospital boats of a "monster" and medley detachment of more than eight hundred Europeans, the senior medical charge of which under the age of twenty-three I had the responsible honour to hold.

In quest of these thirty or more of my severest cases I had to let loose from a weather shore far off, and was fortunate in not drifting past, but pitching upon them and their shelter. The day following, about half-a-dozen of the soldiers' boats came up from leeward, the Head-quarters and Commissariat being "nowhere." Each boat had I believe on board its grog cask in charge of the serjeants, but no provisions. We bought from the Brahmins, through the medium of Mahomedans, a bullock each day, which, to the affected horror of the former, butcher lads among the men quickly reduced to inviting joints. Matters went on quietly for a couple of days, save that I saw the men at night supping on a duck a-piece, with one each also to "the ladies;" and I am afraid, under the teaching and authority of *the blue picture*, all unpaid for; until the discovery was made, that where everything else, living and inanimate, was swarming, self-rescued snakes especially, *arrack* also abounded;—abounded because a Christian Government was then urging upon its revenue officers the extension everywhere of the "*abkaree*," sale of spirit, which under the Mahomedan governments had been repressed. Drunkenness amongst the soldiers followed as a matter of course, and affrays in which, being but a handful amidst thousands, they no doubt fought the more desperately. One of them, half drunk, intruded into a native's Zenana in search of more liquor, and in a quarrel cut his leg half through with a "bill." Victory for the hour was with the European *pupils of the blue picture*. Redress however was sought through the Civil authorities; and not many days after, at Berhampore, from an early hour in the afternoon till towards dusk, it was my painful duty to stand, as the surgeon, over an uninterrupted succession of floggings, from that of the "bill" man, who, if I remember rightly, was sentenced to many hundred lashes, and received most of them, through floggings of others less than his by a third, a half, and down to a hundred lashes or more, the smallest awarded. I did not take note in writing of the number of lashes awarded to each, and given; but I believe that a reference to the Bengal military records would confirm this statement on memory.

The reader may imagine the hospital scene that night—what peace of mind and good will to man was exhibited by men raging under pain, shame, heat, and a sense of wrong! but he will not easily imagine my feelings when, upon endeavouring to soothe the ravings of the chief offender and sufferer, he turned and appealed to me, with a volume of imprecations, against the higher powers and all in authority; those especially who had *posted up that very blue picture*, the object of my former indignation, as put forth to deceive him and other ignorant men into "thinking it nothing to cut down the Moors." I felt that had he, prior to, or during the punishment, called that picture and the system of deception of which it was the type to my recollection, the nerve to witness the inflictions which had well nigh given way would have failed me quite.

Here were ignorant men who, sent out from a Christian and

Protestant realm dominating over a vast heathen population, ought to have been solemnly charged with the duty of exhibiting an example of Christian humanity, compassion, and integrity; but who were, not only recklessly shovelled into India with no such warning and exhortation, but actually, from the first moment, invited out by false temptations of murderous rapine! and who were then visited by punishment so severe and humiliating as almost to unseat reason and endanger life, when, falling into a drunken snare, laid as it were by the government, they carried out the very and only impression implanted in their minds, if not under the countenance of that government, at least with its cognizance!

(O.—Pages 201 and 217)

On the Value of India as a Dependency.

No one can have traced out the misemployment of labour and the lack of enterprise in the various paths of industry in India, without surprise that the gross amount of its products should be as considerable as it is, and without inferring from these facts that the natural resources of the country should be very great. Upon searching into the fertility of the soil, and the minerals to be found beneath it in various localities, this inference must grow into conviction. Such an one, moreover, can scarcely fail to desire earnestly that these resources should be drawn forth, and the defective state of industry corrected. But while these facts might fully be discerned and appreciated, it is far from desirable that the value of India as a possession should be overrated. It can only tend to mislead the continental states of Europe, and excite envy, while it has a pernicious effect upon the minds of the natives of India. It serves only to confirm a notion prevalent amongst them, that Britain derives all her wealth from their country. Significantly placing his hand upon India, in a chart of the World, and his thumb upon England, the native will remark upon the small territorial extent of the latter. It being a current opinion amongst them that the people of England are straitened for food, the great exports of indigo surprise them so much that an old report has arisen, which I understand prevails unto this day amongst the sepoys, that we possess the means of converting indigo into a larger weight of food. Extreme need is, I believe, commonly presumed by them to be the cause which urges Englishmen to seek a life in India, the climate of which is so hostile to them and their children, and renders necessary a separation from these from an early age, and often for life. That such impressions are undesirable must be evident, and that they have operated amongst others more influential towards disposing the minds of the natives to insurrection, I cannot doubt. As a matter of fact, it is also to be desired that more correct opinions should be current than those which have been too hastily put forth, especially of late, as to the value of India as a dependency. It has value sufficient to justify its retention, apart from the obligations which the occupation of it has now imposed upon us; and there is little fear of its being prematurely abandoned by a British Government. But how greatly its value has been overrated will, I think, appear from such considerations as these. Whatever may be the available amount of the public revenue of India, all that *Britain* is beneficially interested in out of this sum is, first the receipts of Her Majesty's and the Honourable Company's Commissioned Officers and covenanted European servants over and above what their professions and industry might have yielded them at home or in other fields. It is to be presumed that one-third of their receipts must be deducted on this account. Secondly, the pensions and salaries paid in England. Thirdly, the *profit and wages* on public stores supplied to India. Fourthly, the *profit and wages* upon that portion of the trade with India which is in excess of what it would have amounted to had the country been independent or in other hands. Then from that estimated total have to be deducted all expenses due to the hostility of the climate, both those incurred in the country, and the heavy expenses of journeys and voyages for change of air and climate, and for sending children to be educated in Europe, and maintaining them at much greater cost than if their parents' home were at hand. Now these charges commonly swallow up all that can be saved by a careful economy during the first twenty years of a residence in India. It is a small minority only who are alive and in possession of anything from India at the end of that time. With all these deductions that must be a strained estimate which would bring the *pecuniary* value of India to England up to six millions sterling per annum. In this, no account has been, or can be, taken of the deductions chargeable upon the climate for destruction of health, premature death, and bereavements, separation of parents from children, and children from parents, from infancy, and often for life—a thing so unnatural, that man in a simpler state of society would not incur it for any consideration.

With respect to the support of the European soldiery of the ranks, nothing can be placed to the credit of India as a possession, but a grievous deduction, as has abundantly appeared in the preceding pages. Lastly, the possession of India renders us at any time liable to a European war, which in these times cannot be waged for any length of time under a cost of fifty or a hundred millions sterling, the interest upon which would represent a *permanent* charge equal, or nearly so, to the *net annual* value of India only until the recurrence of another war. In fact, if the Russian war had been incurred on account of India, the expenditure upon it would have amply sufficed to satisfy and liquidate every existing British interest in connexion with India. Every public servant would have come home with glee (excepting in so far as a moral interest in India might have operated with some), and every planter and merchant closed his concern with high satisfaction upon the seventy or eighty millions, it cost, being showered amongst them. Every prospective hope, also, in the minds of parents, of a provision in India for children now living, might have been abundantly satiated with these ample means.

Greatly surpassed by Australia or America.

Compare with this the value of either our Eastern or Western Colonies—the Australasian or American. Take the former. They contain at least two hundred thousand adults of British birth of both sexes and of different ranks, whose earnings, ranging from thirty pounds at the lowest to some thousands per annum at the highest, cannot average less than 70*l*. a year, or a total of 14,000,000*l*. per annum.* As they are permanent residents in a congenial climate, the whole of their earnings must fairly be estimated as so much gain to the nation. To this has to be added the value to England of the rapidly-increasing

* Or take the annual gross products of their industry in gold, copper, wool, &c., and the amount will rise much higher.

trade to those colonies, which, when the land question is properly settled, will in time far outstrip that with India. Having taken much interest in the question of wholesome colonization, especially in connexion with a settlement in New Zealand, Otago, in the formation of which I was much concerned, I obtained from the New Zealand Company an engagement, as the condition of my friends' and my own support of the settlement, that a system of land sale and allotment should be established there, which I venture to think would have proved of great advantage to every rightful interest, public and private. The fulfilment of this engagement never took place. The Company, indeed, became dissolved not long after. Nevertheless, under any system, New Zealand cannot fail to progress until it alone, when its many natural resources are taken in connexion with its great climatic advantages, will prove of far more substantial value to Britain than India, which has served only as the prison-house and premature grave of the great bulk of the Britons—the soldiers who have gone out, and has exterminated their *British* descendants!

To say then that the loss of India would reduce England to a third-rate power, or even a second-rate, is simply absurd.* It has merely diverted from many choice parts of the world a portion of the enterprise and energy which would have acquired a substantial and permanent growth by this time of much larger amount and value to her; whether such settlements continued a dependency of the Crown, or, like the United States of America, became separated from it. Were *these States* annihilated at this moment, it *may* be a question whether England would not decline at once to a second-rate power, though they cost her nothing in their maintenance and defence. As to the apprehension that the two countries, England and the United States, should ever be engaged in war, the very thought of it ought to be insufferable to the mind of every one, on either side the Atlantic, whose language, literature, and faith are English. War, upon any conceivable grounds which could be named, would exhibit such wickedness and puerile folly, that rulers who drew the Crown of England and the American Union, or allowed them to lapse into conflict, would be guilty of the highest treason—that against

* The *retention* of India is at present having this effect in drawing away nearly all our army, and rendering enlistment into it so undesirable.

Christian Civilization and Constitutional Government. Surely it would be well at such a time as the present, when neither people is on its mettle, honour, pride, or folly, that a mutual and solemn declaration and treaty should be made, pronouncing war between the countries IMPOSSIBLE; providing, for the settling of disputes, a council of arbitration with the choice of an umpire in reserve, and leaving it to the dissatisfied party to record, if it pleased, a *protest*, as its ultimatum. Leaving out of view the wickedness of any war between sections of a kindred people, it is admitted on all hands that no object or right that could be named, excepting the maintenance of honor (!), would be worth to either country the cost of so internecine a war as it would prove. Now the declared IMPOSSIBILITY of war would have settled the point of "*honor*" beforehand, as in the case of a man taking orders. And just as a military man is tenfold more liable to give and receive insults than a clergyman—as the self-same "honor" which puts the former and his opponent on their mettle, prompts the latter and any opponent to mutual forbearance, so would it assuredly prove between England and America, when once it wore the aspect of mere dastardly hectoring for the one Government to speak, or act offensively towards the other. The subjects of the offending state could not but feel themselves degraded and insulted by their own rulers. The reader will, it is trusted, pardon this digression, England and America being mutually, as free colonies, of the greatest value to each other.

A perfect amalgamation with her North American colonies would give real power to England.

If England were ambitious of greatly advancing her power, by increasing largely the surface and population of a consolidated imperial territory, it may be a question, now that Montreal is practically nearer than Dublin was a hundred years ago, whether such a thorough amalgamation with her North American dependency, as would be implied by combining her European and American sections under a new title of "East and West Britain," would not very soon place her far at the head of the nations of the earth.

With respect to India, we have got it and must keep it if we can. The sooner we abandon an opium revenue, which is rendering us abandoned, and will ere long abandon us, and stir the people up, by the *highest taxation* and the *briskest local ex-*

penditure in improvements on every scale, to more productive industry, the sooner will they be raised from their general depression, and be able to support liberally their beneficent trainers and defenders. The convictions of thirty years, long since expressed in various writings, remain more than ever confirmed, that if the Government could, and were to, lower the land rent *to nothing*, the condition of the mass of the people on the land would after a time be not improved but rendered worse. Production would decrease excepting under certain local circumstances of commercial stimulus, the sources of the rent would vanish and those who are supported by the expenditure of it would become destitute.

Remarks on the Causes of the Rebellion.

Distress of landholders a cause of disaffection.

Many years ago while making inquiries into the prevailing distress and decay of irrigation in Bundelkund, of sepoys and zumeendars * from that province, I found them clamorous in their anxiety that the causes which had brought their families into trouble should be inquired into. On another occasion when taking a look into Oude, after having for more than six years repeatedly heard from the opposite bank of the Ganges the sound of guns proclaiming the progress of conflicts, I found villages in desolation and depopulated. On inquiring the cause, of the only inhabitant clinging to the home of his fathers, the usual tale was told of the cruelest oppression under the signature of the Lucknow minister or the King himself. Upon my suggesting that cruelty so extreme would justify a combined resistance more effective than the desultory, commonly practised by them; the old man, the head of the village now in ruins, replied, "What chance have we against the Company's power, have not your arms extended over all lands?" Thus: were the classes yielding our soldiers not disposed to look very favourably towards us; in the latter case as upholding by our troops the misrule they suffered from; in the former as dispossessing their families when defaulters; often deservedly, but in the case of Bundelkund I have no doubt op-

* As many as a thousand *brinjarees* at a time, many of them zumeendars, have come up to me with immense droves of bullocks laden with feldspathic earth and fire-clay, from mines of these earths, I held in Bundelkund in the *Rewar* territory.

pressively, from a mistaken view of the position of the people and the state of their resources. Further inquiry made it plain that by drawing its soldiers from the rent-paying classes it happened in numerous cases that bitter feelings must be created when their families were dispossessed. In Oude indeed it was well known that enlistment took place to a large extent that each family might have in the Company's army a connexion able to speak and to secure for them exemptions, or privileges, protective against oppressions with which the Company's government itself was associated as presenting the ultimate force of suppression against which resistance were vain.

Again the wants of the cultivators for seed corn, &c., had constantly to be supplied by the savings of their relations in the army. There can be no doubt the claim of the collector for revenue was often paid by the accumulated savings of the sepoy. In other cases a zumeendar of substance, whose nephew was receiving ten rupees a month as a sepoy, with a social rank the highest, as a Brahmin of the priestly class, could not but compare such receipts with the two hundred a-month he himself paid as revenue, and which his nephew would tell him, "just equalled the pay of the young ensign who had come in poverty from England, fed perhaps on indigo resolved into food, and a pariah in caste." As time went on this connection of the soldiery with the revenue-paying classes could not, it has always appeared to me, fail to have a prejudicial effect. Indeed on mentioning this apprehension to a field-officer recently returned from India he stated that of late years a recklessness had grown up amongst the sepoys on account of the pressure of their village wants upon them. and its drain on the funds of the sepoy.

Again, while the bigotry and superstition of the Brahmin, which have been much dwelt upon as a cause of the outbreak, are not to be overlooked, it is the *social* position and *prescriptive power*, which his caste confers upon him, for the maintenance of which he is most jealous. The Brahmin does not only stand in a hierarchical, but also in the highest aristocratical position; and he has an authoritative voice in all pursuits of industry. All processes in other arts, as well as agriculture, are supposed to have been prescribed and imparted through the Brahmins. Every newly commenced process of business, every new machine, or even repair of an old one, has to go Jealonsy of the Brahmin for his prescriptive power.

through the ceremony of "*poojah*" with a feeing of the Brahmin.

I very soon discovered the jealousy of the Brahmin towards processes and machines of a kind and on a scale which struck the people with surprise; and which for a time the workpeople desired should be "*poojahed.*" A little reflection must make it plain that if the Governor-General had even sent oblations to their idols daily, it could have availed little towards suppressing the deadly hostility of the Brahmin towards the European system —towards progress of every kind. Not only does Western science put to silence the trash taught by the gravest of them, as their hallowed system of physics, but more palpably in the arts, their authority is suffering daily shipwreck through it. In the locomotive engine they must have seen it run down at the rate of forty miles an hour. In short, their hierophantic aristocracy was going to ruin; in their sight much more certainly and alarmingly by the impertinence of progress, than by the quiet labours of the missionary. To combine the exaltation and conciliation of the Brahmin with the progress of civilization, was an impossible attempt. A European gentleman in my employment, of great ability, and born in the country, taught me early to perceive the expediency of excluding the Brahminical element and spirit as fast as we could from the large establishment employed in the works described under a former head.* We had a curious *grease question* arise, in connexion with the lubrication of the various bearings of machinery, which in weather very hot and dry required more than usual unction. By unusual tact on the part of my friend, instead of a "strike," which in India is peculiarly difficult to overcome, we always gained the ascendency, and, by degrees, destroyed the authority of the Brahmins completely.

THE CONFIDENT RELIANCE of the natives in the destructive effects of their sun upon Europeans, is another cause upon which I have dwelt in former pages.† Without this reliance, it is not probable they would for many years to come, have attempted to throw off our yoke.

Mahomedans encouraged by the deferential bearing towards them.

THE ENCOURAGEMENT given by our studiously conciliating bearing towards the Mahomedans also was likely to foster their pretensions rather than lead them to acquiesce in our ascendency.

* Appendix H.

† Page 14 and elsewhere.

An instance of this effect of rather a striking character came to my notice in connexion with the impression on the Company's rupee. It is well known that up to so late a date as the year 1835, the Company's government maintained the inscription on the last Mahometan sicca rupee, that of the Emperor Shah Allam, with his title on the obverse, and on the reverse a passage from the Koran; and it was thought unsafe to tamper with this impression.

It came to my knowledge, from a conversation respecting this inscription on the rupee that the Mahomedans professed the belief and carefully circulated the report, that the impression was supernaturally maintained by the Deity; as a public evidence of the Mussulman right to rule Hindostan, and as a pledge for a restoration of the right. It was affirmed that the Company had repeatedly sent out dies from England, bearing their own device and that of the King of England, but that when put under the press they uniformly yielded rupees with the Mussulman impression on them. Upon being remonstrated with for their credulity the ready reply of the Mahometans was that a miracle was a possible occurrence, but that it was impossible the Company would continue the impression, and with it the acknowledgment of the right of others to the empire, if it lay in their power to avoid it.

It thus appears, that a measure which might possibly have been politic for a few years after our occupation of the country, was being persevered in, as such, until it was so incomprehensible by the natives, as to encourage a miraculous interpretation of it in favour of Mahomedan right.

Some years afterwards, when in Calcutta, I mentioned the report, at the Mint, to the late General (then Colonel) Forbes, who was at the time endeavouring to induce the Government to substitute an English device for the Persian impression on the coin of India. He was much amused by it, and said, "the next time you see the Governor-General (whom he knew to favour me with interviews on public questions connected with Indian progress) I wish you would mention it to him; he is disposed for the change." I did so; and Lord W. Bentinck, appeared struck with the view the natives took of this act of obsequious policy on the part of the Government. The fact that the existing impression on the coin only served to produce a false impression on the minds of the natives, Hindoos as well as Mahometans, of a character not a little opposed to the policy, upon which alone the retention of it was defended, could not but have been viewed as a reason of some weight in favour of the change contemplated.

A native press free and unbalanced.

ANOTHER cause of disaffection and disrespect will be found in the state of the press of India—a question very difficult to deal with. It were far better to give up India than to sacrifice, were the thought endurable, freedom of the press in England. If a free press is needful for England our countrymen feel the need of it equally in India, where wrong would prevail on all sides uncorrected and even unknown, and where life, dull as it is, would be intolerably so, without it. But if the European press is free it is difficult to put a restraint upon the native press. Yet how far an alien and absolute Government can be maintained over a half-enlightened people possessing an unfettered and most licentious press, while that Government too, disdains to maintain organs of its own, is a problem which remains to be solved, and of which an unfavourable solution has well nigh taken place. It is in fact a question simply of military strength. Whether the Government can sit in a panoply of power with its arms folded in majestic indifference towards shafts from the pen sent forth in daily torrents, will depend upon its ability and care to clothe its British soldiery with an anti-thermal panoply proof against the fiery shafts of the rebel natives' great ally—THE SUN; and also upon what other ethnic resources it has to supply the tropical element in its armies.

A Government periodical recommended.

Knowing how ignorant the natives are of the wealth and power of England, the value of a Government Military Journal has been so strongly impressed on my mind, that I could not refrain from submitting to the attention of the President of the Board of Control, nearly a year ago, the suggestion of such a paper as a 'Native Army Gazette;' which might be edited by some of the ablest of the present hostile native writers, enlightened by, and entertained on, a suitable salary. Would it prove of no value to supply the sepoys of every regiment, free of cost, accompanied with military news connected with the army—its distinctions and promotions, with information as to the speed with which a British army could be conveyed by steam to the most distant parts of the world; with a list of Her Majesty's shipping and armament, and of the steam power of England, royal and commercial; with an account of her revenue and wealth compared with the poverty of India; with tables of her exports and imports, and of the quantity of food consumed per head, and its variety; with an account of her various colonies, and command over other tropical races abundantly able to supply a black army equally sun-proof with themselves? There might be some ground in an objection that its marvellous statements might not receive credit, if it were a single publication; but that an abiding incredulity would be maintained in the minds of the sepoys towards evidence of all kinds—statistical tables, parliamentary reports, &c.,—and persevered in month by month, and year by year, it would be absurd to suppose. It was surely desirable that the sepoy should not think that the whole resources of England lay in India, and up to the hour of his rebellion believe that in their hunger the English had devised the means of converting indigo, and that supplied from his country, into food! It was surely desirable that notions so contracted and little to the dignity of his rulers and officers should be corrected!

The absence of paternal Government.

THERE is a further and powerful cause of disaffection amongst the people: of Hindostan Proper more especially:—a cause which has operated upon the village feelings and interests of sepoys from our own territory—it is the absence of that *paternal* government to which they have from time immemorial been subjected. In the preceding pages will be found copious facts and arguments proving the inability of the natives to husband their industry and the impoverishing effects on many districts of drawing away all the rent from them. To this joint cause I endeavoured, twenty-five years ago, to invite the attention of the authorities as tending to produce "a fearful disaffection in the hearts of millions," and rendering the British system, though so equitable and moderate in its demands, more irksome than the capricious and lawless course of many native rulers, so long as the latter did not amount to rapine, and aided the operations of the husbandman. Native industry has such little power of organization, and is so prone to fall off in productiveness, that it is not simply a light taxation that will avail much. In numerous instances the smaller zumeendars have not the providence to husband the necessary capital, and if they had, would oftentimes not dare to keep it for any time, and very generally would not have the resolution to spend it in keeping their agricultural "plant"—implements, wells, cattle, &c.—in the best order. They need providence from without, supplying the means at the time when they are wanted, and enforcing the employment of them. Amongst instances of this, discernible on all hands by those who will search for them, may be mentioned the state of parts of Bundelkund, as exhibiting the fact in a striking light. The portion of the province in our possession yielded to the Emperor Ackbar far more than it has to the Company. I believe twice as much. Some years ago large tracts were waste, and overrun with "dawk" jungle, and are so still, no doubt. Yet the surface soil is good, much of it said to be excellent, while the ruins of substantial masonry wells show the extent to which it was anciently cultivated. The opportunity of discussing the deteriorated condition of the province from its ancient state with zumeendars from the impoverished part of it, having under particular circumstances been afforded me, the following admissions were elicited by a little persuasive questioning: that their lands possessed high fertility, but could yield no "Rubbee" crops from a lack of water—that water abounded, but as in the case of many parts of India the subsoil was too sandy for any but masonry wells—that there was plenty of brick clay and of "*Kunkur*," stalagmitic limestone, at hand—plenty of "*dawk*" wood for burning both bricks and lime—labour so redundant, that they affirmed the poor Assamees, lacking employment and food, had often to eat a kind of soapy clay to satisfy their cravings, and yet from year to year no attempt was made to construct wells. Moreover, that the remains everywhere of ancient wells testified to the traditional fact, that formerly the land was highly cultivated, and yielded to the "Sircar," the government, a large revenue. The zumeendars one and all explained that none of them had weight sufficient to organize the necessary labour, for, to them, so heavy a work; and that anciently there were government officers for advancing the means and enforcing its performance.

Some such auxiliary system as this would appear indispensably necessary for accommodating the Company's revenue system to the requirements of the people. It would save many, possibly nearly all, zumeendars from becoming defaulters, dispossessed, and then of course, rebels at heart; and there is scarcely a limit to which it might not draw forth the resources of the country. As to the common objections to any measures of interference in Europe, most of them do not apply to the case of India. To the more plausible ones, that the Government has not the means, and that they would be wasted by fraud if they had; the ready reply is that the means are presumed to arise, after, possibly in some cases, one first beneficent expenditure, from a proportionably increased taxation, while waste or fraud merely replaces funds to that amount in the hands of the zumeendars from whom they were levied. The system is that which prevailed to the greatest extent under Ackbar and other governors, who rendered Mahomedan rule acceptable to the people in spite of the unparalleled bigotry and cruelties the Hindoos had endured at the hands of "the faithful." Even under those milder rulers, Hindooism was barely tolerated, and was subjected to wanton insults at the hands of Mahometan officers. Yet the people prospered, and were contented under such reigns, and had Ackbar's successors been like himself, they might have been in power to this day.

Confidence of the natives in our want of detective means.

A FURTHER cause favouring combination will be found in the knowledge the natives had of our profound ignorance of their thoughts and ways; and of the facility with which a plot might be carried on to its maturation unknown by us. They witness, and practise, successful deception every day, and are well aware that the government has not a detective police worth anything excepting for the discovery of such offences as it is convenient to native officials should be discovered. The deception practised towards the civil functionaries, even those of the greatest ability, is the necessary consequence of this want of a detective machinery.

No person can now doubt that the rebellion was organized long previous to the outburst, and that the relations of the sepoys throughout the country, and the zumeendars generally were privy to it. It is surprising that any one should doubt that large numbers of them were also accessary to it, and it is difficult to disconnect so remarkable, mysterious, and general a measure as the circulation of the "*chuppatees*" from the rebellion which immediately followed it; especially as it is said that, on an ancient occasion of a general combination of the fighting population, it had been practised. That the zumeendars in possession should not have risen, is a satisfactory proof that the motives for disaffection were not strong enough to induce them to risk their properties. But nothing more can be said of the majority of them than that, excepting in that they circulated the chuppatees, they were neutral in *action*, but accomplices in knowledge. They acted the part of the signalman or bugler, who is an accessary to the combat though he does not engage in it.

A secret-service corps recommended.

Impressed with the great need in India of a better detective machinery than can be at the command of local officers, I ventured, in one of the communications already referred to, to express the opinion that a secret service corps, of great value for civil as well as political and military purposes, might be formed of dark complexioned half-caste Christians, trained at the Government Schools and selected for their abilities and good principles. To refuse, upon moral grounds, to employ such a machinery in India, would exhibit a squeamishness not enforced in Scripture, nor fairly deducible from its precepts. What! shall a government not be squeamish at the thought that every day in the year all manner of injustice and oppression is being enacted under, and by, its authority acting in ignorance, and affect a moral sensitiveness against the only machinery equal to the detection of it? The difficulty of maintaining integrity in a secret service corps, of any kind, especially in India, is not to be overlooked; but that a large and efficient amount of fidelity might, by suitable provisions, be commanded, there cannot be a doubt. Perhaps the members of such a corps should never be very long resident in one locality; and they ought to have no direct communication with the local authorities, nor acquaintance with their own successors; or, perhaps, even with the names of their whole body. Good pay, fair promotion, and a strict discipline and able superintendence, would ensure an amount of efficiency giving such a machinery incalculable value. Had it existed, the first whispers of the rebellion would have been heard, probably before the country was denuded of troops for the Persian war.

If then we would take such a comprehensive and philosophical view of the causes of the rebellion as shall exclude erroneous impressions, we must not too hastily adopt the suggestions, as to their nature, even of friendly natives, who would not think of naming any displeasing to their rulers to hear; such as the damaging effect of progress to Brahminical pride, &c.; and, least of all, are the statements of the disaffected to be relied on.

The native, subjected from time immemorial to despotic and more or less oppressive rule, and trained in no thoughts of freedom, has no idea of pleading oppression as an excuse for rebellion, unless it should be almost of an exterminating character. Though, on the other hand, his allegiance is not ordinarily such, as a moderate inducement to rebel would not overrule, provided security could be insured to him. But with him, even more than with other nations, religion is a ready rallying cry. Although men of intelligence should place little credit to complaints respecting it, it forms a general excuse for yielding to the impulse, and it ensures combined action. In the present instance it is scarcely credible that any intelligent native should have thought the government had any design, either in the greased cartridges or otherwise, to do violence to his religion. The Mussulmans, whose religion could not be touched by anything but open obstruction, have been quite as loud in the religious cry, and more active in the rebellion than the Hindoos. The latter would feel the use of the greased cartridges, unceremoniously forced upon him, an insult to his caste; not one of design, but of carelessness, contrasting with the former, almost obsequious, conduct of the government towards his prejudices.

Causes of the rebellion in their conjoint action.

For the real ground of the rebellion, we must look to the several causes, already enumerated, in their conjoint operation.

1stly. We find the bulk of the soldiery drawn from the tax paying population, who are sure to have grievances against any Government; especially against one, like the Company's, standing unfortunately in a two-fold position of invidiousness—in its own territory: having renounced that system of paternal discipline which, when not unjust and capricious beyond a certain point, the natives by temperament and custom were disposed to rely on; and which certainly saved them from many of the ejectments attendant upon the British system;—and in Oude: which yielded so large a portion of its soldiery, having the oppressions endured by the same classes referred to the presence of its powerful interference at one period and absence of it at another—oppressions too which the exactors have been doubtless ready enough, though with but partial truth, to persuade the people were consequent upon the large payments extorted from their sovereign by the Company. Each such (*quasi*) loan has probably sufficed as an excuse for the exactions of many a year, and of ten times its amount.

2ndly. We find the army drawn, not only from the tax-paying classes, but from those castes anciently in the highest position of social dignity and prescriptive privilege, and restored to much of it, by our own obsequious policy, befitting us as "*pariahs.*" Our omnivorous, and other habits, are those which distinguish the native pariah; and, like him, we have been sedulous to acknowledge ourselves such, by the great deference we have ourselves shown to the high castes; whose especial characteristic it is to avoid and contemn all these habits and tastes which we have in common with the native outcast.

We have in effect said—"Our tastes and instincts are, alas! swinish and low caste. Though we cannot change our nature, it shall not prevent us from honouring you, the stately roebucks of mankind—pure herbivorous feeders, of exclusive habits." In how many ways has the English functionary, civil as well as military, said by his deference to caste—"Write *me* down a pariah." But not only have we appeared before them as pariahs; but as ravenous ones from a hungry country, migrating to theirs for all we could obtain. It is marvellous that superior knowledge and prowess should have so long sufficed to command for us so large a measure of respect, in the face of such a humiliating deference to caste, and inflation of its pride.

3rdly. While we have lent ourselves to restore and actively uphold the high pretensions of Brahminism, the example of social progress we have set has laid the severest strokes at its foundation; being altogether incompatible with its prescriptive claims and privileges. To preserve their social position, men in Europe are ready to incur any risk. To improve it: is the main object for which wealth is sought with a life of toil. The Brahmin felt the very earth giving way under him. He was persecuted formerly by the Mahometan; but this was approaching extinction. His only chance was to strike at once, and eradicate Western example and teaching.

4thly. While the Mahometan was ready enough, uninvited, to cling with pertinacity and pride to every semblance of dynastic right, we have in various ways fostered such feelings, even to the extent of maintaining his impression on the coin of the country—an open acknowledgment of a right, which was yet being kept in abeyance in perpetuity by ourselves. So inexplicable to the native was an acknowledgment so damnatory of our position, that a miraculous interference in favour of the Mahometan's claim appeared to him less incredible.

5thly. The native mind was left in the power of a vernacular press, everywhere playing to its prejudices, unopposed by any such organs as are found to be necessary by other despotic Governments wherever the art of printing is known, and doubly requisite for the security of the alien Government of India. Hence *the mass* of the natives have remained totally ignorant of the resources and wealth of England.

6thly. The too well grounded confidence of the natives in their power to effect a combination undiscovered by any detective machinery we possess, was a further encouragement to action.

7thly and mainly. Their observation: actually surpassing our own in its correctness, of the power of their sun upon Europeans, has been doubtless the great and determining cause of the present movement; as it will of future, to our ultimate confusion, if the dressing of our soldiery in the Tropics shall continue at the decision of no better qualified minds than at present.

In conclusion. Such an examination of the causes of the rebellion—causes which, if they shall continue to operate, will give final success to a future, if they do not hazard the issue of the present rebellion—forces upon the mind some further examination of the merits of the "traditionary policy" which has ruled in India. Its basis was an endeavour to cherish both the Mahomedan and the Hindoo element, and to rule upon the strength of their mutual jealousies. But this system of backing and bottle-holding to two opponents, involved in it constantly-increasing libations to each, and was sure to issue in their discovering the object, and uniting for the time the very training imparted to them, to destroy the power which was making their prejudices and animosities its tools. It is, in fact, simply impossible to win the good-will of the Hindoo or Mahometan population by courting them as such. The progress, enlightenment, and prosperity which would make them British subjects in substance and feeling as well as in law, must be promoted with a like parental and authoritative course to that pursued in the training of a rising generation amongst ourselves; saving, of course, in the matter of religious instruction. Secular knowledge relating to "things which are seen and temporal" brings with it present experience and fruition, whereas spiritual knowledge —religion, relating to "things which are not seen and eternal," must, in man's sublunary state, rest in faith; and Christianity in love also. Coercion, or even the semblance of temporal authority is destructive of these. It may *change the religion* of a country, but then it must be *thorough* in its action—it must be the exterminating sword of Mahomet; to *convert the heart* it must be kept out of sight altogether.

The Government of India, in refraining from affording any active support, *as a Government*, to Christian efforts did surely right; and it cannot too repeatedly avow the determination, and explain fairly all the reasons for it. But then its functionaries, individually, from the very highest, ought to be found amongst subscribers to the work; otherwise an opposite impression is produced of indifference towards, and disbelief in, our own religion, which we are bound to desire to propagate. It cannot but have a damaging effect to the persuasions of the missionary, if men in authority, professors of the religion he has to offer, exhibit no interest in it whatever. It makes their presence and the Government they constitute, instead of the blessings they might be, the greatest of evils, as limiting the progress of that enlightenment which is of infinite value and the surest basis of all other. As to the policy of courting idolatry by doing homage to its rites, decorating its gods, and offering military salutes to its processions—it is an exhibition of treachery to Christianity, and of political timidity, beyond measure more ignoble and humiliating than would be any flight of our forces from the field of battle! It is the converse error of those who, also failing to take the word of God in its entirety for their guide, would propagate religion by coercion; but it is a far less excusable error in its motives, while it is sure to defeat its object.

THE PATH OF DUTY THE SOUNDEST POLICY.

Favourable state of India when first possessed by us, for a sound policy.

The reader of Eastern history is invited to reflect upon the peculiarly favourable position of India, when it fell into our hands, for a rule of Christian benignity.

Hindooism on the one hand: with its high caste pretensions, and its social extinction, and oppression, of its lowest castes, had been for centuries humbled in the dust by the violence of Mahometan bigotry; though latterly exempt from absolute persecution. Mahometanism, on the other hand: was enduring humiliation by the fall of its dynasties throughout the Continent; and that: not at the hands of the Brahmin raising his head again to spiritual and secular pretensions surpassing those even of Popery. It was the Mahratta—a marauding race of no high caste nor much Hindoo zeal, whom we found everywhere triumphing, though here and there dividing with the Pindarees, mere robbers, the work of Mahometan demolition. We found the Mahratta at the gates of Delhi itself, and saved the Mogul family from extinction at his hands. The Mahratta race had triumphed so far as to have acquired the power, and learnt its interest in establishing orderly government in various parts of India.

Here then was a favourable opportunity for a Christian government, duly valuing the blessings, and impressed with the teachings of its own faith, and sincere in its professions of beneficence, to have adopted that simple, straightforward, English (?) policy which in true wisdom, and happy results, would have indeed surpassed all the wiliness of worldly statesmanship. "We come," it would have said, "to put an end to your contentions, "civil and religious, and to all social oppression. We interfere "with no man's religion, where it does not outrage humanity, "and will allow no one to interfere with it by force or intrusive "insult of any kind, but we leave every one free in his zeal to "propagate his own faith by his best efforts. If the Hindoo is "not a propagator, that rests with himself. We even rigidly "refrain, as a government, from propagating our own faith, "highly as we value it, and convinced as we are that it would "prove the greatest of blessings to this people, but we trust "that none of our servants professing it will be behind men of "other religions in making known what we are assured is the "only truth. As to our army, having no distinction of castes "ourselves, our military service will involve much that would "wound the prejudices of the high caste Hindoo; we are too "considerate therefore towards him to permit him henceforth to "enter it; especially as it is our purpose to raise the low castes "out of their depressed position, and to find occupation for them "in our ranks. We will, therefore, that the former remain "actively engaged in their pursuits of husbandry which it is our "purpose to encourage by all means at our command. Maho-"metans ought to have no castes and no objection to stand in "the ranks with any of their fellow men of like social position. "We shall therefore be ready to receive poor Mussulmans into "the army."

Advantages of a low caste army.

Acting upon this principle an army of low caste men might have been formed, whose feelings of loyalty would have greatly surpassed those of any of them at present in the service: admitted as they are on sufferance merely, and not upon principle. The degraded position and oppressive exactions they are subjected to under Brahminism, render them a class in a state of social humiliation eminently favourable for the operation of such influence as a benign government might have brought to bear upon them; while every step they were raised, would have placed them in an antagonism to Brahminism, and, we might hope, eventually to Hindooism itself, through the permitted efforts of the teachers of Christianity, which would have bound their fortunes up inseparably with those of the government; even where such teaching had gone no further than to produce a moral conviction in their minds of the oppressive and degrading character of the religion to which their class had been contented to remain the social victims through many ages.

If for a generation or two many of them lacked the stately appearance of the bovine Brahmin, their omnivorous habits would be found to introduce into their systems a quantity of nitrogenous food, giving them a nervous temperament far more really fitted for military purposes of every kind than that of the Brahmin. But a large number of low caste men, especially of Chumars, Tèlees, and Mehturs—tanners, oilmen, and sweepers—are to be met with, quite equalling the Brahmin in strength, and surpassing him in endurance and nerve. The castes a step above these, the coomars, danrees—potters, boatmen, and others—now doing with ourselves an increased homage to Brahminism, under our rule, and therefore affecting to be polluted by even an approach of us, self-proclaimed pariahs, to their food, might, had we taken a stand of befitting dignity in the ignoring of all caste, have been drawn into our service with the former. Its good pay on the one hand, and the example of a combined resistance of its ranks to the contumely and exactions of the Brahmins on the other, would have swelled the number of the classes gradually rejecting a system which trod them down, and impressed even the most pretentious of them with a mark of low degradation.* The emancipation and social independence of all these classes would be the downfall of Hindooism, as a social, and very soon therefore as a religious system.

Another signal advantage in a moral point of view, of the circumstances in which we found India, must not be omitted. To the credit of the Mahometan it has to be recorded that his Government had suppressed the incentives to drunken debauchery—alcohol and opium—so carefully, that we found even the lowest caste Hindoos, who have little or no religious compunctions in the matter, so generally temperate, that the occasional excesses of some with the fermented juice of the *Tarree* and with the plant *B'hung* offered no practical obstruction to the social and moral improvement of the population.

Having found the education of the Brahmin, not only in superstition, but more especially in pride, and prejudice, and generally also in indolence, to disqualify him for nearly all useful pursuits, and to make him an obstructive tamperer with others: and having, on the other hand, found low-caste men far more teachable of industrial pursuits, and faithful than others, I have to confess a prejudice in favour of the latter. I have experienced an instance of fidelity in one of the lowest of these, which it would not be easy to find paralleled in any country.

* I have often heard Brahmins decline to admit these several castes even to the name of "Hindoos," or to recognise any appreciable difference between them.

With an army drawn from these castes alone, interspersed or not with the humbler class of Mussulmans, and strengthened with a suitable proportion of African troops, and with a proper machinery for improving the minds of all such soldiery willing to learn, and for enlightening them respecting the country of their rulers, the government might have watched with calm indifference that growth of rancorous hostility in the high-caste Hindoos which is inevitable towards it, and the whole European body, as introducing a progress in art as well as science, which is cutting from under them the high stilts of privileged ignorance and error, and prescriptive claim on which they march over the heads of their countrymen, and are everywhere treading on their toes.

To judge of the opinions of the high castes throughout India generally, by those expressed, and doubtless very much felt, by the *Anglicized*, *semi-Anglicized*, and well-to-do Brahmins of the Presidencies, would be to mislead oneself. They have the discernment to see that progress is inevitable, and they feel the comforts and security of their own position under those who are its representatives and authors. They have made up their minds to accept a new social position, more gainful to them personally than the one which is being undermined. Accepting as inevitable the decline of the prescriptive status it gave them, their devotion to Hindooism is in proportion weakened. Many of them can now perceive in it absurdities, to which it blinded them effectually so long as it was able to flatter their self-importance, and confer upon them gainful privileges.

The traditionary policy its unfortunate contrast.

How unfortunate a contrast to such a policy has been "the traditionary" adopted by the East India Company's governments, and even still clung to by some persons! They entered upon a field in which they found, ready to hand, Brahminism long, and Mahometanism recently, depressed; and drunkenness of no kind prevailing; and they found numerous abject classes needing only an enlightened and resolute encouragement to induce them to throw off the remaining trammels of Hindooism, and to stand in *armed* antagonism to the oppressive pretensions of the Brahmin. But what did the "traditionary" policy? It restored, and even exalted the social pretensions of the Brahmins, and the dynastic of the Mussulman; it helped to depress still lower the social position of men of low and no caste: of its own leper* complexioned authors, therefore, amongst the rest, and to aggravate the intensity of Brahminism by even doing homage to its rites, its idols, and processions; and, to crown the whole, it was at pains to encourage everywhere, for a revenue, a free use of distilled spirit, aggravated by the example of the European soldiery, whom it introduced to a life of reckless despair. At the same time it unavoidably exhibited enough of progress to offend the Brahmins, but not enough to benefit them, and the rest of the agricultural population; and it then drew the soldiery not only from the tax-paying population, but chiefly from these exalted Brahmins. Is it then too much to affirm that it has brought down upon its promoters the very rebellion they have sacrificed so much of their better principles to avoid?

A Word on the Claims of Native Rulers.

One of the most serious questions arising out of our occupation of India, and the most trying to the statesman to handle conscientiously without having his reputation soiled, is to render British responsibility in India compatible with the maintenance of Asiatic rule in the various independent states within our territory; and to form treaties, the observance of which shall not eventually prove a far greater offence against morality and humanity than the breach.

It is not possible for any one habituated to the consideration of public questions to have lived for several years close to Oude, to have heard its continued conflicts, and to have seen its desolation, without having long since reflected upon the policy pursued towards independent native states.

Prevalent corruption of Asiatic rule.

The history of Asiatic rule, especially of Mahomedan over a Hindoo population, is, in general, one of misrule: culminating through a few generations to a point at which the natural remedy for grievous oppression takes place—rebellion aided by treachery, and followed by the establishment of a fresh Government, often under a traitor relative of the murdered or dethroned

* The complexion of a native leper is so like that of a pale European, somewhat heated by exposure, that at a short distance I have mistaken the one for the other. The impression on the native mind of the similarity in connexion with our "outcast habits" is not to be overlooked.

oppressor. The population then enjoy some respite under a Government winning favour by performing a paternal part, but at the same time gradually yielding to corruption and vice and bringing upon itself the fate of its predecessor. Under such Governments, in the advanced stages of their corruption, every one who possesses the strength, rivals the supreme power in wrong. This is a gloomy picture; but it is as nothing compared with the state of a country in which the oppressions of barbarism are supported with the strength of civilization. It is then that profligacy and selfishness run riot: unrestrained by that wholesome fear of reaction, which keeps within some bounds those who are unblest with any feelings of humanity to restrain them.

In connexion with the extension of our arms in the East there are few measures calling for more regret, as inconsiderate and grievous in their consequences, than our defensive treaties binding us to support native rulers against internal commotions; yet leaving the administration of Government in their hands. In the case of Oude, the claims of an unhappy people to our pity were so long merged under our respect for the tenfold forfeited rights of a worthless dynasty, to which we had indignly placed ourselves under obligations for large loans (query, gifts) obtained from its coffers, that the evil of a multitude of sub-oppressors in the persons of marauding landholders had grown up and become superadded to the iniquitous oppressions perpetrated under the authority of the Government itself.

Inconsistently supported by some.

We are wont, in these days, to marvel that the doctrines of Filmer, and the scruples of the non-jurors, should have commanded so much respect; but the homage they paid to an impossibility—a divine right to misrule *—was nothing to that which,

* Strange! that the right of despotic government, irresponsible to man, should have been inferred from a portion of Scripture—the 13th chapter of Romans, written as if to prove the necessity and to authorize the establishment of constitutional government. The great Apostle, wise as a serpent while harmless as a dove, contends indeed for the Divine authority of civil government, in the abstract: as necessary for man's sublunary and social state, and urges the duty, therefore, of an implicit obedience to it; but he is careful not to leave rulers any excuse, or their subjects without a remedy, for oppression. He presumes an excellency of government as the ground, and measure, of the obedience he demands; and he is scrupulous to claim implicit obedience to it on that condition only. He repeats, as if to avoid the possibility of a misunderstanding, the condition again, and

strange to say, some of those whom we honour as the upholders of liberal views in politics have done, surely from a want of acquaintance with the interests concerned, to the claims of native Governments—that of Oude in particular. Why! the bitter plaint of the *industrious, producing*, population of Oude has been, our upholding by our strength, directly at one time, indirectly at another, the oppressions under which they groaned! I cannot doubt, had any one of the feeling men, whose sympathies have been excited for their late rulers and other oppressors, heard their touching plaints, and witnessed the sad scenes confirming them, that he would have felt indignant that such a worthless dynasty as that at Lucknow should be upheld for an hour, and such merciless marauders as the latter not be promptly deprived of all power to oppress.

The duty of the British Government in India as supreme.

How far the position we have taken up in India is one of Divine *sufferance* rather than *guidance* may be a question, but there can, or ought to be, no question as to whether it does not now impose upon us the duty of an enlightened protectorship of the whole people encompassed in our dominion. It were an outrage to humanity and to all Christian principle to concede to barbarous rulers, and chieftains, under our auspices (as all in India must be), the right to oppress and torture their unhappy subjects and dependants without limit. To value *their* dynastic rights at a higher price than the lives and happiness of the people under their rule, and to scruple to sacrifice the former for the preservation of the latter, would evidence a political morality, it is to be hoped, few enlightened minds in England would in these days desire to profess. The policy of weakness may compel us to connive at much evil, but that should never be allowed to form a precedent for wilfully upholding wrong, or even to habituate our minds to an indifference towards the sufferings of the humble and oppressed.

again, with consummate tact, but with singular boldness, considering that he wrote under the dominion of the worst of tyrants—"*for* rulers are not a terror to good works"—"*for* he is a minister of God to thee for good"—"*for* he is a revenger to execute wrath upon him that doeth evil"—"*for* for this cause pay ye tribute also." If rulers, whether Christian or Mahometan in profession, prove hopelessly neglectful of these conditions, they, by a logical deduction from the apostle's teaching, forfeit all right from on high to rule; and neither the inconsiderate treaties of man, nor his power, can rightly countervail that forfeiture.

To annex the territory of a feebler state—to take possession of it in a spirit of ambition, were indeed reprehensible; but, even in the worst instance that could be named, it would be a greater injustice to the people of such a state not to make their interests, and the manner in which they had been ruled, the foremost point for searching inquiry before a decision was pronounced upon the propriety of the measure. The reader of the preceding pages will not charge the Author with any ambition to see the territorial surface of the British dominions in India extended. He would, however, rather see every inch of it annexed than remain under the hopeless misrule of such native governments as that of Oude. He has not been unobservant of the fact (and has referred to it in papers written between twenty and thirty years ago), that the "paternal" character of native governments, which were otherwise tolerably well conducted, rendered them more inviting to the people than the full regulation system of the Company's, and he is no unqualified admirer of the Civil Government the latter has succeeded in affording its subjects; nevertheless, much, in spite of its best intentions, as unremedied evil and ill-doing abound in its dominions, they are an elysium compared with the condition of states under a weak or profligate native ruler sleeping, or rioting, at his ease under the shelter of the British flag.

When, if ever, our Government shall so modify its administration of justice in India as to include in it every educated European mind in its service available, military as well as civil, and in subordinate offices not a few of the less educated, and shall introduce and urge forward improvement with a paternal hand, then will it indeed prove, in all that concerns their secular interests, a blessing to the people of India.

(P.—Page 228.)

Soldiers' service should vary with their ages.

It did not appear necessary or expedient to venture, in the text, into any details while naming what seemed the reasonable pecuniary prospect for the deserving soldier retiring at the end of twenty years' service; but it may be as well not to appear unmindful of the fact, that men, especially in H. M. regiments, come out at various ages. A man going out at the age of 40 has little, and at 50, no chance whatever of living twenty years in India. It might be fair to name twenty as the commencing age of service and to deduct one year of the service required for title to a pension for every two years and a half, men exceeded that age on coming out. Thus a man at twenty would have twenty years to serve and be able at forty to claim his pension of 40*l.* a year. At thirty he would have sixteen years to serve and obtain his pension at forty-six. Entering India at forty he would have twelve years to serve and arrive at his pension at fifty-two.

Non-commissioned officers would of course have a suitable advancement on the privates' pension of 40*l.* a year. In the event of incapacity from illness they might severally be allowed an invalid pension of half the full rates on having served half the several terms.

The total annual charge would be trifling when compared with the rightfulness of the claim, the beneficial effects, and probably the absolute ultimate economy resulting from them.

The following tables of the Company's *good conduct* PAY and *good conduct* PENSION exhibit the best pecuniary hopes the soldier in India has at present!! With the views, or rather no views, which have hitherto prevailed, the scale was doubtless thought to have been liberal; but then it was fixed by those who were not the representatives of *the people's* claims and feelings. *With how much of hope and satisfaction it has inspired the soldier* may be judged from the preceding pages, both in the body of the work, and from the matter under the letters L, M, and N, of the Appendix.

Tables of the scanty pensions allowed European soldiers for services in India.

"REWARDS FOR GOOD CONDUCT.

"*Good Conduct Pay, and Distinguishing Marks.*

"In order to make due distinction between deserving and undeserving Soldiers, the following rewards are granted to the former class, *viz.*

"If a Non-commissioned Officer shall obtain a commission as a reward for distinguished conduct in action with the enemy, he is allowed, in aid of outfit, 100*l.*

"Annuities are granted to Serjeants for meritorious, or

distinguished service, not exceeding 20*l.* each, with a Silver Medal.

		Good Conduct Pay.	Number of Distinguishing Marks.
"To Corporals, Drummers, and Privates.	Having served 5 years, and not having been in the Defaulter Book during the last 2 years	1*d.* a day.	1
	Having served 10 years, and having been during the last 2 years in uninterrupted enjoyment of 1*d.* a day good conduct pay	2*d.* do.	2
	Having served 15 years, and having been during the last 2 years in uninterrupted enjoyment of 2*d.* a day good conduct pay	3*d.* do.	3
	Having served 20 years, and having been during the last 2 years in uninterrupted enjoyment of 3*d.* a day good conduct pay	4*d.* do.	4
	Having served 25 years, and having been during the last 2 years in uninterrupted enjoyment of 4*d.* a day good conduct pay	5*d.* do.	5
	Having served 30 years, and having been during the last 2 years in uninterrupted enjoyment of 5*d.* a day good conduct pay	6*d.* do.	6

"The following are some of the benefits conferred on the deserving Soldier by the East India Company's Pension Regulations.

"Men discharged after 21 Years' Service.

Serjeant Majors	2*s.* 6*d.* a day.
Quarter Master Serjeants—having served 5 years in one or other of the Ranks	2*s.* 3*d.* a day.
Serjeants—having held that Rank during the last 8 Years of Service .. .. or, distinguished for Good Conduct, and disabled by being wounded on actual service	2*s.* a day if at home, or,
If permitted to remain in India	30 Rupees a Month.
Serjeants—not having held that Rank during last 8 Years of Service	1*s.* a day.
Corporals and Privates	1*s.* a day.

"Men discharged as unfit from debilitated constitutions, after 14 Years' Service.

Serjeant Major	1*s*. 4*d*. a day.
Quarter Master Serjeant	1*s*. 2*d*. a day.
Serjeants	1*s*. a day.
Corporals and Privates	9*d*. a day.

"Men discharged on account of Wounds or Injuries received on Service.

	If able to contribute towards a livelihood.	If unable to contribute towards a livelihood.
Serjeant Major—		
After 21 Years' Service	2*s*. 6*d*. a day	2*s*. 6*d*. to 2*s*. 9*d*. a day.
After 14 Years' Service	1*s*. 6*d*. a day	1*s*. 10*d*. a day.
Quarter Master Serjeant—		
After 21 Years' Service	2*s*. 3*d*. a day	2*s*. 3*d*. to 2*s*. 6*d*. a day.
After 14 Years' Service	1*s*. 3*d*. a day	1*s*. 6*d*. a day.
Corporals and Privates—		
After 21 Years' Service	1*s*. 4*d*. a day	1*s*. 10*d*. a day.
After 14 Years' Service	1*s*. 0*d*. a day	1*s*. 6*d*. a day.
Under 14 Years' Service	0*s*. 9*d*. a day	1*s*. 3*d*. a day.

"The Pensions granted by Lord Clive's Fund are included in the above rates, and no man whose service is under 21 years is eligible to the above pensions, unless discharged as an Invalid entitled to the benefits of that Fund, and unless his discharge contain the government's recommendation for his admission to these benefits."

LONDON: PRINTED BY WILLIAM CLOWES AND SONS, STAMFORD STREET, AND CHARING CROSS.